Theatre and Film in Exile

GERMAN ARTISTS IN BRITAIN, 1933–1945

Edited by
GÜNTER BERGHAUS

OSWALD WOLFF BOOKS
BERG PUBLISHERS
Oxford/New York/Munich
Distributed exclusively in the US and Canada by
St Martin's Press, New York

First published in 1989 by
Berg Publishers Limited
– Editorial Offices –
77 Morrell Avenue, Oxford OX4 1NQ, UK
165 Taber Avenue, Providence R.I. 02906, USA
Westermühlstraße 26, 8000 München 5, FRG

British Library Cataloguing in Publication Data
Theatre and film in exile: German artists in Great Britain, 1933–1945.
1. Great Britain. Performing arts, 1933–1945
I. Berghaus, Günter
790.2'0941
ISBN 0–85496–025–2

Library of Congress Cataloging-in-Publication Data
Theatre and film in exile: German artists in Great Britain, 1933–1945
/ ed. by Günter Berghaus.
p. cm.
Includes index.
Bibliography: p.
ISBN 0–85496–025–2: £19.95
1. Theater — Great Britain — History — 20th century. 2. Germans–
–Great Britain — History — 20th century. 3. Performing arts — Great
Britain — History — 20th century. 4. Performing arts — Germany–
–History — 20th century. 5. Exiles' writings, German — Great
Britain — 20th century — History and criticism. 6. Refugees,
Political — Great Britain — History — 20th century. 7. Refugees,
Political — Germany — History — 20th century. I. Berghaus, Günter,
1953.
PN2595. T47   1989
790.2'0941 — dc 19

89–116
CIP

Printed in Great Britain

Contents

Illustrations

Photographs

Text Illustrations

vii

The editor has tried, within reasonable limits, to trace the copyright holders of the material reproduced in this volume. Most of the printed material and photographs were kindly provided, free of charge, by the artists or their families. In some cases copyrights could not be cleared because no existing copyright holder could be traced. Any claims arising out of this omission should be made to the editor via the publishers.

The original material reproduced in the text illustrations comes from the following collections:
Alan Clarke: 1 (© *Evening Standard*), 3
Egon Larsen: 2, 6
Hanne Norbert: 4, 5
Hugh Rank: 7, 8

The photographs and artworks reproduced in the half-tone sections come from the following archives and collections:

Hanne Norbert: 6,7
Hugh Rank: 10, 14, 15
B. Vernon: 11
Egon Larsen: 1, 9
Liselotte Souza: 8
Marjorie Leng: 13
Kevin Gough-Yates: 5
Crescent Theatre, Birmingham: 2, 3, 4
Dartington Hall Trust: 16

Kurt Jooss Archiv, Wiesbaden: Cover illustration
Laban Archive, Laban Centre, London: 12

Acknowledgements

The realization of the plans to organize a conference on German Exile Theatre in Great Britain was only possible through the generous support received from the German Historical Institute, the Goethe Institut, and the Standing Committee of University Drama Departments (SCUDD). I wish to express my gratitude to Gerhard Hirschfeld, Fellow of the German Historical Institute, whose extensive knowledge of the general problems connected with German exile between 1933 and 1945, and the particularities of the exile situation in Great Britain, was an important asset when it came to organizing the conference and setting up the publication. As far back as 1985, when the concept of the conference was first discussed at a reception at the Royal Academy of Arts, the project found encouragement from Günter Coenen, director of the London branch of the Goethe Institut, and his support did not abate when it came to securing finances for the venture. Margaret Shewring, chairperson of SCUDD, provided us with the sponsorship of other Drama Departments in the country; and our gratitude extends to Edouard LeMaistre and Jacqueline Readwin of the Architectural Association for granting us the excellent conference facilities on their Central London premises.

The organization of the conference lay in the hands of the Bristol University Drama Department, and I wish to express my gratitude to the Head of Department, Edward Braun, who supported the project throughout its different stages. Bencie Woll helped with the organization of the conference, and special thanks are due to John Adler, without whose enthusiastic assistance the realization of the conference and of this publication would not have been possible.

Editor's Foreword

The essays assembled in this volume are the outcome of an interdisciplinary symposium held in London in January 1987. Entitled 'German Exile Theatre in Great Britain, 1933–1945', this conference had the aim of bringing together a number of experts from different disciplines in the field of the performing arts in order to discuss the theatrical and cinematic activities of the émigrés from Nazi Germany, and to assess their influence (if any) on British theatre and cinema.

This conference provided the participants with interesting new insights into a little-known chapter in the history of European culture. At the end of the symposium there prevailed a general feeling that the results of the discussions deserved to be made known to a larger public. For this purpose preparations were made for the publication of the papers, and further essays commissioned in order to round off the volume and to cover aspects which — because of limitations of time and financial resources — could not be included in the programme of the conference.

The resulting book, which now lies in front of you, has been designed in such a way that even a non-specialist reader with no knowledge of the German language or of British theatre history will be able to make him/herself familiar with the astonishing range of cultural activities carried out by the German refugees who found asylum in Great Britain during the years of the Nazi régime. A number of readers will have seen the exhibition 'Art in Exile in Great Britain, 1933–1945', held at the Camden Arts Centre from 20 August to 3 October 1986. This publication on Exile Theatre is meant to complement the exhibition and the catalogue 'Kunst im Exil in Großbritannien, 1933–1945', published on the occasion of the first showing of the touring exhibition at the Orangerie of Schloß Charlottenburg in West Berlin from 10 January to 23 February 1986.

When Hans-Albert Walter, the doyen of West German *Exilforschung*, began to publish the first volumes of his series 'Deutsche Exilliteratur 1933–1950', he wrote about some future aspects of the study of German exile culture:

Whilst I am examining — within the framework of what is possible — the inspiration the exile writers received in their host countries, I have to leave out an assessment of their influence on the countries where they found refuge: this complex question — in my view — can only be examined and clarified in these countries themselves by experts who are intimately familiar with the conditions there.[1]

As the individual contributions to this volume reveal, the influence the German exile artists had on the performing arts in Britain differed from field to field. Those artists who relied in their profession on verbal language and linguistic skills had to overcome considerably greater difficulties than those who worked in the media of opera and dance, which are more visual and physical art forms and in any case more international in their general outlook.

The same seems to apply to stage, film and costume designers, although unfortunately it was not possible to secure a contribution on this subject either for the conference or for this publication. The fifteen design historians I approached felt that too little research had been carried out in this field and that, therefore, at the present time it would be impossible to assess the influence the German artists had on British design of the period. My own research has shown that a considerable amount of material survives in British and German archives and collections, and it is to be hoped that in the near future the design *œuvre* of at least some of the following refugees to Britain will be studied: Hans Abarbanell, Alice Berger-Hammerschlag, Käthe Berl, John Heartfield, Hein Heckroth, Carl Joseph, Alfred Junge, Kurt Lade, Ernö Metzner, Litz Pisk, Ernst Stern.

Another subject which proved to be difficult to cover was that of the theatre performances in internment camps. Unfortunately, Michael Seyfert, who studied the cultural activities of the internees for his dissertation,[2] was prevented from participating in our project. I am most grateful to Alan Clarke for his willingness to undertake, at very short notice, the study printed below on pp. 189–222, which is based on material he collected for his unpublished dissertation *Die Rolle des Theaters des 'Freien Deutschen Kulturbundes in Großbritannien' im Kampf gegen den deutschen Faschismus*.[3] The scarcity of surviving or accessible documents on the theatre activities in the internment camps made it seem desirable to include in this volume an eyewitness report of one of the former internees. On pp. 223–9 George Brandt, Professor Emeritus of Radio, Film and Television Studies at Bristol University, gives us a personal account of his involvement with some of the internment camp shows.

Another member of the theatrical profession, Carl Weber, formerly of Brecht's Berliner Ensemble and now Professor of Drama at Stanford University, was so kind as to provide us with a personal recollection of his theatrical experiences in a British PoW camp. This is the first time, to my knowledge, that these activities have been described, and his account will serve, I hope, as an interesting side piece to George Brandt's essay. At this point, some may ask what the theatrical activities of prisoners of war have to do with those of the exiles to whom this volume is dedicated. Unfortunately, the clear distinctions between anti-Fascists and Nazis which we are nowadays able to make was at the time beyond the grasp of large sections of the British population and, indeed, of quite a few government officials as well. Former inmates on internment camps told me the most appalling stories about their detention, when they — as Jews or political exiles — were forced to share a room or even a bed with an arch-Nazi. Similarly, amongst the PoWs there were large contingents of defectors who, because of their anti-Fascist convictions and despite the serious dangers involved, seized on any opportunity to abandon their service in the Nazi Wehrmacht and to surrender to the troops of the Allies.

At a time of jingoism, war hysteria and Fifth-Column paranoia the British regarded any refugee German in the first instance as an alien, and few were willing (or able) to distinguish between a Nazi and an anti-Fascist, between a Hitlerite and a Jew. In this volume, however, we will not repeat the mistake of a Scotsman who was unable to see the difference between the exiles' theatre work and that of the Nazi consulate. He invited his German-Jewish neighbour to a Reichsdeutscher Bildungs-abend and was quite astonished and rather peeved that his friendly invitation did not meet with much enthusiasm. Therefore, the theatre performances organized by the Reichsgerman consulates and Anglo-German Friendship Societies (although in themselves an interesting and under-researched subject) have to be omitted from this volume. The essays will deal, exclusively, with the cultural activities of German anti-Nazis and concentrate on the work carried out by exiles who made Great Britain their home between 1933 and 1945.

Exiles, in our usage of the word in this volume, are people who were persecuted, harassed, threatened or disadvantaged by the National Socialist régime because of their ethnic origin, political convictions, religious faith, humanist ideals or moral principles, and were therefore forced to emigrate from their home country. For the sake of this study it is irrelevant whether this period of exile was 'voluntary', coerced, or the only alternative to certain death. The terms 'exile', 'refugee', 'emigrant' and 'émigré' are basically used here as synonyms. No subtle semantic differentiation is aimed at, and no attempt is made at establishing strictly defined categories of fugitives from Nazi Germany.

No attempt, either, has been made to distinguish between the different nationalities of the refugees from German-speaking countries or countries under German occupation. The term 'German' relates to a culture rather than a nationality. In this volume we classify those exiles as German who spoke German as their first language, or came from a cultural background that had a distinctly German character, or who had spent most of their professional lives in a German-speaking country. The majority of exiles came from the territory of the former Weimar Republic or from Austria, but smaller numbers of refugees arrived in Britain from the Sudetenland and Saarland, from Bohemia and Moravia, from Silesia, Hungary, Romania, Yugoslavia and so on. The historical and political aspects of their fortunes in this country have been discussed in Gerhard Hirschfeld's book *Exile in Great Britain: Refugees from Hitler's Germany*.[4] This volume on Exile Theatre has been conceived as a companion piece, concentrating on a particularly prolific area of the refugees' cultural activities.

Exile theatre, often created under the most adverse circumstances, functioned not only as a means of communication amongst the refugees themselves, but was also addressed to the population of their host country. It enriched the lives of the émigrés as well as those of the British community. Therefore, the refugees can be considered to have been *Kulturvermittler*, or cultural ambassadors, at a time when Britain lagged behind other European countries in most fields of the arts, and displayed a xenophobic attitude which made the cultural exchange with different European countries extremely difficult. This negative attitude towards other European cultures has receded since Britain joined the EEC. However, anyone who has been a regular newspaper reader or followed the news on television will have noticed how certain prominent victims fleeing political persecution are received with open arms and front page coverage, whilst thousands of anonymous refugees from oppressive régimes and economic hardship in countries of the Third World are sent back to their homeland. It seems that the humiliating ordeals in British Immigration Offices have not changed a great deal:

The office was small and, although it was early in the morning, already sour with cigarette smoke. Two men sat at a table. One was a good deal older than the other, almost sixty perhaps, with dark, peaked features. The other, much younger, perhaps thirty-five, was a heavy, muscular man with a complexion like underdone beef. . . .

The immigration officer cleared his throat; 'you claim that your reason for desiring to come to this country is a wish to learn English.'

Hugo didn't say anything. This man was hostile to him and he had not expected hostility in England. Then he said, 'Excuse me . . .' . . .

'*You know English!*' The red-faced man brought the words out like hammer-blows. 'Don't you? Why are you coming here to learn something you know already?!'

Hugo knew this immigration officer hated him. He knew the man was going to hand him over to the police. And the police would keep him locked up until there was another boat going to France and then they would put him on it and send him back to Germany.

. . . 'I have wanted to come to England for a long time,' Hugo said.

'So have a lot of other people. It doesn't mean we're going to let them in,' the immigration officer said grimly. . . .

Hugo . . . knew it was hopeless. He wished the immigration officer would let him go. Arrest him, if he liked; put him back on the ship; send him back to Germany. Anything rather than go on with this.[5]

This extract from one of the stories related by Austin Stevens in his book *The Dispossessed: German Refugees in Britain* could equally well stem from the life story of one of the present-day arrivals on these shores, which the newspapers refer to only in brief notices such as this one from the *Observer* of 20 September 1987:

Desperate Wait
An Iraqi Kurd at Harmondsworth detention centre, Middlesex, while his application to stay in Britain is considered, has tried to commit suicide . . . He is thought to have been depressed about his continued detention. He and his wife have been held for three months without any sign of a decision on whether to grant them political asylum.[6]

It would seem that attitudes towards foreigners have not changed all that much; maybe only the colour of the skin of these foreigners? At a time when 'Paki-bashing' has become a pastime of the New Right and West Indian families have their houses burnt down, when coloured citizens suffer discrimination at work and harassment on the street it may be timely to remind ourselves that refugees do not only mean a burden on the community but also, in the long run, an asset to the country. Britain, in the past, has benefited from the immigration of Anglo-Saxons and Danes, Romans and French, Huguenots and Jews. What will prevent it from doing so in the future? It is to be hoped that this book will fulfil a useful function in the current debate on a multiracial British society, and aid our understanding of the hardship and plight that exile causes and of possible ways to remedy them.

Notes

1. Hans-Albert Walter, 'Bemerkungen zu einigen Problemen bei der Erforschung der deutschen Exilliteratur', in *Jahrbuch für Internationale Germanistik*, vol. 6, no. 1, 1974, pp. 86–108, here p. 89.
2. Michael Seyfert, *Im Niemandsland: Deutsche Exilliteratur in britischer Internierung. Ein unbekanntes Kapitel der Kulturgeschichte des Zweiten Weltkrieges*, Berlin (West), 1984.
3. PhD Thesis, Humboldt University, Berlin (GDR), 1972.
4. Leamington Spa and New Jersey, 1984.
5. Austin Stevens, *The Dispossessed: German Refugees in Britain*, London, 1975, pp. 111–13.
6. *The Observer*, 20 Sept. 1987, p. 2.

1. *My Goodness, My Alibi* at the Kleine Bühne (1944)

2. Ernst Toller's *Masses and Man* at the Crescent Theatre, Birmingham (1937)

3. Ernst Toller's *Masses and Man* at the Crescent Theatre, Birmingham (1933)

4. Ernst Toller's *Masses and Man* at the Crescent Theatre, Birmingham (1933)

5. Elizabeth Bergner in Paul Czinner's *Stolen Life* (Orion Productions, 1939)

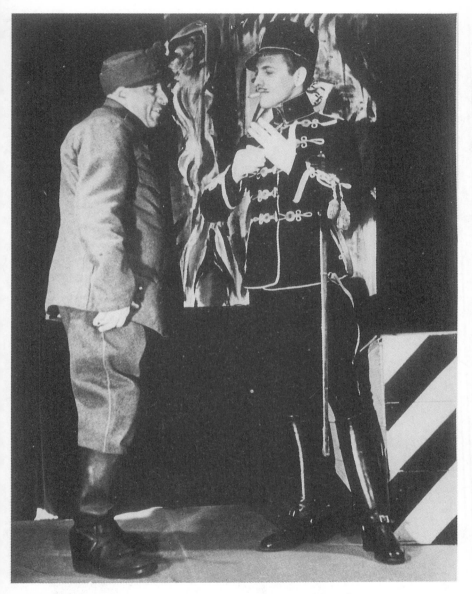

6. Jaroslav Hašek's *The Good Soldier Schwejk* at the Laterndl (1940)

7. Jaroslav Hašek's *The Good Soldier Schwejk* at the Laterndl (1940)

8. J.B. Priestley's *They Came to a City* at the Kleine Bühne (1944)

9. and 10. (*Above and Below*) *Mr Gulliver Goes to School* at the Kleine Bühne (1942)

11. The eleventh programme of the Laterndl, *Wiener Miniaturen* (1942),
presented four one-act plays by Arthur Schnitzler. Above, the scene
Weihnachtseinkäufe from *Anatol*

12. Kurt Jooss's *The Mirror* (1935)

13. Ernst Stern's design for the decorations of the Selfridge Building (Orchard Street frontage) at the time of the coronation of King George VI and Queen Elizabeth (May 1937)

14. R.C. Sheriff's *The Journey's End* at Camp Hay, Australia (1941). Drawing by George Blank

15. At the Laterndl in Eton Avenue, Hampstead (1943)

16. A rehearsal in the Open Air Theatre at Dartington Hall

-1-

Great Britain and the Emigration from Nazi Germany
An Historical Overview

GERHARD HIRSCHFELD

The enforced migration of hundreds of thousands of men, women and children from National Socialist Germany is without precedent in German history. To be sure, the nineteenth century saw the departure of millions of Germans as part of a proletarian mass migration from the old continent to the new promising countries overseas. But this emigration was mostly economically motivated and seemed to follow the general pattern of an overall demographic development, though in many cases migration was the result of individual hardship and misery and often ended in equally miserable and frustrating conditions.

The establishment of Nazi rule after 30 January 1933, the day Adolf Hitler was appointed Reich Chancellor, not only put an end to decades of German-Jewish acculturation but clearly represented a watershed in Germany's political and cultural life. The majority of those who had to leave were Jews, either in denominational terms or according to the Nazi definition of an assumed Jewish 'race', but there were also other categories of refugees and/or exiles: Social Democrats, Communists and members of other political organizations, Catholics and Protestants, intellectuals, artists, pacifists and sundry other groups and individuals. The distinction between 'refugees' and 'exiles', between supposedly non-political Jewish emigrants and political activists fighting National Socialism from abroad, is a pragmatic one and the categories are clearly not exclusive. Numerous 'refugees' were or became active opponents of the Third Reich, while many political 'exiles' later aimed to become fully integrated into the societies of their respective countries of refuge.[1]

Looking at the consecutive periods of Nazi anti-Jewish policies between 1933 and October 1941, when emigration was officially prohibited, one can clearly distinguish two basic patterns: an interplay between Reich-level measures and local or regional pressure, and a strong correlation between intimidation and street violence and legislative acts.[2] Institution-

1

alized terror in the newly founded concentration camps went hand in hand with legal defamation and the exclusion of certain categories of people from the German *Volksgemeinschaft* (folk community). The so-called 'Law for the Restoration of the Professional Civil Service' of April 1933 led to the first dismissals of Jewish civil servants, university teachers, judges and other public servants, while the infamous Nuremberg Laws of September 1935 and subsequent decrees deprived all Jews of their German citizenship rights and helped to remove them from positions they had previously held in local government and public life. Following the pogroms of November 1938, in which ninety-one Jews were killed and 26,000 Jewish men were sent to concentration camps, Jewish communities throughout Germany were fined 1 billion Reichsmark to 'make good' the murder of a German diplomat in Paris by a Jewish student, whose family had been among those 17,000 Polish-Jewish nationals whom the Nazi authorities had previously deported from Germany to Poland.

These brutal actions were followed by a series of economic measures. All Jewish participation in German businesses was soon prohibited and Jewish companies were now systematically 'aryanized': they either became subject to liquidation or were systematically transferred from Jewish to German owners at depressed prices. Wealthy Jews were ordered to deposit their stocks, bonds and other securities with local tax offices. A series of *Berufsverbote* and other decrees further narrowed the sphere of Jewish economic and social activities. At the beginning of December 1938, German Jews were finally excluded from teaching or research at universities and other institutions of higher education and even forbidden to use their libraries. In short: Nazi persecution policy was a many-layered and polymorphous affair, neither consistent nor systematic, but certainly quite effective and comprehensive.

The precise number of individuals leaving Germany on account of 'racial' or political persecution cannot be established. Estimates of the total number of emigrants from Germany, Austria (after March 1938) and the German-speaking region of Czechoslovakia (Sudetenland after October 1938), range up to 500,000 and include all persons not of Jewish religion. The number of non-Jewish refugees who fled solely for political reasons was approximately 30,000, but this figure does not include the war years for which no statistics are available. The number of Jewish emigrants from Germany alone can be estimated at between 270,000 and 300,000 persons, roughly three-fifths of German Jewry. Figures based on German census data and Jewish sources show that the number of Jews emigrating after the initial wave of emigration following the Nazi takeover in 1933 remained relatively stable (between 21,000 and 25,000 refugees per year). Figures increased dramatically only after the 1938

November pogroms (euphemistically called *Reichskristallnacht* — 'Crystal Night' or 'Night of the Broken Glass') and in the wake of Germany's expansionist policies after March 1938, from 40,000 in 1938 to 78,000 in 1939. A mere 30,000 Jews managed to flee Germany during the war years, and around 134,000 were deported to concentration and extermination camps. Another 5,000 stayed in hiding. Altogether, between 20,000 and 25,000, or less than 5 per cent of the original population of 525,000 German Jews, managed to survive the Holocaust within reach of Nazi barbarism.[3]

In explaining the flow and timing of the emigration process in the pre-war years one has to look at a number of factors, above all the economic and social circumstances. The economic development of the Jewish community in Nazi Germany appears to have followed two divergent paths: impoverishment, loss of professional capacity and unemployment on the one hand, and relative recovery from the general economic depression on the other. Poverty stimulated emigration, while recovery, even on a temporary basis, tended to retard it.[4] While many employees, forcefully retired civil servants, and middle-class professionals became increasingly impoverished, Jewish business and manufacturing, especially in the larger enterprises, initially not only succeeded in maintaining its economic position but presumably even shared in the growth of the German economy after 1933. This might explain why many wealthy Jews left Germany relatively late, just before or shortly after the pogroms of November 1938.

The emigration of Jews from Germany was a social movement of individuals and families. In line with the tradition of close family cohesion among Jews, family ties abroad and mutual aid between members of the extended family played a major rôle in the choice of country of refuge.[5] Having children of school age was certainly a factor in delaying the date of emigration. Family cohesion may have also influenced the decision to place a number of older children in home-care placement programmes initiated by a number of national refugee organizations, even before the *Kristallnacht*. Altogether some 18,000 children left Germany as 'unaccompanied children' for foster homes or families abroad; the majority, however, left after November 1938. In the USA, the German-Jewish Children's Aid committee asked that only children from well-to-do families should be selected for placement in US foster homes. Though this was originally designed to minimize the social problems expected from poorer children, it demonstrated an astonishing lack of imagination on the part of the responsible bureaucratic institutions.

After November 1938, the admission of refugee children to Great Britain, on the other hand, was strongly linked with Britain immigration policies on Palestine.[6] The Foreign Office had persistently refused to allow a group of 10,000 German-Jewish children to enter Palestine, but then, with the agreement of the Home Office, had accepted their entry into Britain, on condition that the British Inter-Aid Committee (later known as the Refugee Children's Movement) agreed to maintain them by providing welfare and support. By the outbreak of war in September 1939 some 9,300 children, about seventy-five per cent of them of the Jewish religion, had come to Britain with the help of private refugee organizations.[7]

During the early years of German emigration, Great Britain was certainly not the most favoured country of refuge. France, Poland, Czechoslovakia, and even the small Netherlands, despite its rather restrictive immigration policy towards 'racial' as well as political refugees, admitted many more emigrants than Britain.[8] By the end of 1937 only about 5,500 of the approximately 154,000 people who had fled from Nazi oppression had entered Britain. Meanwhile other countries were beginning to close their doors. Between 1933 and 1936 Palestine, then under a British administration provided for by the League of Nations mandate, had absorbed 35,000 refugees. The outbreak of a serious Arab rebellion in 1936 led the British government to restrict the issue of immigration certificates. As a result, German-Jewish emigration to Palestine in the following years (except for 1939) was reduced by more than half. As Palestine and other countries raised new barriers to entry, the pressure on Britain increased.[9]

The restrictive regulations on immigration and foreign nationals, which the British government applied to German refugees after 1933, were not new. They simply amounted to a continuation of the Restrictions on Immigration and the severe Aliens Legislation introduced by various British governments at the height of the immigration of East European Jews (1905) during and after the First World War. This legislation remained in effect until after the Second World War and, in its application to immigration from continental Europe, was overridden only on Britain's ratification of the Treaty of Rome in 1972.[10]

The restriction on immigrants was politically initiated and publicly supported by fears that any increase in the number of refugees admitted would inevitably lead to rising unemployment and economic difficulties. As early as March 1933 a Conservative MP, the Unionist Member for Tottenham North, had claimed in the House of Commons that 'hundreds of thousands of Jews are now leaving Germany and scurrying from there to this country . . . Are we prepared in this country to allow aliens to come in here from every country while we have 3,000,000 unemployed?'; and, implying that anti-Semitism would increase if Britain admitted more refugees, he added: 'If you are asking for a von Hitler [*sic*!] in this country,

4

we will soon get one.'[11] Though the government initially reacted in a cautious and restrained way and confirmed the traditional right of asylum regardless 'of religious belief or racial origin' (Home Office) it was well aware of the sensitive nature of this problem. Instructing the British delegate at the League of Nations Council in Geneva, the Foreign Secretary told him that with regard to the refugee question, unemployment and the state of the labour market were of 'paramount consideration' to the government.[12] Two months later, at the beginning of December 1933, Britain's representative to the newly established 'High Commission for Refugees (Jewish and Other) Coming from Germany', Viscount Cecil of Chelwood, was given detailed instructions about the possible immigration of German refugees into Britain: 'owing to the acute unemployment . . . there are no prospects for Germans seeking employment in commerce or industry'; there was no guarantee that medical doctors, even after obtaining a British degree, would be permitted to practise; and there was 'little or no possibility of finding useful openings in this country for more refugees of the professional classes'.[13]

From the outset, two social groups had been exempted from the restrictive regulations on asylum because the British government had hoped to obtain direct benefits from their presence. The first group comprised industrialists and businessmen with private fortunes who could help to reduce unemployment by establishing new businesses, particularly in the economically hard afflicted areas of north and north-west England, where unemployment ran high and industries were frequently outdated.[14] The second was made up of well-known artists and scholars. As early as April 1933 the British Cabinet accepted that it was in the public interest

> to try to secure for this country prominent Jews who were being expelled from Germany and who had achieved distinction whether in pure science, applied science, such as medicine or technical industry, music or art. This would not only obtain for this country the advantage of their knowledge and experience, but would also create a very favourable impression in the world, particularly if our hospitality were offered with some warmth.[15]

At the same time the government hastened to make it clear that even in such cases, based on carefully considered utilitarian grounds, the allocation of state funds was not intended. Private organizations and individuals were to be encouraged to bear the burden.

If British ministers and government officials had cherished any hopes that an 'orderly' solution to the growing refugee problem might be achieved by involving all countries concerned, they were soon disillusioned. Nazi Germany showed no interest in an orderly emigration of Jews or in an internationally agreed settlement concerning their immigration into European and other countries. On the contrary, Nazi leaders and Hitler in particular clearly hoped that unregulated Jewish immigration would create economic and social unrest and lead to open anti-Semitism in all countries of refuge.[16] Similar arguments were put forward by a number of Fascist and right-wing, but also by some conservative politicians and organizations in these countries, while demanding a restriction in the admission quota of refugees.

The failure of the Evian conference in July 1938 to bring about international co-operation *vis-à-vis* refugees from Germany, and the refusal of the governments of the British colonies and Dominions to accept any significant number of German emigrants, put additional pressure on Britain. Following the Austrian *Anschluß* in March and the incorporation of the Sudetenland into Germany after the Munich conference in September 1938 the number of refugees seeking to enter Britain increased dramatically. The British government began to adopt a progressively more flexible attitude, first shown in the *en bloc* admission of the Sudeten Social Democrats to Britain after attempts to settle them in some part of the Dominions had failed. By the outbreak of the war some 6,000 Sudeten and Czech refugees had found a temporary home in Britain.[17]

While the Sudeten refugee problem was still very much in the public eye, Nazi Germany created yet another massive wave of emigration. In the wake of the expulsion of thousands of Polish Jews in October and the pogroms in many German towns in November 1938 the number of refugees asking for asylum in Britain reached a new peak. The situation was complicated by the fact that the Jewish voluntary organizations were by then having enormous difficulty in meeting the guarantee they had given the British government in 1933. This guarantee contained a pledge by the Anglo-Jewish community, signed by four of their most prominent representatives, that 'all expense, whether in respect of temporary or permanent accommodation or maintenance, would be borne by the Jewish community without ultimate charge to the state'.[18] Jewish leaders then had put the number of refugees at between 3,000 and 4,000, vastly underestimating the magnitude of the problem, as did everybody else at the time. Although the voluntary aid organizations had virtually reached breaking-point by the summer of 1939, they managed to cope with the flood of refugees, and the Jewish community's guarantee was fulfilled until after the outbreak of the war.

By December 1938 more than ten relief organizations were represented in the Co-ordinating Committee for Refugees, which provided a formal link between the Home Office and private institutions. Among the Jewish organizations which had to bear the main burden were the Council for German Jewry (established in 1933 as the Central British Fund for

German Jewry, a fund-raising body) and the German Jewish Aid Committee. The latter had been founded in the early months of 1933 as the Jewish Refugee Committee by Otto M. Schiff, a German-born City merchant banker. Schiff, who had been involved in relief work since the First World War as President of another aid organization, the Jews' Temporary Shelter in London, maintained close contacts with the Home Office and other government departments, which occasionally encouraged Home Office officials to make some unbureaucratic decisions regarding the acceptance of German-Jewish refugees. The Refugee Children's Movement (formerly the Inter-Aid Committee for Children Coming from Germany), which had been most influential in the admission of more than 9,000 children to Britain after November 1938, was a joint Jewish–Christian body, though much of the local refugee work was organized by synagogue committees.[19] A very successful fund-raising campaign launched by the former Prime Minister, Lord Baldwin, together with *The Times*, attracted donations of more than £500,000, about half of which went to assist the work of the Refugee Children's Movement.

The most active of the non-Jewish organizations was the (Religious) Society of Friends with its Germany Emergency and Austria Committee and offices in Paris, Prague and Berlin. Alongside the Jewish bodies, the Society of Friends often became directly involved in negotiations about refugees with the relevant government departments. Important refugee work was also undertaken by the Society for the Protection of Science and Learning (formerly the Academic Assistance Council) on behalf of émigré scholars and university teachers; the Federation of University Women in England, which aimed to support women university teachers and researchers; the International Student Service, working for the estimated 3,500 students among the German refugees; and the Jewish Academic (Professional) Council, which concerned itself particularly with refugees from the 'professional' classes such as doctors, solicitors and teachers.[20] The target groups as well as the social composition of the voluntary bodies point to the overwhelmingly middle-class character of the German emigration. Though there are no data available on the social and professional background of German refugees it is safe to say that the majority of refugees came from the middle or lower-middle classes. There were only very few members of the working class among the Jewish refugees and only marginally more among some groups of the political emigration, with the possible exception of the German and Austrian Communists. The exiled Social Democrats who had moved their headquarters-in-exile to London (after Prague, 1933–38, and Paris, 1938–40) were initially supported by the Trades Union Congress and the Labour Party until the Vansittartite view among the leadership of the Labour Party, after 1942, became an insurmountable obstacle to their relations.[21] The German Communists, numerically the largest political exile group in Britain, received support directly from Moscow but also from politically like-minded British organizations.

Once it was generally recognized that there were many professing Christians among the German-Jewish refugees, Church organizations like the Church of England Committee for Non-Aryan Christians [*sic!*], similar committees from the Church of Scotland and the Catholic Church, as well as the International Hebrew Christian Alliance joined forces with other voluntary organizations. Most of the Christian groups and committees were represented in the Christian Council for Refugees from Germany, which acted as a fund-raising institution but also maintained direct contact with the Home Office.

The efforts and constant lobbying of voluntary organizations, Jewish and others, on behalf of German, Austrian and Sudeten refugees, were supported by a number of prominent individuals, among them several Members of Parliament such as the Labour MPs Philip Noel-Baker and (Colonel) Josiah Wedgwood. The most forceful advocate of refugees in the House of Commons, however, was an independent Member of Parliament (for the Combined English Universities), Eleanor F. Rathbone, who earned herself the honorary title of 'Member for Refugees'.[22] Time and again Miss Rathbone demanded that the British government ease regulations on admission and strengthen the traditional right of asylum for *all* refugees from Nazi oppression, while at the same time castigating the government's attitude of 'selfish isolationism' and calling upon the public to press for changes in the official refugee policy, 'loudly, insistently and persistently'.[23] The interventions and appeals to support all refugees made by her and other Members were echoed in the House of Lords by the Bishop of Chichester, George Bell, who repeatedly called the government's attention to the seriousness of the refugee problem.[24]

It was thanks to the unceasing activities of British refugee organizations and the calls of prominent individuals, which received a responsive hearing from the public at large, that the government, however reluctantly, lifted the restrictions on immigration after December 1938. At the outbreak of war in September 1939 approximately 55,000 German and Austrian refugees had been officially-granted asylum. A further 20,000 had received a temporary permit upon entry but were told that they had to leave the country immediately after they had been issued with a visa to migrate to another country. That such a large number of refugees — ninety per cent of them Jewish — were admitted in spite of the anti-Jewish and anti-German roots of the British immigration laws still in force at the time was remarkable indeed.

The outbreak of war marked a turning point both in the government's policy on immigration from Nazi Germany and in official and public attitudes towards all refugees already in Britain.[25] On 3 September 1939 all visas granted to enemy nationals were automatically invalidated. No refugees from enemy countries (Germany and Italy) or even from enemy-occupied territories were henceforth admitted into Britain. Although large numbers of citizens of allied countries·occupied by Germany were allowed to enter Britain, the policy of exclusion was applied particularly to German and Austrian refugees, regardless of their political or 'racial' status. A few exceptions occurred only in cases where the relevant person was considered to be of importance to the British war effort. The government did not even refrain from referring to the supposed existence of anti-Semitic fears among the British public when discussing the (theoretical) possibility of admitting '1,000 to 2,000 refugees' during the war years after it had received first reports of the Jewish Holocaust in Eastern Europe. As the Home Secretary Herbert Morrison stated at the end of December 1942, 'there was considerable anti-Semitism under the surface in this country. If there were any substantial increase in the number of Jewish refugees or if these refugees did not leave the country after the war, we should be in for serious trouble'.[26] But Morrison was clearly overstating his case. Although there were, even in later war years, occasional signs of wartime anti-refugee or anti-Jewish feelings, particularly fostered by certain sections of the tabloid press, these derived more from an island xenophobia than from widespread anti-Semitic prejudice.

The near-impossibility of emigration from Nazi-occupied Europe combined with the negative attitude of the British government towards any further immigration of so-called 'enemy aliens' reduced the flow of German refugees to Britain to a mere trickle during the war. But what happened to the 55,000 refugees already in the country? As during the First World War, the suspicion that Germany was attempting to infiltrate agents and spies into Britain led to restrictive moves against all immigrants. Immediately after the declaration of war 112 special tribunals were set up by the Home Office to review all Germans, Austrians and Czechs (Sudeten) in order to determine whether they should be interned. The whole operation included about 73,000 cases and was virtually completed by January 1940; by then a total of 528 aliens had been interned, 8,356 subjected to some restrictions while the overwhelming majority (some 64,000) were left at liberty, although they, too, had to observe certain restrictions.[27] The internees included 350 known German Nazis and 160 refugees, among them the political economist Jürgen Kuszinski and the journalist Sebastian Haffner, author of the anti-nazi polemic *Germany: Jekyll and Hyde* (1940). At the same time about 1,800

British citizens suspected of Nazi sympathies were also detained under Defence Regulation 18b.

The end of the 'phoney war' and the German invasion of Denmark and Norway in April 1940 led to a further change in public opinion. The sudden collapse of the Dutch, Belgian and French armies in the face of the German advance and the British retreat from Dunkirk heightened the 'Fifth Column' panic in Britain. There were frequent outbursts of xenophobia and hysteria resembling certain anti-German demonstrations during the First World War.[28] Anti-alien feelings received a further boost after some newspapers published inflated or wholly invented stories about the danger of foreigners becoming German agents. Even papers like the liberal *Manchester Guardian* and the *Jewish Chronicle* became increasingly worried and argued in favour of mass internment. Responding to the anti-refugee mood (the 'socially done thing') and to an order attributed to the newly appointed Prime Minister to 'collar the lot', the government embarked on a policy of general internment.[29] By July 1940 a total of 27,000 people had been arrested, among them more than 4,000 women and several hundred children along with their mothers. The majority of internees were refugees from Germany and Austria, formerly classed as 'friendly enemy aliens'. Generally excluded were unaccompanied children under the age of sixteen and older people over seventy. Some exceptions were made for scientists and engineers who had been enlisted for research and other work essential for the war effort, while a few others were protected by influential individuals or British refugee organizations. The Isle of Man, where thousands of civilians had been interned during the First World War, once again became a vast metropolis of aliens. For several internees, like the journalist Heinrich Fraenkel, this was the second time they were interned on the same island during their stay in Britain. Housing conditions on the Isle of Man and in dozens of other internment camps varied enormously: tents, holiday apartments, schools, army barracks, disused factories, underground car parks, manor houses and even the winter quarters of the Bertram Mills Circus were used to accommodate the internees. The experience of internment was for many refugees a very depressing one and led — at least in one camp — to a number of suicides. After a while living conditions improved. Refugees were separated from Nazi sympathizers, and most internment camps experienced a flood of educational and intellectual activities. The existence of a rich cultural life behind barbed wire is perhaps one of the most fascinating and surprising features of this otherwise depressing period.[30]

Deportation overseas, however, was generally worse than internment in British camps. In 1940 about 8,000 'enemy aliens' were deported by government order to Canada (2,000) and Australia (6,000), often suffering

WRITE TO YOUR MEMBER OF PARLIAMENT AND YOUR LOCAL NEWSPAPER TO DEMAND THE IMMEDIATE DECLARATION OF A NEW POLICY ON THE LINES SUGGESTED HERE

You will be assisting in the creation of a great company of people of all nations who will help us to achieve a more speedy victory:

(Reproduced by kind permission of the *Evening Standard*)   (*Copyright in All Countries*)

Please make sure

that every person you know and meet reads this pamphlet.

Order further supplies
from the publisher
RAYMOND GAUNTLETT, 10 Gerald Road, London, S.W.I

d by Unwin Brothers Ltd., London and Woking

1. Caricature of British internment policies. From a 1940 FDKB pamphlet

11

abuse and physical ill-treatment during the passage. Some excesses, such as the events aboard the overcrowded troopship *Dunera* on her voyage to Australia, were later strongly condemned in Parliament and punished by military courts. But the British public, which had initially clamoured for strong and effective measures against all 'enemy aliens', soon reverted to a more lenient attitude. Obvious scandals in the setting-up and administration of some internment camps and the unremitting and constant campaign by voluntary organizations and some prominent Members of Parliament, led to a general recognition that the internment of refugees served no rational purpose. The *Arandora Star* catastrophe in particular marked a significant reversal in public opinion on the treatment of emigrants from Nazi Germany. On 2 July 1940 the Blue Star liner *Arandora Star*, on her way to Canada with nearly 1,200 deportees on board, was struck by a German torpedo and sank off the north-west coast of Ireland. Of the passengers, 600 deportees drowned, many of whom, as was later shown, were German and Austrian refugees and non-political Italian immigrants.[31]

The British government again responded to the shift in public opinion and soon began ordering the release of certain categories of internees, who were thought to be of immediate use for the British war effort. Apart from engineers and scientists, these included those working on BBC broadcasts to Germany, or the support staff of various British intelligence services. About 4,000 interned refugees were allowed to join the Auxiliary Military Pioneer Corps, a non-combatant unit under the command of the Marquis of Reading. (At a later stage of the war, refugee soldiers were permitted to serve with other Army units and many took part in military actions on all fronts.)[32] By mid-January 1941 about one-third, and half a year later two-thirds of the former 27,000 internees had been released. Those who had been deported to Canada and Australia, however, had, for the time being, to stay in internment camps, since no ships were available to take them back to Britain, which meant that some internees did not return until the end of 1942. By April 1944 only twenty-five refugees were reported to be still interned in Britain, a further sixty-eight were kept in Australia, while all deportees in Canada had been released.

It has repeatedly been said that the British record of admission of German emigrants between 1933 and 1939 was relatively generous by contemporary international standards.[33] Although this might be the case, at least for the critical years of 1938 and 1939, this assessment needs some qualification. Like other Western parliamentary democracies Britain did not pursue any real refugee policy that would have had to be predicated upon the scope and character of Nazi persecutions. Instead, it merely followed a traditional immigration policy which was based first and foremost on its own economic and political interests. Most refugees from Nazi oppression were not spared the personal experience of this important distinction.

Notes

1. See Werner Röder, 'The Political Exiles: Their Policies and Contribution to Post-War Reconstruction'. Introduction to *International Biographical Dictionary of Central European Emigrés 1933–1945*, vol. 2: *The Arts, Sciences, and Literature*, Munich, 1983, p. xxvii.
2. Herbert A. Strauss, 'Jewish Emigration from Germany. Nazi Policies and Jewish Responses (I)', in *Leo Baeck Institute Year Book*, vol. 25, 1980, p. 332.
3. Ibid., pp. 316–27.
4. Ibid., p. 339.
5. Ibid., p. 338.
6. A. J. Sherman, *Island Refuge: Britain and Refugees from the Third Reich 1933–1939*, London, 1973, p. 211.
7. See Mary R. Ford, 'The Arrival of Jewish Refugee Children in England, 1938–1939', in *Immigrants and Minorities*, vol. 2, 1983, pp. 135–51.
8. For the Netherlands see the instructive case study by Bob Moore, *Refugees from Nazi Germany in the Netherlands 1933–1940*, Dordrecht, 1986.
9. For emigration to Palestine see Strauss, 'Jewish Emigration from Germany. Nazi Policies and Jewish Responses (II)', in *Leo Baeck Institute Year Book*, vol. 26, 1981, pp. 343–57.
10. Bernard Wasserstein, 'The British Government and the German Immigration 1933–1945', in Gerhard Hirschfeld (ed.), *Exile in Great Britain: Refugees from Hitler's Germany*, Leamington Spa, and New Jersey, 1984, pp. 64–5.
11. *Hansard*: House of Commons Debate, vol. 275, col. 1351–1354 (E. Doran).
12. Simon to Ormsby-Gore, 3 October 1933, Public Record Office (PRO): FO 371/16757, C. 8669/6839/18.
13. Simon to Cecil, 1 December 1933, PRO: FO 371/17698, C 39/23/18.
14. See Herbert Loebl, 'Refugee Industries in the Special Areas of Britain', in Hirschfeld, *Exile in Great Britain*, pp. 219–49.
15. Cabinet conclusions, 8 April 1933, PRO: Cabinet 27/33.
16. On the Nazi policies towards refugees see John P. Fox, 'Nazi Germany and German Emigration to Great Britain', in Hirschfeld, *Exile in Great Britain*, pp. 29–62.
17. See Sherman, *Island Refuge*, pp. 131–65.
18. 'Proposals of the Jewish Community as Regards Jewish Refugees from Germany', Appendix I to the Memorandum by the Home Secretary, 7 April 1933, PRO: Cabinet Papers 96/33.
19. Ford, 'Arrival of Jewish Refugee Children', p. 142.
20. See Gerhard Hirschfeld, 'German Refugee Scholars in Great Britain, 1933–1945', in *Refugees in the Age of Total War*, London, 1988, pp. 152–63.
21. See Anthony Glees, *Exile Politics during the Second World War: The German Social Democrats in Britain*, Oxford, 1982.
22. Francis L. Carsten, 'German Refugees in Great Britain 1933–1945: A survey', in Hirschfeld, *Exile in Great Britain*, p. 14.
23. Thus in her letter to the *Manchester Guardian*, 6 April 1939. See M.D. Stocks, *Eleanor Rathbone: Biography*, London, 1949, pp. 257–8, 300; Sherman, *Island Refuge*, pp. 33, 225–6.

24. See Sherman, *Island Refuge*, pp. 79, 122, 245.
25. See Wasserstein, 'The British Government and the German Immigration', pp. 76–8; for a more detailed account see Bernard Wasserstein, *British and the Jews of Europe 1939–1945*, London/Oxford, 1979.
26. Cabinet Committee on the Reception and Accommodation of Jewish Refugees: Minutes of meeting, 31 December 1942, PRO CAB 95/15.
27. See Wasserstein, *Britain and the Jews of Europe*, p. 85.
28. See C.C. Aronsfeld, 'Jewish Enemy Aliens in England During the First World War', in *Jewish Social Studies*, October 1956.
29. For Britain's internment policy during the Second World War see Peter and Leni Gillmann, *'Collar the Lot!': How Britain Interned and Expelled its Wartime Refugees*, London, 1980; Ronald Stent, *A Bespattered Page? The Internment of His Majesty's 'Most Loyal Aliens'*, London, 1980. For the views of former internees on this period see Miriam Kochan, *Britain's Internees in the Second World War*, London, 1983.
30. See Michael Seyfert, '"His Majesty's Most Loyal Internees". The Internment and Deportation of German and Austrian Refugees as "Enemy Aliens". Historical, Cultural and Literary Aspects', in Hirschfeld, *Exile in Great Britain*, pp. 163–93.
31. On the *Arandora Star* catastrophe see P. and L. Gillmann, *'Collar the Lot!'*, pp. 185–201.
32. See Norman Bentwich, *I Understand the Risks: the story of the Refugees from Nazi oppression who fought in the British Forces in the World War. With a Foreword by the Marquis of Reading*, London, 1950.
33. Wasserstein, 'The British Government and the German Immigration', p. 79; Sherman, *Island Refuge*, p. 267.

-2-

Producing Art in Exile
Perspectives on the German Refugees' Creative Activities in Great Britain

GÜNTER BERGHAUS

Following Hitler's appointment as Chancellor on 30 January 1933 a number of laws were passed which enabled the Nazis to assume total control over the German population: a Law for the Reconstruction of the Civil Service (7 April), a Denationalization Decree (14 July), a Law for the Protection of German Blood and Honour, and a Reich Citizenship Law (13 September: the so-called Nuremberg Laws) and a Law for the Establishment of a Reich Cultural Chamber (22 September), to name just a few. A few weeks after Hitler's seizure of power the *Große Säuberung* began, the clearing out and elimination of left-wing and Jewish art and culture. On 10 May 1933 a burning of books was held, and in September 1933 Joseph Goebbels was charged with the formation of a *Reichskultur-kammer*, a guild-like organization with compulsory membership for all artists working in the media of literature, theatre, music, film, radio, fine arts and journalism. In order to qualify for membership a proclamation of loyalty to the new régime was required; those who were not prepared to support the new cultural policy were barred from exercising their profession and having their work shown in public.

As a result of these measures many artists were arrested, deported or killed in prisons and concentration camps. Others went into so-called 'inner emigration'; but the majority of Germany's critical intelligentsia and creative artist community went into exile. Some of them were forced to leave Germany because they found themselves on the *Ausbürgerungslisten* (lists of expatriation) on account of their ethnic background or political record. For them, fleeing Germany was the only way to secure their physical survival. However, famous artists found themselves, generally, in a much more secure position than the so-called man on the street who was caught and put through the mangle of the Gestapo without anybody but his nearest friends and relatives knowing about his disappearance. The number of well-known artists who ended up in concentration camps or died in the torture chambers of the SS was very small indeed. A few prominent left-wing or Communist intellectuals fell into the hands of the Gestapo (e.g. Willi Bredel, Berta Lask, Egon Erwin Kisch, Ernst Busch, Wolfgang Langhoff, Hermann Duncker, Karl August Wittfogel), but none of them shared the ill fortunes of Carl von Ossietzky or Erich Mühsam. Many artists were made extremely tempting offers by the new government in order to ensure their loyalty. Actors, for example, were given long-term contracts, paid holiday leave, free medical treatment and generous social security and superannuation schemes.[1] The Nazi rulers themselves must have been rather unsure about who could be classified as their supporter or enemy. The well-known case of Fritz Lang who was offered the chair of the *Reichsfilmkammer* and then decided to leave Germany, just a few hours after his audience with Goebbels,[2] may have been an extreme example, but it was indicative of the Nazis' attempt to prevent a cultural famine following their take-over. They were perfectly aware that the loss of one Thomas Mann could not be redeemed by the retention of ten Ernst Jüngers, Ernst Wiecherts or Hans Carossas.

The attitude of those artists who could be persuaded to stay in Germany after 1933 ranged from open support for the Nazis or restrained loyalty, to passive resistance or inner emigration. In the field of theatre one could mention the playwrights Gerhart Hauptmann and Max Halbe; the directors Gustav Gründgens, Heinz Hilpert, Erich Engel, Jürgen Fehling and Karl Heinz Martin; the designers Caspar Neher, Traugott Müller and Cesar Klein; the dancers Mary Wigman and Harald Kreutzberg; the actors Heinrich George, Werner Krauß, Paul Wegener, Eduart von Winterstein, Horst Caspar, Lothar Müthel, Friedrich Kayßler, Paul Hartmann; the actresses Käthe Gold, Marianne Hoppe, Käthe Dorsch and Paula Wessely. Although a number of prominent artists and a few of international repute stayed behind in 1933, their creative output over the next twelve years could not make up for the intellectual bloodletting caused by the exodus of no fewer than 2,000 writers (420 of them dramatists) and 4,000 theatre practitioners.[3] Some were overtaken by events at a time when they were travelling abroad and found 'that while one is away one's country is running away somewhere and one can't get hold of it anymore'.[4] Others were *Spätexilanten* (late emigrants) who initially tried to come to some kind of arrangement with the new régime but then decided to leave when the full extent of Nazi oppression and the cultural implications of their take-over dawned on them. Whether exiled by design or coincidence, few of the emigrants conceived of the possibility that their 'prolonged trip abroad' would actually last ten to twelve years. What initially looked like a short interlude in their lives soon grew into a veritable nightmare. Even the most starry-eyed artists, who had to experi-

16

ence the November pogroms of 1938 (*Kristallnacht*) and German expansion into Austria, Czechoslovakia and Poland to see clearly what was afoot, eventually became aware that the Nazi régime was proving to be a durable factor in German politics and was, in fact, developing into a major political force threatening European peace and security. The sooner they came to terms with the fact that their exile was more than just a passing phase the easier it was for them to build up a new existence abroad and to find a new purpose for their art.

Many artists, when they arrived in France, England, Sweden or wherever, expected to be received with the same friendliness they had experienced on their former trips to these countries. However, after 1933 things turned out to be very different. The friends, who had invited them to their country (and it was usually personal contacts that determined the artists' choice of exile country), may have given them a warm welcome, but the rest of the population was usually less enthusiastic about the possibility of a large refugee community in their midst.

Once-famous artists suddenly had to realize that they were virtually unknown figures in their guest country. The self-importance they had always attached to themselves, and the notion of international repute they thought they had achieved following an exhibition in Paris, a lecture tour in Scandinavia, or the granting of an honorary degree in Oxford, suddenly fell apart when an unimportant magazine declined to publish one of their poems because it was not considered 'good enough', or when they tried to secure the commission of a portrait or some book illustration, and their offer was rejected because nobody wanted to buy the work of an 'unknown artist'. This experience is reflected in Max Herrmann-Neiße's poem 'Ein deutscher Dichter bin ich einst gewesen' (Once I was a German poet), where he says:

> . . . hier wird niemand meine Verse lesen,
> ist nichts, was meiner Seele Sprache spricht;
> ein deutscher Dichter bin ich einst gewesen;
> jetzt ist mein Leben Spuk wie mein Gedicht.[5]

> (No-one will read my poems here,
> The language of my soul has no meaning.
> Once I was a German poet,
> Now my life is a spectre, just like my work.)

Most artists were not able to survive by their creative work alone. Many were forced to take any job offered to them in order to supplement their meagre income. They had to join the queue of other refugees on the labour exchange and compete with the native unemployed on the job market. As a result of this, the population's indifference towards these artists often turned into open hostility. The frosty atmosphere caused by xenophobia and anti-Semitism, the loss of self-esteem, and the sudden realization that they had been cut off from their old public and stood little chance of gaining access to a new market, led many artists into severe personal crises. Some were driven into isolation and despair and committed suicide (Kurt Tucholsky, Walter Hasenclever, Ernst Weiß, Carl Einstein, Stefan Zweig and Walter Benjamin, to name just a few), which seemed to be the only logical answer to Hasenclever's question: 'We are banished, we are homeless, we are cursed. What right do we have to live?'[6] Stefan Zweig confessed that after his move into exile 'I felt that I didn't quite belong to myself anymore. Something of my original and real self had been destroyed forever.'[7] As early as 1937, Ernst Stern wrote a book on this phenomenon entitled *Die Emigration als psychologisches Problem* (Emigration as a Psychological Problem). Klaus Mann, in his *Emigrantenroman Der Vulkan*, called this attitude 'Entwurzelungsneurose' (neurosis caused by uprooting a person), and Alexander Granach coined the term 'Emigrantenpsychose' (emigrant psychosis) for this.[8]

Artists who relied on language as a medium of expression (writers, actors, etc.) found it invariably frustrating to see themselves reduced to stuttering in a foreign language when their accomplished command of the German tongue had brought them justified acclaim in their homeland. One might assume that artists who used a visual language might have been in a better position and more able to transcend any national barriers and to continue their career in exile without too much of a hiatus. But this was far from being the case. The living and working conditions forced nearly all artists to relinquish their personal style and interest and to produce whatever might find a buyer on the market. For example, one painter who had come to England in the 1930s still remembers how his works were considered too expressionistic and how he was constantly asked to tone down his colours:

> As much as I have an accent in my language I have an accent in my painting. In German art of our century, expression and feeling comes into it a lot. Whereas mainstream art in Britain is more good taste and playing down feelings. The majority of English people find my paintings too emotive, too direct. English art is a refined understatement.[9]

The modes of expressions that had prevailed in the Weimar Republic (e.g. Expressionism, *Neue Sachlichkeit*) were known to only a few admirers abroad. When a courageous gallerist was prepared to organize an exhibition of one of these artists, the show was often greeted with consternation and revulsion by the local population and turned into what Ludwig Meidner called in his case 'a second class funeral'.[10]

Theatre artists did not fare any better, as the examples quoted on p. 33–41 reveal. The artistic traditions in the countries of exile were so different from those that had existed in Germany before 1933 that many artists felt that they could not elicit any desired response from their addressees, or that they were, as Leonard Frank put it, 'playing on a violin of stone, a piano without strings.'[11] As a result of this, artists had to turn to menial tasks in order to make a living. Stage designers had to do window decoration for department stores; painters worked in china factories and sculptors in toy shops; poets wrote advertisement slogans and composers little ditties for the radio. There were few who could agree with Schoenberg when he said: 'If immigration to America has changed me — I am not aware of it.'[12]

On the other hand, it would be misleading to assume that exile had only negative experiences to offer. The life of an émigré artist may have been hard but it also granted valuable lessons, which some of them later would not have missed for anything. Bertolt Brecht saw exile as a school for life and reminded his fellow emigrants that 'the Chinese poets and philosophers are wont to go into exile just as we are used to going to an academy'.[13] Egon Schwarz came to appreciate his exile experience as a blessing in disguise 'which led me away from the insularity, provincialism, the narrow-mindedness full of resentment and hostility of my middle-European existence'.[14] Alfred Kerr rhymed in a similar vein:

> Manchmal fühlt das Herz sich sehr erheitert
> (trotz der zugeschlagnen deutschen Tür):
> Weil die Flucht den Horizont erweitert,
> Ja, du dankst den Jägern fast dafür.[15]

> (Sometimes my heart cheers up
> (Despite the German door being closed):
> Because exile widens the horizon —
> I could nearly thank my persecutors for this.)

Hermann Kesten adjudged that 'we have found plenty of knowledge and experience of the ways of the world during our exile, which we can now use to enrich German literature with'.[16]

These quotations show that artists did not necessarily consider their exile a purely negative chapter in their lives. Therefore, Peter Laemmle's challenge: 'Shouldn't the exile scholars for once admit that exile, or the experience of exile, has changed the quality of literary texts, and has changed them in a negative sense?'[17] has to be treated with care. It is true that artists did not always create their best and most enduring works during their exile, but it was not always exterior circumstances which prevented them from achieving a level of quality which otherwise they would have been capable of. In many cases exiled artists continued a process already set in motion during the Weimar Republic, one which might roughly be described as 'deconstruction of High Culture'. New genres had sprung up in the 1920s (e.g. reportage, *Lehrstück*, photomontage, collage, etc.) because they were more flexible and versatile, and therefore more suitable to express contemporary artistic concerns. The small, 'operative' forms preferred by the exile artists must be seen in a similar light. Works of art should not be judged by 'absolute' aesthetic standards. Using criteria derived from other historical periods and applying them to creations which differ from those of previous centuries in aim and function will, by necessity, lead to distorted judgements. Any artistic product has to be assessed within the parameters or historical conditions which determine its creation, otherwise its specific qualities will easily be overlooked and misinterpreted. Since the circumstances under which the exiled artists were creating their works differed so fundamentally from those in pre-1933 Germany, these conditions have to be examined first before one can arrive at a critical, objective assessment of the artists' achievements in the various countries of exile. In our case this means that we have to study the political and cultural climate in Britain before we can come to a proper understanding of the theatrical activities generated by the German exiles.

Exile in Great Britain

Britain is a country with a high tradition of hospitality to foreigners and has, for centuries, offered refuge to those of every rank and station who sought asylum on her shores from persecution and economic plight in their own lands. During the nineteenth century, many Germans had to flee their country because of the anti-revolutionary backlash following the defeats of the 1830 and 1848 revolutions. Others decided to emigrate because of Germany's backwardness with regard to economic and scientific development. Because of her acclaimed liberalism Britain was a classic country of refuge for these men and women disenchanted with their homeland, and many Germans settled here, especially in London around Soho and Leicester Square, in St John's Wood and Camberwell.

Two of the most famous Germans to arrive in Britain were Karl Marx and Friedrich Engels. Other political thinkers and philosophers included Arnold Ruge, Gottfried Kinkel, Wilhelm Wolff, Eduard Bernstein and Wilhelm Liebknecht. Amongst the poets one can mention Ferdinand Freiligrath, Georg Weerth and Moritz Hartmann; amongst the publishers

Nikolaus Trübner and Julius Reuter; amongst the scholars the orientalist Friedrich Karl Müller and Theodor Goldstücker, the Germanists Karl Buchheim, Eugen Oswald, Robert Priebsch, and many more. Some immigrants such as the engineer Wilhelm Siemens or the architect Gottfried Semper decided to return to Germany; others made England their permanent home and founded institutions which are still with us today (e.g. Johannes Ronge, who introduced the first kindergarten in England in 1851, or Karl Halle, who founded the distinguished Hallé Orchestra in Manchester).[18]

Between 1826 and 1905 there existed practically no restrictions on immigration to Britain and, by all accounts, the reception refugees found in this country was very friendly indeed. Lord Malmesbury, in a speech to Parliament on 5 April 1852, sums up the prevailing atmosphere of hospitality by saying:

> I can well conceive the pleasure and happiness of a refugee, hunted from his native land, on approaching the shores of England, and the joy with which he first catches sight of them; but they are not greater than the pleasure and happiness every Englishman feels in knowing that his country affords the refugee a home and safety.[19]

According to a census in England and Wales the number of foreigners resident in those two parts of the country rose from 50,289 in 1851 to 118,031 in 1881.[20] Most of these exiles had arrived in England on their own or with their nearest relatives. They found the political climate here more liberal and the economic structures more advanced than in their home country and therefore decided to stay and start a new life as British citizens. The situation changed drastically with the mass emigration of Russian Jews at the end of the nineteenth century. By 1901 the number of aliens resident in the country had risen to 247,758, nearly half of them being East European Jews who had arrived in Britain during the past two decades.[21] This large influx of an ethnically and culturally diverse group of immigrants and their settlement in a relatively small, confined area (the London East End) gave rise to anti-Semitism, which soon turned into general xenophobia during the Boer War (1899–1902). As a result of this, the Aliens Act of 1905 was passed and soon afterwards was reinforced by the Aliens Restrictions Bill of 1914, curtailing the right of asylum and giving the immigration officers the power to refuse entry to those immigrants they considered 'undesirable'. The outbreak of the Second World War caused an outbreak of Germanophobia and led to the internment of about 40,000 of the 50,000 Germans living in this country.

The restrictions of the Aliens Act of 1905 and 1914 were further reinforced by the Aliens Order of 1920 which stated that no alien was to be given leave of entry unless he was in the possession of a work permit or some visible means of support. These restrictions being still in force during the 1930s prevented Britain from becoming a country of mass exile after Hitler's seizure of power. The initial wave of emigration from Nazi Germany caused the British Cabinet to set up a committee under the chairmanship of the Home Secretary in order to consider the question of German refugees. It was judged to be in the public interest to

> try and secure for this country prominent Jews who were being expelled from Germany and who had achieved distinction whether in pure science, applied science, such as medicine or technical industry, music or art. This would not only obtain for this country the advantage of their knowledge and experience, but would also create a very favourable impression in the world, particularly if our hospitality were offered with some warmth.[22]

Since many of the applicants for exile status were neither prominent nor wealthy, they tried to enter the country as 'visitors'. Consequently, the Foreign Office instructed the Passport Control Department that 'such persons, especially those who appear to be of Jewish or partly Jewish origin, or have non-Aryan affiliations, should be discreetly questioned as to their family circumstances, and how their business or employment has been affected by recent events'.[23] Further instructions were to the effect that whilst any 'distinguished persons, i.e. those of *international* repute in the field of science, medicine, research or art' were to be granted a visa, those applicants who were not 'likely to be an asset to the United Kingdom' were to be refused entry. Amongst those regarded as *'prima facie* unsuitable' were

(1) Small shop-keepers, retail traders, artisans, and persons likely to seek employment.
(2) Agents and middlemen, whose livelihood depended on commission and, therefore, on trade activity.
(3) Minor musicians and commercial artists of all kinds.
(4) The rank and file of professional men — lawyers, doctors, dentists.[24]

As a result of these restrictions, only 5,500 of the 154,000 refugees who left Germany between 1933 and 1937 were granted asylum in Great Britain. Most of them were professionals, industrialists, scholars and academics who had personal contacts or family ties in Britain and who also managed to transfer a substantial part of their personal possessions from Germany to Britain.

This development took a drastic turn in 1938 following the invasion of

Austria, the occupation of the Sudentenland and the anti-Jewish pogroms after the *Kristallnacht*. In 1938/39 more than 25,000 mainly Jewish refugees were admitted to Britain, and by the time war broke out the number of exiles from countries under Nazi rule had risen to 55,000. Nearly 90 per cent of them had left their home country because of the anti-Semitic coercive measures, and the rest were political exiles.

Because of the rather diverse ethnic, political and cultural background of these refugees it is difficult to speak of *a* German group of exiles in Great Britain. Besides the Reichsgermans there were the Austrians,[25] Czechs,[26] Hungarians, Poles, Rumanians, Yugoslavs, etc. Because of the apolitical nature of most of these refugees and because of the interdiction against forming political parties, most exiles organized themselves around *Kulturvereine* based on the emigrants' country of origin. Other popular meeting places were the clubs and coffee-houses, as well as the social events organized by the approximately 200 refugee charity bodies. Many English people looked at these refugee organizations with amusement and regarded the endless number of societies and associations that sprang up all over the country as a typical outgrowth of German club mania. Although this mentality cannot be completely denied, one should, however, not underestimate the cultural, political and social functions these innumerable clubs had.

A social analysis of the German emigrant population in Britain reveals that 27 per cent of the men and 17 per cent of the women had an academic profession, and 33 per cent were entrepreneurs and businessmen.[27] These refugees had been eager participants in the cultural life of their home countries, but a continuation of their former life-style was often out of the question when they arrived in Britain, partly for financial reasons, partly because they lived outside the centre of London where most of the cultural life was concentrated. But even when they had access to a theatre or music hall, a cinema or an art gallery, many of the immigrants did not avail themselves of these facilities. Their unfamiliarity with the English language and with English artistic traditions made it very difficult for them to appreciate cultural events aimed explicitly at British audiences.

This loss of a cultural identity came as a shock to many emigrants, since they had not expected that the process of adaptation to their new surroundings would be so difficult and long-lasting. The refugees' desire to keep in touch with their cultural traditions led to the foundation of several cultural associations which soon became a vital element in the life of the German émigré community. Out of the *Kulturbünde* grew a large number of projects and ventures such as journals, theatres, exhibitions, concerts, lectures, etc. which operated in two directions: they helped the refugees to overcome the feeling of loss inevitably connected with their emigration to another country, and they served to communicate the emigrants' concerns and interests to the native population. This latter element was, of course, of immense political importance. In most instances it was the left-wing artists and intellectuals who set up these enterprises. They had the self-confidence and political experience, and often the organizational skills, to build up a network of contacts with local parties and societies and to bridge the gap between the refugees and the British population. A strong anti-Fascist attitude served as a common ground to unite the socially and politically diverse members of the refugee community. However, when it came to formulating a more precise programme for action, the differences of opinion and beliefs often proved to be an insurmountable obstacle for creating a popular front against Fascism. The economic, social and political causes for the rise of Fascism in Europe and National Socialism in Germany were interpreted and analysed by the émigrés in rather diverse terms. This often led to arguments and friction and caused serious ruptures within the organizations. Personal animosities, formations of cliques and coteries, ideological quarrels and political sectarianism enhanced the potential for discord and conflict. Not infrequently this led to the formation of splinter groups, which seriously weakened the effectiveness of the refugee organizations:

> For most of the Social Democrat refugees it was out of the question to get involved with the *Kulturbund* because of the active participation of Communists in the organization. Rejecting co-operation with the *League* (which, after all, was the largest and most effective organization of the German emigrants in Great Britain) even implied, for the SPD leadership, the boycott of purely cultural or literary events.[28]

In their initial stages, however, the refugee organizations knew few of these problems. The thousands of émigrés who had just arrived in Britain often led a lonely existence in tiny flats and dingy bed-sits; so if nearby there was a Refugee Centre they went there 'because there was a restaurant, so in that sense people met and I mean during the war, any restaurant where you got food and especially food to your liking, was a great attraction and I would say most people were attracted by that sort of thing, the dancing and the social events'.[29]

Whilst the first wave of immigrants had found it relatively easy to integrate into British society, the majority of the new arrivals in 1938/39 found the conditions of exile more difficult. They arrived in a country where few of them had any family ties, and where because of high unemployment it was extremely difficult to make social contact through work. According to Gabriele Tergit, 'around 1943 many refugees — at least in London — had never been in an English home, didn't know an

English soul except the milkman, the postman and the greengrocer'.[30]
Due to this lack of social contacts their command of the English language
improved only slowly and they found it difficult to entertain normal
relationships with the people who lived around them. As a result of this,
most of the refugees hoped that their stay in Britain would be a short one
and that soon they would be able to return to their native country:

> Each man might say to himself, or each woman for that matter, I've just come
> from Düsseldorf, I've just come from Mannheim, the war will finish, and I'll go
> back, because I'm a stranger here — I am truly a refugee. So it's better to keep
> together, and to retain each one's own culture, one's own interest, one's own
> language, one's own behaviour and so on because I don't know, tomorrow I
> might be able to go back. So you keep yourself to yourself.[31]

The only people many of them knew were other refugees who showed
similar reactions to their new surroundings and went through similar
experiences. Hence they frequented the same meeting places which offered
social contacts and psychological support in a society which appeared
alien and often hostile to them. When being asked why they spent so much
of their spare time in the refugee clubs their typical answer was: 'When
meeting other refugees one does not feel an outsider.'[32] This lack of
integration into British society bred loneliness and depression, and without the Refugee Centres many of the emigrants would have ended their
lives in utter despair. If there was no Centre near, a restaurant or a café
could fulfil the function of acting as a social focal point for the local refugee
population: 'The majority were refugees who were at a loose end with
language difficulties here anyway and that was the only way they could
spend a Sunday afternoon or a Saturday afternoon to get some strudel and
a bit of music but it was as innocent as that.'[33]

Erich Fried, in a recent interview, remembered the refugee organizations 'as a basis of our existence, as employment agency, as cheap
restaurants where you could have a decent meal, and as cultural organizations',[34] but he also underlined their political importance, especially for the
younger generation of emigrants:

> The exile organizations had been called into existence by the political move-
> ments. There were Zionist ones (amalgamated with the English Zionists) who
> had a great run from the Jewish refugees. Then there were communist ones,
> who were the biggest. Not that the communist parties — the Austrian or
> German ones — had all that many members, but their propaganda was very
> efficient. The communists opened up restaurants, founded culture clubs, organ-
> ized cultural programmes, lectures, cabarets, etc. in order to reach as many
> emigrants as possible, especially the young ones. . . . The youth organization of
> the communists — not the Kommunistischer Jugendverband, although that

was the core — had immense influence. The mass organization Young Austria alone had about 2,000 members, which was quite a number. And with the German communists it was similar.[35]

The Refugee Clubs were, in the first instance, social meeting places, but since political discussions were a regular event, they often gained a reputation which put off some of the older, apolitical émigrés:

I know my parents used to say, you know that's quite a left-wing club you go to and I said nonsense, nonsense because I was not a bit interested and I didn't want to know, all I was interested in was that I could meet some young people of my age and I was quite happy with that, I didn't want to get involved.[36]

Many of the younger refugees were less opposed to political activities, and they liked to come to the Centres because of the opportunity they offered for political debates and education:

Questions such as what had all this been about, you know, Hitler coming to power and the war breaking out and where was all this leading and what was going to happen and in those days socialism certainly seemed a way out of all these difficulties and so our activities at the centre and the cultural activities were geared towards widening our knowledge about what that really meant and we had some marvellous programmes. We participated in a young group of actors and we participated in a choir and when the War broke out we went right up to the north of Scotland where we took songs from Czechoslovakia, songs from the Spanish War, from Germany and then we had 'Sprechchöre' but we didn't only do that, we wanted to let the Scots know how much we appreciated living here. We recited Burns at them with rather strange accents and they bore with us with a great deal of pleasure and even more tolerance.[37]

The biggest and most important exile organization in Britain was the Freier Deutscher Kulturbund (Free German League of Culture). Besides theatrical activities they organized exhibitions, concerts, readings, lectures, courses, published journals, books and pamphlets, and so on. Membership in the FDKB was open to British citizens, and in their public events directed at the native population the émigrés made the voice of 'the other Germany' heard in the country. They tried to explain to the British that 'Germans' and 'Nazis' were not the same, that Hitler and the NSDAP had seized power and were holding it largely through the use of terror and intimidation. They pointed out that there were Germans inside the Reich who were resisting the Nazi régime (as for example in the 1942 exhibition 'Allies Inside Germany', which had no less than 30,000 visitors[38]).

This 'two Germanies' doctrine found support amongst some members of the British government. In April 1941, the Foreign Office explained the

ALLIES INSIDE GERMANY

EXHIBITION

Showing the underground struggle of
the German Anti-Nazis against Hitler.

Organised by the Free German League of Culture
in Great Britain.

From JULY 3rd to JULY 26th
at 149, Regent Street, W.1.

Open from 10 a.m. to 10 p.m. daily.
ADMISSION 6d.   (H.M. Forces 3d.)

2. Leaflet for the FDKB's 1942 exhibition on the German resistance movement.
Design by René Graetz

reason behind their support for the German-language newspaper *Die Zeitung* by saying: 'It is part of [our general propaganda line] that we must admit the existence of two Germanies (a 'good' one and a Nazi one).'[39] But others held the opinion that while there were 'other Germans' there was no 'other Germany'. Many refugees found it more and more difficult to defend their position when it became evident that even at times of increasing war-weariness Hitler's hold over the German people remained strong and that there were few signs of a widespread and effective resistance movement. Especially amongst the exiled politicians of the Social Democratic Party (SPD) this led to a reconsideration of the political line to be taken with the British government. Instead of seeking a rôle of representing the German opposition against Nazism they regarded themselves as representatives of the 'better Germans' who were going to erect a new German state after the defeat of the Hitler régime.

The government's attitude towards the Hitlerites or the exiles depended largely on the political expediencies of the day and the opinions which gained influence in Parliament. In March 1933, immediately after Hitler's seizure of power, there were debates in Parliament as to what attitude the government ought to take towards the stream of Germans who were forced to leave their country. Some MPs maintained that Britain had always welcomed exiles from anti-democratic countries, whilst others supported a Conservative MP who proclaimed that 'hundreds of thousands of Jews are now leaving Germany and scurrying from there to this country . . . Are we prepared in this country to allow aliens to come in here from every country' while we have 3,000,000 unemployed?'[40] In June 1933, the Marquis of Reading, a member of the House of Lords and himself a prominent British Jew, warned: 'We have well in mind, in our duty as British citizens, that we must take care that we do not add to the great unemployment existing in this country.'[41]

The refugees who tried to gain entry to Britain were at the mercy of the vagaries of the official line the government was taking towards Nazi Germany. During the period of appeasement the attitude towards the German refugees was 'carefully restrictive',[42] which meant that the exile question was handled in a manner avoiding any possible clashes with the diplomatic representations of the Hitler régime in Great Britain. The situation began to change after the Munich agreement, when Hitler's expansionist policies threatened the peace in Europe and eventually led to the Second World War. Germanophobia became rampant in Britain and sentiments against anything or anyone German were expressed even by educated people and by politicians who should have been able to distinguish between Nazis and the German victims of this régime. Sections of the British government spurred these anti-German feelings, and Robert

Vansittart, Under-Secretary at the Foreign Office, proclaimed a doctrine according to which '80 per cent of the German race are the moral and political scum of the earth. You cannot reform them by signatures and concessions. They have got to be hamstrung and broken up . . . They are a race of bone-headed aggressors . . .'[43] The Foreign Secretary, Anthony Eden, stated in 1941: 'I have no confidence in our ability to make decent Europeans of the Germans and I believe that the Nazi system represents the mentality of the great majority of German people.'[44] Even William Gilles, International Secretary of the Labour Party, who had invited part of the SPD leadership to form a German shadow government in London, lost his trust in the German comrades and stated in 1943:

> The HQ regards these émigrés as individuals and does not accept that they are representatives of a party. The Germans' spirit is not really democratic. They are too easily led, much more prone to follow any warlord to the conquest of their neighbours' lands. An insignificant part of the SPD leadership became exiles . . . and there is not much basis for the opinion that they will have any influence after the war.[45]

In 1943 the British Institute of Public Opinion tested the British public's feelings towards Germany and reported that in reply to their question: 'What are your feelings towards the German people?' 45 per cent answered 'bitterness, hatred and anger', 20 per cent 'the Germans are getting what they deserve', and only 15 per cent stated any feelings of friendliness or pity.[46] These attitudes can be compared to an opinion poll carried out in the summer of 1939 when 70 per cent stated that refugees from Nazi Germany should be allowed to enter Great Britain (although 80 per cent of those in favour of giving these refugees leave of entry wanted to see restrictions attached to their entry permits in order to safeguard British workers and taxpayers[47]). Andrew Sharf, who analysed the British press's attitude towards the German refugees, sums up his findings by saying that public opinion displayed 'an anti-Semitic substratum lightly covered over by a mixture of vague humanitarianism and fear of German conquest'.[48]

The Jewish refugees who had sought asylum in Britain found themselves in the ironic situation that after having had to leave Germany because of their Jewish origin they were now treated as Germans and subjected to the same enmity as their Nazi oppressors. Erich Fried, when questioned about his experiences of xenophobia in those years, stated that on the whole the English had been friendly to foreigners, but exceptions to the rule occurred fairly regularly: 'Only occasionally one heard someone saying "Bloody German". Then one replied: "But I'm not really a German. I am a Jew." Then one could hear: "Worse still, bloody German Jew!"'[49] This inability to distinguish between Nazis and anti-Fascist

exiles is mentioned again and again in the refugees' memoirs and personal
recollections. The following statement of an exile employed in a Scottish
household is typical of this experience:

> They had four sons in the British army and one of them was shot down by the
> Germans and I got the blame for that. I find Scottish people very nice people
> and I wouldn't change my life but all the time of the war they hated us, they
> could not understand the difference between a Jew and a German.[50]

Marion Berghahn interviewed a large number of Jewish exiles on the
question of xenophobia and sums up her findings:

> In general, though, they were convinced of the fundamental decency of the
> English people, and were confident that the liberal traditions of England would
> retain the upper hand — although some expressed doubt, because 'after all, we
> believed that in Germany too'.[51]

The ambivalent feeling many refugees had towards the British population was further exacerbated when they looked for employment to match
their professional training and expertise. Some were lucky enough to be
issued with a work permit; but this still did not mean that they could find
a position where they could use their professional training or which gave
them an income comparable to what they had earned in Germany. Only a
few of them were able to continue their secure middle class existence in
Britain. More typical were the personal histories I was told by London
émigrés, such as the case of a lady of good society who once commanded a
large household with several servants in Berlin-Wilmersdorf and then
became a maid in Putney; of a well-known lawyer from Vienna who had
to work as a bank clerk; of a doctor from the *Charité* who became employed
as a nurse at St Bartholomew's; or of a Germanist from Humboldt University who served as a farm hand in Cornwall. One can imagine how
humiliating it felt for the mainly middle-class refugees to be pushed into
the only work sector where a shortage of labour existed: domestic service.
No fewer than 21,000 of the émigrés became employed as domestic
servants[52] (usually the women, since many men refused to lower themselves to become members of the 'serving classes'). I quote from two
interviews to give an impression of how reduced in their value these
middle-class refugees felt:

> And I really must say, they wanted to exploit us all! At home, we'd all had
> maids of our own. And it wasn't so easy, suddenly to become maids ourselves.
> But they made no allowance for this, I must say.[53]

> [My wife found a] position in Glasgow. It was a large tailor's workshop

producing women's uniforms. Her job was at the sewing-machine. There were large rooms with a lot of people and a lot of noise, dust and dirt. She really got to know proletarian working conditions there. She accepted this with her usual courage, but it wasn't nice. . . . I often used to pick her up from work and would wait for her in front of the house in the city centre, in a narrow and rather unpleasant-looking street near the Clyde. After work the female workers would pour out. They were mostly very young girls who looked pretty dirty and unkempt. As a class they were below the shop employees, but gradually she even got used to these surroundings . . .[54]

The employment situation improved after 1940. The acute labour shortage caused by the outbreak of the war made it easier for the refugees to find work. Many of the exiles contributed to the war effort on the side of the anti-Fascist allies. No fewer than 9,000 men and 1,000 women volunteered for the British forces and 'conducted themselves', as Col. Arthur Evans, MP, told the House of Commons, 'in the best traditions of the British Army'.[55]

Similar praise and distinction were earned by a number of scientists who had come to Britain. In 1933 some 1,200 scholars had been dismissed from German universities, and by 1934 about 650 of them had decided to emigrate. Within two years, 287 of them had been placed permanently in some thirty countries, and 336 temporarily. The British share was fifty-seven permanent and 155 temporary appointments.[56] Most of them remained after 1945 and contributed to the advancement of science and learning in Britain. By 1955, no fewer than twenty-five had been awarded fellowships of the Royal Society, and three, Born, Chain and Krebs, had won the Nobel Prize. By 1977, fifty-three of them had become Fellows of the Royal Society and twenty-eight Fellows of the British Academy. Art History in British universities gained international status by the arrival of the Warburg Institute and of celebrated scholars such as Nikolaus Pevsner, Ernst Gombrich, Frederick Antal and Rudolf Wittkower.[57] The British publishing world profited from the arrival of George Weidenfeld, André Deutsch, Bruno Cassirer, Oswald Wolff, Walter Neurath (founder of Thames and Hudson), or Bela Horovitz and Ludwig Goldscheider (who transferred the Phaidon Press from Vienna to London). British sociology took a new course through the enormous influence exercised by Karl Mannheim. There was hardly any university or academic discipline which did not benefit from the exodus of the cream of German scholarship; in fact several pages could be filled if one were to compile a complete list of all German scholars who became distinguished professors, heads of department, directors of medical schools, or chairmen of scientific research institutions in Great Britain.[58]

Similarly beneficial to the country was the arrival of about 4,000 to

6,000 German industrialists, businessmen and entrepreneurs. Most of them were directed into regions of severe unemployment, and by 1939 about 300 firms had been established by refugee manufacturers, creating about 15,000 to 25,000 jobs. By 1947 this number had been increased to about 1,000 refugee manufacturing firms employing about 250,000 people.[59]

There are no exact figures available on how many of the émigrés went back to their country of origin after 1945. Most of the political exiles returned to their homeland in order to participate in the reconstruction of a democratic Germany, whilst the majority of the Jewish refugees made Britain their home. Their break with Germany remained final, partly because of their distrust and reserve towards the Germans; partly because their family ties had been broken up by the Nazis and there were no relatives left in Germany to go back to. When Karen Gershon questioned these émigrés about their attitude towards Germany,[60] even thirty years after the war many of them still felt bitter:

When I go back to Germany I smell blood. (p. 154)

I wish them all to hell, do unto them what they did unto others. (p. 135)

As late as 1951, when I paid my first visit to Germany since leaving in 1938, I murmured, when actually seeing the mounds of rubble that were once cities: 'Serves them right, serves them right, serves them right'. (p. 139)

I have found that on a few visits to relatives my emotions have got the better of me. The old fears returned from the moment I set eyes on the man who inspects the passports. (p. 139)

My attitude to Germany and the Germans is rather mixed. It varies between cynical admiration of their revival, to deepest revulsion about their past deeds. (p. 136)

I do sometimes find myself resenting West German affluence and efficiency, and our recent purchase of a Volkswagen took some doing. (p. 136)

All émigrés I spoke to over the last ten years see themselves as loyal Britons; yet culturally they have not broken with their past. They regularly frequent the German Film Seasons at the National Film Theatre, come to poetry readings at the Goethe Institut, or visit the performances of German theatre companies touring Great Britain. Many of them never set foot again on German soil. Some of Gershon's interviewees visited their old home town and found that 'the home is destroyed by bombs, a new generation lives in the town, their social and economic culture is alien . . . There is nothing there for me' (p. 140); or, 'I went back to my home town last year. It was completely destroyed and rebuilt and seemed to me like a strange place' (p. 141). Some of the Jewish émigrés occasionally return to Germany in order to visit a friend or relative, but their attitude towards the Germans as a people still remains ambivalent: 'I know quite a few individual German people whom I like very much, but as an anonymous nation I hate and fear them' (p. 140). Another former refugee explains why he takes a more philosophical view: 'How can I hate the Germans; my worst enemies, but also my best friends were German.'[61] They certainly feel more comfortable in Britain, although they cannot refrain from the occasional jibe about the British way of life. Marion Berghahn has studied the assimilation of German refugees into British society[62] and has found that their attitude towards their new home country is overwhelmingly positive. They have become integrated into British life, but socially they still carry the stigma of being 'Continental'. Their homes tend to exude a typical German notion of *Gemütlichkeit* and their eating habits are distinctly non-British.

Even the second generation of immigrants is still aware of their German-Jewish background. They were born in England, their friends are mainly English, but at the most they can say: 'I am British, though I shall never be English.'[63] In Marion Berghahn's study, even in the third generation, 99 per cent stated that they do not feel English. They see themselves above all as Jews, but different from the English Jews. One of Gershon's interviewees explains this by saying: 'We do not fit in completely because we are Jewish, yet not Jewish enough for English Jews.'[64] They do not feel German either, but then German-Jewish culture has always been different from the official German 'high-culture'. Berghahn describes their identity as 'German-Jewish ethnicity', where the German component becomes more diluted and the Jewish element merges more and more with the Anglo-Jewish culture. But at the present, forty years after the Holocaust, an important part of German culture of the past still survives in Britain because, as Marion Berghahn says, 'in England the Jews are permitted to be what, in the final analysis, they could not be in Germany: German Jews.'[65]

German Exile Theatre: The British Experience

In 1945, when many of the exiled theatre artists returned to their home country, they were greeted by a population which was crying out for theatrical entertainment. Between 1945 and 1948 no fewer than 419 theatre enterprises were called into existence,[66] but the fare the audiences were provided with consisted mainly of comedies, operettas and classical plays. Contemporary anti-Fascist drama accounted for only a small fraction of the repertoire. Hans Daibler has estimated that of the circa 500 plays written during the period of exile only 5 per cent were performed after 1945,[67] and most of these in the Soviet Occupied Zone.[68]

One of the few plays to be given repeated runs in several West German theatres was Friedrich Wolf's *Professor Mamlock*. Obviously audiences were interested in the play's political message — much to the distaste of the cultural establishment. On 13 December 1946 the *Kölnischer Rundschau* wrote: 'What are we to do with tendentious plays such as *Professor Mamlock*? We have been fed with this kind of stuff during the Third Reich . . . Now we want to see works which lift us out of the narrowness of our poor existence into higher spheres . . .'[69] While anti-Fascist drama was being pushed into the background the protagonists of National Socialist drama, such as Erwin Guido Kolbenheyer or Hanns Johst, experienced a renaissance in West Germany. The political climate of the Cold War and restoration period led to a situation where the exiles, just as the resistance movement, 'became for a second time victims of a political situation'.[70] A similar fate lay in store for the historians who had studied the cultural activities of the exiled artists and who wanted to inform the German public how the progressive and humanist traditions of German culture had been upheld and continued by the exiles outside the confines of the Third Reich. When Walter Berendsohn offered his manuscript of *Die humanistische Front* to the Munich publisher Kurt Desch the book was rejected because it was considered

> a sort of pamphlet of an émigré against the writers who remained in Germany. We have to and want to object to this book most emphatically because of its sad and disgraceful tendency . . . which not only obstructs our attempts of bridging the gap between us and the émigrés, but also contaminates the atmosphere between Germany and her neighbours with new poison.[71]

The theatre artists returning from exile with the intention of informing their fellow countrymen about their activities abroad received a fairly similar reception, i.e. total disinterest or distinct hostility. Apart from a few articles and brochures published immediately after the war,[72] no major study on exile theatre appeared until the early 1970s.

In 1973, the Academy of Arts in West Berlin organized an exhibition 'Theater im Exil' and a symposium on the same subject, and in the same year published the papers given at the conference. These events coincided with a research project organized by the Academy of Arts in Berlin (GDR) and the issuing of an *Arbeitsheft* containing a survey, entitled *Das antifaschistisch-demokratische und sozialistische deutsche Theater im Exil*. In West Germany the Hanser Verlag published Hans Christof Wächter's dissertation *Theater im Exil*. From then on, a major monograph on exile theatre has appeared nearly every year (see the bibliography in the appendix). This sudden upsurge of interest in the exile period brought to a halt the irretrievable loss of valuable documents which had still been in the possession of the artists once involved with the exile theatre, or at least decelerated the rapid disappearance of material without which the history of exile theatre cannot be reconstructed. Since many of the theatre productions were badly documented in the first place, the personal scrapbooks of actors, directors or designers, containing texts, music sheets, photographs, or newspaper clippings are of considerable importance for the theatre historian. Unfortunately, many of these memorabilia do not have much of a sentimental value for the relatives of a deceased artist, which means that a large amount of unique documents has been destroyed and will no longer be available for future research.

It has been estimated that between 1933 and 1945 the exiled playwrights and theatre artists created about 724 dramatic works and 800 theatre productions, 108 radio dramas and 398 film scripts.[73] Only a few of the texts survive, and many productions were never reviewed in the exile or foreign press, which leaves us with very little evidence of how extensive the theatrical activity was and what artistic quality it did achieve. A systematic study of those documents that have been preserved in various archives and private collections makes us aware that an enormous variety of theatrical activities was instigated by the exiled artists. It is therefore misleading to speak of *the* exile theatre, when the diversity of theatrical ventures appears to be one of the most salient traits of the émigrés' theatre activities. The particular organizational or artistic shape of a theatrical enterprise depended on the artists involved, the composition of the exile community, the theatrical traditions of the host country, the financial and material conditions of the theatre, the political and legal framework under which they were operating and so on. Hence it is wise to avoid generalizations and sweeping judgements and to concentrate on specific descriptions and analyses of the theatrical work carried out in individual countries or theatres or by particular ensembles or artists.

The ten studies assembled in this volume offer an impressive picture of the range of activities carried out by the exiled theatre artists in Great Britain. Arising out of these essays a number of conclusions can be drawn. (These, of course, only reflect my own opinions and do not necessarily coincide with the views of the contributors to this volume.)

When comparing the German exile theatre in Great Britain with that in other English-speaking countries, especially the USA, it becomes apparent that the cultural climate in a receiving country was always more important for an artist's successful career than his or her command of the

English language. While in the USA the refugee artists had relatively good chances of becoming integrated into the existing theatre structure, in Britain the co-operation with professional theatre institutions could be achieved only to a limited degree. Initially, the situation looked fairly promising. Many actors who were fleeing Nazi Germany seem to have regarded London as a favourite city in which to continue their theatrical career. On 21 December 1935, the exile journal *Das Neue. Tage-Buch* reported: 'The transplantation of the Berlin theatre of old makes constant progress. After Elisabeth Bergner, Lucie Mannheim, Grete Mosheim, Oskar Homolka, Fritz Kortner, Conrad Veidt, Paul Grätz and others, Ernst Deutsch is now also making his passage to the English stage.' It is interesting to note that between 1933 and 1938, when only a limited number of refugees had found asylum in Britain and only a small exile community existed in London, there were more productions of German plays in regular English theatre than in the following six years. Nick Furness, in his article 'The Reception of Ernst Toller and His Works in Britain' in the volume *Expressionism in Focus*, lists no fewer than nineteen productions of this dramatist, presented between 1933 and 1939, in British theatres. Toller, certainly, was the most widely performed German playwright in the country; but one should also mention some other notable productions of the pre-war era:

1933   Friedrich Schiller, *Kabale und Liebe* (perf. in German), Duke of York's Theatre, dir.: Leopold Jessner, des.: Caspar Neher

1933   Hermann Sudermann, *Heimat*, ditto

1934   Carl Zuckmayer, *The Golden Toy*, Coliseum, dir.: Ludwig Berger

1935   Kurt Weill, *My Kingdom for a Cow*, Savoy Theatre, dir.: Felix Weissberger, des.: Hein Heckroth

1936   Bruno Frank, *Young Madam Conti*, Savoy Theatre, dir.: Benn W. Levy, des.: Ernst Stern

c. 1936/37 Leo Lania, *Der Held* (mentioned in Wächter, p. 41)

1937   Walter Hasenclever (under the pseudonym Axel Kjellström), *Scandal in Assyria*, The London International Theatre Club at the Globe Theatre, London, dir.: John Gielgud, des.: Motley

1937   Walter Hasenclever, *What Should a Husband Do?* Theatre unknown; dir.: Robert Klein

1938   Bertolt Brecht, *Señora Carrar's Rifles*, Unity Theatre, dir.: John Fernald

It was a great loss to the English theatre that internationally renowned actors such as Fritz Kortner, Oskar Homolka or Ernst Deutsch could not be won permanently for the London stage. The same applies to directors such as Berthold Viertel, who directed only one major production in London, Max Catto's Gothic thriller *They Walk Alone* (1939: Shaftesbury Theatre).[74]

Only after 1938, when the mass immigration of German refugees to Britain set in, did an exile community with an active cultural life come into being. Whenever the exiled actors, directors, designers etc. did not find employment in the theatre, the film industry or at the BBC they offered their service to one of the exile theatre ventures that had sprung up after 1939: the Laterndl, the Kleine Bühne des FDKB, the Blue Danube, the Österreichische Bühne, the Lessing Theater, the Spieltruppe der Freien Deutschen Jugend, the Kulturbund-Spielgruppe, the Austrian Youth Players, the Oxford Refugee Theatre Company, the Kleinkunst-bühne der Jacob Ehrlich Gesellschaft.

Due to the limited facilities these companies had at their disposal, short plays and revue shows were performed more frequently than full-length plays with large casts. The artists drew heavily on the traditions of cabaret and agit-prop, although some reviews indicate that even within the limitations of small budgets and restrictive technical apparatus attempts in the direction of psychological naturalism were undertaken. Experiments with new dramatic forms or innovatory theatrical languages are never mentioned. Even the three Brecht productions of the FDKB (the 'Informer' scene from *Fear and Misery of the Third Reich* in 1939 at the West Central Hall, the *'Rechtsfindung'* scene from the same play in 1941 at the Toynbee Hall, and *Señora Carrar's Rifles* in the same double bill as *Rechtsfindung* in 1941) had been chosen solely for their political subject matter and were performed in a style that gave no indication of Brecht's importance as a radical innovator of the German stage.

The artistic quality of a production was largely determined by the technical facilities and the personnel available, and its formal characteristics were always subservient to the function of the production. The restrictions imposed by poor working conditions forced the exile theatres in their initial phase to use an Epic style similar to the one used by the working-class theatre collectives of the Weimar Republic. But later, when the facilities and finances allowed it, the style of many productions resembled those of a traditional Stadttheater of the Weimar period (see, for example, the last productions at the Kleine Bühne (Little Theatre) and the Laterndl).

The relationship between function and format of the exile theatre productions can be summarized under five headings:

(1) The performances were organized by refugee clubs and took place in the early evenings or at weekends, when there were no curfews and few

work commitments. The theatres served as a meeting point for the refugees and fulfilled important social functions within the exile community.

(2) Many performances were given in the German language in order to help the refugees retain a cultural identity and serve as a reminder of the Weimar years when theatre had always played an important rôle in their lives. The retention of a cultural heritage reduced the feeling of loss which characterized other parts of the refugees' existence. Hence the emphasis on plays and scenes stemming from the traditional repertoire and the nostalgia which pervaded many performances.

(3) The rediscovery of the humanistic and democratic traditions in German theatre served to emphasize the existence of an 'other Germany' and to counterbalance the appropriation of part of the classical repertoire by the Nazis. Since these performances were directed at an exile as well as an English audience they were given in the English language.

(4) Plays and scenes written by authors living in exile often dealt with the everyday life of the refugees and offered help in coping with the exile situation and the innumerable problems attached to the émigrés' attempts at building up a new existence for themselves in a foreign country. These problems were dealt with in humorous little vignettes or sketches, but sometimes whole revues or serious plays were dedicated to this subject matter.

(5) Anti-Fascist plays and scenes performed in English served to enlighten the British public about what was happening in Nazi Germany. They tried to reveal the true nature of the Hitler régime and served as a counterbalance to the propaganda of the Nazis and their British allies. These performances aimed at having a strong emotional appeal, which was usually achieved by offering the spectator the opportunity to identify with the victims of Nazi oppression. The Brechtian method of appealing to the spectators' rational capacities and making use of the Alienation Effect was rarely employed.

It is difficult to assess what kind of response these productions received outside exile circles. Reviews in the national as well as exile press tended to be very positive because many of the reviewers were personal friends or acquaintances of the performers, and they tried to support these theatrical activities by writing encouraging reviews. Therefore, one cannot attach too much significance to their assessment of the artistic qualities of the productions. From most reviews it transpires that the critics were so impressed by the mere fact that the refugees were creating theatre under such adverse circumstances that they would not discourage these undertakings by petty carping or fault-finding, even if they thought that the productions left a lot to be desired.

The attempts of the National· Socialist embassy and consulate to suppress the activities of the émigrés and to hinder the performances of anti-Fascist plays (successful, for example, in the case of Bruckner's *Die Rassen*, which Robert Klein, former director of the Deutsches Theater in Berlin, planned to produce in London in 1934[75]) can be interpreted as a sign that the exiles' influence on public opinion abroad was taken seriously by the government in Berlin. The exile theatres were considered to have a detrimental effect on the image the Nazi régime sought to propagate abroad, and they tried to counteract it by founding a Truppe für Auslandsgastspiele (Foreign Touring Company) under the auspices of the Reichsministerium für Volksaufklärung und Propaganda (Propaganda Ministry).[76]

But it is rather doubtful that the importance the Berlin government attached to the exiles' activities can serve as a truthful indicator of the actual effect the émigrés' propaganda work had on the population of their host country. In 1943, the Foreign Office requested MI5 to investigate the political activities of the German refugee organizations and was content to find, after they had received the secret service's report, 'First, that German exiles were very much on their good behaviour and less outspoken than their colleagues in the USA and second, that whatever their views, they had in fact been able to gain little influence on any action of British public life not excluding the Labour party with which their contacts are strongest'.[77] Although the majority of the population was aware of the presence of a considerable number of German immigrants in their country, only a few of them took an active interest in their political and cultural activities. Until the outbreak of the Second World War, the arts programme of the Nazi consulates exercised a considerable influence in Britain, and it was not only the Mosleyites who were impressed by the glamour of Nazi culture and admired Hitler's solution to the economic crisis of the early 1930s.

Amongst those members of the public who felt sympathy for the émigrés, only a few attended their theatre performances, and if they did, they did not necessarily find them to their taste. For obvious reasons, the performances in the exile theatres did not compare favourably to productions in the West End. But even when the German theatre artists managed to break into the commercial theatre world, only a few of them received a favourable reception. The gap between the German and British theatre traditions was immense: the works of Expressionist playwrights such as Ernst Toller were greeted with consternation, atonal music of the Viennese School was slated as 'sewing machine counterpoint', Jessner's famous *Treppen* were gazed at in disbelief, and many spectators found Kortner's acting style downright revolting.[78] The revolutions in European theatre from Craig and Appia onwards had left virtually no trace in Britain. Even the productions in 'experimental' theatres such as the Gate or Cambridge Festival Theatre were tame compared to what had been performed in Germany, Russia, France or Italy in the early part of the century. In Britain, the *pièce-bien-faite* variety of theatre reigned supreme, and the production methods can only be described as slapdash. Friedrich Richter, later to become one of the few commercial success stories of German émigrés working in the British commercial theatre, draws a vivid picture of this type of production:

> The Oxford Playhouse opens every week with a new play. How is it possible that the actors in Oxford can churn out a play in no less than six days (the seventh day is a Sunday when the theatre is dark and no rehearsals take place)? How is this in the long run possible? Well, first of all these plays are pure conversation pieces, and secondly these actors are incredible *routiniers* and play without director. True, the programme always mentions a director, and this person is also sitting in the stalls during rehearsals, but he very wisely keeps his mouth shut. He can't afford to hold up rehearsals by giving any hints or advice. There are six times four hours of rehearsals, half an hour of which is always taken up by a coffee break, when you go over into the foyer, have a cup of coffee, and become absorbed in a conversation with the charming English colleagues.[79]

The six days rehearsal period also applied to arts theatres such as the Gate or Festival Theatre,[80] which despite the Continental flavour of their repertoire do not hold any comparison to the Art Theatre in Munich or Moscow.

Kurt Schwitter's judgement on the English art scene: 'Nobody in London cares about good art. Only a few foreigners know what art is'[81] would have been fully endorsed by the German theatre folk. For anybody who had grown up with the richness and diversity of the Weimar art scene London must have looked like a cultural desert in the 1930s and 1940s. However, it would be unfair to fault the British for not lapping up the 'artistic manna' which the German exiles were dispensing to a 'culturally impoverished' country. There were enlightened, cultured, sympathetic visitors to the performances created by the German exiles, and they found many productions lacking in artistic quality and unsuccessful in evoking the gripping emotional experience the executing artists had aimed at. A plausible explanation for this is given by Brooks Atkinson in an analysis of the genre of anti-Fascist drama on the occasion of the New York première of Friedrich Wolf's *Professor Mamlock*. He finds that the persecution of the Jews and the atrocities committed by the Nazis are so appalling that a mere description on stage turns them into Grand Guignol or a horror show. In order to avoid this danger anti-Fascist theatre has to lay bare the causes of this evil and the mechanism that enabled it to grow to these proportions: 'The province of the playwright goes beyond surface events to the causes of action. What we need to know is how this relapse into ignorance and barbarism came about in one of the major nations of the world. . . . What the playwright should explain to us is not what, for we know that, but why.'[82]

The reason for the lack of response which many productions received cannot be explained solely by the audiences' lack of appreciation or by the poor technical facilities in the exile theatres. Amongst the artists there existed a misconception of how art could operate under the conditions of exile. In the theatre this not only applied to the format of a stage show, but also to the communication structure of a performance and the stage–audience relationship. Productions that would be a reasonable success in Germany cannot be expected to receive a similar reception in England, because the audience has a different cultural background and goes to the theatre with different expectations and references in mind. The mixture of agit-prop and nostalgia which characterized so many productions in the exile theatres was bound to be anathema to an English audience raised on French farces and West End comedies.

These critical notes do not mean to detract from the fact that despite many faults the productions organized by the exiled theatre artists, taken in their entirety, did have considerable political effect and did amount to a remarkable artistic achievement. But at the same time one has to be aware of their limitations. Exile theatre can be assessed objectively only by examining the productions within the framework of the social and cultural conditions of the country where they were presented. If the artistic quality of many performances in the exile theatres was not always of the highest standard, one can find good reasons for it. If the political effect was not always as powerful as expected, again — with hindsight — one can see why. To write a history of exile theatre, therefore, also means to write a history of the obstacles and restrictions under which the artists were operating. It is astonishing to see how much — despite the most detrimental circumstances — was actually achieved by the exiled theatre artists and how many traces this activity has left behind to the present day.

Notes

1. See Wolf-Eberhard August, *Die Stellung der Schauspieler im Dritten Reich*, Ph.D Thesis, Munich, 1973.

41

2. See his own account of the event in an autobiographical sketch, published by Lotte H. Eisner, *Fritz Lang*, London, 1976, pp. 14–15.
3. See Curt Trepte, 'Deutsches Theater im Exil der Welt', in Helmut Müssener and Gisela Sandqvist (eds), *Protokoll des II. Internationalen Symposiums zur Erforschung des deutschsprachigen Exils nach 1933 in Kopenhagen*, Stockholm, 1972, pp. 520–56, here p. 522.
4. Quoted in Peter de Mendelssohn, *S. Fischer und sein Verlag*, Frankfurt, 1970, p. 1253.
5. Max Herrmann-Neiße, 'Ein deutscher Dichter bin ich einst gewesen', in *Um uns die Fremde: Gedichte*, Zurich, 1936, p. 84.
6. Walter Hasenclever, *Gedichte, Dramen, Prosa*, ed. Kurt Pinthus, Reinbek, 1963, p. 407.
7. Stefan Zweig, *Die Welt von Gestern: Erinnerungen eines Europäers*, Stockholm, 1944, p. 466.
8. See Ursula Ahrens, 'Bericht über Alexander Granachs sowjetische Exiljahre 1935–37. Aus Briefen im Archiv der Westberliner Akademie der Künste erstellt', *Europäische Ideen*, no. 14–15, 1976, pp. 127–30, here p. 129.
9. See the interview in Marion Berghahn, *Continental Britons: German-Jewish Refugees from Nazi Germany*, Oxford, 1988, pp. 94–5.
10. Quoted in Michael Nungesser, 'Die bildenden Künstler im Exil', in *Kunst im Exil in Großbritannien 1933–1945*, Exh. cat., Berlin (West), 1986, pp. 27–34, here p. 31.
11. Leonard Frank, *Links wo das Herz ist*, Munich, 1952, p. 191.
12. See 'The Sounding Board: The Transplanted Composer', *Los Angeles Times*, 14 May 1950, part IV, p. 5.
13. Bertolt Brecht, 'Geburtstagsbrief an Karin Michaelis', in *Gesammelte Werke*, vol. 19, Frankfurt, 1967, pp. 477–8, here p. 478.
14. Egon Schwarz, 'Was ist und zu welchem Ende studieren wir Exilliteratur?', in Peter Uwe Hohendahl and Egon Schwarz (eds), *Exil und Innere Emigration II: Internationale Tagung in St. Louis*, Frankfurt, 1973, pp. 155–64, here p. 160.
15. Alfred Kerr, 'Exil', *Neue Weltbühne*, 4 Nov. 1937, pp. 1422–4, here p. 1423.
16. Hermann Kesten, 'Erinnerungen und Erfahrungen: Schicksale der Deutschen Literatur 1933–1953', *Deutsche Universitätszeitung*, vol. 8, 1953, no. 4, pp. 12–15; no. 5, pp. 14–17; here no. 5, p. 15.
17. Peter Laemmle, 'Vorschläge für eine Revision der Exilforschung', *Akzente*, vol. 20, 1973, pp. 509–19, here p. 518.
18. The history of the German exiles in Victorian England has recently been re-examined by Rosemary Ashton, *Little Germany: Exile and Asylum in Victorian England*, Oxford, 1986. Still informative on the subject is C.R. Hennings, *Deutsche in England*, Stuttgart, 1923. For a general characterization of German emigration to Britain in the nineteenth century see C.C. Aronsfeld, 'German Jews in Victorian England', in *Leo Baeck Institute Year Book*, vol. 7, 1962, pp. 312–29.
19. See *Hansard's Parliamentary Debates*, Third Series, vol. 120, London, 1852, col. 675.
20. See Bernard Porter, *The Refugee Question in Mid-Victorian Politics*, Cambridge, 1979, p. 4.
21. In 1850 the Anglo-Jewish community in Britain numbered about 35,000 persons. The 1871 census counts 32,823 Germans and 9,569 Russians and Poles in a foreign population of 105,000. The 1891 census counts 50,599 Germans, 21,448 Russian Poles and 23,626 Russians. In 1901 the Russian-Jewish population is believed to consist of 95,245 persons with 43,000 of them living in Stepney, where they form 18.19 per cent of the population. The census of 1911 lists 272,204 foreigners, 51,165 of them being German and 106,082 Russian and Polish Jews. All figures are taken from Lloyd P. Gartner, *The Jewish Immigrant in England, 1870–1914*, London, 1973, p. 49; Colin Holmes, *Anti-Semitism in British Society, 1876–1939*, London, 1979, p. 5; Colin Holmes, 'Immigrants, Refugees and Revolutionaries', *Immigrants and Minorities*, vol. 2, 1983, pp. 7–22, here p. 8.
22. Home Secretary's Memorandum to Cabinet Committee on Alien's Restrictions, 6 April 1933, Public Record Office, Kew, CAB 24/239; quoted in Bernard Wasserstein, 'The British Government and the German Immigration 1933–1945', in Gerhard Hirschfeld (ed.), *Exile in Great Britain: Refugees from Hitler's Germany*, Leamington Spa and New Jersey, 1984, pp. 63–81, here p. 68.
23. Foreign Office Circular to Passport Control Department Concerning Visas for Holders

of German and Austrian Passports Entering the United Kingdom, 27 April 1938, Public Record Office, Kew, FO 372/3284/9, quoted in Wasserstein, 'The British Government and the German Immigration', p. 72.

24. Ibid.
25. Werner Röder, *Die deutschen sozialistischen Exilgruppen in Großbritannien: Ein Beitrag zur Geschichte des Widerstandes gegen den Nationalsozialismus*, Hanover, 1968, p. 23 gives their number as 12,000 in 1940.
26. A.J. Sherman, *Island Refuge: Britain and Refugees from the Third Reich 1933–1939*, London, 1973, p. 264 sets the number of Czech refugees in Britain at 6,000. Leopold Grünwald, *In der Fremde für die Heimat: Sudentendeutsches Exil in Ost und West*, Munich, 1982, p. 13 estimates that 3,000 of them were Sudentendeutsche.
27. See Röder, *Die deutschen Exilgruppen*, p. 25.
28. Ibid., p. 87.
29. Interviewee, quoted in Rainer Kölmel, 'Problems of Settlement: German-Jewish Refugees in Scotland', in Hirschfeld, *Exile in Great Britain*, pp. 251–83, here p. 272.
30. Gabriele Tergit, 'How They Resettled', in *Britain's New Citizens: The Story of the Refugees from Germany and Austria*, ed. the Association of Jewish Refugees in Great Britain, London, 1951, pp. 61–9, here p. 63. On unemployment and living conditions in Britain in the 1930s see Noreen Branson and Margot Heinemann, *Britain in the 1930's*, London, 1971. The refugee question is also dealt with in Malcolm Muggeridge, *The Thirties: 1930–1940 in Great Britain*, London, 1940.
31. Interviewee quoted in Kölmel, 'Problems of Settlement', p. 264.
32. Interviewee quoted in Karen Gershon (ed.), *We Came as Children: A Collective Autobiography*, London, 1966, p. 155.
33. Interviewee quoted in Kölmel, 'Problems of Settlement', p. 273.
34. 'Gespräch mit Erich Fried', in Michael Seyfert, *Im Niemandsland: Deutsche Exilliteratur in britischer Internierung. Ein unbekanntes Kapitel der Kulturgeschichte des Zweiten Weltkrieges*, Berlin (West), 1984, pp. 151–6, here p. 155.
35. Ibid., p. 154.
36. Interviewee quoted in Kölmel, 'Problems of Settlement', pp. 274–5.
37. Ibid., p. 275.
38. See Cordula Frowein, 'Ausstellungsaktivitäten der Exilkünstler', in *Kunst im Exil in Großbritannien*, pp. 35–48, here p. 44.
39. Report in Public Record Office, Kew, FO 371/26554 c 1930, quoted in Anthony Glees, *Exile Politics During the Second World War: The German Social Democrats in Britain*, Oxford, 1982, p. 149.
40. E. Doran on 9 March 1933. See *Hansard Parliamentary Debates: House of Commons*, Fifth Series, vol. 275, London, 1933, col. 1352.
41. Quoted in Austin Stevens, *The Dispossessed: German Refugees in Britain*, London, 1975, p. 119.
42. Sherman, *Island Refuge*, p. 259.
43. Memorandum of 11 March 1940 in Public Record Office, Kew, FO 371/24418 c 5304, quoted in Glees, *Exile Politics*, p. 51.
44. Quoted in Glees, *Exile Politics*, p. 155.
45. Labour Party Archives, International Department, Middleton Papers, (M), Box 9, Letter to S.W. Smith and R.J. Davies of 21 September and 6 May 1943, quoted in Glees, *Exile Politics*, p. 103.
46. Public Record Office, Kew, FO 371/34461 c 12764, quoted in Glees, *Exile Politics*, p. 201.
47. See Andrew Sharf, *The British Press and Jews under Nazi Rule*, London, 1964, p. 199.
48. Ibid., p. 206.
49. Fried in Seyfert, *Im Niemandsland*, p. 153.
50. Interviewee quoted in Kölmel, 'Problems of Settlement', p. 261.
51. Marion Berghahn, 'German Jews in England: Aspects of the Assimilation and Integration Process', in Hirschfeld, *Exile in Great Britain*, pp. 285–306, here p. 295.
52. See Francis L. Carsten, 'German Refugees in Great Britain 1933–1945: A Survey', in

Günter Berghaus

Hirschfeld, *Exile in Great Britain*, pp. 11–28, here p. 13.
53. Interviewee quoted in Kölmel, 'Problems of Settlement', p. 259.
54. Ibid., pp. 263–4.
55. Quoted in Francis L. Carsten, 'German Refugees', p. 24. See also the statistics in Norman Bentwich, *I Understand the Risks: The Story of the Refugees from Nazi Oppression Who Fought in the British Forces in the World War*, London, 1950, pp. 176–7.
56. All figures are taken from Norman Bentwich, *The Rescue and Achievement of Refugee Scholars: The Story of Displaced Scholars and Scientists 1933–1952*, The Hague, 1953, pp. 1–2 and 13. See also Kurt R. Grossmann, *Emigration: Geschichte der Hitler Flüchtlinge 1933–1945*, Frankfurt, 1969, p. 217.
57. See Dieter Wuttke, 'Die Emigration der Kulturwissenschaftlichen Bibliothek Warburg und die Anfänge des Universitätsfaches Kunstgeschichte in Großbritannien', in *Kunst im Exil in Großbritannien*, pp. 209–15.
58. The most important names are mentioned in *Britain's New Citizens*, pp. 35–43 and Bentwich, *Rescue and Achievement*, pp. 80–92. See also Gerhard Hirschfeld, 'Die Emigration deutscher Wissenschaftler nach Großbritannien, 1933–1945', in Gottfried Niedhart (ed.), *Großbritannien als Gast- und Exilland für Deutsche im 19. und 20. Jahrhundert*, Bochum, 1985, pp. 117–40; and Bernard Wasserstein, 'Intellectual Emigrés in Britain, 1933–1939', in J.C. Jackman and C.M. Borden (eds), *The Muses Flee Hitler: Cultural Transfer and Adaptation 1930–1945*, Washington DC, 1983, pp. 249–56.
59. See Herbert Loebl, 'Refugee Industries in the Special Areas of Britain', in Hirschfeld, *Exile in Great Britain*, pp. 219–49, here pp. 221 and 246.
60. See Gershon, *We Came as Children*.
61. Quoted in Berghahn, 'German Jews in England', pp. 297–8.
62. See idem, *Continental Britons*.
63. Interviewee quoted in Gershon, *We Came as Children*, p. 168.
64. Ibid., p. 155. In the wake of the Jewish emancipation in the eighteenth century many German Jews had become integrated into German society and given up their Jewish culture. They despised their non-assimilated co-religionists, especially if they were *Ostjuden*. Many of these Eastern Jews had settled in Britain at the turn of the century and regarded the new influx of German Jews after 1933 with suspicion, resentment or aloofness. One refugee remembers: 'The Glasgow Jews took just as little interest in us. On the contrary, they to a certain extent resented the German-Jewish refugees. Most of the Glasgow Jews had come from Russia or Poland; their families had emigrated in the 1880s and 1890s, at the time of the pogroms there. Earlier, German Jews had looked down on them; now they avenged themselves by being very reserved towards us.' (Quoted in Kölmel, 'Problems of Settlement', p. 267. See also the interviews in Berghahn, *Continental Britons*, pp. 231–4.) These distinctions account for the fact that to this day there are culturally different Jewish communities living in Britain.
65. See Berghahn, 'German Jews in England', p. 304.
66. See Hans Daibler, *Deutsches Theater seit 1945*, Stuttgart, 1976, p. 90.
67. Ibid., p. 57.
68. See Werner Mittenzwei *et al.*, *Theater in der Zeitenwende: Zur Geschichte des Dramas und des Schauspieltheaters in der Deutschen Demokratischen Republik 1945–1968*, vol. 1, Berlin (GDR), 1972, pp. 82–136.
69. Quoted in Gerhard Roloff, *Exil und Exilliteratur in der deutschen Presse 1945–1949*, Worms, 1976, p. 203.
70. Hans-Albert Walter in an interview with Heinz Ludwig Arnold, in *Akzente* vol. 20, 1973, p. 483. See also Erhard Bahr, 'Das zweite Exil: Zur Rezeption der Exilliteratur in den westlichen Besatzungszonen und in der Bundesrepublik Deutschland von 1945 bis 1959', in Donald G. Daviau and Ludwig Fischer (eds), *Das Exilerlebnis: Verhandlungen des Vierten Symposiums über deutsche und österreichische Exilliteratur*, Columbia, 1982, pp. 353–66; and Martin Mantzke, 'Emigration und Emigranten als Politikum in der Bundesrepublik der sechziger Jahre', *Exil*, vol. 1, 1983, pp. 24–30.
71. See the facsimile documents in Walter A. Berendsohn, *Die Humanistische Front:*

44

Einführung in die deutsche Emigranten-Literatur. Zweiter Teil: Vom Kriegsausbruch 1939 bis Ende 1946, Worms, 1976, pp. 229–30.

72. See Curt Trepte, 'Freies Deutsches Theater in Schweden 1938–1945', *Theater der Zeit*, vol. 1, no. 2, 1946, pp. 22–4; Erich Freund, 'Deutsches Theater im Londoner Exil', *Theater der Zeit*, vol. 1, no. 4, Oct. 1946, pp. 20–4; Paul Walter Jacob (ed.), *Theater: Sieben Jahre Freie Deutsche Bühne in Buenos Aires*, Buenos Aires, 1946; Kurt Stern, 'Eine Bühne im Exil: *Deutsches Theater in Mexiko*', *Theater der Zeit*, vol. 2, no. 4, 1947, pp. 23–6; Erich Freund, 'Studio 1934: Die erste deutsche Bühne im Exil', *Theater der Zeit*, vol. 2, no. 7, 1947, pp. 30–2; Egon Larsen, 'Deutsches Theater in London: Ein unbeschriebenes Kapitel Kulturgeschichte', *Zick-Zack*, vol. 2, 1948, pp. 13–15; Paul Walter Jacob (ed.), *Theater 1940–1950: Zehn Jahre Deutsche Bühne in Buenos Aires*, Buenos Aires, 1950; Karl Otto Paetel, 'Deutsches Theater in Amerika', *Deutsche Rundschau*, vol. 81, 1955, pp. 271–5.

73. See Curt Trepte, 'Archiv Deutsches Theater- und Filmschaffen im Exil', *Mitteilungen der Deutschen Akademie der Künste zu Berlin*, vol. 5, 1967, no. 1, pp. 11–12, here p. 12 and Curt Trepte, 'Deutsches Theater im Exil der Welt', in Müssener/Sandqvist, *Protokoll des II. Internationalen Symposiums*, p. 522.

74. See Friedrich Pfäfflin (ed.), *Berthold Viertel (1885–1953): Eine Dokumentation*, Munich, n.d. [1969], p. 35; Berthold Viertel, *Schriften zum Theater*, ed. Gert Heidenreich, Munich, 1970, p. 531; Konstantin Kaiser, 'Theater im Exil: Das Beispiel Berthold Viertel', *Wiener Tagebuch*, no. 11, Nov. 1986, pp. 22–4; Eberhard Frey,'Ethisches Theater: Berthold Viertels Theatertätigkeit im Exil', in Wolfgang Elfe et al. (eds), *Deutsches Exildrama und Exiltheater: Akten des Exilliteratur-Symposiums der University of South Carolina*, Berne, 1977, pp. 77–84, here p. 78.

75. See Joseph Wulf, *Theater und Film im Dritten Reich: Eine Dokumentation*, Gütersloh, 1964, p. 245.

76. See Georg Wilhelm Müller, *Das Reichsministerium für Volksaufklärung und Propaganda*, Berlin, 1940, p. 28.

77. Quoted in Glees, *Exile Politics*, p. 189.

78. In his autobiography, *Aller Tage Abend*, Munich, 1959, pp. 386 ff., 428 ff., 465 ff., Fritz Kortner paints an amusing picture of the London theatre world and describes how the British tradition of underacting (he calls it 'Gefühls-Tiefstapelei' [p. 466] or 'Ausdrucksanämie' [p. 429]) forced him, who had always strived for expressiveness, to forgo his best qualities as an actor and to adapt to the 'charming virtuosity of a non-committal acting style' (charmante Virtuosität der Ausdrucksunverbindlichkeit, p. 428) which the British audiences favoured. See also the sources quoted by Alan Clarke in this volume, pp. 100–7.

79. Friedrich Richter, 'Auf Theatertour in England', in Renate Seydel (ed.), *. . . gelebt für alle Zeiten: Schauspieler über sich und andere*, Berlin (GDR), 1978, pp. 293–306, here pp. 296–7.

80. See Richard Cave, *Terence Gray and the Cambridge Festival Theatre*, Cambridge, 1980, p. 14.

81. Schwitter in a letter of 1 April 1947 to Louise Spengemann, in Kurt Schwitter, *Wir spielen, bis uns der Tod abholt: Briefe aus fünf Jahrzehnten*, ed. Ernst Nündel, Berlin (West), 1974, p. 272.

82. Brooks Atkinson, 'Culture under the Nazis', *New York Times*, 25 April 1937, Section X, p. 1.

45

– 3 –

German Theatre and Cabaret in London, 1939–45

HUGH RORRISON

Our story starts when Hitler's occupation of Czechoslovakia and the annexation of Austria, both exile lands of first resort for Nazi target groups in Germany, triggered a second move for many émigrés and turned the trickle of refugees coming to Britain into a flood.

There are thought to have been about 2,500 German refugees in Britain in 1935. By the end of 1938 there were 11,000 and by the end of 1939 the total reached 55,000. This refugee community fluctuated as a result of re-emigration to the US and dispersal to the colonies. The reasons for the sudden influx were increased persecution in the Reich itself in the two years before the Second World War, the annexation of Austria on 13 March 1938 and the occupation of the Sudetenland in the first ten days of October 1938, and then of the remainder of Czechoslovakia in March 1939.

Mrs Liselotte Souza (a former refugee who was present at the conference where this paper was originally given) tells a story that is typical of many. When Chamberlain handed Czechoslovakia to Hitler at Munich she was at drama school in Prague, where she at one point shared a teacher with Herbert Lom. She left Prague in March 1939, ten days after the German take-over. In Britain she settled with her first husband near Pontypridd where a colony of entrepreneurs from Northern Bohemia had already set up factories with government backing to combat unemployment in South Wales. It was a bourgeois enclave without much thought for the arts, she recalls. In 1943 she escaped to the Royal Academy of Dramatic Art and back to acting, so that she was just in time to participate in the dying fall of all three refugee theatres, the Blue Danube, the Kleine Bühne and the Laterndl in the last year of the war. After it ended she pursued a career with the BBC and in films until 1956; she appeared, for example, in Herbert Wilcox's *Odette* in 1950. Life in this situation was a matter of finding a niche rather than making one's mark. Establishing a career was a process of adaptation and assimilation, marked, in Mrs

Souza's case, by horror at hearing her first recording test which exposed a thick accent in what she had fondly supposed to be her perfect English. Her efforts were finally crowned by acceptance by the BBC and the film industry as a supporting actress.

The British attitude to the refugees fluctuated, but by and large visa restrictions were relaxed after the Czech débâcle, and there were intitiatives on the British side such as the Czech Refugee Trust Fund which provided a living allowance, which amounted more or less to dole money, for Czech refugees until they found employment. Among the refugees there were around 400 artists of all sorts, including actors like Josef Almas, Erich Freund, Amy Frank, Charlotte Küter, Paul Lewitt and Friedrich Richter, the cabaret artist Annemarie Hase, writers like Kurt Barthel (whose pen-name was Kuba), Jan Kopplowitz and Max Zimmering, and artists like John Heartfield and Oskar Kokoschka.[1]

While names are being named, perhaps some of the early luminaries of the Weimar stage to arrive in London should be mentioned: Albert Lieven, Lucie Mannheim, Grete Mosheim, Oskar Homolka, Fritz Kortner, Conrad Veidt, Paul Grätz, Ernst Deutsch, Elisabeth Bergner, Adolf Wohlbrück. All I think, apart from Albert Lieven, Anton Walbrook (as he became) and Lucie Mannheim, moved on to the USA.[2] Herbert Lom arrived young and unknown and became a British star. Part of the brief for the conference at which this paper was first given was to identify the impact which people like these had on their host country, coming as they did from the German stage which had been far bolder, more experimental and in every way more modern than the British theatre in the 1920s and 1930s. In the case of stars like Bergner, Walbrook and Lom the answer seems to be none. Bergner was a star in Berlin from the early 1920s and she was welcomed and used as a star by C.B. Cochrane, but she did not alter the concept of stardom or the style of acting. Foreign actors made their careers by fitting in and they present, at best, cases for biographical study with sidelights on the psychology of exile and the pattern of native prejudice. There is no evidence of stylistic innovation or any real impact on the course of theatre in Britain. It would be strange if it had been otherwise.

The Free German League of Culture

With the growing pool of refugee talent in London it was only a matter of time before an outlet for self-expression could be found. On the organizational front the Freier Deutscher Kulturbund (FDKB = Free German League of Culture) was set up in December 1938 to provide a framework and a forum for the energy and creativity of the refugees.[3] It was constituted as 'a German, anti-National-Socialist, anti-Fascist, non-party refugee organization' with the aim of nurturing 'free German culture'. The initial impetus came largely from the Communists, whose policy of a Popular Front against Fascism at this time was designed to combine and co-ordinate the efforts of all the oppositional groups. The refugees in Britain were not allowed to form political organizations, so the FDKB was originally a surrogate for political activity, even the smokescreen behind which political interests were pursued. It became the social and cultural centre of the German community for the duration of the war. It had 1,000 members soon after it was founded, and 1,226 by May 1940, 102 of them being British.[4]

The FDKB had a threefold aim: first to represent the interests of the refugees and to provide a venue for activities that would help to keep up their spirits in a demoralizing and materially difficult situation; secondly, to explain their predicament to the British, to disseminate as widely as possible information about the real situation in Germany; and thirdly, to persuade their reluctant hosts that Hitler's Fascism was not the real Germany but a temporary and distasteful aberration.

The FDKB had writers, musicians, actors, painters and sculptors, and scientists among its members. They had their first public appearance with *Going, Going — Gong!*, a revue which was staged even before war was declared. It opened at the Arts Theatre on 21 July 1939, attracted 5,000 paying customers and made a loss of £150, which was a burden on the FDKB for many years. The directors were Wolpe Wooping and Heinrich Fischer. Wolpe Wooping (pronounced 'Whooping', according to contemporary witnesses) was a one-eyed Berlin cartoonist. The revue consisted of a series of unconnected turns. Under the headline 'Refugees satirize life in new show', the *Daily Worker* (24 July 1939) commented: 'Songs, sketches, burlesques, dancing, were presented with a wealth of wit and satirical force, subtlety and fire very rarely combined in a show of this kind. Indeed a show of quite this kind has never been seen in London.'

Alfred Kerr reported: 'The mixture is good. They blithely make fun of their own worries — and, more pointedly, of the author of those worries. They even gently pull the host country's leg' (*Pariser Tageszeitung*, 25 July 1939).

John Heartfield used *Iron for Butter*, one of his old photomontages, to illustrate Goering's contention that 'butter only ever made the German people fat, whereas iron made it strong'. Kerr inserts an English word into his German review, telling us that the natives in the audience were 'startled' to see a German family in the Third Reich tucking into their bicycles at the dinner table. Eddie Regon impersonated Goebbels. Li

3. WolpeWooping's drawing for the programme of *Going, Going—Gong!* at the Arts Theatre, 1939

Nolden sang Brecht's *Ballade von der Judenhure Marie Sanders* (*Ballad of the Jew-lover Marie Sanders*). The 'Schattentänzerin' (shadow-dancer) Senta Born danced. There was a German folksong whose impact on himself Kerr registered with surprise:

> *Daß du mein Liebster bist* (*That You Are My Darling*) Lili Hard sings it quite simply; a pure, engaging voice. A curious feeling hits you suddenly, the past seems to flood in, in its entirety; at one time, not long ago, all that existed. The critical faculties are disarmed, you try your damnedest to resist. Lili Hard sang wonderfully. (*Pariser Tageszeitung*, 25 July 1939).

Kerr manages to capture the feeling of the whole show in a nutshell here: the choking homesickness coupled with the realization of how much has gone. At the same time he clearly identifies the satire, and puts his finger on the unmasking of the National Socialist myth of masculine toughness as the revue's prime target.

In 1939 the FDKB was given the use of a room in a house at 36 Upper

Park Road, Hampstead, by the Church of England through the good offices of the Bishop of Chichester. It had club status which meant that it was exempt from censorship and taxation. It was here that the Kleine Bühne opened in 1940. (Contemporaries told me that nobody ever spoke of it as the Kleine Bühne, but it seems to have become the accepted historical label for the shows staged by the FDKB and it is convenient.) In 1942 the FDKB took over the entire premises. There was a library, a coffee-room, a restaurant, and a room for meetings.

The Laterndl

It was, however, the Austrians who got their act together first. Their predicament was identical with that of the German refugees, but they set up a separate refugee centre, where they performed their own shows which were essentially and authentically Viennese in character. One might think that their problems were simplified by the fact that they could look upon Austria as an occupied country for whose liberation they were fighting. But this does not seem to be how their situation was perceived at the time, for the British were unable to distinguish Austrian refugees from German ones.

Rudolf Spitz has given an account of the foundation of the Laterndl which reads as if the project was conceived as a cabaret sketch.[5] He suggests that it was called the 'Lantern' not as a pale reflection of Karl Kraus's *Die Fackel* (The *Torch*) but after a *Beisl* or cheap eating-house in the Landgerichtsstraße where one of the Austrians, a sweet-toothed Communist writer called Albert Fuchs, used to take his *Mehlspeisen* (Viennese pastries). Hanne Norbert-Miller recalls that the participants thought of it as having come into being quite casually. Rudolf Spitz, Fritz Schrecker and Maximilian Schulz (who later went to the USA) were chatting at the Austrian Centre: 'Now that we are here we ought to found a theatre. Incidentally, I hear Martin Miller is in London, too.' At this point Miller joined the conversation and that remark became a project which was soon realized. The Laterndl was set up with club status at the Austrian Centre at 126 Westbourne Terrace. It seems to have been viewed from the start as a *Kleinkunstbühne*. There is no real translation for this. Whereas *Cabaret* or *Kabarett* as a feature of Vienna's night-life embraced the whole spectrum of small-scale performance from literary and political satire and sophisticated songs to stand-up comics and striptease, *Kleinkunst* was a term invented in the 1930s for anti-Nazi cabaret. *Kleinkunst* was therefore the serious end of the comic market, and although it used the revue format to string together solos, songs and

51

sketches, it eschewed the more frivolous and bohemian elements of cabaret. It took advantage of the fact that in Vienna auditoria with forty-nine seats and under needed no licence, and via this loophole *Kleinkunst* made the voice of protest heard until the *Anschluß* in 1938. It all began when Stella Cadmon set up Der liebe Augustin in 1933. It was political revue with high artistic standards which produced at least one writer of lasting importance, Jura Soyfer.[6]

The Laterndl circulated a leaflet which explained what the organizers meant by the term *Kleinkunstbühne*:

IT is a LANTERN
    BUT there are no stars.
IT is a novel form of theatre
    BUT there is no formal theatre.
IT is not musical comedy
    BUT there is music and comedy.
IT is fighting with the weapon of wit
    BUT it is a serious fight.

The Lantern continues the tradition of the Viennese *Kleinkunstbühne* as represented by Der liebe Augustin, Die Stachelbeere, Literatur am Naschmarkt and ABC. These were small inexpensive theatres producing shows which neglected luxurious scenic effects, but concentrated on wit, topical satire, and progressive outlook. They formed a vital part of the intellectual life of Austria which was interrupted in March 1938.

All the collaborators at the LANTERN worked at one of those theatres. It may be hoped that THE LANTERN will preserve one of the characteristic forms of Austrian culture.[7]

Before the theatre opened, the founders heatedly debated whether the auditorium should be laid out with café tables (as was the custom in Vienna where the venue was often a café cellar and the owner charged no rent but expected to make it up on drinks) or with rows of seats. They opted for the latter. One should perhaps remark here that satirical cabaret had been the natural medium for political comment on the continental stage since the beginning of the century. Erika Mann could be said to have initiated anti-Nazi cabaret in 1933 in Munich when her Pfeffermühle opened in one hall while Hitler made his maiden speech as Chancellor next door. She then, as is well known, took her 'Peppermill' into exile in Zurich and from there toured France, Holland and Belgium until Nazi sympathizers in Switzerland contrived to have it closed.

At the Laterndl, according to the leaflet, Martin Miller was responsible for production, as well as being a character actor of note. The writers were Franz Hartl, Hugo Königsgarten (who was later, as H.F. Garten, to publish a work called *Modern German Drama* on which a generation of post-war British students of German cut their dramatic teeth), Rudolf Spitz and Hans Weigel. Music was in the hands of Kurt Manschinger, décor was by Carl Josefovics and costumes by Käthe Berl. The actors were Lona Cross, Grete Hartwig, Willy Kennedy, Jaro Klüger, Fritz Schrecker, Sylvia Steiner and Marianne Walla.

The productions were numbered by programme, and number one was a revue which opened on 21 June 1939. It contained six sketches, one of them by Rudolf Spitz called *Bow Street* which wrily evoked the tense atmosphere in the waiting-room and interview-room at the Aliens' Office where all refugees had to register. There was another sketch called *Memories* by Hugo Königsgarten in which two geriatric refugees, Mrs Greenfield and Mr Silverstone, meet forty years on and recall the Vienna of their childhood, to the bafflement of their grandchildren to whom the very name Hitler means nothing. (The implication in this sketch that some people might never go back is uncommon, and may not even have been noticed, since the time-shift to the distant future was a comic device to enable the refugees to laugh at themselves.) Martin Miller sang *Das Lied des einfachen Menschen* (*Song of the Man in the Street*) by Jura Soyfer, Jaro Klüger recited the Lutheran hymn *Ein' feste Burg* in honour of Pastor Niemöller, and Fritz Schrecker sang a Viennese ballad, *Pfüat di Gott*.

The opening was reviewed in *The Spectator*, where Goronwy Rees wrote:

> We have no form of theatre so intimate, so direct as this; it has all the charm of amateur theatricals without the amateurishness. Anyone who saw the skill with which the actors used their tiny stage last week realised how much art there was in their spontaneity. The theatre is a room on the first floor divided in half by the proscenium and seating 50–60 people. There is little scenery, the simplest of lighting; this necessary economy in equipment is half the charm of a theatre in which the gap between audience and stage is reduced to a minimum and illusion is no more necessary than a charade . . .(7 July 1939)

The Laterndl moved after this to a defunct music school at 153 Finchley Road where there was a large hall that was converted into a 160-seat theatre. It then moved on to its final location, 69 Eton Avenue, NW3, which was opened with Zuckmayer's *Captain of Köpenick* on 13 November 1941.

In the second programme, *Blinklichter*, there was a sketch by Albert Fuchs called *Wo liegt Deutschland?* in which a public meeting on Mars, chaired by the President, discussed the need to intervene in earthly affairs as a matter of cosmic justice. A Martian professor (Fritz Schrecker) was despatched to gather 'inside information' about 'the so-called Germans', a rogue mutation in the normally rational species known as man, recognizable by a large mouth and constant twitching of the right arm. The professor meets Lessing (Martin Miller) who explains that he has been dead for 150 years but is out of favour anyway for writing a play in which a Jew delivers a verse parable on tolerance, whereupon the 'Ring Parable' from *Nathan the Wise* was performed. The professor is picked up in the street at night by an SA squad rounding up Jews. He is in the congregation when a church is closed by the SS for the duration of the war. A prayer by Matthias Claudius was recited here. He has a propaganda-machine demonstrated to him at the Propaganda Ministry:

Question: What is a Czech?
Machine's Answer: The Czechs are a Jewish-Bolshevik-Hussite horde whose origins among the rachitic-luetic-paralytic dwarf races of central Asia have recently been identified by racial biologists.

The professor finally visits a labour-camp where the girls sing him their own version of the *Horst Wessel Song* when the Supervisor is called away. The professor, reassured that the spirit of reason is alive below the surface of the Third Reich, returns to advise the President that Martian intervention will not be necessary and the elimination of Nazism can be left to its opponents on earth.

Wo liegt Deutschland? established the model which was later elaborated by Egon Larsen and Fritz Gottfurcht in *Mr Gulliver Goes to School*. A total stranger of unquestionable moral integrity and objectivity samples life and culture in the Third Reich, establishes that there is underground opposition, and diagnoses the evil as temporary.

Martin Miller also performed a sinister impersonation of Hitler, called *Der Führer spricht*, in the first revue. He repeated his Hitler impersonation in the George Formby film, *Let George do it*, and again in perhaps the most famous achievement associated with the Laterndl, his spoof Hitler broadcast on the BBC on April Fool's Day, 1940, in which Hitler claimed that Columbus had discovered America with the aid of German science and technology, giving Germany a territorial claim to the United States which he intended, in the near future, to make good. So authentic was the impersonation that CBS contacted the BBC in great consternation to ask where it had picked up the broadcast.

The third Laterndl programme was called *Von Adam bis Adolf*. It contained Jura Soyfer's *Der Lechner Edi schaut ins Paradies*. Soyfer (1912–1939), a young Jewish Social-Democrat who joined the Communist party in 1934, had written regularly for the ABC and developed the 'centre-piece' (*Mittelstück*), a political sketch which would form the heart of a revue. *Eddie Lechner looks at Paradise* is a good example. Soyfer was arrested soon after the *Anschluß* in 1938 and died in Buchenwald of typhus which he contracted from carrying corpses. He has slowly come to be recognized as

News Chronicle

ONE PENNY   TUESDAY, APRIL 2, 1940   *

MARTIN MILLER
(as he impersonates Hitler in a British film) last night reproduced the Fuehrer's fury of speech

B.B.C.'s April Fool on Germans

Hitler's Voice Claims U.S.A.

TO celebrate All Fools' Day the B.B.C. in its German programme broadcast a bogus Hitler speech yesterday.

It was written in language typical of the Fuehrer.

The speaker, Herr Martin Miller, well - known Austrian actor, faithfully reproduced all peculiarities and mannerisms of the Fuehrer's speech.

In his address the bogus Fuehrer reminded his German audience of the discovery of America, which had only been possible by Columbus using German-made instruments and the result of German science.

Germany had been cheated out of her rightful part in the exploitation of America.

PATIENCE STILL EBBING

Now the Fuehrer had to right this wrong and to give back to Germany what belonged to her.

"Ever since 1492 I have remained silent. But now my patience is at an end. I hereby firmly declare that I have now made my last territorial demands in Europe, but beyond that I have now to state certain claims of a maritime nature.

"America is a big country and the Americans are a great nation. They certainly need access to the sea.

"I've never denied that, either in my speeches or in my book.

"But it is a fact that in the United States there are national minorities closely connected by race and tradition with German Reich.

"In Chicago alone there are 324,000 Czechs, and those Czechs keep asking themselves : 'Why can't we come under the Protectorate?'

"In the well-known city of New York there are 476,000 Poles. They have a right to be protected by Germany, and I shall enforce that right, not only theoretically but also practically.

"I am very grateful to Mr. Roosevelt for his interest in European affairs ; I am proving my gratitude by declaring the German Protectorate over the United States

"I shall make America a blossoming garden.

"New York, today an insignificant port, will become a centre of world trade. I shall remove all the mean shacks now representing the architecture of that city."

The speech was frequently interrupted by recorded heiling.

4. Newspaper report on Martin Miller's Hitler impersonation on the BBC, 1 April 1940

one of the clearest commentators on inter-war Vienna, as well as one of its leading writers.

The Laterndl had included one of Soyfer's songs in its first programme. In January 1940 there was a *Jura-Feier*, an evening devoted to his work and his memory, after which Fritz Gross wrote a cycle of verses entitled *Jura*. After these revivals it was to take twenty years and more for Soyfer's work to receive the recognition it merits.

The fourth programme was *Der unsterbliche Schwejk*, and this was followed by Brecht's *Dreigroschenoper* and Zuckmayer's *Der Hauptmann von Köpenick*. The pawky, anarchic humour of Hašek's Schwejk and Zuckmayer's Shoemaker Voigt afforded plum comic parts in which Martin Miller excelled.

Up to this point at the end of 1941 the shows can be called critical: certainly Prussian officialdom (and servility) is the target in Zuckmayer's play which could be turned against Hitler's régime with its plethora of

DAS LATERNDL

WIENER
KLEINKUNSTBUEHNE
IN LONDON

153, FINCHLEY ROAD, SWISS COTTAGE, N.W.3.

Telephone: PRIMROSE 5548

KLEINES WELTTHEATER

Das "Laterndl" wird an Montagabenden wertvolle Werke der Literatur zur Auffuehrung bringen und betrachtet es als Pflicht, den ersten Abend dem Werk des jungen Wiener sozialistischen Dichters JURA zu widmen, der vor Jahresfrist im Konzentrationslager Buchenwald — ein tragisches Opfer des Naziregimes — gestorben ist.

Die Stuecke

"Der Lechner Edi schaut ins Paradies"
"Vineta, die versunkene Stadt"
"Der treueste Buerger Bagdads,"

eigenartige literarische Produkte, unter dem Druck der engstirnigen Zensur der Schuschnigg-Regierung—scheinbar nur fuer den Tag-geschrieben, sind heute wie damals geisselnde Anklagen gegen Faschismus und Reaktion. Ihr scharfer Witz, ihre ergreifende Lyrik, ihre packende Dramatik gehoeren zum schoensten, was das Theater unserer Zeit zu sagen hat.

Das "Laterndl" spielt diese drei Stuecke zum ersten Mal am

Montag, den 15 Jaenner 1940 um 7.15 Uhr abends.

Wiederholungen am Montag, 22 und 29 Jaenner.

Normale Eintrittspreise : 1/–, 1/6, 2/6.

DAS LATERNDL SPIELT JETZT TAEGLICH.

Literarische und Musikalische Samstagnachmittage.

Sonntag nachmittags Tee und Tanz.

Verlangen Sie unsern Kalender fuer Jaenner.

5. Publicity sheet for the 1940 Jura Soyfer celebration at the Laterndl

uniforms. *The Immortal Schwejk* was not a straight adaptation of Hašek's novel *The Good Soldier Schwejk*, like Erwin Piscator's 1928 Berlin production, but a kind of revue. Schwejk was transplanted from the Habsburg Empire in the Great War to occupied Czechoslovakia, so his simple-minded willingness to carry out any order or observe any regulation to the very last letter now served to send up Nazism. It was clearly a stepping stone from Piscator's *Schwejk* to Brecht's *Schwejk in the Second World War.*

After this, apart from the thirteenth programme, *No Orchids for Mr Hitler* which had a sketch called *Is Your Journey Really Necessary* by Franz Hartl, and a finale called *Tiefer geht's nimmer* (*You Can't Get Any Lower*) which featured Hitler, Lord Haw-Haw, Mrs Hihi (Lady Astor), Laval and Pétain, the Devil and Beelzebub's Apprentice (Beelzelehrbub), the repertoire begins to look more literary, with Stefan Zweig's version of Ben Jonson's *Volpone*, Karl Schönherr's *Weibsteufel*, Arthur Schnitzler's *Anatol*, Johann Nestroy's *Der Talisman*, and Hermann Bahr's *Das Konzert*. These are all Austrian (as opposed to German) plays. The last three all have many good parts for actresses, and may have been chosen for casting reasons. Of Bahr's play one anonymous reviewer wrote, '*The Concert* is proof that when it comes to putting together a new season, there are enough Austrian plays available to provide a varied repertoire. To have put this to the test and given actors and audience alike something enjoyable to get their teeth into, must rank as the Laterndl's literary achievement.'[8]

This writer's concern for a varied, Austrian, literary repertoire is shared by K.R., another reviewer, and the critics in general are concerned in a quite conventional way with literary merit and acting standards. On this occasion the stalwart Fritz Schrecker was felt to be miscast as the philandering concert pianist, but the rest of the cast, particularly Marianne Walla, were praised: 'Most striking in this meticulously directed production by Paul Hardtmuth is the returning Maria Walla who achieves powerful effects both with the overall structure and with the detailing of her role.' There is a sense of normality in the reviews, of people going about the normal business of culture, unconcerned about avant-gardism or political content but with a keen eye for artistic standards and, in the case of the Laterndl, for the Austrian-ness of what was being offered.

What the audience and the performers had in common at the beginning were their disorientation, their homesickness and their problems with the host language, and these concerns faded with time. This may have contributed to the turn from satirical revues and plays with a critical slant to a conventional comedy of manners like *Das Konzert*, as may casting problems when the demands of the West End, the BBC, US radio and anti-Nazi films took their toll of the company.

Egon Larsen, in his 1948 account of German theatre in London, saw the achievement of Fritz Schrecker and Martin Miller at the Laterndl as 'cultivating the flame of German theatre art in Central Europe's darkest years'.[9] This seems just, and it serves to underline that alongside its politically critical rôle it had culturally conservative concerns rather than innovative ones. The Laterndl, like the Blue Danube, but unlike the Kleine Bühne, was a permanent theatre, open all week. It closed in August 1945.

The Österreichische Bühne

Another Austrian enterprise, Arthur Hellmer's Österreichische Bühne, opened in 1942, produced Lessing's *Nathan der Weise* and Friedrich Wolf's early anti-Nazi play, *Professor Mamlock*, and collapsed. It is a pity that no information about the venture has come to light since the pairing of Lessing's parable play on the theme of tolerance in which the central figure is a Jew, with Wolf's *Zeitstück* in which the central figure is a Jewish surgeon who is forced, painfully, to recognize that liberal tolerance of the kind advocated by Lessing has no place in any part of the political spectrum in Hitler's Germany in 1933, has polemical implications which are intriguing. Did Hellmer fail because his programme was too serious? Or did he just fail? It would be good to know.

The Blue Danube Club

The third Austrian theatre was the longest lived. The Blue Danube played from 1942 to 1954. Its origins lay in an internment camp on the Isle of Wight where Peter Herz founded the Stacheldraht Cabarett in the camp mess.[10] It featured people like Ravitz and Landauer, later household names on 'Housewife's Choice', and a magician called Kalanag. The speciality of this venue was that you had to bring your own chair. After internment was phased out Herz tried to repeat his success at the Austrian Centre, but it was latterly, he says, 'under Communist management'.[11] So he set up the Blue Danube Club in the converted music school recently vacated by the Laterndl at 153 Finchley Road. The Blue Danube Club played five nights a week in the 160-seat theatre. Assessing his own intentions he writes,

As I have already stated, the Blue Danube never deviated from its policy of exposing the full horror, the brutality, the reign of terror and the manipulation of the law under the brown Nazi hordes, while at the same time keeping hope alive and combating any resignation and any sign of defeatism in the face of the Nazis' initial successes by demonstrating the vulnerability of the Nazi death-machine, and satirizing this whole system of inhuman cruelty in its full, revolting illegality as a colossus with feet of clay.[12]

It is surprising to find Peter Herz describing his activities in these highly charged, political terms. He was speaking at a symposium on 'Austrians in Exile' in June 1975 in Vienna and perhaps felt the occasion deserved a little rhetoric.

As a producer-manager Herz believed in the liberating power of laughter. His revues were located firmly at the entertainment end of the *Kleinkunst* spectrum and had titles like *Lease and Lend Revue*, *Tales of Mr Nobody*, *Vagabond Street*, *Spring Parade*, *Circus Continental* and *The Importance of Being Funny*, all of which suggests that he had a lighter touch in his productions than in his self-assessment. In summing up he perhaps finds the right tone when he calls his work: 'A struggle against the Nazi régime, against the crimes of the Brownshirts, with wit, words and music!'[13] The stress here should be on wit, words and music rather than struggle. Herz notes in an aside that not only was the *Völkischer Beobachter* aware of his existence, it once stated that the Nazis would come and get these cheeky chappies ('diese frechen Burschen in der Finchleyroad') one day soon.

Herz's posters were always in English so as not to provoke hostility.

The Kleine Bühne at the Free German League of Culture

The FDKB kept up a constant flow of activities and events. On weekdays there were talks, readings, musical evenings and so on, while the theatrical performances provided the highlights at weekends. The theatre was just a room with a minute stage at one end, and this, coupled with the restricted number of actors available, limited the scope of what could be put on.

Like the Austrian companies this was a professional ensemble, and Erich Freund, who was one of the leading lights in the company, made it clear that to introduce amateurs would constitute a dilution which might prejudice the whole enterprise. This was meant as no slight to amateur theatricals, but as an affirmation of the Kleine Bühne's professionalism. The company had to cope with defections as the BBC and the London stage recruited players. Those who remained had to make a living elsewhere, and this could lead to withdrawals once a play was cast. It also meant that rehearsals had to be late in the evening and lasted for an average of two and a half hours. Plays were rehearsed for several weeks, and there were inevitable absentees. Egon Larsen commented:

> It took a high degree of artistic commitment after a day in a draughty factory or a chilly room to race through the damp, dark, foggy streets of Hampstead and squeeze into the last corner of a primitive, crowded dressing room in time. But it is no exaggeration to say that for many of our friends it was taking part in that pocket theatre that gave their lives meaning in that endless wartime winter.[14]

Freund was a stickler for quality. Great efforts were made to get the productions right, and he thought it better to have a few good productions than to run continuous performances if that meant lower quality, and in any case supply probably met demand adequately, since, as Freund noted, the circle that came to the Kleine Bühne was a only small segment even of the refugee community.

It is worth noting that although there were plenty of *Theatermacher* (as current jargon has it) — that is to say, actors, directors, designers — not to speak of critics, there were no theorists, nobody to develop the ideas of innovators like Brecht or Piscator. John Heartfield, who had worked closely with Piscator since their 1920 agit-prop days, was on hand but does not seem to have tried to influence things. Whether or not this matters is a moot point. The Kleine Bühne was working within its means and its budget, doing what the situation required. What they were trying to do was keep body and soul together by developing their own variety of community theatre. As Hugh Rank remarked recently when I consulted his records from the 1940s, people had no idea at the time that what they were doing would ever be of historical interest, so to see the London refugee theatre as a potential growth point for progressive strands from the Weimar Republic is a polemical distortion of historical fact. In Zurich things were different: several of the plays Brecht wrote in exile were first staged there. But Zurich is part of the German speaking world, and the Theater am Pfauenplatz was part of the German theatrical circuit. Piscator's political theatre and Brecht's *Lehrstücke* were targeted, the former perhaps not very accurately, at an identifiable public in an identifiable political context. Brecht felt that Germany by 1930 was ripe for revolution, and the *Lehrstücke* were his way of telling that to the Berlin proletariat. With the Hampstead refugees it was more a question of sustaining their morale than of raising their political consciousness.

The main thrust of the Kleine Bühne was in the field of satirical revue. Topicality and political relevance were major considerations in the initial planning, and there were writers who could write sketches and cabaret scripts. Few plays by anti-Fascist dramatists were to hand (Wolf's *Professor Mamlock* was, as was noted above, but it had already been produced in Warsaw and Zurich by 1934), and no recognized dramatist had taken refuge in England. (Ernst Toller had by this time been and gone.) Only two plays actually written in England were even given a reading: Heinz Karpeles' *Flieder* (*Lilac*) and Max Zimmering's *Familie Blanchard*.[15]

Satirical Revues at the Kleine Bühne

The first revue in the FDKB's new house in Hampstead was *Was bringt die Zeitung* (*What's in the News*), a satirical appraisal of the press, written by Egon Larsen and Fritz Gottfurcht who were to become the first-string scriptwriters. Editorial manipulation of the news, sensational and fictitious reporting, escapism in the readership (readers to whom a newspaper was merely a vehicle for the daily crossword puzzle clearly baffled the refugees), and gossip columns came under fire. There were also topical foreign reports: a sketch called *Kriminelle* showed how Communist prisoners in German concentration camps managed to resist, in spite of the brutal way they were treated. There was Brecht's *Ballade vom Baum und den Ästen* (*Ballad of the Tree and the Branches*), and a sketch which pilloried Tucholsky's archetypal Jewish philistine Herr Wendriner, who had contrived to transplant his opulent Berlin life-style to Hampstead in its totality. As a contrast to Wendriner's smugness Agnes Bernelle as *Die Kosmopolitin* presented the anguish of a disorientated twenty-year-old who longed for home. The young Agnes Bernelle was the company's own discovery, and *Kosmopolitin* became her theme song. Reviews suggest that this revue managed to be serious with a light comic touch. It coincided with the beginning of internment — indeed Manfred Fürst and Margarete Hruby, who were to have appeared in it, were taken into custody on the day of the première, 17 April 1940.

Internment caused a twenty-one month gap in activities before the next revue, *In den Sternen steht's geschrieben* (*What the Stars Foretell*), opened on 30 January 1942. It included Egon Larsen's adaptation of *Erna Kremer of Ebenstadt* by John Bishop (a pseudonym for Ted Willis) which had run at the Unity Theatre in 1941.[16]

In *Wir rufen Erna Krämer* the Soviet German Service broadcasts a touching report on Ludwig Krämer's death in a Russian hospital and couples it with an appeal to his widow to do her bit to stop the German working class from fighting the peace-loving Soviet Union. Erna Krämer, listening at home in Germany, is shattered by what she hears, and is then subjected to the threats of the block Party representative, who has been notified of the broadcast by HQ and warns her of the penalties for listening to foreign propaganda. This effective little piece of agit-prop was set in a series of sketches and songs, some of which again satirized the press.

61

In Hampstead Heath ist Holzauktion (*Wood is Being Auctioned on Hampstead Heath*) was the next revue. It opened on 10 April 1942, and the title alluded to a Berlin song, *Im Grunewald ist Holzauktion*. The piece was scripted by Gottfurcht and Larsen and directed by Gottfurcht. It was an evening of Berlin nostalgia in which the scriptwriters' material provided a framework for well-known *Kabarett*-songs from the 1920s by Marcellus Schiffer (*Wenn die beste Freundin*), Kurt Tucholsky (*Mutters Hände*) and Felix Holländer (*Wenn ick ma doht bin*, which Blandine Ebinger had made famous in Berlin). This evening was entirely in German for a refugee audience, but since the songs were by artists whom the Nazis had branded as degenerate, the nostalgia was making a clear point, as Eva Priester pointed out in her notice:

> It brought back something we had almost forgotten in these bitter years — the brilliance and the laughter that once was Germany, and can be again, the fact that in that country whose name has become a curse on the lips of mankind, there was, and still is, something whose rebirth is worth fighting for — because the world will be a more beautiful place when it is free to live again. (*Zeitspiegel*, 18 April 1942)

This was followed on 28 November by the most interesting of the Kleine Bühne revues, *Mr Gulliver Goes to School*, which will be examined in detail below.

The final revue was *My Goodness, My Alibi*, the title a take-off of the long-running Guinness advertisement. It was written by Richard Wiener, Erich Freund, Fritz Gottfurcht and Egon Larsen 'in true Hampstead dialect — German, and English with a soupçon of French', and opened on 8 January 1944 in a Kleine Bühne that had just been reconstructed. The stage had been moved to the opposite end of the room and the seating capacity increased to 100.

This time the revue used a spoof investigation by Sherlock Holmes as the thread on which the individual numbers were strung. Holmes is on the track of the 'minor offenders of this war, the coughers-and sneezers, the squanderers, and the escapists'. An anonymous reviewer reports,

> Topical? — it is right up to the minute with allusions to the Jet Plane, Mosley ('Somebody must have let somebody out!') and Basic *Englisch* — sorry, English. Despite the wide range of the revue — one moment we are in on a BBC Brains Trust, the next in Nazi-occupied Paris, the theme is never lost. . . .
> The revue does not hesitate to poke fun at the refugees themselves: Annemarie Hase's portrayal of the 110 per cent Britisher who wants her husband and maid to learn English for the sake of Winston Alexander Montgomery, her English-born child, is *sehr komisch* . . . Basic German, too, provides great fun — 'voll von Bohnen' having not quite the same meaning as 'full of beans' . . .
> Frederick Nietzsche and Karl May are even unable to enjoy Heaven, their

cloudy sojourn marred by their cross-examination as to their responsibility for Hitler's crimes.

But underneath this lightheartedness runs a deeper vein — that of 'Noch ist es Zeit' . . . time for the German people to rise against the Nazi regime.[17]

The musical numbers by E.H. Meyer were singled out for special praise, the public liked it all and it ran for three months.

These revues derived from a Continental tradition and their presence in London raises the question of reception and possible emulation. Revue in London was not an interface between politics and the stage. It was suppertime entertainment and tended to be modish, even snobbish. Noël Coward springs to mind as the trendsetter, at least in the West End. To find something akin to the spirit that animated the Kleine Bühne we have to look at Unity Theatre. Unity had in a sense pre-empted the FDKB when it formulated its response to Chamberlain's appeasement policy with a Living Newspaper which opened under the title *Crisis* on 29 September 1938. This agit-prop piece ran, with its material constantly updated, through October. This was followed by *The Babes in the Wood*, 'a pantomime with a political point'. The idea came from Robert Mitchell, but the writing is credited in the programme to the 'Unity Theatre Play Department'. The idea was brilliantly simple — the fairy-tale figures represented countries and politicians, so the babes were Austria and Czechoslovakia, the Wicked Uncle was Chamberlain, his robber accomplices were Hitler and Mussolini, while the goodies, Robin Hood and Maid Marion, were the Popular Front against Fascism and the People respectively. *The Babes in the Wood* was seen by 50,000 people during its run from 15 November 1938 to 22 May 1939.

The only other political pantomime at Unity was *Jack the Giant-Killer* in 1941, though there were political revues like *Sandbag Follies* (1939), *Get Cracking* (1942), and *Let's Be Offensive* (1943). Panto is, of course, archetypically British. It is low, popular comedy which treats its audience with a collusive directness which is akin to Continental political *Kabarett*, so it is intriguing to see it pressed into service for political satire. Unity's activities are clearly a parallel development to the FDKB in a native idiom, but it has yet to be proved that there was any cross-fertilization, though there were personal contacts, and the Kleine Bühne was a venue at which Unity appeared. On 16, 17, 23, and 24 October 1943 it presented its topical revue *A Stitch in Time* there.[18]

The Return to Straight Drama

After *My Goodness, My Alibi* a change of policy at the Kleine Bühne becomes evident. One reason may be that after the Russian breakthrough at

Stalingrad and the decision to open a second front, the Germans in Britain were allowed to form their own political organizations, and the FDKB's function as surrogate political centre ended. The Kleine Bühne now began to concentrate on straight plays. A start had been made when the company performed Goethe's *Iphigenie* at Toynbee Hall in the East End on 2 April 1944. This was followed by Kleist's *Amphitryon*. The shift to the classics was not achieved without opposition, and Monty Jacobs mounted an eloquent defence of the project.[19] The Nazis had built Kleist into their programme as an officer, a Prussian and a patriot. The last line of *Prinz Friedrich von Homburg* springs to mind as something of a gift for them — 'Into the dust with all the foes of Brandenburg'. The jingoistic ethos of *Die Hermannsschlacht (Hermann's Battle)* is also deeply suspect, but Jacobs managed to turn one of that play's lines to advantage. Accusing the Roman invader Septimus, the hero Hermann says,

> You came to Germany without grievance, villain,
> To oppress us? Take a club of double weight
> And strike him dead.

Jacobs turned these words neatly against the Nazis.

Amphitryon is a difficult verse drama, but so successfully did the company perform it that it ran for nineteen performances, which means that it was possibly seen by 1,900 people. It was performed against simple drapes, and classical costumes were simulated with old curtains. The size of the room imposed on intimate, conversational style on the delivery of the lines. The impact of *Kultur* after long abstinence was profound, as Ernst Sommer reported: 'It is a joy to hear Kleist's verse. One devours it avidly. When was the last time one heard the like? Its firm, decisive flow arouses a kind of sad delight. Where is one? How did one get here? Suddenly, in a flush of certainty, one realises what one has missed most.'[20]

Oskar Kokoschka was in no doubt where he was and felt impelled to write a long, ecstatic letter to the director, H.W. Litten. It is nothing if not flowery and offers an interesting sidelight on the native theatrical landscape.

> Dear, revered Herr Litten,
> Before the solemn rapture is sullied (the trip in the Tube, past the billboards announcing the theatrical mission of this most unintellectual of cities is enough in itself to give cause for concern — sheer murder), let me offer to you my most heartfelt congratulations for the miracle made manifest to you, and to us who were privileged to hear you. What can have guided you to enable you to find the one spot in this parched wilderness of sand where the crystal stream flowed underground?[21]

The impact of the performance is as clear as Kokoschka's contempt for British culture, which is partly to be explained by its failure to welcome him and the manner to which he had become accustomed on the Continent before the war, and partly by the deplorably trivial state of West End theatre. His pomposity of course allows us mere British to smirk at him in our turn. Kokoschka goes on, however, to give an eloquent appreciation of Kleist's concept of freedom.[22]

> It is the true, democratic freedom, unaffected by the pseudo-democracy of pulpit, money or force of arms. It is the cultural mission of the good European, that, as an underground movement that is now impinging on the consciousness of those who previously, before the war, only registered it subconsciously, and which tomorrow will lead us out into the world of light that is humanism . . .

Kokoschka sees in Kleist a model for the rejuvenation of post-war Europe, and his reflections on the evening at the Kleine Bühne, airily equating true democratic liberty with the cultural mission of good Europeans, echoes the Expressionist calls for the New Man that followed the Great War.

The plays that followed sustained the high level of performance achieved by *Amphitryon*, but apart from that all we need do here is mention them. In December 1944 there was J.B. Priestley's *They Came to a City*, a play with a utopian theme which had been successful in the West End. The fact that the Kleine Bühne made it available in German for its Hampstead regulars may indicate that the future after Hitler was now exercising the refugees' minds. This was followed by Max Zimmering's *Familie Blanchard*, a contemporary piece written in Britain but set in France among the Resistance, which explored the nature of loyalty and patriotism.[23] It was presented as a reading by Josef Almas, and was poorly received. (The only other play written in Britain to get a hearing was an anti-Fascist piece by Heinz Karpeles, *Flieder (Lilac)*. It was a variation on Büchner's *Woyzeck* and was set in South Germany in 1943. It went down well at a reading in 1943.) After *Familie Blanchard* came Sternheim's *Die Hose*, three grotesques by Curt Goetz with the overall title *Menagerie*, and finally Oscar Wilde's *Bunbury* as the Germans, apart from Peter Zadek, call *The Importance of Being Earnest*. It opened on 16 March 1946, and Mrs Souza, then Liselotte Kristian, played Cecily. After that the Kleine Bühne was turned over to an amateur group organized by Erwin Jacoby. It finally closed in 1947.

Mr Gulliver Goes to School

Mr Gulliver Goes to School opened on 28 November 1942. It was a revue with nineteen numbers (which I shall call scenes), comprising eight songs and eleven sketches. Four of the sketches had songs in them. There was an interval after Scene 10, and in the second half there were three unnumbered interludes when Ariel appeared in front of the curtain to establish a measure of continuity.

The evening was billed as 'A Topical Revue'. It was written by Fritz Gottfurcht and Egon Larsen, with music by Allan Gray. The songs were directed by Annemarie Hase and the sketches by Paul Hardtmuth. Sets were by Günther Wagner and the music was played by Paul Lichtenstern at the piano. Three of the songs, *In Deutschland fehlt eine Scheuerfrau, Die Ballade vom Riesen Koschchei* and *Second Front* were by Rolf Anders (a pseudonym for Rolf Thoel), one, *Geography, 1943* was by Max Zimmering, and another, *What is a Gentleman?*, was by Agnes Bernelle.[24] The music contributed greatly to the success of the revue.

The Larsen–Gottfurcht team used Swift's Gulliver as a time-traveller. In the establishing scene he has just returned from 1942, and his friends at Lloyd's coffee-house in 1704 are having fun with the exotic grab he has brought back from his trip. They press him to tell them about the lands where the quaint (1940s) clothes are worn. Gulliver was played by Peter Cozens, a young amateur actor from the East End who was working in a munitions factory at the time. Egon Larsen still refers to him as the star of the show, pointing out that it took courage, given that he neither spoke nor understood a word of German, to step into this company. Complicated misunderstandings arose which spiced rehearsals and performances alike.

The second scene, *How Grand is the 20th Century*, is a song in which Gulliver wittily lists the achievements of the age while pointing out that modern man has not discovered how to exploit these for the common good. At the end of the song he invites them to see for themselves, and subsequent scenes show us his trip in flashback.

In the third scene, *English without Tears*, Gulliver meets Ariel, borrowed from *The Tempest* to serve as his guide and interpreter on his journey through time. Ariel offers to take him to 1939 and gives him his first instruction in the manners and speech of the time. All these three scenes are in English.

In the fourth scene, *Never Say Lie*, which is partly in English and partly in German, they alight at the Hotel Adlon, that landmark of inter-war Berlin, to see 'the most revolting creatures in the whole of creation'. (Ariel has by now — since the Kleine Bühne's talented young discovery, Agnes Bernelle, was cast in the part — mutated into Miss Ariel.) They meet a Berlin charwoman who is a German variant of Tommy Handley's Mrs Mopp,[25] an Essen industrialist, Dr Klump from Deutsche Maschinenwerke, and a high NSDAP (Nationalsozialistische Deutsche Arbeiterpartei) official, *Regierungsrat* Dr Schwersenz, who presents Gulliver, as an honoured guest, with an historic chair as a gift from the Führer. The disparity between the apparent popularity of the Nazis, and the sceptical charwoman's assertion that the Nazis are liars and ordinary Berliners like her son are all politically like 'englischet Biefstück' (beefsteak), brown on the outside, but otherwise red to the core, baffles Gulliver.[26]

When the antique chair Hitler has sent him turns out to be the one from the opening scene at Lloyd's coffee-house, Gulliver astonishes Dr Schwersenz, who has the Kaiser-Wilhelm-Museum's appraisal in his hand, by accurately assessing its historical provenance at a glance, adding that it is a truth chair which strikes dead anyone who tells lies while sitting in it. Schwersenz, who has a heart condition, when forced to sit down duly reveals what he has been covering up before: the Nazis intend to conquer Europe in 1942, and the world by 1945. Klump then in his turn confesses that he has paid a million marks to have his grandmother aryanized. This corroborates the charwoman's views, and Gulliver's education in the true nature of Nazism has begun.

The fifth scene is a song, *In Deutschland fehlt eine Scheuerfrau* (*What Germany needs is a Charwoman*), which tells us that not just the Adlon, but all Germany needs a charwoman to clean it up. The charwoman was played by the accomplished actress Annemarie Hase who had made her name with appearances at Fritz Gottfurcht's Larifari, in Friedrich Holländer's Tingel-Tangel-Theater, and in the Küka in the Budapester Strasse in Weimar Berlin. She was the seasoned trouper in the company whose experience held everything together, and at this period in the war she had a series on the BBC German service called 'Frau Wernicke', which relayed the woes of Frau Wernicke, a woman of the people from the Berlin working-class district of Wedding, to occupied Europe. The charwoman was therefore tailor-made for her wonderful talent.

The sixth scene moves to the Citizen's Advice Bureau in Hampstead, where Gulliver sees his first refugee.

The seventh scene is *Der Song vom Bernhardiner* (*The St Bernard Song*) in German. It tells of a little Pintscher in a zoo who, back in Germany, had been a full-sized St Bernard.

Mr Gulliver then goes to school in a four-scene parody of the Hampstead School for Refugees. In *Geography Lesson* (eighth scene, in English) the charwoman from the Adlon, who has fled to Hampstead via

Shanghai and Rio, instructs him in contemporary political geography. She amplifies this with a song, *Geography, 1942* (ninth scene, in English).

Scene 10, *Singing Lesson*, features an anti-Fascist medley in which Snow White, Alice, Rübezahl, Kleiner Moritz, Awful Audrey and Schwejk sing in turn of the opposition to the Nazis which is growing everywhere.

In Scene 11, *Shopping Lesson*, an old Continental English teacher corrects Gulliver's pronunciation of his own name (to Gölliver) and instructs refugees in the arcane practice of queueing.

Scene 12, *Die Ballade vom Riesen Koschchei* (*The Ballad of the Giant Koschchei*), tells of the immortal Russian giant, symbol of the peace-loving Russian soul against whom Hitler's troops are powerless.

In an Interlude in English Ariel wants to move on, but Gulliver now insists on staying to fight Fascism.

In Scene 13, *German Harvest* (in English), set in 1942, Gulliver, who has parachuted into Germany to blow up a munitions factory, is helped to escape by a group of farm workers, some German, some foreign, a demonstration of anti-Nazi solidarity which is the cue for *Second Front* (Scene 14), a song (in German, refrain in English) announcing the closing of ranks and the convergence of liberating forces on Germany from East and West.

In an interlude in English Ariel seeks out Gulliver: they have to board the time-ship again.

In Scene 15 the song *Heute trägt man alles unverpackt* (English and German) (*Today We Wear no Packaging*) recalls the days when common liquorice was sold 'boxed glamorously in cellophane and paper-lace', then turns packaging into a metaphor for a wider self-deception, the prime example of which was Chamberlain's claim after Munich to have ensured 'peace in our time'.

> We were wrapped up in sweet non-intervention.
> But now we have discovered: if Freedom is to win,
> Down with all wrappings — in the salvage bin!

It concludes with a Churchillian exhortation to take off the kid gloves and show a clenched fist.

In an Interlude Ariel asks the previous singer the way to Upper Park Road, but he is no gentleman and refuses to help her.

Scene 16 is a song entitled *What is a Gentleman?* (in English) which dismisses the understated toff in his sagging Sunday clothes, and the gent of elegant exterior in favour of a Churchillian gentleman whose salient characteristics are pugnacity, determination and intelligence.

In Scene 17 Ariel tries to buy a travel outfit in a tailoring establishment in Hampstead, providing a cue for scene 18 which is a song, *Utility* (in English). Prominent in the set was a utility label of the kind found on all goods manufactured according to stringent official wartime regulations, and the song is full of praise for this egalitarian approach to distributing the available goods. It ends with vision of a utilitarian future where there are no shirkers. A review in the *Leicester Mercury* on 19 April 1943 singled out this scene for the effectiveness with which 'the girls sew on imaginary buttons, hem imaginary seams, and thread imaginary needles to music and with the most convincing artistry'.

In Scene 19, *Victory Bar*, two married couples in a pub sing of everything returning to normal after the war. The middle-class couple will go back to golf and holidays at Biarritz, the working-class couple to coping bravely, if need be with unemployment. It is left to Gulliver to suggest that after all that has happened the classes in Britain should move closer together. The wall that separates the lounge bar from the public bar is removed and the four sing:

> We'll need each other,
> We'll know each other
> We'll help each other after this war!

The revue thus ends on a note which invites its audience to reflect on the kind of society that victory will bring.

The perspective from which the revue is presented is a reflection of the spirit of wartime Britain rather than anything more polemical, though it does have traces of European rather than British thinking, and also reflects the hopes which were to lead to Labour's victory in the first post-war election.

When Gulliver first appears, the customers at Lloyd's express their admiration for Churchill: 'He's tough as ever he was, and if there's anyone to see us through this mess, it's him.' The joke is that they are referring to John Churchill, Duke of Marlborough, who was Gulliver's contemporary. As Gulliver flashes through time with Ariel, the landmarks are 1789 ('A revolution sweeps away the powers of mediaeval tyranny') and 1848 ('There's another revolution') suggesting history seen from a Continental, rather than an English, viewpoint, though Gulliver is liberal enough to be curious about these events. In Berlin the charwoman's song *In Deutschland fehlt eine Scheuerfrau* tells us,

> Only our foreign guests harbour any doubts,
> Never having seen like vermin ever before.

Everybody in Germany, she implies, knows the Nazis for the scum they are. The charwoman is a female Schwejk, a subversive with *Schnauze*, as the special Berlin brand of impudence is called, who presents a satirical analysis, in which Germany's docile masses are trundling to hell, led by Nazis and exploited by 'Generals, Kruppites, Junkers and Steelowners'. She says,

> The fat cats suck the thin ones dry
> In spite of their dream of a national community

The National Socialist ideal of all pulling together for the common good is a sham. Hitler may have found employment for her son Emil, but only as permanent cannon fodder. This is substantial, analytical political comment in the best tradition of Weimar *Kabarett*-songs.

In the *Geography Lesson* Gulliver learns that the finest city in the world is not Paris, New York or London, but Stalingrad, as well it might be since it had just worn down and stopped Hitler's war machine. The pupils in the *Shopping Lesson* refuse to hear about the Crimean War when Britain fought Russia. Now that the two countries are allies they want to hear about 'the soul of Russia', and this is the cue for the *Ballade vom Riesen Koschchei* which is generalized hymn to Russian strength, quite free from ideology. Koschchei is a mythical incarnation of Russia whose only characteristics are ubiquity and immortality. Only in 'German Harvest' is the Soviet Union's political structure touched upon when Pavel, a Russian prisoner of war, movingly evokes life on his kolchos in a manner that recalls Brecht's idealized picture of collectivized agriculture in *Der kaukasische Kreidekreis*. The general perspective is, however, one of allied solidarity. Gulliver sums it up when he describes his escape from German territory to Ariel as 'A miracle of human kindness and solidarity among the victims of Nazi oppression'. Even the exhortation in the finale is for class co-operation and not for class struggle, and, taken with the egalitarian message of the *Utility* song, suggests modest reform rather than revolution. In British terms it is Labour rather than Tory in bias, but instead of offering a specific political vision the revue constantly returns to the theme of solidarity. Churchill's toughness (Scene 1), Pavel's idealism as well as his willingness to help the Polish countess working alongside him on the farm, the countess's desire to turn her back on her old life and do something useful after the war (Scene 13), the new Gentle Man in *What is a Gentleman?* (Scene 16) who will bring two fists, a will and a brain to building the peace, and the last stanza of the *Utility* song (Scene 18):

> If we all fall in, and no one shirks,

Our pattern for the future works

all bespeak the refugees' hope that the wartime spirit will be harnessed to build a better future, but a future so vaguely hinted at that all we can say about it is that it is to be more egalitarian than the past.

Mr Gulliver Goes to School is not a political polemic, but an entertainment, albeit a critical and stimulating one. English peculiarities and eccentricities provide many of the laughs. One client at the Citizen's Advice Bureau (Scene 6) is a girl who wants to know if at twenty-one she can still be prevented by her parents from buying a new frock. She confesses, when pressed, that she needs it to go to Buckingham Palace to receive the George Medal she won when she ruined her old frock scrambling into a neighbour's garden to defuse a time-bomb. It is explained to Gulliver that she could not tell her parents this because 'It simply isn't done'. This admiring little comedy of manners is followed by a lady who wants her iron gate repaired by her landlord so that she can turn it over to the scrap collection in good repair. She is a refugee who has caught a dose of eccentricity. The *Shopping Lesson* reduces shopping to a technique for queueing, a peculiarly British exercise in self-discipline that foreigners all marvel at. Tongue in cheek, the principles are expounded: a shopper must always join the longest queue and take what he gets, even if he has no use for it. Should he want fish and find that there is no queue at the Hampstead fishmonger he must take the bus to Kilburn, where there will certainly be the desired queue. Irony and self-irony alternate in passages like these, most clearly perhaps in *Der Song vom Bernhardiner*, which starts by reflecting on the refugees' drop in status:

> He was a director — he was a judge
> 'How goes it then?' — they smile cheerfully:
> 'Nowadays we're munitions workers!'

but then reflects that the process also works the other way:

> The goldfish, that I used to own,
> Has become an aquarium somehow.

There are also in-jokes whose humour reconciles the refugees to their difficulties. The best of these is in the *Geography Lesson*:

CHARWOMAN:	What lies between this country and the USA?
1ST PUPIL:	The Atlantic Ocean, Miss.
CHARWOMAN:	Very good. And what else?
2ND PUPIL:	The Affidavit, Miss.

71

CHARWOMAN:	Excellent.
GULLIVER:	The affidavit? What's that?
PUPILS:	(burst out laughing)
CHARWOMAN:	I'm afraid that doesn't concern you Mr Gulliver.

Finally there are naughty, nostalgic, little jokes, like,

> Once upon a time — you'd see a pretty girl
> laden with packages and parcels;
> it made the male heart beat a little faster —
> he dreamt of satin, silk and lacy edges
> filling those lovely parcels — the imagination could
> run riot . . . Ah yes, once upon a time!

> (Es war einmal — da sah man hübsche Mädchen,
> beladen mit Paketen und Paketchen;
> da mußte sich ein Männerherz erhitzen —
> da träumte man von Seide, Samt und Spitzen
> in all den schönen Päckchen — da blieb freie Wahl
> der Phantasie . . . Ach ja, es war einmal!)

which comes from the best of the songs, *Heute trägt man alles unverpackt*; or in English,

> Once we dressed with grip and squeeze,
> so we had to strip with tease;
> Progress brought quick zip with ease . . .
> Zip has gone — and what now, please?

which comes from *Utility*.

With a bilingual audience translation itself could become a comic device. In *English Without Tears* the translation offered for 'a continent gone nuts' is '*Verboten — Herrenvolk — Ersatz*', with nuts rhyming with Ersatz. It was clearly easier then to say '*Scheiße*' in London than to use its English equivalent as Gulliver's coyness in Scene 4 shows:

CHARWOMAN:	Na meine Herrn Volksjenossen, da ham Se sich aber scheen in die Scheiße jesetzt!
KLUMP:	Bis zum Hals
ARIEL (to Gulliver):	They say that they are now up to their necks in the . . . now let me see, what did they call it in the eighteenth century?
GULLIVER:	Never mind — I know exactly.

Uwe Naumann, who was the first to analyse *Mr Gulliver Goes to School*, tends to underrate the comedy and labour the revue's 'anti-Fascist message' to suit his general thesis.[27] *German Harvest*, which Naumann makes the centrepiece of his interpretation, is a playlet with elements of pathos and suspense that set it apart from the rest of the piece. It demonstrates a Brechtian type of cunning for survival, and Clara, the heroine of the sketch, is a figure reminiscent of Kattrin in *Mutter Courage*. She is a Westphalian farm-worker and at first plays dumb. When Susi, the pert Berlin landgirl, asks if she heard the sirens the previous night, Clara has to be pressed to even mumble no. However, when Gulliver appears with the SS on his heels, a remarkable lucidity descends upon her and she takes charge of the situation. She prevents Susi from turning Gulliver in by threatening to expose her hanky-panky with the French PoW, shows Gulliver the way to the frontier and gives him the address of a safe house, indicating that she is part of an underground group.

The other characters represent a range of Europeans. There is Edouard, the French forced labourer, and Pavel, the Russian PoW who, to her surprise, helps Elena, the Polish aristocrat with her work. She cannot remember ever having helped the peasants back home, but in the course of the scene she is infected by Pavel's vision of a future Europe where they will all be pulling together.

Will Gulliver escape? Will Susi spill the beans, attracted as she is both to the French PoW (*'hübscher Junge'*) and to the SS man (*'fesch'*)? She thinks the others are mad to let the 100,000 marks reward slip through their fingers. She, like Clara, is a folk-type, albeit negative; a flighty, flirtatious, unreconstructed lower-class girl with no principles and only pleasure in mind. She does not learn, but is deterred by threats. Gulliver's departure brings an affirmation of solidarity, and the message for the Hampstead public is that Allied bombing has support on the ground. Even the Westphalian woman who owns the farm they are all working on turns a blind eye — she does not want any trouble. It is a solid piece of morale-boosting.

Gulliver's exit was followed by the sound of bombers overhead, whereupon the remaining characters looked up and launched into the *Second Front Song*, adding their voices to the campaign which had to wait for satisfaction until the Normandy landings. The message was that the second front was imminent:

> Von Osten — sie kommen!
> Von Westen — sie kommen!
> Laßt Helfer und Kämpfer der Freiheit uns sein!.

Naumann suggests that Gulliver's education is complete by this point, so that the later scenes are superfluous, but this overlooks the fact that we are dealing with a revue, not a *Lehrstück*, and the last scenes develop the theme of solidarity and project it hopefully into the post-war era.

Gulliver was premièred on 28 November 1942, ran for nine months and was seen by some 5,000 people, more than any other of the exile revues. There were guest appearances at the Austrian Centre and the Blue Danube, and the revue toured·to Guildford and Leicester. The *Observer* on 3 January 1943 noted that London could offer 'no exact parallel to this type of production', the Herbert Farjeon revues of the day not having the 'same depth of feeling'. It also praised the 'ingenious framework' and the 'unfailing gusto of the performers'. Monty Jacobs in *Die Zeitung* (4 December 1942) wrote:

> Never before has the League of Culture shown fresher, crisper acting . . . but more than that, none of the refugee stages in London has ever before managed so successfully to be combative and artistic at the same time. The right attitude alone is not enough, we have seen that before and suffered. But here skilful hands have been busy, grafting art happily on to the message.

In one of the earliest accounts of refugee theatre in Britain, Egon Larsen suggests that the London stage benefited in various ways from 'the Continental style', and that the stage, the BBC and the British film industry recruited many actors, writers and musicians from the ranks of the exiles.[28] The latter is undisputable, and names like Herbert Lom, Elisabeth Bergner, Martin Miller and Anton Walbrook spring to mind. Whether much can be made of this is doubtful. There had always been a flow of talent from Germany to the US, and the advent of the Nazis briefly turned the flow into a flood, some of which spilled over into Britain. The gain in skilled personnel is clear, the impact of the 'Continental style' more problematic. The straight productions done at the Austrian Centre and at the Kleine Bühne were of a high professional standard, but the technical resources of the theatres were limited. The style was perforce non-illusionistic, with no box sets and no naturalist detail. The little referential 'backcloths' at the Kleine Bühne no doubt derived from Expressionism and *Neue Sachlichkeit*, but the natives probably perceived them as making the best of a bad job, or clever bricks made without straw, rather than advanced staging. And they were probably right. It really took the visit of the Berliner Ensemble in 1956 to make people realize that there was a modern principle at work here.

Satirical *Kabarett*, too, should have been influential, for here was an entirely new theatrical mode right on the West End's doorstep. In fact it did not take root. The refugee theatres like Unity Theatre were fringe events which did not impinge on the mainstream. It was only in the 1960s and on television, that satire established itself in Britain.

Notes

1. For a full account of this phase, see Ludwig Hoffmann *et al.* (eds), *Exil in der Tschechoslowakei, in Großbritannien, Skandinavien und in Palästina*, Leipzig, 1980, pp. 168–9.
2. For details see ibid., p. 239. Lucie Mannheim's entry in C. Trilse, K. Hammer and R. Kabel (eds), *Theaterlexikon*, Berlin GDR, 1977, indicates that she played Nora in *A Doll's House*, and the title rôle in Bruno Frank's *Nina* between 1933 and 1949 in England, where she returned to live after retiring from the West Berlin stage in 1958.
3. The foundation of the FDKB is described in detail in Hoffmann, *Exil*, pp. 197–203. Survivors remember the FDKB as beginning in 1939, but Hoffmann has documentary evidence that it was founded the previous year (cf. notes, p. 649). The FDKB would have been impossible without support from British well-wishers. There were twenty-two patrons, among them J.B. Priestley and Sybil Thorndyke. The Bishop of Chichester arranged for the house in Upper Park Road. Hannen Swaffer went out of his way to report Kleine Bühne productions. But these were exceptions. On the other hand the internment programme in 1940–41 had widespread approval, and Lord Vansittart's indiscriminate anti-German views were given wide exposure from 1940, understandably in view of the state of the war. Among the refugees themselves there were those who wanted to be totally assimilated, and they wanted nothing to do with the FDKB. There was also the Communist reputation of the group, and that kept away some people, though there were prominent non-Communist figures like Oskar Kokoschka, Alfred Kerr, Berthold Viertel and Stefan Zweig among the founders of the FDKB. Egon Larsen comments that the revues were independent, that in fact they exploited the Communists who did the organizing and left the artistic side to the creative members who belonged to no party.
4. Hoffmann, *Exil*, p. 200.
5. Lothar Schirmer (ed.), *Theater im Exil 1933–45: Ein Symposium der Akademie der Künste*, Berlin (West) 1979, pp. 129–32.
6. Rudolf Weys in his survey of Cabaret in Vienna defines *Kleinkunst* very broadly: 'The genre *Kleinkunst* takes in everything. The banal and the literary, coarse jokes and literary aspirations, street ballads, *chansons*, *couplets*, protest songs and operatic arias, beautiful girls and fat comedians, Viennese waltzes and New Orleans jazz, timeless satire and transient bitching, *Tingel-Tangel* with a touch of the bohemian, smart revue and literary workshops, politics and culture, sex and striptease, the whole lot served up with hot and cold cuisine, champagne and soda water, in short, anything goes.' (R. Weys, *Cabaret und Kabarett in Wien*, Vienna/Munich, 1970, p. 7.) He also quotes a 1908 definition by Peter Altenberg: '*Kabarett — Kleinkunsttheater*, the art of creating effects on a small scale that usually only big productions in full-scale theatres can achieve.' Survivors from the Laterndl prefer to restrict the term *Kleinkunst* to serious anti-Fascist cabaret, as developed in Vienna by Der liebe Augustin, Literatur am Naschmarkt, Die Stachelbeere, and the ABC.
7. The founding of Der liebe Augustin (Our Dear Augustin) in 1932 by Stella Cadmon, for which Hugo Königsgarten supplied literary parodies, marks the beginning of *Kleinkunst*. In 1933 Rudolf Spitz founded the Stachelbeere (The Prickly Gooseberry). Hans Weigel and Rudolf Spitz wrote sketches for Literatur am Naschmarkt from 1934, and it was here that Jura Soyfer's first pieces were done. Soyfer then became the main writer for the ABC where Martin Miller appeared in the première of *Astoria* in 1937. In 1939,

therefore, a choice selection of seasoned anti-Fascist cabaret artists from Vienna were available in London.

8. For this and the following quotation I am indebted to Hugh Rank's collection of cuttings, which in these cases have no source data.
9. 'Deutsches Theater in London', *Zick-Zack* (Hanover), vol. 2, 1948, p. 15.
10. Herz's own account is published in *Österreicher im Exil*, Vienna, 1977, pp. 450–8.
11. Ibid., p. 452.
12. Ibid., p. 454.
13. Ibid., p. 455.
14. *Zick-Zack*, p. 15.
15. An account of the readings of *Flieder* and *Familie Blanchard* can be found in Hoffmann, *Exil*, pp. 660–1.
16. In his introduction to *Erna Kremer of Ebenstadt* in *Two One-act Plays*, published by the Russia-Today Society, André van Gyseghem writes: ' . . . now is the time when people are more readily disposed to *see* the connection between our theatre and our life. These two plays [the other was *According to Plan* by Geoffrey Parsons] are for such a purpose. They deal pungently and expertly with contemporary events . . . They shock, they stimulate, they make the blood beat faster . . . The idea of the broadcast to Frau Kremer is one of the most brilliant examples of Soviet war propaganda — the idea of showing the effect of its reception on the family concerned is as good a theatrical device as ever came out of an experienced dramatist's bag.' This programmatic statement applies aptly to the FDKB. Egon Larsen comments in his article in *Zick-Zack* (p. 14) that *Erna Cremer of Ebenstadt* had been done by amateur groups up and down Britain — not that it had been launched by Unity.
17. Quotation by courtesy of Hugh Rank whose contemporary clipping has no source data.
18. I am indebted for the information on Unity to Colin Chambers who lent me the manuscript of the book he is preparing on Unity Theatre.
19. Monty Jacobs, 'Zur Aufführung auf der *Kleinen Bühne* des FDKB', in *Freie Deutsche Kultur*, London, April 1944; reprinted in Hoffmann, *Exil*, p. 260
20. Quotation by courtesy of Hugh Rank whose contemporary clipping has no source data.
21. *Freie Deutsche Kultur*, June 1944, quoted in Hoffmann, *Exil*, pp. 666–8.
22. Ibid., p. 668.
23. *Familie Blanchard* was published in Hansjörg Schneider (ed.), *Stücke aus dem Exil*, Berlin (GDR), 1984, pp. 199–246. The Blanchards run the inn in a small French town. The plot suffers from well-intentioned obviousness. The father, Paul, is pro-German for business reasons. When the inn is searched for pamphlets one day, Hilbert, a German sergeant, shows interest in the daughter Marie. Marie's boyfriend Marcel persuades her to string him along and collect military intelligence for the Resistance while she is about it. Marie feels vaguely guilty because Hilbert is such a decent sort. In the *dénouement* her patriotic brother Gaston shoots Hilbert during a British raid which he mistakes for the invasion. Hilbert writes down the name of another German contact and explains with his dying breath that he is in the German resistance network and has only approached Marie to make contact with the *maquis*. Nobody asks why he did not say so in the first place. The theme is similar to the 'German Harvest' scene in *Mr Gulliver Goes to School*. Even in the German army opposition to the Nazis lies just below the surface, waiting for an ally to solidarize with.

    Familie Blanchard was read at the Kleine Bühne on 12 January 1945 by Josef Almas. *Die Zeitung* commented: 'The spirit is honest and upright, but a new form of dramatic expression is needed to lift the action above the level of the everyday. The play is well constructed, the characters are clearly drawn — and if it does not really get going, it is because we are too close to events. The audience followed Josef Almas's masterly reading attentively. . . .'
24. J. Thunecke's contribution on pp. 86–93 reconstructs the music. [See Thunecke, note 37, below regarding the number of songs in the revue — Ed.]
25. Mrs Mopp was the charwoman in the long-running wartime BBC comedy series ITMA

('It's That Man Again') which starred Tommy Handley. Her catchphrase was 'Can I do you now sir?'. The Berlin charwoman has one too: 'Da muß ick heiser kichern.' (That's good for a hoarse giggle.)

26. This derives from a joke current in Germany in the early 1930s. It also recalls the Tucholsky/Eisler song, *Feldfrüchte* (in Kurt Tucholsky, *Gesammelte Werke*, vol. 2, pp. 508–9) in which the SPD are 'darling little radishes, red on the outside but white on the inside'.

27. In Uwe Naumann, *Zwischen Tränen und Gelächter*, Cologne, 1983, pp. 169–215.

28. *Zick-Zack*, p. 13.

-4-

'Das Hübscheste sind die Lieder'
Allan Gray's Contribution
to the FDKB Revue
Mr Gulliver Goes to School

JÖRG THUNECKE

By the end of 1937 only a relatively small number of refugees from Nazi Germany had reached Britain;* yet, in the wake of events following the *Anschluß* of Austria (March 1938), the horrors of the *Reichskristallnacht* (November 1938), and the annexation of parts of Czechoslovakia (March 1939), the trickle became a steady flow, forcing Britain to relax her previously rigid immigration laws[1] and to grant refuge to a large number of German-speaking emigrants. These included many prominent artists, who, on arrival in London, were instrumental in setting up a number of cultural institutions, amongst them the Free German League of Culture (FDKB)[2] (December 1938) based in Hampstead (December 1939), and the Austrian Centre based in Paddington (March 1939).[3] Of these, the FDKB-HQ in Hampstead became the main 'cultural, intellectual, and social centre of anti-Fascist German emigration'[4] in England, and its 'Little Stage' (Kleine Bühne) the forum for the implementation of a four-point programme, whose principal aims were to:

— rescue German cultural heritage from Nazi barbarism;
— discuss the future of Germany after the defeat of Fascism;
— air problems encountered by German-speaking emigrants in Britain;
— employ satire as a political weapon in the struggle against Fascism.[5]

Although Continental-style cabaret was a particularly suitable artistic medium for conveying the political message of the FDKB[6] to a mixed audience of German-speaking refugees and native English, conditions in war-torn London — except for the period of the so-called 'phoney war' in 1939/40 — were far from ideal for sophisticated theatrical performances. Only the first of six FDKB revues, entitled *Going, Going — Gong!*,

Mr. Gulliver

Free German League of Culture

in Great Britain

Anti-Nazi

Refugee

Organisation

36 Upper Park Road, N.W.3

Tube Station: Belsize Park. Buses 24, 187

Phones: Office—PRI 0151/2.   Restaurant—PRI 5869
Office Hours : 10—6.

PROGRAMME

Goes to School

6. Programme for the FDKB revue *Mr Gulliver Goes to School* in 1942

premièred in the London West End at the Arts Theatre in July 1939, and performed by a group of actors calling themselves 'Four and Twenty Black Sheep', encountered mildly favourable conditions, whereas circumstances surrounding the staging of later revues at the Hampstead HQ of the FDKB on Upper Park Road (1940–44) could hardly be described as adequate:[7] the stage was barely six square metres in size;[8] actors had to enter it from the auditorium which — prior to improvements in 1943 — had a seating capacity of barely eighty; stage design had to be extremely simple; and artists on the whole participated on a part-time basis, often

80

after a hard day's work and under severe constraints imposed by the Blitz.
Topical revues, consisting of a fixed number of scenes, sung or spoken
in English or German, with or without accompaniment, were the FDKB's
answer to such adverse conditions, a type of political-satirical cabaret
based on a tradition popular in Austria and Germany in the 1920s and
1930s (*Nummernkabarett*).[9] Such revues were the result of collective efforts
by *all* participating artists: authors, composers, actors, musicians and
stage-designers alike. They guaranteed continuity for a form of cabaret
launched just over a decade earlier on the continent (*Kleinkunstbühnen*),[10]
allowed for the inclusion of topical political material,[11] and provided
entertainment for an English as well as a German-speaking audience.[12]
A total of six such topical revues was performed by FDKB cabaret
members:[13]

— *Going, Going — Gong!* (première: 21 July 1939);[14]
— *What's in the News?/Was bringt die Zeitung?* (première: 17 May 1940);[15]
— *What the Stars Foretell/In den Sternen steht's geschrieben* (première: 30
  January 1942);[16]
— *In Hampstead Heath ist Holzauktion* (première: 10 April 1942);
— *Mr Gulliver Goes to School* (première: 28 November 1942);
— *My Goodness, My Alibi* (première: 25 December 1943).[17]

By far the most successful of these revues, both in terms of public
acclaim[18] *and* artistic achievement,[19] was *Mr Gulliver Goes to School* which
opened on the Kleine Bühne on 28 November 1942, played until 27
March 1943 (on tour until July 1943), and is the sole FDKB revue for
which a complete typescript of the text still exists.[20] However, despite the
good fortune of a working script having survived, it took scholars some
forty years to rediscover and evaluate this text, starting with Alan Clarke's
1973 doctoral dissertation,[21] followed in 1983 by Uwe Naumann's book
Zwischen Tränen und Gelächter. Satirische Faschismuskritik 1933–1945,[22] which
devotes a whole chapter to the discussion of *Gulliver*, and more recently the
present author's article 'Humorous Ideology or Ideological Humour? *Mr
Gulliver Goes to School* (1943)',[23] as well as the contribution by Hugh
Rorrison in the current volume.[24]
These interpretations of *Gulliver*, based almost exclusively on the extant
text of the working script, contributed valuable information to our understanding of FDKB revues, pointing out that on this occasion[25] co-authors
Gottfurcht and Larsen broke with established cabaret tradition, replacing
the usual pattern of loosely connected scenes with a central plot based on
the hero of Swift's novel *Gulliver's Travels* (1726);[26] that they structured
the plot along a vertical time-axis and a horizontal space-axis

('*Montagetechnik*');[27] and made the revue's political message more palat-
able by occasionally adopting a light-hearted approach, encouraging a
re-examination of the link between humour and ideology in this type of
cabaret.[28] Contemporary reception of *Gulliver* in both the German exile
press and in British newspapers[29] also reveals that team-work had
reached new heights of achievement by those involved in the production of
this revue: Fritz Gottfurcht and Egon Larsen (text), Allan Gray (music),
Paul Lichtenstern (piano accompaniment), Günther Wagner (stage design), Paul Hardmuth (stage direction), Peter Cozens, Annemarie Hase,
Charlotte Küter, Agnes Bernelle, Gerhard Kempinski, Ellen Mogner,
Mowgli Sussmann and others (cast).[30]

Until recently, however, claims of a highly successful interaction between text (Gottfurcht/Larsen) and music (Gray)[31] were difficult to
substantiate: Gray's musical accompaniments for *Gulliver* had been un-
available since 1943;[32] eyewitness accounts tend to be unreliable; and
conjectures by modern critics are at best speculative[33] — a situation
aggravated by the fact that extremely little was known about the person
and the career of Allan Gray,[34] the only source of reliable information
about the composer and his work for the period 1940–43 being contemporary FDKB programme leaflets.[35] These show that Gray had *not* been
involved in the production of the first FDKB revue *Going, Going — Gong!*
(1939) — the music was written by Fred Manfeld[36] — but that in 1940 he
composed most of the accompaniments for *Was bringt die Zeitung?/What's in
the News?* (jointly with Ernst Hermann Meyer and Hanns Eisler); that in
1941/42 he wrote some of the music for *What the Stars Foretell/In den Sternen
steht's geschrieben* (jointly with André Asriel, E.H. Meyer, Kurt Passer, and
Arthur Sullivan) and for *In Hampstead Heath ist Holzauktion* (jointly with
Friedrich Hollaender and Mischa Spoliansky); assuming sole responsibility for the accompaniments of only one FDKB revue: *Mr Gulliver Goes to
School*, in the second half of 1942. For this revue Gray wrote no fewer than
twelve original tunes[37] (the 'quodlibet' of Scene 10: *Singing Lesson* is
probably also his arrangement), eight of which have now been redis-
covered, and only four songs, *How Grand is the 20th Century* (Scene 2), *In
Deutschland fehlt eine Scheuerfrau* (Scene 5), *Der Song vom Bernhardiner* (Scene
7), and *Second Front* (Scene 14) are still missing and must be assumed lost.

Having completed the work on *Gulliver*, Gray appears to have resumed
his pre-war career as a composer of film music, joining producers Michael
Powell and Emeric Pressburger in 1943.[38] The accompaniments of the
final FDKB revue, *My Goodness, My Alibi* were written by Friedrich
Holländer, Ernst Hermann Meyer and Harry Ralton in the second half of
1943, without Allan Gray's involvement.

Undoubtedly, the single most significant discovery following research into the life and work of Allan Gray is the fact that he too — like other prominent members of the FDKB ensemble who contributed to the success of the six revues staged in London[39] — had been no newcomer to cabaret. Born Josef Zmigrod in Tarnow (Poland) on 23 February 1902[40] Gray received his university education in Berlin and Heidelberg,[41] before becoming one of Arnold Schoenberg's master pupils at the Berlin Academy of Arts in the late 1920s.[42] Prior to that he had already made a name for himself as a highly accomplished composer of theatre music, having written accompaniments for Georg Kaiser's play *Von morgens bis mitternachts* and the German version of Diderot's *Ist er gut, ist er böse?* at the Berlin Schiller-Theater in the mid-1920s, and having been Max Reinhardt's musical director (writing the music for a production of *Julius Caesar*), while at the same time receiving tempting offers from Trude Hesterberg and Rosa Valetti to work as a permanent in-house composer for the cabarets Wilde Bühne and Rampe.[43]

Due to Schoenberg's dislike of popular music, Zmigrod appears to have chosen the pseudonym Gray, the name of Oscar Wilde's fictional hero,[44] composing chansons to texts by Erich Kästner, Kurt Tucholsky, Joachim Ringelnatz, Marcellus Schiffer, Karl Schnog, Karl Kinndt, etc., sung by such artists as Margo Lion, Paul Grätz, Curt Bois and Gertrud Kolman. In addition he also wrote chansons for Werner Finck's cabaret Katakombe;[45] composed an operetta called *Gloria*; supplied the musical arrangements for radio plays and revues like 'Kleine Revue', 'Der Tag zweier Menschen', 'Wie bleibe ich arm und glücklich', 'Jahreszeiten der Liebe', 'Die fleißige Leserin' and 'Schreckenskammer' for various German broadcasting corporations. Kate Kühl sang his 'Moritaten und hochtragische Balladen' and many of his most popular tunes were adopted for revues in places as far apart as Berlin, Königsberg and Breslau.

In 1931 Gray embarked on a new career as composer of film music,[46] writing tunes for such well-known UFA films as *Berlin Alexanderplatz* (starring Heinrich George and Maria Bard); *Emil und die Detektive*; *Die Gräfin von Monte Christo* (starring Brigitte Helm, Rudolf Forster, and Gustav Gründgens); *F.P.1 antwortet nicht* (starring Hans Albers, Sibylle Schmitz, Paul Hartmann, and Peter Lorre); *Mensch ohne Namen* (starring Werner Krauß, Maria Bard, and Mathias Wieman); *Brennendes Geheimnis* (starring Willy Forst, Hilde Wagener, and Alfred Abel); *Hände aus dem Dunkel* (starring Karin Hardt and Hans Brausewetter); *Rund um eine Million* (starring Camilla Horn and Gustav Fröhlich); and *Ihre Hoheit, die Verkäuferin* (starring Liane Haid and Willy Forst). Some of the film music composed by Gray eventually became very popular indeed, and a number of his songs even became hits, like *Flieger, grüß mir die Sonne*; *Ganz dahinten*, *wo der Leuchtturm steht*; *Niemand fragt uns*; and *Liebe kommt — Liebe geht*. By 1933 he had established himself as one of Germany's most promising young song-writers, but — being of Jewish origin — was forced to leave the country when the Nazis came to power at the beginning of that year.[47] He first went to Paris and later emigrated to England, finally settling near London where he resumed his musical career, writing accompaniments for three Shakespeare productions: *Love's Labour Lost* in Stratford-upon-Avon, *Much Ado About Nothing* with Robert Donat, and *Twelfth Night* at the Arts Theatre in London.[48] He was interned on the Isle of Man (Huyton Camp) in June 1940,[49] and following his release in 1941 collaborated for just under two years with the FDKB, until — at the end of 1942 — the film industry reclaimed his talents.

In 1943 Gray was commissioned to write film music for the Powell/Pressburger production of *The Life and Death of Colonel Blimp*.[50] According to his own *Vita*[51] he composed the full scores of almost one hundred English, French, German, and American feature films, as well as those for the first series of thirty-nine television films of 'Douglas Fairbanks Presents' (NBC), having worked with such famous film directors as John Huston and Billy Wilder.[52] His *Vita* lists him as having composed the music for such well-known films as: *First Offence*, *The Marriage of Corbal*, *The Secret of Stamboul*, *The Challenge*, *School for Husbands*, *Latin Quarter*, *Mr Perrin and Mr Trail*, *Madness of the Heart*, *The Woman with no Heart*, *The Late Edwina Black*, *The African Queen*, *The Planter's Wife*, *The Iron Mask*, *The Last Voyage* etc., and also for one more German feature film *Solange es hübsche Mädchen gibt* (1955), starring such internationally acclaimed actors and actresses as Claudette Colbert, Katharine Hepburn, Deborah Kerr, Humphrey Bogart, David Niven, Douglas Fairbanks, Ellen Kessler, Georg Thomalla and Anton Walbrook (i.e. Adolf Wohlbrück).

For the greater part of his life in exile Gray resided in Chesham Bois, just outside London, and died, rather unexpectedly, in nearby Amersham on 10 September 1973.[53] His widow, Lissy Gray, returned to her native Aachen (Aix-la-Chapelle), where she died on 5 July 1980.[54]

Mr Gulliver Goes to School is a revue comprising nineteen numbers (scenes): eight songs and eleven sketches (including five songs),[55] making a total of thirteen songs, if the 'quodlibet' of Scene 10 (*Singing Lesson*) is counted as a song. The distribution of songs and sketches in *Mr Gulliver Goes to School* is as follows:

| Scene 1: | *Where was Mr Gulliver?* | Sketch and Song |
| Scene 2: | *How Grand is the 20th Century* | Sketch and Song |

Scene 3:	*English Without Tears*	Sketch and Song[56]
Scene 4:	*Never Say Lie*	Sketch
Scene 5:	*In Deutschland fehlt eine Scheuerfrau*	Song
Scene 6:	*Citizens' Advice Bureau*	Sketch
Scene 7:	*Der Song vom Bernhardiner*	Song
Scene 8:	*Geography Lesson*	Sketch
Scene 9:	*Geography 1942*	Song[57]
Scene 10:	*Singing Lesson*	Sketch and Songs
Scene 11:	*Shopping Lesson*	Sketch
Scene 12:	*Die Ballade vom Riesen Koschchei*	Song
Scene 13:	*German Harvest*	Sketch
Scene 14:	*Second Front*	Song
Scene 15:	*Heut trägt man alles unverpackt*	Song
Scene 16:	*What is a Gentleman?*	Song
Scene 17:	*I can't take you with me*	Sketch
Scene 18:	*Utility*	Song
Scene 19:	*Victory Bar*	Sketch and Song

The show followed a pattern of regularly alternating songs and sketches, with a concentration of songs at the beginning (three) and at the end (five) of the revue. This is more or less what one would expect if an audience's attention is to be captured from the start, and if a revue was to finish with a rousing finale.

The introductory song of the opening sketch *Where was Mr Gulliver?* — sung in English, like well over 50 per cent of the songs — is lighthearted and humorous, compared with later scenes from *Gulliver*, which are often characterized by ideological aggressiveness and clumsy didacticism, and no doubt helped to quickly familiarize the audience with the political situation in Europe. The background is Mrs Lloyd's coffee-house in London in 1704, following Gulliver's return from his most recent adventure, a journey into the future aboard a time-machine. Everywhere twentieth-century clothes are on display, brought back by Gulliver as presents for the café's regular customers. The cheerful tone of the scene is beautifully supported by Allan Gray's music, concealing the seriousness of Gulliver's most recent experience. Gray's brisk melody, accompanying four sets of paired couplets — a feature commonly used in cabaret — linked by the chorus *Where was Mr Gulliver?* has a distinct pre-war quality, and echoes the boisterous atmosphere at the inn and the storm of laughter generated by the comments with which the various gifts are received.[58]

There immediately follows the sketch *How Grand is the 20th Century*, in which the gentle irony of the opening scene soon gives way to a more sinister form of humour, evoked by Mrs Lloyd's naïve question:

Jörg Thunecke

> Cannot the people who are so wise
> make of the world a paradise?

and reflected in the scathing criticism of Gulliver's reply:

> Oppressors in their cruel rage
> put back the clock to darkest age.
> The wonders of communication
> are used to preach annihilation.
> The climax of this hellish brew
> is reached in 1942.[59]

Unfortunately, this is one of four songs for which Allan Gray's music is missing, leaving us to surmise what the melody may have sounded like,[60] a situation somewhat compensated for by the fact that Ariel's song in the following sketch, *English Without Tears*, gives a good indication of the quality of the accompaniments in the opening section of the *Gulliver* revue (Scenes 1–4).

Ariel's song occurs in a number in which Gulliver, accompanied by a female figure (!),[61] travels from 1704 via 1750, 1789, and 1848, to the year 1938, in an attempt to acquaint the English-speaking section of the audience with details of the anti-Fascist struggle in Continental Europe. Such efforts run concurrently with Ariel's insistence that Gulliver, equally ignorant of modern history, is also given a quick lesson in contemporary politics and its terminology, taking the form of a song, each stanza ending in a chorus containing the advice:

> Be 'Swift' and learn the ABC
> of up-to-date philosophy.

None the less, Allan Gray's musical accompaniment for this number must be classed as only a partial success: the gaiety of the melody quite adequately fits the flippant and irreverent tone of the first stanza (a lesson in twentieth century love-making), but hardly suits the serious political message of the following one:

> And now, before the coast appears,
> I'll teach you English without tears.
> I guess you'll be a bit surprised
> Old English has been modernised.
> Translate: 'The world is torn to bits!'
> [Gulliver shrugs his shoulders]
> The answer: 'Führer — strafen-Blitz!'
> Translate: 'A Continent goes nuts!'
> 'Verboten — Herrenvolk — Ersatz!'

Lighthearted and serious issues are contrasted rather successfully in the text itself, whereas the recurring melody for both stanzas fails to convey the changing mood between the first and second verse, with the result that the interaction between text and music encounters serious obstacles, which even Gray's ingenious composition failed to overcome.

Gulliver's 'learning process' — initiated in Scene 4 (*Never Say Lie*), the first in a series of overtly political numbers, which continue until Scene 14 (*Second Front*)[62] — is dominated by ideological considerations, often to the exclusion of humorous entertainment. At the same time the middle section of the *Gulliver* revue occasionally still contains irony, counterbalancing highly obtrusive didactic passages: the hilarious background to *In Deutschland fehlt eine Scheuerfrau* (Scene 5), for example, which seems to have inspired one of Allan Gray's most successful contributions for the *Gulliver* revue.[63] But unfortunately, the music for this song, too, is missing, and we still have to rely on the judgements of contemporary witnesses regarding the effectiveness of this number.[64]

However, in general the humour in the middle section of *Gulliver* becomes increasingly laboured (see for example the sketches of Scene 6: *Citizens' Advice Bureau*, Scene 8: *Geography Lesson*, and Scene 11: *Shopping Lesson*, the last two scrutinizing the refugees' attitudes to their host country); and consequently the song in Scene 9: *Geography 1942* comes as quite a relief, showing Allan Gray at his best. In fact, the accompaniment for *Geography 1942*, a number written by Max Zimmering,[65] fully justifies Peter Noble's claim that Allan Gray's music was 'gay and tuneful':[66] its wistful melody captures the flight of the imagination reaching out to distant and somewhat exotic lands, which contrasts sharply with the refugees' plight in a foreign country, where they struggled to overcome the difficulties of day-to-day existence:

> If you should ask me for the shortest way
> to Hyde Park Corner, Charing Cross, or Zoo,
> I tell you frankly, between me and you,
> I could not say — I could not say.

> But if you ask me: have you any notion
> about some island somewhere in the ocean,
> let's say New Guinea, Madagascar — well,
> there is no secret which I could not tell.

Consequently, the rather melancholy tune, which so eminently fits the fanciful geographical details of the first stanza, may have compensated the audience to some extent for Gray's failure to harmonize text and music in the following two: for the sweet melody and blunt political message are at odds, even when the tune is sung faster and given a more syncopated rhythm, demonstrating that no stretch of the imagination is able to bridge discrepancies between crude texts, like Zimmering's chorus in the final stanza of *Geography 1942*, and congenial music, as composed by Allan Gray:

> But if you ask me: where is Hitler going,
> where to is Mussolini's vessel rowing,
> where will they end, and when, please tell me!
> [Well?]
> I tell you: soon and certainly in Hell!

Fortunately, the 'quodlibet'[67] of the following scene, *Singing Lesson*, offers additional distraction, apart from throwing new light on how well text and music occasionally were combined.

Critics have, of course, known these songs — five English and three German, all popular ones — for some time, since they were listed in the working script of the *Gulliver* revue. The only question which therefore remains[68] is how closely on this occasion the political message echoes the original words, and equally, how well such texts had been adapted to the melody and rhythm of the original tune. The answer to both questions is that a successful blend of the various strands was indeed achieved, and that in each case the association of legendary figure and song, the nexus between old and new meaning, as well as the adaptation of the rhythmic and melodic pattern of the song is near perfect, leading one to suspect that in this instance, too, Gray may have lent a professional hand in the arrangement of the medley.

This critical evaluation applies equally to:

— the song by Snow White, heroine of *Grimms' Fairytales*, about the illegal and subversive activities of her dwarfs in Nazi Germany, to the tune of *My Bonny lies over the Ocean*;
— the song by the giant Rübezahl from the Riesengebirge on the border of Germany and Czechoslovakia, witnessing the looting and ransacking of the Sudetenland, to the tune of *Was kommt da von der Höh*;
— the song by Lewis Carroll's Alice in Wonderland, refusing to be scared by the Nazis, to the tune of *Loch Lomond*;
— the song by Little Moritz, a familiar Jewish joke figure, reminding the audience of its responsibility to ask awkward questions to avoid future political catastrophes, to the tune of *Ein Männlein steht im Walde*;

— the song by Awful Audrey, a popular 1930s cartoon figure, showing how economic pin-pricks could thwart the powerful Nazi machinery, to the tune of *Little Brown Jug*;

— the song by Good Soldier Schwejk, the hero of Hašek's novel, witnessing the assassination of Reinhard Heydrich, Governor of Nazi-occupied Bohemia and Moravia in May 1942, to the tune of *Good King Wenceslas*;

— the song by Frau Holle of *Grimms' Fairytales*, predicting the defeat of the German armies in the East by the Russian winter, to the tune of *Das Wandern ist des Müllers Lust*;

— the chorus in praise of fairytale figures of all nations and ages, serving the cause of justice while engaged in defeating the forces of evil, to the tune of the Scottish New Year's Eve song *Auld Lang Syne*.

Highly illustrative of Allan Gray's work is also his accompaniment to the *Ballade vom Riesen Koschchei* by Rolf Anders,[69] the legend of a giant — representing the Spirit of Russia — whom invaders can never destroy. From a literary point of view this is one of the more polished texts of the *Gulliver* revue, and Gray's music enhances the attraction of this number even further, conjuring up a Russian atmosphere, reminiscent of tunes by Mussorgsky: slow and ponderous melodies echoing the vastness of the country, gigantic like the legendary figure itself. In addition, the melody fits the text of each stanza equally well, since the balladesque account of the heroism of two Russian patriots did not necessitate progress from atmospheric beginnings to an ideological conclusion, helping Gray to avert problems encountered in connection with Ariel's song and *Geography 1942* — which in turn leads one to suspect that Gray often only knew the first stanza of songs for which he was asked to write accompaniments; this suspicion is supported by the fact that his musical scores never make any mention of other verses.

Gulliver's 'education' being completed in Scene 14 (*Second Front* — another of the four songs for which Gray's accompaniment unfortunately is missing) the revue moves on to a discussion of political conditions in Europe, past and present, and the outlook for the future, especially for emigrants living in Britain. The first of the songs in this section occurs in Scene 15 (*Heut trägt man alles unverpackt*), in which changing shopping habits are compared to changing political habits. Gray's musical response to the lively iambic verse pattern of the main part of each stanza, expressing an urgent need for change, is highly innovative, using jazz rhythms in the style of Count Basie, who by 1938 had become internationally famous, and whose music Gray must have known, since he had lived in England since the mid-1930s:[70]

In olden times we were so much impressed
when things were nicely labelled, wrapped,and dressed;
and so it happened that the phoniest muck,
in splendid covers, by its glamour struck.
In politics the gangsters dressed in lies their crimes,
and got away with it . . . In olden times!

In olden times we used to shield our minds
with blinkers, plug our ears, and draw the blinds.
Our house was burning — we paid no attention;
we were wrapped up in sweet non-intervention.
But now we have discovered: if Freedom is to win,
down with all wrappings — in the salvage bin!

By contrast, Gray quite sensibly changed the rhythm and speed of the melody in the accompaniment for the chorus starting with 'Heut kauft man nicht die Katz im Sack', a refrain expressing satisfaction about changing attitudes, and suggesting the dawn of a new era.

The undisputed climax of the *Gulliver* revue, according to eyewitness accounts, as well as the evidence of Gray's music, was the song *What is a Gentleman?* (Scene 16), written and sung by Agnes Bernelle, daughter of Rudolf Bernauer.[71] Although the lyrics of this song leave a lot to be desired and lack the political aggression of Messrs Gottfurcht and Larsen, Gray's accompaniment is a small masterpiece, which may well have been a big hit under different historical circumstances. The text compares two types of people: educated bourgeois speaking 'posh' English, and ignorant Cockneys dropping their h's. Gray used this contrast quite cleverly for his music, adopting the division within each stanza into two separate halves, using the first as introduction for the second: a woman's wistful yearning for the right kind of man is followed by a marvellous chorus, abounding with romantic sentiments:

That's what I call a gentleman
of very high degree;
he's got to know exactly when,
and where, and what, to be.
He has to show incessantly
his gentlemanly touch;
with ladyfriends he has to be
correct — but not too much.
That's what I call a gentleman,
a gentleman as such.[72]

Soon afterwards, however, the cutting irony of the so-called *Utility Song* (Scene 18) abruptly, and quite deliberately, brings us back to earth:

90

> Dreams of love and of romance
> are to-day not left to chance:
> not the moonlight's silver beams —
> Utility now rules the dreams!

It is in this song, which ridicules the design of utility utensils, manufactured during a period of great austerity at the end of the Second World
War, that Allan Gray once again shows his deep empathy for the authors'
intentions, adopting the existing division within each stanza and using
quite a slow melody for the main part of the song, almost as though
looking back nostalgically to the 'good old days', gone for ever, along with
all the things once appreciated and now replaced by modern gadgets:

> Laces, trimmings, pleats, and cuffs,
> trains, embroideries, and muffs,
> things that seemes [*sic*] so dear to us:
> now they seem just queer to us.
> Miles of ribbons, rows of bows,
> lapels, buttons, all that goes
> overboard — gone with the storm:
> we're informal, but in form!

This slow tune, however, imparting deep-seated resentments, is
superseded in due course by a melody of such infectious quality that the
audience was apparently still humming it when leaving the Hampstead
theatre of the FDKB.[73] Once again the iambic verse pattern seems to nave
inspired Gray: the brisk melody echoes the numerous sharp vowels (i's
and e's) and creates a feeling of urgency for a new era to be ushered in:

> Utility, Utility,
> the end to all futility!
> And no more knick-knacks, no more frills,
> we're sick of such old-fashioned thrills.
> Utility, Utility
> means charm and spells beautility;
> and when returns stability
> we'll stick with all ability
> to beautiful Utility, Utility, Utility.[74]

This chorus in turn paves the way for the last — and most complex —
song of the *Gulliver* revue, contrasting customers in the saloon of an
English public house with those frequenting the bar, while at the same
time comparing ladies with 'ordinary' females, and gents with men in the
street, a song in which nothing at all stays the same except the chorus,[75]
supposedly giving musical vent to people's frustration that there might be

no change even when the war is won: class structures will remain as they are, and nobody will alter his or her habits.

Gulliver's prognosis of life in post-war Britain echoes precisely this attitude, possibly mirroring the pressures exerted by the leadership of the Communist-dominated Free German League of Culture on the authors of the *Gulliver* text to conclude the revue with a few blunt warnings of the dire consequences if the social and economic structures in Europe remain the same:

> How dreadful to think that after this war
> Life should be just as it was before;
> How dreadful to think:
> Life should be cruel,
> Life should be senseless,
> Life should be just as it was before!

Gray for his part wrote a highly accomplished victory march, using a melody which echoes the sentiments of the upper middle classes during their celebrations (in Stanza 1), who — as the song suggests — suffered least from the ravages of war, a tune which by contrast is singularly, and deliberately, at odds with the way the working classes conduct their V-Day celebrations, being once again the losers. The melody for the chorus, on the other hand, has none of the emphatic qualities of the preceding march, returning to tunes of the 1930s, implying — in musical language — that in the composer's opinion little has changed during the intervening years:

> Life will be just as it was before.

As suggested in the title of this essay, one contemporary critic, who attended a performance of *Mr Gulliver Goes to School* in 1943, claimed that Allan Gray's songs were by far the 'nicest' part of the revue,[76] a view difficult to substantiate in later years due to the lack of evidence. Suddenly, however, the discovery of most of Allan Gray's music for the *Gulliver* revue has created an opportunity to subject statements like these to a more rigorous test.

The result of such an investigation shows that Gray's musical accompaniments must in fact have been the life and soul of the *Gulliver* revue, that they were of far higher quality than previously assumed, and certainly more accomplished than most of the lyrics, which were stifled by ideological considerations and often lacking in humour.[77] In addition, such a critical scrutiny of text and music proves conclusively that attempts by erstwhile members of the FDKB ensemble to play down the importance of Gray's contribution, to the point of ignoring his part in the successful staging of the *Gulliver* revue, are totally unjustified: in fact, one feels inclined to hazard a guess that Allan Gray's accompaniments could have been even better had he been briefed more thoroughly about the precise nature of the content of the texts for which he was commissioned to write the music. Allan Gray's songs are indeed the best part of the *Gulliver* revue; moreover they are still worth listening to — something which can *not* be said for most of the lyrics, interest in which has all but disappeared.[78]

Notes

* ep. (= Eva Priester): 'Mr. Gulliver geht zu den Refugees', *Zeitspiegel*, 5 Dec. 1942.
1. See A. J. Sherman, *Island Refuge. Britain and Refugees From the Third Reich 1933–1939*, London, 1973; Werner Röder, *Die deutschen sozialistischen Exilgruppen in Großbritannien 1940–1945*, Hanover, 1968 [recte: 1969]; and Helene Maimann, *Zur Politik der österreichischen Emigration in Großbritannien 1938–1945*, PhD thesis, Vienna, 1973.
2. For the history of the FDKB see the works listed in the bibliography at the end of this volume.
3. On the Austrian Centre and Austrian emigration to Britain see the works listed in the bibliography of this volume.
4. Josef Schleifstein, 'Selbstlose Arbeit für das Bündnis aller antifaschistischen und humanistischen Kräfte der Kultur. Zum Gedenken an Hans Fladung', *Die Tat*, no. 39 (24 Sept. 1982), p. 10.
5. See Egon Larsen, 'Deutsches Theater in London. Ein ungeschriebenes Kapitel Kulturgeschichte', *Zick-Zack*, vol. 2, no. 3, 1948, p. 14; see also Fritz Gottfurcht, 'Gedanken zur Zukunft des Deutschen Theaters', in Fritz Weinert (ed.), *Die fatale letzte Patrone*, London, 1943, pp. 23–5.
6. Uwe Naumann, 'Bühnen-Reise zu den abscheulichsten Wesen: Die Londoner Kulturbund-Revue "Mr. Gulliver Goes to School"', in *Zwischen Tränen und Gelächter. Satirische Faschismuskritik 1933 bis 1945*, Cologne, 1983, p. 172.
7. See Jan Hans, 'Über Produktionsbedingungen des Theaters im Exil', in Lothar Schirmer (ed.), *Theater im Exil 1933–1945*, Berlin (West), 1979, pp. 165–71.
8. See Egon Larsen, 'Deutsches Theater in London 1939–1945. Ein unbekanntes Kapitel Kulturgeschichte', *Deutsche Rundschau*, vol. 83, 1957, p. 380.
9. The pattern of cabaret was changing in the mid-1920s; loosely connected scenes were abandoned in favour of a more coherent theme; for further details see Rainer Otto and Walter Rösler, *Kabarettgeschichte. Abriß des deutschsprachigen Kabaretts*, Berlin (GDR), 1977, pp. 93f., esp. p. 98 ('Die Hollaender-Revuen'): 'Hollaender . . . suchte nach neuen kabarettischen Formen. Das thematische Kunterbund der Kabarettprogramme sollte durch eine vereinheitlichende Grundidee verbunden werben. . . . [Ein] rote [r] Faden wird zum künstlerischen Prinzip von Hollaenders Kabarettproduktionen seit Mitte der zwanziger Jahre.'
10. See Rudolf Weys, 'Was ist Kleinkunst?' and 'Ära Kleinkunst 1931–38', in *Cabaret und Kabarett in Wien*, Vienna/Munich, 1970, pp. 7–8 and pp. 25–63 respectively; see also Ingeborg Reisner, *Kabarett als Werkstatt des Theaters. Literarische Kleinkunst in Wien vor dem*

Jörg Thunecke

zweiten Weltkrieg, PhD thesis, Vienna, 1961.

11. See Naumann, 'Bühnen-Reise', p. 177.
12. Most of the FDKB revues contain scenes both in English and in German; some of the sketches in *Gulliver* were even written bilingually (see Erich Freund, 'Deutsches Theater im Londoner Exil'. *Theater der Zeit*. vol. 1, no. 4, 1946, p. 21).
13. See Egon Larsen, 'Kleine Bühne des FDKB, London. Chronologie' (typescript), pp. 1–2; see also Egon Larsen, 'Die Revuen des "Freien Deutschen Kulturbundes" in London 1939–1945' (typescript), pp. 1–8 (*Gulliver* is dealt with on p. 7).
14. That is, just prior to the start of the Second World War.
15. That is, during the period of the so-called 'phoney war', and just prior to the start of mass internment in June 1940; for further details on the 'phoney war' see Ursula Adam, *Zur Geschichte des Freien Deutschen Kulturbundes in Großbritannien (Ende 1938–Mai 1945)*, PhD thesis, Berlin (GDR), 1983, chpt. III: 'Zur Tätigkeit des Freien Deutschen Kulturbundes nach Ausbruch des zweiten Weltkrieges (September 1939–Juni 1941)', pp. 81f.; see also Larsen, 'Deutsches Theater in London', pp. 13–14; Larsen, 'Deutsches Theater in London 1939–1945', pp. 379–80; and Freund, 'Deutsches Theater', p. 20; on British policies of mass internment see the works listed in the bibliography at the end of this volume.
16. That is, immediately after the first internees were released at the end of 1941 (see Adam, chpt. IV: 'Das Wirken des Freien Deutschen Kulturbundes nach dem faschistischen überfall auf die Sowjetunion (Juni 1941–November 1942)', pp. 129f.).
17. See Larsen, 'Revuen', p. 8.
18. See Freund, 'Deutsches Theater', pp. 21–2; see also R.P. (= Rudolf Popper), 'Von Gulliver zu "Toni"', *Einheit* (19 Dec. 1942), p. 16.
19. See Larsen, 'Deutsches Theater in London 1939–1945', p. 381, and M. J. (= Monty Jacobs), 'Mr. Gulliver Goes to School', *Die Zeitung* (4 Dec. 1942).
20. The working script of *Gulliver* was made available by Mrs D. Gotfurt (London), the widow of co-author Fritz Gottfurcht.
21. Alan Clarke, *Die Rolle des Theaters des 'Freien deutschen Kulturbundes in Großbritannien' im Kampf gegen den deutschen Faschismus (1938–1947)*, PhD thesis, Berlin (GDR), 1973.
22. See Naumann, 'Bühnen-Reise' as in above note 6.
23. Jörg Thunecke, 'Humorous Ideology or Ideological Humour? *Mr Gulliver Goes to School* (1943). A Topical Revue at the "Free German League of Culture" (London) by Fritz Gottfurcht and Egon Larsen', in D.F.L. Nilsen (ed.), *WHIMSY VI: International Humor. Proceedings of the Sixth (1987) Conference*, Tempe, 1987, pp. 230–1;
24. See pp. 66–75.
25. Another attempt was made in the following and last FDKB revue: *My Goodness, My Alibi* in 1943/44.
26. See Clarke, *Die Rolle des Theaters*, p. 279; see also Jennifer Taylor, 'The Critic in Exile: Monty Jacobs in London 1939–46', *New German Studies*, vol. 14, no. 3, 1986/87, pp. 240–1.
27. See Naumann, 'Bühnen-Reise', p. 185.
28. See Thunecke, 'Humorous Ideology', p. 240–1.
29. See Naumann, 'Bühnen-Reise', p. 207–15 ('Reaktionen').
30. See Clarke, *Die Rolle des Theaters*, p. 279.
31. See Rorrison in this volume p. 66: 'The music contributed greatly to the success of the revue.'
32. Clarke claims to have had access to Allan Gray's musical accompaniments (made available by Egon Larsen in the early 1970s); unfortunately this material seems to have been lost in the archives of the East Berlin Academy of Arts (see Naumann, 'Bühnen-Reise', p. 355, fnt. 220), but see also Robert Sandall: 'Teaching a Revolutionary New Tunes' [*sic*], *The Sunday Times* 12 Feb. 1989, p. C14, on the recent record release of Hanns Eisler songs by Dagmar Krause ('Tank Battles') and the problems she encountered during her research: ' . . . despite his [Eisler's] tremendous popularity then and the success he achieved later in his American exile . . . Eisler's musical legacy today

is a well-kept secret. Though Weill is seldom far away, much of Eisler is still under lock and key at the Eisler archives in the city where he spent his declining years, East Berlin. Krause's applications to the archive for sheet music were, for the most part, courteously stone-walled. The official reason, that a complete catalogue is in preparation, sounded less plausible when she heard unofficially that many of Eisler's early militant numbers are not now considered "relevant" by the East German authorities — a posthumous irony that seems grimly appropriate for a man whose seditious populism led him into trouble at regular intervals throughout his life.'

33. Naumann at least expressed doubt regarding the quality of Allan Gray's accompaniments for *Gulliver* ('Bühnen-Reise', p. 205).

34. Not even Allan Gray's real name was knówn at the outset of the current investigation.

35. The extant programme leaflets list authors, composers and actors who partook in the production of each revue.

36. See Larsen, 'Revuen', p. 8; and Reinhard Hippen, *Satire gegen Hitler. Kabarett im Exil*, Zurich, 1986, p. 112.

37. Rorrison, p. 66 (above), and Larsen, 'Revuen', p. 7, both missed out Ariel's song in *English Without Tears*, and consequently wrongly calculated the total number of songs.

38. See *Who's Who 1987*, p. 1411; see also the entry on Michael Powell by Stephen L. Hanson in C. Lyon and S. Doll (eds), *The International Dictionary of Films and Filmmakers*, vol. 2: 'Directors/Filmmakers'. Chicago/London, 1984, p. 425–6.

39. Both main text-writers, Fritz Gottfurcht and Egon Larsen (Lehrburger), composers Fritz Hollaender and Mischa Spoliansky, and actress Annemarie Hase played a prominent part in the Berlin cabaret scene in the 1920s.

40. Details on Gray's life and work were made available by Günter Vollmann in '75. Geburtstag: Eine Erinnerung an Allan Gray', in *artist* (Düsseldorf), vol. 95, no. 4, 1977, pp. 4 and 6 (reprinted in *expertise* (Munich), vol. 2, February 1980, p. 14.

41. See Gray's own typescript, made available by Günter Vollmann.

42. According to information supplied by the 'Arnold Schoenberg Institute' (Los Angeles), Josef Zmigrod was a student of Schoenberg's in Berlin from 1 April 1926 to 31 March 1929.

43. See Heinz Greul, *Bretter, die die Zeit bedeuten. Die Kulturgeschichte des Kabaretts*, vol. 1, Munich, 1971 (2nd edn), pp. 205–10; see also Rudolf Hösch, *Kabarett von gestern nach zeitgenössischen Berichten, Kritiken und Erinnerungen*, vol. 1; 1900–1933, Berlin (GDR), 1967, pp. 213–25; and Rainer Otto and Walter Rösler, *Kabarettgeschichte. Abriß des deutschsprachigen Kabaretts*, Berlin, 1977, pp. 88–90.

44. *The Picture of Dorian Gray* (1891).

45. See Greul, *Bretter*, pp. 269–77; see also Otto and Rösler, *Kabarettgeschichte*, p. 115–19.

46. The era of the sound film had just begun (see David Robinson, *The History of World Cinema*, New York, 1981 (2nd rev. edn), esp. chpt. 5 ('Revolution'); according to this (pp. 170–1), '[t]he patents owned by Tobias-Klangfilm permitted Germany a brief Indian summer before the onset of the Third Reich.').

47. The 'Erste Durchführungsverordnung' of the 'Reichskulturkammergesetz' of 1 November 1933, Section II, §§ 4 and 5 stated: 'Die Befugnis der Reichskulturkammer und ihrer Einzelkammern, ihre Reihen von unzuverlässigen und ungeeigneten Elementen freizuhalten, bedeutet *eine* wichtige Voraussetzung für den Erfolg der neuen Kulturpolitik' (see Hans Hinkel (ed.), *Handbuch der Reichskulturkammer*, Berlin, 1937, p. 21); and the President of the 'Reichsmusikkammer', Peter Raabe ('Wege und Aufgaben der Reichsmusikkammer', p. 93) decreed in his introduction to the section on the RMK (pp. 95–134): 'Es gilt da freilich, die Augen offenzuhalten und wohl zu unterscheiden zwischen dem, was wirklich als . . . *künstlerische* Betätigung anzusehen ist und was als Kitsch und Schund ausgemerzt werden muß. . . . Es gibt noch manchen Charlatan . . ., der nicht in den Stand der deutschen Musiker hineingehört. Hier gilt es durchzugreifen, ohne jede Rücksicht auf Person oder Bindungen welcher Art auch immer.'

48. See John Huntley, '*The African Queen* — The Composer and the Film', *Film Music Notes*, vol. 11, no. 4, March/April 1952, p. 22.

49. See typescript (made available by Günter Vollmann) of Allan Gray's brief autobiography, entitled *Komponist und Europäer*, chpt. IV: 'England 1939–46', pp. 8–9, according to which Gray was interned on 26 June 1940.

50. Hanson, *International Dictionary of Films and Filmmakers*, p. 425, mentions five films produced by the Archer Company between 1943 and 1946 for which Gray composed the music: *The Life and Death of Colonel Blimp* and *The Volunteer* (1943); *A Canterbury Tale* (1944); *I Know Where I'm Going* (1945); *A Matter of Life and Death* (1946). He probably also wrote the music for another Archer film, *The Silver Fleet* (1944); and according to information supplied by Michael Powell, the last music Gray wrote for the Archer Film Unit was for *A Matter of Life and Death* (see also the filmography in Powell's autobiography *A Life in Movies*, London, 1986, pp. 680–2). This information tallies with an entry on Gray in John Huntley's *British Film Music*, London, 1947, p. 206, and that in the *British Film and Television Year Book 1958/59*, ed. Peter Noble, p. 118.

51. See note 41.

52. Other well-known film directors Gray collaborated with were: Max Ophüls, Lads. Vajda, Ken Annakin, Robert Siedmak, Karl Hartl, Walter Resich and Willy Forst.

53. See obituaries in *The Times* on 15 Sept. 1973, and in the *Bucks Examiner*, on 21 Sept. 1973.

54. According to information supplied by Günter Vollmann.

55. Larsen, 'Revuen', p. 7, refers to 12 songs and 13 sketches, Rorrison (in this volume, p. 66) to 8 songs and 11 sketches (4 with songs); both figures are in need of correction in the light of new evidence.

56. Rorrison (p. 66) classes this scene as sketch without song.

57. According to the extant FDKB programme leaflets, the title of this song was *Geography 1942*, which fits the chronology of the FDKB revues; however, the heading of Allan Gray's music sheet of this song reads *Geography 1943*.

58. See, for example, the comment of one young girl on receipt of her present, a pair of tight knickers:

    The land of Giants can't have been
    this undergarment's origin.

59. Final stanza.

60. See the BBC Programme 3 of 15 July 1976, produced by Hugh Purcell, entitled 'Cabaret in Exile', in which Lisa Appignanesi, author of *The Cabaret*, London, 1975, chaired a discussion group, including Egon Larsen (Kleine Bühne) and Rudolf Spitz (Laterndl); in the course of this programme (p. 5 of the transcript) Agnes Bernelle and Michael Mellinger sang a 'satirical duet from *Mr Gulliver Goes to School*', entitled *How Grand is the Twentieth Century*.

61. The co-authors of the text changed Shakespeare's Ariel to a female figure.

62. See Naumann, 'Bühnen-Reise', p. 200.

63. See ibid., p. 199: 'Hier lebt beste deutsche Kabarett-Tradition aus den 20er Jahren weiter, und der mitreißende sprachliche Rhythmus dürfte bei entsprechender musikalischer Begleitung noch eindrucksvoller gewirkt haben.'

64. See, for example, Monty Jacobs' review in *Die Zeitung* of 4 Dec. 1942: 'Das Fidele aber ist seines Erfolges sicher, wenn *Annemarie Hases* Scheuerfrau unwiderstehlich auftrumpft. . . .'

65. See Harry Riedel, 'Max Zimmering', in Hans Jürgen Geerdts (ed.), *Literatur in der DDR in Einzeldarstellungen*, Stuttgart, 1972, pp. 113–29, esp. p. 127 ('Kurzbiographie').

66. Typewritten copy (supplied by Egon Larsen) of Peter Noble's review in *What's On* (1943).

67. Parodistic cabaret form superimposing satirical-political lyrics on popular tunes, often melodies of folk songs (for details see Reinhard Hippen (ed.), '*Sich fügen — heißt lügen*'. *80 Jahre deutsches Kabarett*, Mainz, 1981, Anhang, p. 176).

68. See Naumann, 'Bühnen-Reise', p. 201: 'Die Szene nimmt die bewährte Kabarett-Tradition auf, bekannte Figuren und Melodien in aktuellem inhaltlichen Gewand zu präsentieren.'

69. Rolf Anders was the pseudonym used by Rolf Heinrich Thoel (see Hans W. Eppels-

heim (ed.), *Deutsche Exil-Literatur. Eine Bio-Bibliographie*, Heidelberg/Darmstadt, 1962, p. 330).

70. In Germany, jazz music would hardly have been available to Gray.
71. Rudolf Bernauer was one of the most active figures on the German cabaret scene during the years of the Weimar Republic.
72. Stanza 1.
73. According to Agnes Bernelle during an interview in June 1987.
74. The chorus part varies slightly; the cited lines are those following the first stanza.
75. The message of lines 3–6 of the chorus changes with the spokesman/-woman.
76. See note * above.
77. One of Egon Larsen's complaints, voiced in an interview with the author in November 1986, concerned the exclusiveness with which Naumann's doctoral dissertation (see note 6) focuses on ideological aspects in the *Gulliver* revue, neglecting, according to Larsen, the fact that this revue had also provided a lot of entertainment (see also Thunecke, 'Humorous Ideology', pp. 230–1).
78. Allan Gray's musical accompaniments for *Mr Gulliver Goes to School* were kindly made available by Dr Günter Vollmann (Lüdenscheid), who also holds the copyright.

–5–

'They Came to a Country'
German Theatre Practitioners in Exile in Great Britain, 1938–45

ALAN CLARKE

At 7 o'clock on the evening of Saturday, 9 December 1944, the first German-language performance took place of a two-act drama by the well-known English author, J.B. Priestley.* The play, *They Came to a City*, portrayed the various reactions of a representative cross-section of British society to a new Utopian way of life and had already met with great success on the London stage the previous year. Now it was being shown in a tiny theatre set up in a private house in the unfashionable part of Hampstead, loaned to German refugees by the Church of England. The original première, planned for September, had had to be postponed partly due to the danger from Nazi V-bombs but also through the loss of some of the original cast to professional theatre, film and radio engagements.[1] The production was one of the last of the many full-length evenings arranged by the Free German League of Culture, the 'Freier Deutscher Kultur-bund' (FDKB), since its formation in December 1938. The impact of the occasion is captured in a letter sent to the performers by the great English actress, Sybil Thorndike:

> I wanted to tell you what a deep impression the playing of the German company made on me — somehow or other one was not bothered with too much 'Setting', one got the bare bones of the play and what it intended to say in a way that I felt was missed in the West-end performance. The sincerity, the vigour — the brilliant characterizations were so clear and true — and what was done with that tiny little stage is a tribute to any producer . . . may I thank you for a truly satisfying and deeply moving performance . . .[2]

This production was in many ways typical of the work of German refugee theatre practitioners during their period of exile in Britain. Firstly, it was within such institutions as the Kleine Bühne (Little Theatre) of the FDKB and the Austrian Centre's Laterndl that émigré actors and directors found most of their opportunities to practise their craft, for pro-

99

fessional work in British film, theatre or with the BBC was only occasionally available. Secondly, Priestley, like Sybil Thorndike an FDKB patron, was one of the numerous British writers and actors without whose consistent support and encouragement the theatre émigrés would never have survived so productively. Thirdly, the play was a fine example of the kind of literary drama 'discovered' by the refugees during their exile which helped to broaden their cultural horizons. Fourthly, the event underlined how crucial the theatre was within the refugee context as a focal point for ideological debate and social interaction. Finally, the play's theme of facing up to a totally new kind of existence was as relevant in 1944, when the respective merits of returning to a post-Hitler Germany devastated by war or staying on permanently in a foreign country were being hotly debated, as it was for the period some half a dozen years earlier when most of those involved in the production first arrived in Britain as 'aliens' from mainland Europe. Ironically, the least typical aspect of this occasion was that it took place in the German language, for most of the theatre work involving émigré performers was directed as much towards their British hosts as their own compatriots.

Whilst, therefore, much of this study will be concerned with the efforts of individuals to function as professional actors, directors and writers within a foreign context — both on the English stage and with the BBC — consideration will also be taken of the interaction which occurred between German theatre people and their British counterparts and the importance of this in determining the quality of the work which resulted.

'Dressed up and in respectable company': German Emigrés in the Professional British Theatre

Before 1938 relatively few Germans had arrived in Britain as refugees; those who had were mostly established international figures like Sigmund Freud or respectable middle-class professionals with enough independent resources to maintain themselves or with influential British patrons to vouch for them. Only a tiny proportion of these, probably less than a hundred, had any direct connection with the performing arts. Some German-speaking artists, it is true, did make an impact in British theatre and film during the 1930s: internationally recognized stars like Oskar Homolka, Fritz Kortner, Conrad Veidt and Richard Tauber, whose popularity lay more in the effect of his renowned singing voice than in the quality of his stage and screen appearances; newcomers like Peter Lorre who soon moved on to Hollywood; actresses like Lucie Mannheim, the young Lilli Palmer and Elisabeth Bergner, whose appearances in plays like Shaw's *Saint Joan* and *The Constant Nymph* helped to make her one of the most celebrated actresses in England during the pre-war years.

But these were exceptions. Even before the major influx of refugees into Britain following the Nazi invasion of Czechoslovakia, most foreign theatre professionals had to struggle to gain a footing on the London stage or, like the director and writer Berthold Viertel, find occasional film and radio employment before eventually moving on to America. And whilst the British film industry showed an interest in what their Continental equivalents had to offer, the English theatre was barely conscious of the existence of a German theatre tradition. Even Max Reinhardt, who made frequent visits to England during the early 1930s, including a production of *A Midsummer Night's Dream* for the Oxford University Dramatic Society which a participant described as a 'true eye-opener',[3] seems to have left no lasting impression on mainstream British theatre, and it was not until after the end of the Second World War that European drama really began to be taken seriously on this side of the channel.

The main characteristics of the West End stage at that time were its conservatism, its superficiality and its insularity, not only from influences abroad but even from much of its own culture. The newly arrived émigrés were struck by the contrast with their own experiences on the Continent. Amy Frank, one of the few refugee performers who 'made it' in the West End, described what she encountered there as 'a superficial form of entertainment unconcerned with real problems',[4] whilst the playwright Julius Berstl succinctly summed up a typical drama of the period as 'Act 1 — tea is served. Act 2 — cocktails are served. Act 3 – whisky is served.[5] Berstl, who made strenuous, if ultimately unsuccessful, attempts to break into the London theatre scene, outlined the main differences between German and English theatre practice. In Germany, audiences were used to a didactic as well as an aesthetic experience; in Britain, the theatre was primarily regarded as a social institution, not to be taken too seriously: 'You don't go to learn anything or experience literary experiments or to be involved in solving problems but simply to relax after a day's work — and that, if possible, dressed up and in respectable company.'[6] Commercial interests dominated the choice of play with — unlike the planned, partly subsidised, programmes of many German companies — productions running as long as they could pay their way. Amy Frank, who experienced such a run in the inconsequential comedy *Claudia*, commented later: 'If you were lucky and the play you were in was a success with the public you had the doubtful pleasure . . . of playing it 900 (!) times without a break (Sundays excepted).'[7]

As well as noting differences in production conditions, Berstl also remarked on the typically English style of acting:

101

> Like the English in general, the English actor avoids any strong outbursts of temperament and shows his strength through under-emphasizing. He is completely in his element when he can play himself . . . This private approach to acting is nowhere better demonstrated than in the English social comedy where, as soon as he dons his costume, the English actor becomes restricted, even stiff.[8]

Berstl did acknowledge that amongst the male actors there were some outstanding personalities like Laurence Olivier, Ralph Richardson and John Gielgud; amongst the actresses, however, he found few striking individuals. He gives this dearth of female English acting talent as one of the chief reasons for the immense success of Elisabeth Bergner, who numbered even Queen Mary amongst her admirers. Whilst this negative view of English actresses was somewhat over-generalized — Sybil Thorndike for one provided a notable exception — the stock plays of the time tended to cast women in a position of passive submission, though many of the male rôles were almost as limited. For most home-grown actors and actresses the situation was a dubious one, condemned as they were to forming part of the vast reservoir of character types waiting to fill the few available vacancies in the commercial West End. The chances, therefore, of newly arrived German performers finding appropriate openings were even more negligible, especially given their extra disadvantages. Most of them at first spoke little English, and that with marked accents, whilst their strange-sounding names could also be a hindrance — especially if you were called Adolf Wohlbrück, although he did, however, become very successful as Anton Walbrook. Also, they were accustomed to a more externalized and emotional style of performance, a repertory system offering a regular turn-over of plays, and a professional status accorded serious respect. Added to this was the lack of plays in the commercial theatre dealing with anything resembling a serious contemporary theme in which authentic Continental representations might be required. It is to the credit both of the commitment and persistence of the émigrés themselves and of the support of sympathetic British colleagues that so many German-speaking actors eventually managed to find work on the professional stage.

But in 1938/39, when the vast majority of refugee performers entered Britain — out of a total of about 55,000 émigrés roughly 400 were professional artists, with the theatre practitioners forming the largest proportion[9] — they had virtually no possibility of continuing a theatrical career, even though some jobs were available in other fields. It was not until well into the war, following the Nazi invasion of the Soviet Union, that the situation began to improve: partly as a result of the call-up of younger British actors into the armed forces, giving more opportunities for foreign performers, and partly due to a change in the character of the plays being presented on the commercial stage.

In an article written in September 1942 for the anti-Fascist Sudeten-German magazine, *Einheit,* Dr Rudolf Pepper highlighted this change by pointing to six current West End productions dealing seriously with aspects of the war. Two of them actually identified German opposition to Hitler: in *Escort,* a drama about the fighting at sea, a clear difference was drawn between the attitude of a captured German officer and that of a Gestapo official, and in *Watch on the Rhine* by the young American author, Lillian Hellmann, the hero is a German anti-Fascist who fought in Spain.[10] That same month, writing in the British government-supported *Zeitung,* Peter Bratt saw reflected in such plays a clear development in the public's perception of the refugee position from the anti-German hysteria which had led to internment two years before: 'None of these . . . is an inflamatory piece. The experiences of [the] war have not been able to blur the authors' visions. On the contrary, these playwrights could teach certain politicians that Nazis and Germans are not identical.'[11]

Whilst the scope of this awareness should not be exaggerated, especially as so many of the plays concerned were American in origin, there is nevertheless evidence that the fundamental shift in the war situation and the campaign to release the interned refugees had found some reflection on the English stage. Certainly, attitudes towards émigré actors and directors being involved in commercial productions had improved. The lead in *Watch on the Rhine* was played by the previously mentioned Anton Walbrook, Gerhard Hinze returned from a Canadian internment camp to feature in Terence Rattigan's *Flare Path* whilst earlier in the year Lilly Kann and Martin Miller had appeared in the Arts Theatre Group's production of *Awake and Sing* by another emerging American playwright, Clifford Odets. And a year later, in August 1943, we find Julius Gellner directing Frederick Valk as Katusov in an important production of *War and Peace* with other refugee contributions from Peter Illing as Napoleon, Henry Oscar as the narrator and Heinz Heckroth designing the set and costumes.

Thus an encouraging element of this development towards serious contemporary drama on the British stage was that émigré performers were involved in so much of it. This even extended to film where, for example, the 1942 adaptation of *Thunder Rock,* the thought-provoking drama by yet another American, Robert Ardrey, included Valk, Hinze, Lilli Palmer and Milo Sperber in leading roles. Whether because of the unavailability of suitable British actors or because Continental performers were able to provide the emotionally fuller characterizations demanded by more serious works — and the American theatre from which so many of these plays originated tended to be less inhibited in portraying full-bloodied conflicts — a growing number of refugee theatre professionals were finding fulfilling outlets for their talents in Britain.

The greatest impact though was made by Julius Gellner and Frederick Valk. They so dominated much of the serious theatrical scene in England in the early 1940s that the drama critic of the *Daily Worker* could write: 'It is a sad commentary on the state of our drama that . . . the best production of Shakespeare [has been] by a foreign director with a foreign lead.'[12] For it was in one of the traditional British institutions, the Old Vic Theatre Company, that Gellner and Valk made their mark. At that time the Old Vic, enjoyed the status virtually of a 'national theatre', not only for its classical Shakespearean performances in London but also through its policy of touring outlying areas of the country. These tours, partly funded by the recently formed CEMA — the Council for the Encouragement of Music and the Arts (forerunner of the modern Arts Council), which had been set up to improve arts provision in wartime — not only demonstrated the benefits of regular arts subsidies but did much to pave the way for the rapid growth of regional theatre after the war. The effect of the visit of such a prestigious company to the industrial areas of northern England, where the 'legitimate theatre' was hardly known, was described by another refugee member of the Old Vic, Friedrich Richter, who replaced Valk as Shylock on tour:

> The attempt to present a Shakespeare week met with great resistance in these towns. The population was used to an uninterrupted diet of 'music shows' and variety programmes. People were afraid that only a few would be interested in Shakespeare. But just the opposite was the case: the actors encountered . . . a sympathetic and enthusiastic public. At the end of each performance an epilogue was presented, asking the question: 'Do you like Shakespeare's plays?' The answer was always an overwhelming yes.[13]

But even the more hardened theatre-goers in London were impressed by Gellner and Valk, especially with their *Othello* which was first seen in 1942. Gellner's 'cultured production'[14] introduced the British public to what for most of them seems to have been a new approach to staging:

> [He] used every modern stage technique to create a sense of the present in the illusion . . . Gellner had the courage to use colour and understood how to employ lighting to make the figures stand out against a black background. A three-tiered row of pillars, then closed curtains, then a bright perspective demanded rapid scene changes. Twice tumultuous street scenes captured the pulse of everyday life.[15]

It is ironic that such an approach, clearly influenced by the ideas of the English designer and theoretician Edward Gordon Craig, should appear so innovative when presented by a Czech refugee some thirty years after

Craig himself had gone into exile, albeit voluntarily. And Craig's notorious contempt for actors notwithstanding, he would probably have admired Valk's talents too, seeing in them shades of his mentor Henry Irving. For, despite the problems of language and accent, which Valk seems to have turned to advantage in his portrayal of the two classical outsiders, Shylock and Othello, the immense personality of this Austrian-born actor and his ability to produce 'virile masculine acting'[16] seem to have lost none of their force when transferred to an English stage. To an audience more accustomed to the effete qualities of a Gielgud or the controlled bravado of an Olivier, Valk's performances must have been overwhelming, and even four years later he was still 'shattering English stages with his presence and acting'.[17] That this was not just a demonstration of brute force in the barnstorming tradition of a Donald Wolfit is shown by his ability to control his emotions in order to bring out the underlying dramatic sense of a situation. This quality particularly impressed the experienced German drama critic Monty Jacobs, writing about Valk's Othello in the *Zeitung*:

> This broad-shouldered sturdy athlete with the look of an emperor conquers the heights before his downfall. He lends the Moor the dignity of a commander, the strength of mature manhood, the power of a bridled temperament. How strongly he holds himself in check — to maintain his position of power in a world of whites — is shown as soon as he allows his barbarism to get out of control and turn into passion and savagery. But Valk's artistic sense does not allow him to leave this outburst as the final impression. At the bitter end his dignity returns: not as a brutal executioner but as a convinced purveyor of justice does he bend in his blindness over Desdemona's bed ...[18]

Just as impressive had been his portrayal of Shylock the year before, again under Gellner's direction. It was a rôle of particular significance to the refugee community, so many of whom were Jews and who themselves had been treated until recently as undesirables. Richter describes the character he inherited from Valk:

> I played the man who'd been treated unjustly, who'd been jeered and insulted by a society of idlers, and in whom a burning hatred for his persecutors had grown. This hatred ruled Shylock, all his actions were directed towards satisfying it, he insisted on his bond, and he, who loved money so much, refused it, wanting only revenge. The public understood that, their sympathy was completely with Shylock.[19]

The refugees amongst the audience, who had not even been granted exemption from internment as victims of racial persecution, must have identified closely with the bitterness of this portrayal.

How much thought and understanding Valk brought to his rôles is revealed in an article he wrote on 'Acting and Poetry' for the progressive theatre magazine, *New Theatre*. After emphasizing the need to 'live the verse', to convert the poetry into physical action, he goes on to counter the prevalent tendency towards cold detachment in the declamation of verse which he found in his English colleagues:

> Shakespeare's tragedies are born in hell and an actor, who dares to play them, must make a trip to hell. He can't return from there in a very orderly manner! If he does not come back with bloodshot eyes, wild, and screaming with agony, he missed Lucifer's bus!
>
> But most of the actors don't go down to hell. Either they don't know the way, or they don't want to go at all. They prefer a temperate ante-room where one can sit and behave like a gentleman, delivering a declamation beautifully, with legs nicely crossed, in well-pressed trousers. Surely they will deliver the poetry — not a word will be lost — but it will be a dehydrated poetry and you will not hear the voices of Macbeth, Lear, or Othello — baked in hell.[20]

If today Valk's approach seems just as dated as the preoccupation with the beautiful voice and studied detachment which he criticized — especially in light of the innovative work of Piscator, Brecht and others in the late 1920s — this should not be allowed to devalue the relevance of his comments. Whilst Stanislavsky's principles of 'truthful acting' were already well established on the Continental stage, they did not really gain significant credence in Britain until after the war. Valk's influence at that time was therefore an important one and when we consider some of his major post-war rôles — as Ibsen's *Master Builder* in 1947, in Peter Brook's production of *The Brothers Karamasov* in the same year (for which he was awarded the theatre critics' prize for the best performance) and in 1949 in Tolstoy's *Power of Darkness* — we can more fully appreciate his contribution to the encouragement of serious European drama on the British stage.

Valk's unique position within England's major classical theatre company allowed him the freedom to challenge accepted approaches: most of his fellow performers from abroad had however no such opportunity. Some, like Hanna Norbert, were refused work permits, whilst even for those who were permitted to seek professional employment in Britain, opportunities were limited.

> The difficulties I met professionally as an actor in London were due to my accent. And that meant . . . that there was only a certain number of rôles available . . . I played a great number of SA and SS men in films, where the accent was appropriate. Personally I did not find this work very satisfying, but a day's filming was . . . highly paid and that was of course the decisive factor, if only to be able to exist.[21]

The film industry seems to have offered the refugee actors more opportunities than the theatre. Though fewer than thirty émigré performers managed to find work in professional theatre during the war, well over fifty gained employment in the movies. One reason, apart from the differences in scale and funding between the two media, was that problems of acting style and projection were less of a factor in film, where the intimacy of performances, strong directorial control, the fragmented nature of production and the limited scope of the parts enabled foreign actors to adapt more easily. (The work of German refugees in the British film industry will be dealt with at more length elsewhere in this volume.)

'A sense of fair play': German Emigrés in the BBC

The third medium in which refugee performers could work professionally involved a different set of problems and restrictions from either theatre or film. Since the establishment of the British Broadcasting Corporation in 1922, radio had been the major growth area for information and entertainment: 'The universal feature was the wireless set, symbol of the interwar period, especially towards the end when nine million sets were licensed; in other words, in nine homes out of ten.'[22] During the war the radio became even more important. At home its chief concern was to maintain public morale, and it is significant that one of the most influential broadcasters was the FDKB patron and staunch supporter of the refugee cause, J.B. Priestley, who commanded almost as large an audience as the Prime Minister, Winston Churchill: '. . . his speeches were more representative in their cheerful understatements, more representative also in their assumption that a people's war would be followed by a people's peace.'[23]

This tolerance towards progressive views at home did not, however, extend to the BBC's increasing number of foreign transmissions, which by 1942 were in thirty-nine foreign languages with eleven broadcasts to Nazi Germany daily. Antonia White, in her book *The BBC at War*, defined the main aims of these foreign service broadcasts as entertaining British troops abroad, sending news reports from Britain and the battle zones to the rest of the world, and transmitting information and propaganda to countries under German and Italian occupation.[24] Clearly, this last function offered potential employment to German-speaking refugees, but there were serious restrictions on their participation, especially given the politically sensitive nature of such operations. The British authorities went to great pains to put across their ideological standpoint and even set up a special Executive for Political Warfare to keep tight control over foreign-language activities. One section, 'Sender der Deutschen Revolution', came under the direct charge of the Foreign Office itself until it was shut down in 1943.[25] English broadcasters filled the positions of authority and, though a statement in the House of Commons in 1941 listed sixty-one Germans and 303 other aliens in employment with the BBC as announcers, translators, monitors of incoming transmissions and in minor capacities,[26] the scope for exiled anti-Fascists to put across their views was extremely limited. Any direct contacts between the BBC and refugee organizations, especially those deemed 'political', like the FDKB, were frowned upon, so that the majority of the regular German contributors came from the more 'respectable' section of the émigré community.

One example of this approach was the great efforts made by the BBC to arrange for the transmission of Thomas Mann's addresses from America to the *Deutsche Hörer* in the Third Reich, which occurred regularly between 1940 and 1945. At first Mann cabled his texts to London, where they were read out by a German-speaking announcer. Later he spoke onto a disc at the Recording Department of NBC in Los Angeles, from whence it was sent by plane to New York to be played over the telephone into a microphone in London.[27] To the lesser-known German contributors in England the BBC showed less tolerance: towards the end of the internment period, for instance, a number of refugees engaged in radio work were released by the Corporation because their orientation was regarded as being more towards their fellow exiles abroad than to the mass of Germans who still supported Hitler. No wonder the refugee organizations felt that 'the BBC would never be a place through which we could put forward socialist propaganda'.[28] This did not stop them trying, as is shown by a competition organized by the FDKB for the best five-minute radio drama in order to 'improve the radio propaganda to Germany'.[29] And Friedrich Richter, who was able to find some work with the BBC, felt that it was at least an attempt to put across anti-Fascist ideas in Nazi Germany and as such was 'worth the effort'.[30]

The general guidelines laid down for broadcasts to Germany were identified by Heinrich Fischer, who worked on the cultural aspects of the programmes between 1941 and 1945:

(1) Unfavourable events were never concealed . . .
(2) Broadcasts were always to reflect the English character. The main contributors were English who spoke German with a definite accent.
(3) The mistrust that German listeners had towards enemy propaganda was never forgotten and therefore emotional appeals were avoided as much as possible.[31]

It is interesting to see, in a couple of scripts broadcast to Germany some four and a half years apart, how such guidelines worked in practice. The first, transmitted on 20 June 1940 and aimed specifically at German women, was written by Fritz Eberhard on the theme of the weekly newsreels shown in the cinemas of the Third Reich. Its intimate, chatty style conveys the impression of being in close touch with the experiences and feelings of those living under Nazi rule, without losing sight of the political point to be made:

> Soon you'll be seeing pictures of the victorious entry of German troops into Paris in the newsreels. Will you feel happy about it? Look how empty the streets are. Nazi troops will be received in Paris differently from two years ago in Vienna — with silence, the silence of contempt. This contempt is not directed against the individual German soldiers who fought bravely. It is directed against the Nazi leaders who are trampling with brute force on all culture and all freedom in Europe. These leaders do not always tell the truth. But what is true is that they feel happy looking at such pictures of war. This lack of culture, this barbarism, this is the enemy which we English are fighting until it is destroyed.[32]

Whilst Hitler's boast of creating a thousand-year empire still seemed a real prospect to many inside Germany, such an appeal — which does not once mention Hitler by name — must have seemed to the British tactically sound, reflecting current official policy, if not entirely putting across the views of all the anti-Fascist refugees.

In November 1944, on the other hand, with Germany on the verge of defeat, a very different tone was adopted. The 'German Show' used speakers introduced as having fought for their homeland during the First World War but who were later driven out when the Nazis came to power. One such was an Austrian poet whose specially written 'Dance Macabre' was performed by a choir of professional and amateur émigrés. It opens:

> With Hitler comes death, with Hitler comes death
> Black death, brown death, white death — death
> With Hitler comes hell, with Hitler comes hell
> Black hell, brown hell, white hell — hell
>
> A sea of tears rolls onwards, the untold sorrows unheeding
> Millions of corpses stacked up high, broken hearts are bleeding
> Voices are hoarse from cursing, eyes flow blind from weeping
> Martyred old folk, orphaned children amongst the rubble creeping
>
> Gassed, beaten . . . under torture
> Going along with him for ever
> Tightly fastening themselves to the apocalyptic horseman's
> tether . . .[33]

If this melodramatic appeal contradicts the last guideline indicated by Fischer, another contribution to the same programme displayed a chilling Brecht-like simplicity. It was a poem purportedly found in the pocket of a fallen German soldier on the Russian front and set to music by the refugee composer and FDKB activist, Ernst Hermann Meyer:

1. Soldier, ask the man next to you how long he's been there on his own,
   why for so long a time he's not been allowed to go home?

2. Soldier, ask the man next to you how often he's been able to rest,
   perhaps he in turn will ask you if to relieve him there's anyone left?

3. Soldier, ask the man next to you why his hands are shaking?
   He knows that in the next attack most of their lives will be taken.

6. Soldier, ask the man next to you why he's so silent and grim?
   At home a bomb has ripped to pieces the child belonging to him.

7. Soldier, ask the man next to you, 'How long will it be till we know
   who's to blame?' Point the finger at Hitler, who's done this to you,
   for Hitler's the one who must go . . .[34]

How effective such efforts actually were in changing attitudes inside enemy territory is difficult to assess, although the Nazi leadership certainly regarded such activities as dangerous enough to make Broadcasting House a major target of their bombing raids.[35] This assessment is reinforced in an article which appeared in 1942 in the Austrian refugee journal *Zeitspiegel*, which saw in the reactions of the Nazi press an indication of the deep impact made by such transmissions:

> . . . three reasons are given for the popularity of the BBC [within Nazi Germany]: 'the reputation for decency, the sense of fair play, which has attached itself to the English and their methods'; the fact that Germans tend 'to regard anything from abroad as the only correct version' or at least contained a 'kernel of truth' . . . ; and finally the desire to orientate themselves better.[36]

On the other hand, the English historian A.J.P. Taylor provided a more cynical view of the service's effectiveness:

> There was little to show for all this effort. The reliable news . . . no doubt helped to sustain spirits in conquered Europe. The resistance was a rich source of intelligence and information . . . However, [the BBC's] activities did no harm and maybe a little good. They were conducted largely by refugees and thus cost little more than keeping the refugees in internment camps.[37]

For the German émigrés in Britain, though, there was no doubting the importance of radio in the ideological struggle to win support for the anti-Fascist viewpoint within the occupied countries. This is reflected in the frequency with which such broadcasts featured in stage productions of the time, from the negative propaganda of the Franco radio general in Brecht's *Señora Carrar's Rifles*, presented by the Kleine Bühne of the FDKB, to the positive influence of a Radio Moscow transmission in inspiring John Bishop's *Calling Erna Cremer*, performed by the left-wing Unity Theatre with whom the German anti-Fascists had forged close links.[38] A BBC foreign-language broadcast also featured in one of the few original dramas written by a German exile in Britain, Max Zimmering's radio play *Razzia* set in occupied Prague: '. . . Always, when the English radio reports large-scale air-raids I think about [my brother] . . . How often he might be sitting in one of those planes, and even be flying over Prague . . . How I envy him being able to fight openly against the Fascists . . . not as earlier, in hiding, with unequal weapons . . .'[39]

Whatever reservations might be made about the actual effect of such broadcasts, they did provide intermittent and in certain cases regular work for refugees. Under the guidance of their British controllers — including Hugh Carleton Greene, brother of the novelist Graham Greene and later Director General of the BBC, as section head, and Marius Goring, Lucie Mannheim's actor-husband, in charge of scripting — such well-known figures as Julius Gellner, Fritz Wendhausen and Berthold Viertel (before he left for America) were engaged on the directing side; Fischer, Bruno Adler and Richard Friedenthal as writers, translators and editors; Karl Anders, Walter Rilla and Albert Lieven as announcers; and amongst the many actors used were Mannheim, Valk, Annemarie Hase, Peter Ihle, Herbert Lom, Sybille Binder, Paul Demel and Friedrich Richter. Richter, who was even able to move permanently from Manchester to London on the strength of regular radio work, found the conditions fairly monotonous: 'Every week the same thing happened. You stand in front of the microphone and read something or other, sometimes an acting part, then something political.'[40]

Despite the routine nature of much of the broadcasting, there were occasional highpoints when the abilities of the performers could be used to fuller advantage: a German adaptation of James Bridie's *Tobias and the Angel*; an original play by the refugee writer Jan Petersen, *Labour Enslaved*, set in modern-day Germany; and the immensely popular *Frau Wernicke Talking*, in which the FDKB stalwart, Annemarie Hase, portrayed an ordinary Berlin housewife chatting about the situation to other ordinary Germans at home.[41]

Alan Clarke

'Building bridges':
German Theatre Refugees and their English Friends

Though in general émigré performers found only limited opportunities in British theatre, film and radio, there was plenty of scope for them to practise their craft within the wide range of cultural activities organized by the Kleine Bühne, the Laterndl, the Blue Danube, the short-lived Österreichische Bühne and other refugee stages. Not only did such participation — varying from serious drama to satirical review, from literary recitations to play-readings, from English adaptations to German classics, and from intimate stagings to large-scale productions — enable both the experienced professionals and the up-and-coming actors to maintain and develop their theatrical abilities, it also brought them into contact with their English counterparts and the broader British public. Most of the important refugee productions were aimed at an English audience; the material was written in English or made easily comprehensible to their non-German friends — 'We shall play in German and Englishmen will understand . . . we shall play in English and Germans will understand';[42] publicity material, press releases and programmes were bilingual; and a special invitation to attend the performances was sent to 'all fellow artists in the English theatre'.[43] The wide and sympathetic press coverage which resulted is a good indication of the success of these efforts.

Another link with the British cultural tradition was in the choice of 'straight' drama. The FDKB's first production after the outbreak of war was an evening of two one-act plays, *The Twelve-Pound Look* and *The Old Lady Shows Her Medals*, by the Scottish writer J.M. Barrie, whilst six years later, after the war had ended, the Kleine Bühne's final thank-you to their British friends was *Bunbury*, an adaptation of Oscar Wilde's *The Importance of Being Earnest*. Amongst the highpoints in between was, of course, *They Came To a City*, although many more modest occasions were used to promote better understanding and respect between the two nations.

One of the most successful ways of winning British support for the refugee cause was the frequent visits of the London-based émigré troupes to nearby towns in the south of England. One such visit took place in July 1941, when the FDKB took its successful programme of Shakespeare extracts to Bedford on the invitation of the local refugee committee. The trip included a performance for local schoolchildren:

> We were very nervous and full of expectation. For at midday our first engagement was to liven up the usual German lesson for English children with our production, an experiment which was as new to us as our audience. Well, the

112

attempt was exceptionally successful. The English children followed our presentation with great attention and laughed and clapped with special enthusiasm during the comic scenes. I talked to many of the children and was astonished how well they understood everything.[44]

The evening performance in support of the National Air-Raid Distress Fund went equally well, with the Mayor of Bedford addressing the audience and emphasizing how appropriate it was for German refugee actors to be supporting this cause. The effect of the visit seems to have been similar to that experienced by Richter on his Old Vic tour of the industrial north, with the production being the talk of the town, the actors being warmly greeted on their way to the station the next day, and lengthy discussions and photographs of selected scenes appearing in the local papers. For the German performers, still experiencing the consequences of internment and isolation, it was an unforgettable experience: 'As we made our way back to our lodgings at the end of the performance, dead tired . . . we all had the same thought: "High above all the struggles of a suffering humanity stands a bridge built out of the communion of spirits, a picture in miniature of the future at large".'[45]

Other visits included a performance of the FDKB revue, *What the Stars Foretell*, in Guildford before 300 people in April 1942, and in the same year the Austrian Laterndl performed Goethe's *Iphigenie auf Tauris* in both Oxford and Cambridge, a production later revived by the Kleine Bühne company at the Toynbee Hall in London's East End. In April 1943 the FDKB presented its most successful revue, *Mr Gulliver Goes to School*, at the Little Theatre, Leicester, before an audience which included the Mayor and Mayoress.[46] But the most important event outside London involving German performers took place at the New Theatre, Oxford, on 21 June 1942. As part of a large propaganda rally arranged by the Ministry of Information to promote the war effort, the FDKB was invited to put on *The Four Freedoms*. Specially written by the English playwright Montague Slater from original material supplied by Arthur Koestler, this short play seems to have been an allegory on the basic freedoms denied under Fascism. Gerhard Hinze was asked to direct and the cast included such notable refugee actors as Friedrich Richter, Erich Freund, Arnold Marlé, Paul Lewitt and Gisa Liedtke. Considering the status of the other participants in the rally (Roger Livesey as the narrator, Eric Portmann and Robert Beatty performing extracts from the successful Pressburger film *The 49th Parallel*, individual contributions from Leslie Howard and Lt.-Com. Ralph Richardson, and the well-known broadcaster Raymond Glendenning commentating the finale, together with the Central Band of the Royal Air Force) the inclusion of German anti-Fascists in such a prestigious event was a major breakthrough. There is no doubt about the success of the refugees' contribution, as is underlined by a letter to Hinze — who was unable to attend the actual performance as he was appearing in a matinee of *Flare Path* on the same day! — from a representative of the Campaigns Division of the Ministry of Information: '. . . we owe a great debt of thanks to you and your troupe which we can scarcely repay. Your production on Sunday was truly wonderful . . . I hope that I will have the great pleasure of working with you again in future events.'[47] Unfortunately no such opportunities appear to have arisen — whether from political, organizational or other reasons — but the occasion does show how much the attitude towards the German émigré community in Britain was changing.

Another consistent factor in improving the links between the two nationalities was the efforts of the many English friends of the refugees, especially amongst leading theatre practitioners. Priestley's support has already been mentioned, but other respected and influential artists also gave their time and commitment to help their fellow performers in exile: actors and directors like Michael Redgrave, Roger Livesey and Ursula Jeans, his wife, Gwen Ffrangcon-Davies, Constance Cummings, Beatrix Lehmann and Herbert Marshall. They acted as patrons to the refugee organizations and their theatre groups, sent messages of support and encouragement during times of particular hardship, attended events organized by the émigrés and even arranged their own cultural contributions in aid of their German colleagues. Typical of the reciprocal approach which continued throughout the war were a few evenings organized by the FDKB in 1940: in February English actors hired the Embassy Theatre in Swiss Cottage to perform scenes from Shakespeare, in June the German refugees provided an evening of recitation and song 'to express our gratitude for so much help and encouragement received from our English patrons and friends',[48] whilst in August Beatrix Lehmann and Frederick Valk took part in a joint programme to help those still in internment camps.

Many British artists contributed directly to émigré productions: the young English actress Diana Barry performed Viola — in German — in the Shakespeare programme previously mentioned, and Peter Cozens played the title role in *Mr Gulliver Goes To School*, his lack of understanding of the German language being used to good effect. A particularly stimulating example of the creative interaction between English and German artists was the production of Brecht's *Rechtsfindung 1934*, from *The Fear and Misery of the Third Reich*, and of *Señora Carrar's Rifles* at the Kleine Bühne in 1941. A specially composed prologue by Sylvia Townsend-Warner was recited by Ann Davis, presenting with great clarity and insight the feelings of the anti-Fascist exiles:

> Here in this narrow room . . . by distillation
> Of exile, by pride, sorrow, resolve, constancy
> Of purpose fuelled and held in concentration
> Is Germany —
>
> *Über alles*! Above all traitors, all charlatans,
> Above the enormous shadow of the spy,
> Above the smoke curling from books burning,
> Above the fog-bank of time-serving and complacency,
> Above the flaunt of swastika banners waved
> For the vain victory of the enslaved
> Stands our true country, and is, to all your truest,
> Your ally.
>
> We are not new to this warfare, we ask no welcome,
> He was our enemy before he was yours.
> The blood ran in our streets while you in London
> Still walked dry-foot, still believed his bunkum.
> We fight beside you as seasoned warriors . . .[49]

The culmination of the mutual efforts between German refugees and British artists came on 10 May 1943, the tenth anniversary of the Nazi book-burning on the Opera Square in Berlin, an important occasion for all German exiles. This year the FDKB hired the Scala Theatre in central London, and under the title 'Fires in May' included dramatic presentations from Heine, Toller, Heinrich and Thomas Mann, Büchner, Brecht, Viertel and many others. The centre-piece of the occasion was a shortened version of Johannes R. Becher's *Battle for Moscow*, written two years before in the Soviet Union. The production was again by Hinze with Josef Almas particularly impressive, whilst other contributions to the evening came from Valk, Anton Walbrook, the violinist Max Rostal and Charlotte Küter. Alongside these prominent Germans, J.B. Priestley gave the opening address and Beatrix Lehmann provided the English narrative to the Becher extract. The event attracted 1,100 people — German and English — and was the largest audience for a single refugee performance during the whole period of exile in Britain. They were celebrating the belief that however much destruction the Nazis might bring about 'the spirit cannot be destroyed and Germans [will] continue to create in freedom in order to re-establish their country's honour'.[50]

No account of the support for the German exiles in Britain would be complete without special mention of three theatre people who untiringly backed the FDKB and other refugee causes throughout the war. The first was not a performer himself but the General Secretary of the professional actors' union, Equity. Even before most of the émigrés arrived in Britain, Llewellyn Rees had travelled to Prague to hand over money collected from British actors for the rescue of German anti-Fascists; eight years later, when many of those refugees were plannning their return to the Continent, he was involved in arranging for the most active amongst them, including Erich and Nina Freund, to be made honorary members of Equity. In between, his efforts to bring the plight of exiled performers constantly to the attention of his members and the general public were unceasing. In an address to the FDKB in October 1941 he stressed his commitment:

> We of British Equity think particularly of those Trade Unionists in the German theatre who have suffered under Hitler and who have carried on the fight for freedom under every sort of persecution. We hope that, just as German and British artists are performing together . . . , so in the near future the artists of all lands will be united and work side by side in a world of constructive freedom and peace.[51]

The second supporter was Walter Hudd, actor and director who was soon to play a major part in the post-war upsurge in the British theatre. His energy and commitment to the FDKB and the Kleine Bühne were exemplary: in 1939 he offered his own house as the FDKB's first administrative base and was a crucial contact with the British theatre for the production of *Going, Going — Gong!*; in 1941 he introduced the evening of one-act plays by Brecht; in 1942 read from the works of English authors at the anti-Nazi rally, 'They cannot burn the spirit'; in 1943, together with Llewellyn Rees, he was on the organizing committee of the Lessing Bühne, 'representing the co-operation with the English theatre',[52] and borrowing costumes from the Old Vic for its performance of *Don Carlos*; and in the same year he was even preparing to play the lead in *Mr Gulliver Goes to School* — to be performed at the Everyman Theatre — until a professional engagement intervened. The frequent warm references in the FDKB literature to 'our patron and friend Walter Hudd' were richly deserved.

And finally there was Sybil Thorndike, at that time regarded as one of Britain's leading actresses but, together with her actor-husband Lewis Casson, still able to find time to support the anti-Fascist cause. The enormous impact that her frequent appearances made on the refugees is reflected in a review of the Barrie one-acters early in the emigration period, when the exiles from Germany were still finding their feet in an alien society beginning to show them hostility:

> The loveliest moment was, however, when Sybil Thorndike, the great English

actress, came onto the stage at the end and congratulated the actors. She had sacrificed one of her few free evenings, spent two hours in a tiny hall listening to a performance in a strange language, and was now standing up there, embracing Lilly Kann, shaking her colleagues' hands, and speaking from the fullness of her heart to them and the listeners below, constantly interrupted by loud applause. She spoke of their mutual language of art and humanity which knows no barriers, of the fraternity of the love of freedom and goodness which triumphs over hunger, war and banishment and will build a new world . . . Everyone left the hall feeling that not all is lost as long as there are such people around.[53]

This deeply felt support and concern from their professional peers in the English theatre did much to keep the spirits and ambitions of German refugee actors alive and surely played a part in ensuring that so many of them continued in the profession after the war. But the question raised in *They Came to a City*, 'stay or return', eventually demanded a definite response when peace finally came. Some could maintain their established positions in Britain: Valk's stage success continued unabated, Walbrook developed as a major film actor, Elisabeth Bergner played the title role in *Miss Julie* in 1947, and Lucie Mannheim followed a three-month tour of Germany by directing Gogol and Chekhov at the same Arts Theatre where the 'Four and Twenty Black Sheep' had been performed eight years before.[54] Other former émigrés also began to make names for themselves in their adopted country, like Martin Miller, Herbert Lom and Ferdy Mayne. Many decided to return to Germany — West and East — fully aware of the problems and even dangers facing them. And many thrived: Josef Almas, Lilly Kann and Arthur Hellmer had successful careers in West Germany, as did a large number who decided to work in theatre and film in the GDR — Friedrich Richter and Amy Frank, the Freunds, Annemarie Hase.

It is difficult, however, to assess the actual contribution to the new German theatre which developed in both parts of the former Reich by refugees returning from Britain. Around Europe at the end of the war a number of modern English plays were performed, the most popular being, somewhat surprisingly, by Priestley with productions in Berlin, Vienna, Prague and Budapest, including three versions of *They Came to a City*. Other contemporary British writers then on view included Somerset Maugham, Aldous Huxley, A.J. Cronin, Sean O'Casey and Patrick Hamilton. Such authors might have been suggested by former exiles returning from Britain, but there is no direct evidence to support this. In Hamburg an 'English Theatre' was set up 'to build bridges between Germans and English', and in 1947 *The Dover Road* was performed to British troops stationed there, but none of those involved appear to have been refugees from England.[55] The inspiration for the German theatre revival came from other countries of exile, although refugees from Britain certainly played a part.

In Britain after the war, however, with the impressive exception of Valk and the few other actors already referred to, there was little direct influence from German-speaking exiles. Even Brecht was scarcely known outside a few intellectual left-wing circles: an article in *New Theatre* in October 1947 credits only Kurt Weill for the success of *The Threepenny Opera*, and not until May 1949 does a small piece from Charles Laughton in America indicate any real interest in Brecht's ideas on this side of the Atlantic.[56] On the other hand, the involvement of Valk, Bergner and Mannheim in important productions of European naturalist writers like Ibsen, Strindberg, Tolstoy and Chekhov would seem to indicate a more serious approach to drama in Britain, directly influenced by Continental practice. And a contribution of this nature is a fitting tribute to the work of the many professional German actors and directors who spent the war in exile on British soil.

Notes

* The basic information used in this article was gathered for my unpublished thesis, *Die Rolle des Theaters des 'Freien Deutschen Kulturbundes in Großbritannien' im Kampf gegen den deutschen Faschismus (1938–1947)*, Berlin (GDR), 1972, which was substantially used by Birgid Leske and Marion Reinisch in the British chapter of *Exil in der Tschechoslowakei, in Großbritannien, Skandinavien und Palästina*, Leipzig, 1980. However, much of the material used here, especially the sections on professional theatre in England and the BBC, was not included in my original project and is published in this form for the first time. Translations from German have been undertaken by myself and are indicated by an asterisk.
1. Erich Freund, 'Hinter den Kulissen . . .', *Freie Deutsche Kultur*, Nov. 1944.
2. Letter from Sybil Thorndike to Siegfried Zimmering, February 1944 (unpublished).
3. Felix Felton, 'Reinhardt in England', manuscript in possession of the German Academy of Arts in Berlin (GDR), p. 8 (unpublished).
4. 'Leben und Arbeit der Schauspielerin Amy Frank', *Theaterdienst*, 13 June 1953.*
5. Julius Berstl, *Odyssee eines Theatermannes*, Berlin (West), 1963, p. 177.*
6. Ibid., p. 186.*
7. Frank, 'Leben und Arbeit'.*
8. Berstl, *Odyssee*, p. 186.*
9. Kurt Trepte, *Deutsches Theater im Exil der Welt*, Berlin, 1970 (unpublished).
10. Dr. Rudolf Pepper, 'Umwandlung Englands', *Einheit*, 26 Sept. 1942, p. 21.
11. Peter Bratt, '*Das Zeitstück auf der Londoner Bühne*', *Die Zeitung*, 11 Sept. 1942, p. 8.*
12. 'Are American Plays the Best', *Daily Worker*, 14 Sept. 1942, p. 2.
13. Friedrich Richter, 'Eine Tour mit dem Old Vic', *Zeitspiegel*, 23 May 1942, p. 3.*
14. *Daily Worker*, 14 Sept. 1942.

15. M.J. (Monty Jacobs), 'Othello', *Die Zeitung*, 31 July 1942, p. 9.*
16. *Daily Worker*, 14 Sept. 1942.
17. *New Theatre*, July 1946, p. 10.
18. Jacobs, 'Othello'.*
19. Friedrich Richter, unpublished manuscript in the possession of the German Academy of Arts in Berlin (GDR), p. 13.*
20. Frederick Valk, 'Acting and Poetry', *New Theatre*, July 1946, p. 10.
21. Interview with Michael Rittermann, London, 18 August 1988; also interview with Hanna Norbert, London, 1 June 1988.*
22. A.J.P. Taylor, *English History 1914–1945* ('Oxford History of England', vol. 15), London, 1965, p. 307.
23. Ibid., p. 489.
24. 'Das BBC und der Krieg', *Zeitspiegel*, 3 Jan. 1942, p. 9.
25. Walter A. Berendsohn, *Die Humanistische Front*, II. Teil, Zurich, 1953, p. 102 (unpublished).
26. Norman Bentwich, *The Rescue and Achievement of Refugee Scholars*, The Hague, 1953, p. 37.
27. Thomas Mann, Foreword to *Deutsche Hörer!*, Leipzig, 1970, p. 5.
28. Werner Röder, *Die deutschen sozialistischen Exilgruppen in Großbritannien 1940–1945*, Hanover, 1969, p. 182.
29. Mentioned in *Freie Deutsche Kultur*, Mar. 1942.
30. Richter, unpublished manuscript, p. 11 *
31. Quoted in Berendsohn, *Humanistische Front*, p. 100.*
32. Quoted in Röder, *Die deutschen Exilgruppen*, p. 261.*
33. Stenographed text in possession of Ernst Hermann Meyer, p. 3 (unpublished).*
34. Meyer, p. 5.*
35. I.M. Maiski, *Memoiren eines sowjetischen Botschafters*, Berlin, 1967, p. 600.
36. From an article in *Zeitspiegel*, 21 Feb. 1942, p. 4.*
37. Taylor, *English History*, p. 516.
38. Max Zimmering, 'Braches Land', *Freie Deutsche Kultur*, Feb. 1942.
39. Idem, *Razzia*, pp. 1–2 (unpublished manuscript).*
40. Richter, unpublished manuscript, p. 11.*
41. For further information on the work of the BBC German Service during the war, see *'Hier ist England'* — *'Live aus London': Das Deutsche Programm der British Broadcasting Corporation 1938–1988*, BBC External Services, 1988, esp. pp. 1–36.
42. Interview with Heinrich Fischer, *Star* (London) 10 July 1939.
43. FDKB handout, July 1939.
44. G.L. (Gisa Liedtke?), 'Gastspiel der "Kleinen Bühne des FDKB" in Bedford', *Freie Deutsche Kultur*, Aug. 1941.*
45. Ibid.
46. See 'Revue by German Refugees in Leicester', *The Leicester Mercury*, 19 Apr. 1943.
47. Quoted in 'M.O.I. dankt Refugee-Schauspielern', *Zeitspiegel*, 4 July 1942, p. 7.*
48. 'We entertain English Friends', *Freie Deutsche Kultur*, June 1940.
49. Sylvia Townsend-Warner, 'Here in this Narrow Room . . .', *Freie Deutsche Kultur*, Feb. 1942.
50. Komo, 'Brände im Mai', *Zeitspiegel*, 29 May 1943, p. 7.*
51. Llewellyn Rees in *Freie Deutsche Kultur*, Oct. 1941.
52. 'Das deutschsprachige Theater in London', *Die Zeitung*, 22 May 1942, p. 9.
53. 'Sybil Thorndike im Hause des Kulturbundes', *FDKB Nachrichten*, Apr. 1940.*
54. Information on refugee actors in Britain after 1945 from *New Theatre*, July 1946 to May 1949.
55. 'Englisches Theater im Hamburg', *Theaterdienst*, June 1946, p. 13, and 13 Jan. 1947, p. 8.
56. Charles Laughton in *New Theatre*, May 1949, p. 2.

–6–

The Dramatist as Exile
Ernst Toller and the English Theatre

N.A. FURNESS

Ernst Toller was one of the first victims of the National Socialist régime in Germany.* He had achieved fame, and even notoriety, as the charismatic author of plays and poems reflecting an uncompromising pacifist, socialist and idealistic ethic, and as a political activist who had served a five-year prison sentence for his part as one of the leading revolutionaries in the Munich Soviet Republic of 1919. In 1933, he was fortunate to escape arrest when the Nazis carried out their purge of the political opposition, following the burning of the Reichstag, for quite by chance he was in Switzerland for a radio programme, and friends warned him not to return to Germany; but he was in the first group of those who, in August 1933, were formally deprived of their German citizenship and had all their possessions in Germany confiscated.

As a result, Toller experienced many of the common exigencies of exile: not merely the loss of an audience that shared his mother tongue, but the pressing need to keep earning by writing, even in the foreign environment, together with concern at the loss of income from unauthorized translations of his earlier works; there was also anxiety that he might be physically attacked or even abducted by Nazi agents still wishing to silence his critical voice, worry about his physical health and the fear that illness could interrupt his writing, and his dismay that booksellers outside Germany were under pressure not to handle his works. He was also concerned for his fellow exiles, and especially for those worse off than himself, and for the wives and children of fellow writers who were imprisoned in Germany or who had died in Nazi concentration camps. And he was concerned, too, that exiles were often severely restricted in their freedom to travel because their conventional documentation had expired and could not be renewed or replaced, and that many countries were reluctant to allow them to settle.

In addition, Toller was determined to warn the Western democracies of the evils of Nazism, even though, as a refugee, he had to exercise extreme discretion in making speeches that could be considered political. He carried out a number of engagements in Britain, addressing enthusiastic audiences up and down the country from Maidenhead to Manchester, from Halifax to Bristol. For the most part he talked about German drama or his own works, or about the problems of pacifism, but at the same time he stressed the predicament of writers who were imprisoned in Germany, not because they had broken any law of the country, but because their beliefs were unacceptable to the government. And repeatedly he warned his audiences of the threat that Fascism posed to the peace of the world.[1]

Drama, therefore, represents only a fraction of Toller's activities and interests in the last six years of his life. In England, apart from his public appearances as lecturer, or speaker, or chairman of meetings, he was an active correspondent, arranging for the translation and publication and performance of his own works, seeking help for fellow refugees or the victims of Nazi persecution or their dependents, keeping in contact with colleagues in a range of organizations both literary and political, and maintaining a circle of friends and acquaintances in Britain and overseas. The zest with which he threw himself into causes evoked resentment and hostility in some of those who knew him, for they suspected that he was more interested in creating a rôle for himself than in the good work he was ostensibly engaged in. Those who knew him best emphasize rather his utter sincerity, and the selflessness with which he dedicated himself to the causes he took up. Toller's life as an exile was evidently marked by all manner of complexities and distractions, and it is hardly surprising that between 1933 and his death in 1939 he wrote relatively few new literary works.

For most critics, Toller's reputation rests on the plays and poetry that he wrote during the period of his imprisonment, from 1919 until 1924. English-language accounts of his life often refer to his being held in a fortress-prison, but the term is misleading, for Niederschönenfeld, where he was held for the greater part of the time, was never a fortress, but a former young offenders' institution built on to the delicate seventeenth-century fabric of a Cistercian convent. *Festungshaft* (i.e. 'detention in a fortress') is a technical term for a specific category of 'detention without loss of honour', invoked especially for army officers (for instance, for duelling), and for certain categories of political offenders. In theory it was less severe than either 'hard labour' or simple 'imprisonment', although Toller frequently complained that his own treatment was far more severe than the law prescribed. He was nevertheless entitled to have books in his cell, and to receive visitors, as well as letters and newspapers, so that his period of detention became a most fruitful opportunity for him to reflect on and come to terms with the confusion of events and activities of the previous five years, to clarify his ideas, and to exorcize his sense of frustration and disappointment by projecting both ideas and emotions in the intense yet disciplined language of poetic drama. Thus of his first three plays, *Die Wandlung* (*Transfiguration*, 1919) formulates his rejection of imperialism and militarism; *Masse Mensch* (*Man and the Masses*, 1921) attacks capitalism, yet questions whether violence is justified in order to effect social reform; *Die Maschinenstürmer* (*The Machine-Wreckers*, 1922) stresses the need for workers to collaborate to ensure that technology is used to improve their lives, rather than to enslave them. Other major issues dealt with in early plays are the corruption of Justice in *Draw the Fires!* (1930) and *The Blind Goddess* (1932), the readiness of communities on both sides of the Atlantic to follow false prophets in *Der entfesselte Wotan* (1923) and *Miracle in America* (1931), and the need for genuine 'solidarity', compassion and understanding among ordinary working people if human misery is to be reduced to a minimum in *Hinkemann* (*Brokenbrow*, 1923).

Speeches and articles in the 1920s and 1930s reflected similar interests and a political attitude that was more radical than that of the 'majority' socialists of the SPD, but divided in principle from the Communist commitment to the class struggle and strict party discipline. Toller insisted instead on the responsibility of the individual, on the need for social cohesion rather than division, on the reform of society taking place through the will and through the social commitment of the individual to the community, as outlined by Gustav Landauer, rather than through subordination to an externally imposed régime.

After 1933, there is a shift of emphasis: Toller is much more concerned with the fundamental problem of the ascendancy of the dictatorships, the need to mobilize the free world to prevent the further spread of Fascism. There is therefore a refocusing of his work and activities, to maintain contact with and to hearten his fellow refugees, to warn, to inform, to animate his audience in the Western democracies, as well as to earn something to live on. The more reflective, lyrical Toller of the *Swallow-Book* and the early sonnets disappears in the face of the practical problems posed by the increasing threat that he saw in the consolidation of Nazi power in Germany.

Of his earlier plays, *The Machine-Wreckers* was performed in London as early as 1923 by the Incorporated Stage Society, in Ashley Dukes' translation, and *Man and the Masses* (translated by Louis Untermeyer), also by the Stage Society, in the following year; both productions were widely reported in the press. There were also other performances of Toller's plays in London and elsewhere throughout the 1920s. He visited London and Cambridge in 1921, giving a reading of his poetry at the Goethe Society, and attended the performance of *Hoppla!* at the Gate

Theatre in 1929, so that when he settled in London in 1933 he was already well known to admirers in a range of intersecting circles, theatrical, literary and political.

It is understandable, given the sudden dislocation in his life, that many of Toller's major literary publications in Britain after 1933 were translations of works written and published in Germany before his exile. These included six of the *Seven Plays*, published in London in 1935,[2] and his autobiographical *I was a German*, which was published in German by Querido in 1933, but which he had begun writing in 1929.[3] However, he soon started work on a new piece for the theatre, apparently in 1934, *No More Peace! A thoughtful comedy*, translated by Edward Crankshaw, with lyrics adapted by W.H. Auden, and music by Herbert Murrill. It was first published in English in London in 1937, following its performance at the Gate Theatre, London, in 1936.

No More Peace!, ironically inverting the title of the world-wide 'No More War' movement[4] begins, like Goethe's *Faust*, with a wager in Heaven — or at least, in Olympus: Napoleon, who is getting bored with the uneventfulness of his life there, living 'in peace', makes a bet with St Francis that the people in the most peace-loving place on earth (which he invites St Francis to name) can be induced to declare war. He sends a telegram to Dunkelstein, a mythical tiny state lying between Spain and France (an unenlightened antipode to Lichtenstein, perhaps?), where a festival of peace is being celebrated, and instantly the country is mobilized, even though the telegram fails to explain who the enemy is. The leading financier, Laban, makes Cain, a barber, into an all-powerful dictator who, like the Nazis, makes his appeal to chauvinism and mass hysteria, and relies on a Minister for Propaganda and Enlightenment to make the necessary arrangements. Socrates attempts, characteristically, to reason with the people, and is first put in prison and then into a lunatic asylum. Finally, a further celestial message declares the war to have been a mistake, and peace is restored, but St Francis suggests that a good deal more thought is needed about what 'peace' really means, and what peace *could* amount to.

Although Toller referred several times in letters to friends to the success of this production, it was not well received by the critics. Indeed there is a certain irony in the contrast between Toller's international reputation as a dramatist, his eminence as a public figure in 1933, and the extent to which his plays were actually performed. He was never a box-office success in the London West End. His plays attracted the interest of theatre companies which specialized in more experimental forms of drama, such as the Gate Theatre in London, which was a theatre club and therefore not subject to censorship by the Lord Chamberlain, or the Cambridge Festival Theatre, which had very similar interests, and for a time the two companies entered into an arrangement for the exchange of productions. Both theatres offered a season of plays, with the run of each show limited usually to a week or two, while the Incorporated Stage Society, which originally introduced Toller to London in 1923 and 1924, gave only one or two performances of each play. Apart from a few productions in civic theatres in the provinces in later years, all other performances of Toller's plays in Britain appear to have been by amateur groups, who found his work interesting either because of the novelty of form and technique, or because of his political philosophy, or both. The translation of *Masse Mensch* by Vera Mendel, under the title *Masses and Man*, was by far the most frequently performed work (see note 1).

From a theatre manager's point of view, and no doubt from that of many of the influential critics of the day too, Toller's work suffered from a number of disadvantages: it was German, it was serious, it was political, it was socialist, and some of it was Expressionist as well. Sheila Grant Duff, however, in her account of the 1930s, recalls the enthusiasm for Germany and Austria that she experienced in the Oxford of 1932:

> Their films, their plays, their music, their art galleries, the qualities of life in places like Berlin, Hamburg, Munich and Vienna, with their great stretches of water and their free and emancipated youth, seemed to suggest the dawn of a golden age for us all . . . Every new person I met seemed to have just returned from Germany. Stephen Spender, W.H. Auden and Christopher Isherwood were the heroes of the Oxford literary scene, and all were surrounded by a German aura of something new and exciting.[5]

This sense of discovery and excitement seems to have been experienced especially by the younger generation, but hardly to have been shared by the older established theatre critics, who no doubt still carried some of the immensely strong anti-German feelings of the 1920s. At least it seems clear that relatively few German plays were successful in the London theatre in the 1920s and 1930s. George W. Bishop, writing in 1933, reflects the stereotype expectation of German drama in seeking to account for the lack of success of *Caravan*, an adaptation of 'Carl Zuckmayer's famous circus drama *Katherina Knie*. It is possibly part of the explanation of the complete failure that she [i.e. the translator] kept too closely to the original and retained most of the Teutonic rhetoric and verbosity', and he draws the firm conclusion: 'There seems to be no doubt that German plays need very thorough revision for England . . .'[6]

Repeatedly, Toller's name is coupled with that of Georg Kaiser as representative of German Expressionist drama, which was anathema to many of the established critics, who were only too pleased to pronounce it 'dead' in the 1930s, 'as old-fashioned as hobble skirts'.[7] Other writers who were felt to be working along similar lines were similarly rejected. W.A. Darlington's record of the reception of O'Casey confirms the views shared by the theatre-going public and the critics of the day:

> When Cochran staged *The Silver Tassie* in the West End in 1929, with Charles Laughton in the lead, bewildered audiences had found that the war scenes were treated symbolically in what sounded suspiciously like verse, and passed the word round that this play was beyond comprehension. From that time onward the gap between O'Casey and the London public widened steadily, and after *Within the Gates* had failed in 1934 ('Beyond the Agates' was the heading in the *Sunday Times* notice) it became impassable.[8]

Darlington is no less disapproving of the sort of plays performed by the Incorporated Stage Society:

> It was the lame, or neglected, or ferocious dogs that needed assistance over stiles — not the ones which a pat on the head converted instantly into docile domestic pets. The society's leaders began therefore to fall back upon the more unusual kind of foreign play, such as Pirandello's *Six Characters in Search of an Author*, Elmer Rice's *The Adding Machine*, or Ernst Toller's *Man and the Masses*.[9]

James Agate, for many years the *doyen* of London theatre critics, despite his warmly appreciative account of the Stage Society's production of *Man and the Masses*, was in general not sympathetic towards Expressionism, and dismissively critical in particular of Kaiser's *From Morn to Midnight*, Elmer Rice's *The Adding Machine* and their 'successor', J.B. Priestley's *Johnson over Jordan*.[10] St John Ervine, too, found himself unable to respond sympathetically to this form of drama, writing in 1924:

> The whole European theatre is now in distress, and that distress is reflected in the state of the American theatre. In Germany, theatrical activity consists largely of crude experiments in production, most of which derive from experiments made years ago by Mr. Craig, and in cruder experiments in drama, largely neurotic, by overwrought people such as Georg Kaiser and Ernst Toller . . .[11]

In 1933 his views, though now retrospective, were in no way changed: '. . . authors produced dreary works on people who had neither character nor purpose, not even names.'[12]

Sydney W. Carroll, who contributed a weekly column on the theatre in the *Daily Telegraph*, demonstrated condescension, chauvinism and professional pique in his response to Toller's address to the British Drama League in October 1934. Toller, speaking at short notice, had suggested that the commercial theatre was too much dominated by time-killing entertainment which required huge investment and was therefore based on long runs, and that it had forgotten its cultural task; there was need, he suggested, for more serious drama, for more repertory theatre, and for bigger theatres that could attract bigger audiences at lower prices. And he praised the non-professional theatre for its serious and enthusiastic work and its support of young dramatists, and wished that professional drama critics would take more interest in their productions as well as those in the West End.[13']

Carroll rejected Toller's assessment as 'Valueless Criticism', to which Toller replied with composure and dignity, provoking a further rather pompous retort from Sydney Carroll:

> I have no wish to be unjust to anyone, least of all a dramatist of international repute like Herr Toller . . . but I do know that our professional English theatre compares more than favourably at the present time with any of the Continental theatres. I was only concerned that it should not be made a cockshy by a stranger within our gates to gratify a conference of amateurs.[14]

Norman Marshall regards such attitudes as symptomatic of the isolation of the commercial London stage in the 1920s and 1930s, despite the proselytizing efforts of the Stage Society and the brief venture into Expressionism at Birmingham Repertory Theatre.[15] It was only in the experimental theatres, such as the Gate Theatre, and the Cambridge Festival Theatre, run by Peter Godfrey and Terence Gray respectively, that new forms of production and examples of 'advanced' drama could be seen. Nevertheless, when Toller arrived in London in 1933 he was generally thought of as an Expressionist dramatist, in particular as the author of *Masses and Man*, which was performed by numbers of groups, including the Cambridge Festival Theatre, in the 1920s. *Feuer aus den Kesseln*, with its documentary realism, had not yet been translated, while the very different *Hoppla!*, despite performances in Dublin and Cambridge, as well as in London, in 1929, had not supplanted the earlier impression. The Dublin production ran to only two performances, while the entire cast at the Gate Theatre was stricken with mumps, so that the run had to be broken off abruptly after nineteen performances and a replacement brought in at short notice to fill the unexpected gap.[16]

In the years following Toller's arrival in England, London saw productions of *Miracle in America* (Gate Theatre, October 1934), and of *Draw the Fires!* (one performance only, Cambridge Theatre, 12 May 1935). *No More Peace!* was very different, and perhaps in some ways too close to the conventional, light-hearted West End entertainment to be taken as seriously as Toller had meant it to be, for he had deliberately given it the sub-title 'A thoughtful comedy'. There seem to have been several factors involved. Some people took offence at the setting, for while Toller is careful to describe the opening scene as taking place in Olympus rather than in Heaven, it was felt to be indelicate to introduce a female angel or a figure like St Francis, especially when the dialogue itself appeared to be facetious. But it also seems possible that criticism was linked with the political outlook of the critic (and/or the newspaper) to a greater degree than had been apparent in the past. The London Letter of the *Manchester Guardian* was for the most part positive, and certainly sympathetic, yet concluded nevertheless: 'The play itself . . . never quite made up its mind whether to be funny, sad, or just pathetic. Probably it was only meant to be a charade and should be taken as such' (12 June 1936, p. 12).

The *Daily Herald*, by contrast, had no doubts about Toller's intention, or about his theatrical technique:

> Refugee-Dramatist Ernst Toller, exile from Nazi Germany, outstanding figure in the contemporary theatre, has disturbed the dovecotes once more by the vigour of his expression in his new play 'No More Peace!'. Ending a brief run at the Gate Theatre Studio tomorrow 'No More Peace!' is unique as an anti-war play which achieves its object by a brilliantly satirical exposure of complacent pacifism (17 June 1936, p. 6).

While *Time and Tide* and the *New Stateman* seem to have kept a discreet silence, the establishment papers were scornfully dismissive, no doubt recognizing that Toller, despite his convinced pacifism, was critical of the official British policy of appeasement, and resenting his direct link between capitalism and dictatorship in the play. In the *Sunday Times*, G.W.B. (no doubt George W. Bishop) judged it to be a 'clumsy little skit which pokes awkward fun at things sacred and profane', 'a farrago of obvious satire' (14 June 1936, p. 4), and the *Observer* was hardly more enthusiastic, comparing it with 'one of those unevenly inspired charades of our youth, in which flashes of brilliance tempered colloquies more spontaneous than sparkling' (14 June 1936, p. 17). The audience, it suggested, was altogether too indulgent. *The Times* found the dialogue 'mildly entertaining', but 'then satire slips on hob-nailed boots', and there was 'little else to feed the sense of comedy or to minister to moral indignation' (12 June 1936, p. 14). The *Daily Telegraph* was a good deal more outspoken:

> In reality, it is a blatantly obvious satire of things on earth and in Heaven. Some of the lines are in doubtful taste and many of the jokes are cheap. In construction it resembles a charade in which the climaxes come in the wrong places. Amusing lyrics by W.H. Auden, with music by Herbert Murrill, are thrown in at odd moments, and these provide some amusement, but the piece itself is a silly little rehash of the most elementary satire about war and peace (12 June 1936. p. 12).

The *Saturday Review* (20 June 1936, p. 792) went one better:

> The trouble about Ernst Toller is that he has very little to say and that what does appear to be on his mind has been better expressed by more able satirists, among whom I would include Professor Stephen Leacock. To the unsophisticated it is no doubt deliciously funny to see Napoleon betting St Francis five shillings that he can start a war on the earth by the simple means of despatching a celestial telegram, and the groundlings were vastly amused when Socrates was thrown into prison for being Socratic.
>
> To the seasoned playgoer, however, all this was very thin stuff and very poor satire. There were laughs here and there, but they were mostly of the nursery variety.
>
> The music by Herbert Murrill was quite the best thing of the evening . . . Apart from this it was a waste of time.

Michael Sayers, who in 1936 could think of 'no better and more stimulating model for the young dramatist' than Toller[17] was now entirely critical. Writing in *Life and Letters Today*, he agreed that the lyric interludes were the only redeeming feature, and that 'the dialogue is feeble, the satire tame and confused', it 'betrays a pitiful bankruptcy', it is 'obscurantist twaddle'. 'Outraged, frantic, helpless, like a tardy traveller left behind by some punctual train, Toller stands on his pacifist platform, hurling reproaches after the thundering express of history which would not stay while he dawdled.'[18]

The judgments and the language of these critics seem to have dated more than the play itself, and it is curious that three of them should have seen it as a 'charade'. While it was evidently Toller's intention to treat what he saw as a serious problem lightly and with humour, there can be no doubt that his purpose was serious, that the comedy was not intended to be simply light-hearted entertainment. It may be that those members of the audience who sympathized with the author's message found the play entertaining, and that those who did not transferred their ill-will to the fabric of the play, rather than reflect, as Toller had intended, on mankind's capacity to worship false gods and to follow false prophets.

Toller sought to create a parable by placing the 'action' in a fictionalized setting. There are are close parallels with his earlier comedy *Der entfesselte Wotan*, where humour is also used to denounce the gullibility of ordinary people when confronted with the grandiose ambitions of a messianic leader. In both plays, the analogy with the emergence of Nazism in Germany is apparent to those who are familiar with the course of events in the Weimar Republic, but by seeking to generalize his message, Toller may unwittingly have placed a double obstacle to its understanding by a British audience. Just as Charlie Chaplin's *Great Dictator* ran the risk of reducing Hitler to a figure of fun, and thus making him appear harmless, a British audience in 1937 would find it hard to grasp the full significance of the irrational fervour that was evoked by Cain (or indeed by Hitler himself), and setting the action in Olympus and in a purely fictional Dunkelstein undoubtedly implied for many that it was intended to be a Ruritanian romp and must be judged as such.

It may be that the introduction of song, music and dance confirmed such expectations, yet music and song were being used increasingly in the 'serious' drama of the 1930s — in O'Casey's *Within the Gates*, for example (Royalty Theatre, London, February 1934), André Obey's *Noah* (New Theatre, London, July 1935), O'Neill's *Ah Wilderness* (Westminster Theatre, London, May 1936), or Kjeld Abell's *The Melody that Got Lost* (Embassy Theatre, London, December 1936) — quite apart from Brecht's adoption of music, song and dance as devices for 'de-familiarization' in the late 1920s. Toller, too, uses the lyrics in part as a 'distancing' device, but in part also to provide a concise statement of the essence of the principal characters. The lyrics are not just 'thrown in at odd moments', for there is still something of the Expressionist approach in the reduction of the characters here to types, whether representative of different epochs (classical antiquity, the Middle Ages, the modern world), or different temperaments (the rational intellectual, the altruist, the rapacious businessman, the power-hungry individualist), as well as in the desire to seek a new solution to old problems.

The message of *No More Peace!* is by no means out of date, for Toller gives a shrewd analysis of the mechanisms by which power is exercised in the state, a timely warning of the inability of mankind to learn from experience, and of the danger in believing that the future course of events can be foreseen or planned. The parable suggests a direct link between authoritarian rule and war, and pillories the willingness of the mass of the people to be manipulated by slogans and by appeals to their primitive instincts, which are exploited by the rulers for their own ends: greed and self-interest disguised as patriotism, chauvinism and racism supplanting a genuine sense of community, their ready acceptance of the assurance that this war will be a war to end all war and of the ensuing ruthless suppression of opposition or independent thought in the interest of national survival. It is clear that the appeal to honour, glory and self-sacrifice is made to the ordinary people while those with influence scheme to avoid any risk of having to undertake military service themselves. Rational values are inverted: all the cornfields around Dunkelstein are set alight, because an enemy spy might be hiding there, and the Fire Service is made responsible for ensuring that nobody attempts to put out the blaze. Cain, the Dictator, assures them — and his view is accepted without challenge — that it is better for Dunkelstein to be destroyed by their own incendiary bombs than by those of the enemy. Socrates' claim that he knows nothing is seen to be only too true when it comes to worldly wisdom. The philosophical tramp Noah advises him: 'What it proves is that some people are in clover in war-time and some in peace. But the some in war and the some in peace are always the same some!'[19] This insight is demonstrated by the entrepreneur Laban, for he not only makes a fortune with his jam-factory in wartime, he also uses inside knowledge to sell his warehouse at the best possible price when peace 'breaks out'.

Toller evidently gave much thought to making his play appeal to a British audience and developing a technique that was quite new for him, even though, with the benefit of hindsight, it is possible to see both the consistency of thought with earlier works, and the development of stage technique from elements employed in *Der entfesselte Wotan* and *Hoppla!* some ten years before. In particular, he took some pride in his use of humour. Norman Marshall recalls: '"I must thank England for one thing", said Toller when making a speech on the first night, "I have learned to see the very bitter things of life from the angle of comedy."'[20] For no matter how gloomy the picture Toller paints in this work of the foolishness of mankind, of the lack of moral scruples and sense of social responsibility, the ending is nevertheless, if only very guardedly, optimistic. Ultimately, he is convinced, man will learn to behave differently, the values symbolized by St Francis will be recognized and adopted, and there will be peace on earth. It remains a vision, bathed in soft, gentle music, but it implies no facile optimism; rather it reflects one of Toller's enduring convictions, expressed in his first play *Transfiguration* (1919) and repeated in succeeding works: society *can* be changed, but only if there is a change of heart in man first. In the closing lines St Francis anticipates, ultimately, such a transfiguration.

No More Peace! was the only play written and performed during Toller's years of exile. Just a few months after the production at the Gate Theatre, Toller began a lecture tour in the United States which he evidently hoped would be more effective in alerting public opinion to the dangers posed by Fascism in Europe. He was also interested in exploring the possibilities in writing for the new medium — new at least for him — of the film. (In 1930 he had experimented, successfully, with writing a radio play, *Berlin — letzte Ausgabe!*) Despite a contract with MGM, he had no success with film scripts, although his last play, *Pastor Hall*, written in the United States, was subsequently made into a successful film. The play was first performed in English, in Stephen Spender's translation, by Manchester Repertory Theatre in November 1939, and it ran for a second week 'owing to exceptional success' (see *Manchester Guardian*, 25 November 1939). Soon after (December 1939), it received its first amateur production at Bradford Civic Playhouse, where it was also extended for a further week (see *Yorkshire Evening Post*, 16 December 1939).

Whereas *No More Peace!* deals in more general terms with the mechanisms by which an authoritarian régime establishes its hold and, with the people's consent, crushes all opposition, *Pastor Hall* specifically depicts the Nazi régime, its philosophy and methods, while emphasizing the courage needed by the individual who dares to dissent. And whereas in 1927 (in *Hoppla!*) it was the dedicated, unspectacular work of party members (party unspecified) that was to overcome the corruption amongst the Socialists and overturn the reactionary groups on the Right, in 1939 the emphasis is again on individual commitment and individual responsibility and, if necessary, individual self-sacrifice in the cause of humanity.

In technique, too, *Pastor Hall* represents a reversion to conventional form which, after the lukewarm response to *No More Peace!*, Toller may well have felt held greater prospects of success with audiences in America and Britain. Toller was certainly aware enough of contemporary taste to recognize that the more experimental works in the 1930s had met with a very patchy response, but he had no opportunity to see how his last drama worked in the theatre. Both plays from the exile years have been performed more recently in Germany, where they have had interested and appreciative audiences. Nevertheless, Toller must have been disappointed at their reception in his own day — at the dismissive reviews of *No More Peace!*, and at the lack of interest in *Pastor Hall* — which contrasted so markedly with the succession of theatre scandals and triumphs of his earlier years.

It is not easy to identify the specific contribution that Toller made in his host country, either in terms of dramatic technique or theatrical innovation. Breon Mitchell has argued that Toller is the most plausible source of a 'German influence' in the plays written in collaboration by Auden and Isherwood in the 1930s, but that both Auden and Isherwood believed that the 'German' characteristics of their works stemmed from other influential writers, including Ibsen, Shaw, Cocteau and H.C. Andersen, as well as from the traditional English Christmas pantomime.[21] Nor is it possible to identify direct influence in Stephen Spender's *Trial of a Judge* (1938), despite certain superficial similarities with *Masses and Man*, or in plays by Sean O'Casey (*Within the Gates*, 1934) or by J.B. Priestley (*Johnson over Jordan*, 1939), where some comparable characteristics also appear. It is in any event the 'Expressionist' Toller of the 1920s who might most readily be supposed to have been influential, in part, no doubt, because his earlier works were distinctively different from the staple diet of British drama, but at the same time in tune with other innovative works in the contemporary theatre, such as Pirandello's *Six Characters in Search of an*

Author, Čapek's *R.U.R.* and *The Insect Play*, Sutton Vane's *Outward Bound*, or Elmer Rice's *The Adding Machine*. Yet Toller was also innovative in his development of the revue-type political satire (*Hoppla!*, Gate Theatre, 1929), or the documentary drama (*Draw the Fires!*, Manchester Repertory Theatre, 1935), as well as in *No More Peace!*, without receiving the same recognition for these works.

Toller's main purpose, to use a variety of dramatic form and theatrical technique to address serious social and political issues, is not one that has generally found favour in the theatre in Britain. Such drama has tended to remain the preserve of a limited number of writers and producers, with a limited audience. During his own lifetime, however, Toller undoubtedly acted as a potent stimulus to a wide public up and down the country, through the performance of his plays, and perhaps even more through his personal appearances, as well as through his autobiographical works. His popularity with a range of socialist organizations has been well documented by Richard Dove;[22] the English translation of the autobiographical *I Was a German* was reprinted twice in the first months after publication in 1934, and soon ran to a second edition. In technique it, too, was innovative: English readers were fascinated and moved by the arresting combination of realism and stylization, of unpretentious narrative simplicity and emotional intensity.

Post-war interest in Toller has been fitful, but persistent. He evidently has no more appeal for the commercial theatre in Britain today than he had in his own lifetime, but there have been several successful productions of *Masses and Man*, *The Machine-Wreckers*, *Hinkemann*, *The Blind Goddess*, and *Hoppla!*, in more experimental theatres. The Glasgow Citizens Theatre, which has been particularly resourceful in presenting Continental, and especially German, drama (in translation), mounted an imaginative production of *The Machine-Wreckers* in 1984 which brought out very well how relevant Toller's play is to contemporary society. Perhaps there are the seeds there of a fresh and potentially fruitful appreciation of Toller in the British theatre: of the versatility of the poet, the imagination of the playwright, and the humanity of the man, but above all, seeing the theatre as Toller did, not merely as an agreeable place for killing time, but as the very locus of social conscience.

N.A. Furness

Notes

* My sincere thanks are due to the staff of the Wiener Library, London, for valuable help with information and materials.
1. See N.A. Furness, 'The Reception of Ernst Toller and his Works in Britain', in Richard Sheppard (ed.), *Expressionism in Focus*, Blairgowrie, 1987, pp. 171–97.
2. Ernst Toller, *Seven Plays*, London, 1935.
3. Idem, *I Was a German* (i.e. *Eine Jugend in Deutschland*, trans. by Edward Crankshaw), London, 1934.
4. See Fenner Brockway's account of demonstrations in eleven countries, in *Fellowship of Reconciliation News Sheet*, Sixth Series, no. 3, Sept. 1922.
5. Sheila Grant Duff, *The Parting of Ways. A Personal Account of the Thirties*, London, 1982, p. 38.
6. G.W.Bishop, *Barry Jackson and the London Theatre*, London, 1933, p. 135.
7. Ibid., p. 80.
8. W.A.Darlington, *Six Thousand and One Nights, Forty Years as a Critic*, London, 1960, p. 168.
9. Ibid., pp. 136–7.
10. James Agate, *The Contemporary Theatre 1924*, London, 1925, pp. 122–6; *The Contemporary Theatre 1926*, London, 1927, pp. 78–82; *Their Hour upon the Stage*, Cambridge, 1930, pp. 30–4; *The Amazing Theatre*, London, 1939, pp. 231–4.
11. St John Ervine, *The Organised Theatre*, London, 1924, p. 36.
12. Idem, *The Theatre in My Time*, London, 1933, p. 159.
13. See *Drama*, vol. 13, no. 4, Jan. 1935, pp. 50–2.
14. Carroll, *Daily Telegraph*, 1 Nov. 1934, p. 9; Toller, *Daily Telegraph*, 3 Nov. 1934, p. 11; Carroll, *Daily Telegraph*, 5 Nov. 1934, p. 9.
15. Norman Marshall, *The Producer and the Play*, London, 1957, p. 91.
16. Idem, *The Other Theatre*, London, 1947, p. 47.
17. 'A Year in the Theatre', *Criterion*, July 1936. p. 651.
18. *Life and Letters Today*, vol. 18. no. 11, Spring 1938, pp. 202–4.
19. Ernst Toller, *No More Peace!*, London, 1937, p. 62.
20. Marshall, *The Other Theatre*, p. 113.
21. See Breon Mitchell, 'W.H. Auden and Christopher Isherwood: The "German Influence"', *Oxford German Studies*, vol. 1, 1966, pp. 163–72.
22. See Richard Dove, 'The Place of Ernst Toller in English Socialist Theatre 1924–1939', *German Life and Letters*, vol. 38, 1985, pp. 125–37; also 'The British Connection: Aspects of the Biography of Ernst Toller', *German Life and Letters*, vol. 40, 1987, 319–36.

-7-

The British Feature Film as a European Concern
Britain and the Emigré Film-Maker, 1933-45

KEVIN GOUGH-YATES

In the late 1920s and early 1930s many German film-makers found work in Britain. Some had first tried their luck in Hollywood, only to discover that the difficulties were insuperable. Others had come directly from Germany, under contract to British production companies. After 1933, many more arrived as refugees, but with less certainty of finding employment. They sought work wherever they could and, sometimes, rather desperately; often they looked to their compatriots, who had established their own production organizations. Their reputations as skilled craftsmen frequently led to their being offered work whilst British-born technicians were passed over. The history of British cinema of the period is inextricably linked with that of the exiled European film-makers.

British Cinema and Immigration in the 1930s

The 'internationalists', as Thorold Dickinson euphemistically calls them,[1] are generically listed under a single name, Alexander Korda; Korda himself is considered to have initiated the boom of the mid-1930s and precipitated the consequent slump. George Perry describes how the 'extravagant success of Alexander Korda's 1933 picture, *The Private Life of Henry VIII*, . . . set in train a period of excessive speculation with City firms almost falling over themselves in the rush to get a stake in the new booming business.'[2] Quickly, the story reverses itself. Korda's losses and his too rapid expansion led his financial backer, the Prudential Insurance Company, to withdraw its support and take over the enormous studios he had built at Denham. 'The crash', writes the socialist film-maker Ralph Bond, 'did one good thing: it drove out many of the questionable characters who had infiltrated it.'[3] These oversimplifications encourage the confusions which still surround an understanding of the period. The names of foreign-born producers other than Korda rarely appear — these are the 'Korda Years' — but there were others: Max Schach, Gabriel Pascal, Ludovico Toeplitz, Arnold Pressburger, Erich Pommer and Filippo del Giudice among them. Some, like Korda, had reputations for profligacy, but most did not. Similarly, there were the writers, cinephotographers, directors, composers, designers, and actors and actresses which circumstances had brought to Britain, most with impeccable reputations.[4] The list is long, but includes some notable figures: Elisabeth Bergner, Nicholas Brodsky, Curt Courant, Hanns Eisler, Walter Goehr, Paul Grätz, Allan Gray, Karl Grune, Günther Krampf, Lucie Mannheim, Alfred Junge, Lilli Palmer, Ernst Hermann Meyer, Emeric Pressburger, Walter Rilla, Günther Stapenhorst, Berthold Viertel, Oscar Werndorff and Wolfgang Wilhelm. They were not all German but the great majority had worked and received their training in Germany, and they introduced a combination of technical skill and aesthetic confidence to Britain and its backward industry.

The proliferation of amusing anecdotes and novels from the period indicate the perceived difference between the ways émigré producers were able to run apparently flourishing enterprises on borrowed money and the ways in which their British equivalents had to struggle. Not only were their financial escapades highly questionable, but they were considered to be employing foreign technicians, foreign writers and foreign directors in preference to their equally skilled home-grown equivalents. Throughout the 1930s, the émigré was both admired and resented. Only the outbreak of war brought this to an end. Enlistment, other official duties or reserved occupations and internment reduced the competition for the British technician. Also, fewer Americans crossed the Atlantic to work in Great Britain. Whilst there was a shortage of both materials and staff and fewer films were actually produced,[5] the war, partly because the government allowed film budgets to expand, created opportunities for the British film-maker.

German cinema of the 1920s set cinematic standards for both European and American films. Alfred Hitchcock, who was at the beginning of his career in 1930, had directed his first two films in Munich as co-productions with Emelka Productions. His experience was characteristic: 'My models were forever after the German film-makers of 1924 and 1925. They were trying very hard to express their ideas in purely visual terms.'[6] Paul Rotha, who was to become one of the major forces of the British documentary film in the 1930s, wrote perceptively, as early as 1929:

The German cinema has been a great cinema. It has produced principles and processes that have been all-important contributions to the cinema of the world. From its individual development there have come the freedom of the camera, the feeling of completeness, and the importance of architectural environment as part of realisation. These have been brought about by the national aptitude for craftsmanship, for structure, for studioism. They have been a means to an end that in itself has not yet been discovered. .[7]

Numerous films made by émigrés during this period which were rooted in operetta, European history and literature, would never have seen the light of day had only British interests been involved: *City of Song* (1931), the first of the big international films to be made in Britain and featuring the singer Jan Kiepura, was an entirely Continental production; *Abdul the Damned* (1935) was produced by Max Schach, directed by Karl Grune and starred Fritz Kortner, Nils Asther and Walter Rilla; *Escape Me Never* (1935) was a Paul Czinner vehicle for Elisabeth Bergner, a reworking of the play by Margaret Kennedy in which Bergner had earlier appeared; *The Robber Symphony* (1936) was Friedrich Feher's 'pre-scored' or 'composed' film, which was a box office disaster but is now frequently revived. An astounding number of German, Austrian, or Hungarian plays and novels were adapted for the screen by writers who had learnt their craft in Germany. The designers Alfred Junge, Oscar Werndorff, and the Russian-born Andrei Andrejew, as well as the photographers Curt Courant, Otto Heller, Günther Krampf and Mutz Greenbaum, brought a specifically European eye to British film-making. The composers Allan Gray, the Polish-born émigré, and the ubiquitous Mischa Spoliansky had composed for Max Reinhardt as well as for cabaret in Berlin; they incorporated classical and popular themes into their arrangements for the cinema. Writers too, for example Wolfgang Wilhelm and Emeric Pressburger, neither of whom arrived in Britain with any confidence in the use of English, brought with them, as part of their baggage, a creative imagination which had been born abroad.

Three factors reduced the dominance of German cinema. First, as John Grierson argued, 'Hollywood by suddenly buying up Murnau and Freund and Pommer and Lubitsch broke the back of the German School.'[8] These talents were 'joined by a whole crowd, including the star directors E.A. Dupont, Ludwig Berger, Lupu Pick, Paul Leni ; . . and such actors as Veidt and Jannings. . .'[9]

Second, the advent of sound in 1928/9 destroyed the possibility of the German film as an international movie. Actors were, in general, tied to a foreign tongue. The clearest and most celebrated British example of this is Anny Ondra's performance in *Blackmail*, the 1929 film directed by Alfred Hitchcock, which was initiated as a silent film, but finally included sound sequences. Anny Ondra's voice had to be doubled by the English actress, Joan Barry, who stood off camera and spoke into the microphone. Anny Ondra did not again appear in a British film. Difficulties with language were to persist for both actors and writers.

The British film industry's response to sound was twofold. It produced and co-produced a number of multi-lingual films, whereby films were shot 'back to back' in more than one language and sometimes, but not always, with the same performers. The first of these was E.A. Dupont's *Atlantic*, for British International, in November 1929. Most of the films were to be made at UFA studios, Berlin, under the direction of Erich Pommer and with the advantage of German technicians. But Pommer drew 'almost exclusively from European sources for his material — mainly German — and the stories he chose were all too often largely incapable of proper translation' into English.[10] The alternative to this somewhat dislocated method of filming was to bring the key film-makers to Britain. Mutz Greenbaum came in 1929, as chief photographer to Gaumont-British at Lime Grove Studios; he had worked in Germany since 1914 and rapidly established himself as one of the handful of expert cine-photographers in Britain. Alfred Junge, who had been a scenic artist at the Berlin Staatsoper and the Staatstheater was, perhaps, the most important of all art directors in Britain during the 1930s and 1940s. He had first worked in England in 1928, for British International on Dupont's *Moulin Rouge* and *Piccadilly*. After a short period in Paris and Berlin, he returned to London in 1932 under contract to Gaumont-British and remained in Britain until after the war.

The third factor in the decline of the German film industry was the rise to power of the Nazis. In 1933, *The Kinematograph Yearbook* observed that German studios had produced 120 feature films.[11] There was a fall of approximately 25 per cent from 1932, to a figure of ninety-four films in 1935. *Kinematograph Weekly* noted a general decrease in the German film trade for the whole period 1930–36 and commented: 'The drop in German production was primarily attributed to difficulties experienced in putting into execution the programmes projected by various companies owing to shortage of suitable artists.' It argued that 'the political and cultural principles of National Socialism implied by such measures as the removal of Jewish producers, authors, directors and actors . . . [have] . . . militated against the preservation of an atmosphere in which a new and delicate industry can thrive.'[12] In a strongly worded article,[13] the writer and producer Ivor Montagu observed that the 'colossal decline' of the German film industry in the years 1932 to 1934 partly paralleled the plight of its foreign trade in general, but, with more than a little sarcasm, he also drew attention to the legislation which prevented Jews and politically unacceptable figures from finding employment. Of the approximately eighty artists listed by Montagu, who were unable to work in Germany, roughly half worked in Britain during the 1930s. Some of these eventually made their way to Hollywood, but many remained and worked in Britain throughout the war.

Recent literature on British cinema has examined the relationship between film and social structures of the period. Jeffrey Richards has tended to emphasize the imperial perspective apparent in films like *The Drum* (1938), *Sanders of the River* (1935), *Rhodes of Africa* (1936), *The Great Barrier* (1936) and *King Solomon's Mines* (1937).[14] The 'cinema of Empire', as he calls it, advocated, through its plots, 'a view of the British Empire as beneficent and necessary.' There was no direct official influence on them, but they offered 'patriotism with profit' in a form which was highly acceptable to the British government. There has been a special emphasis on the way in which censorship gave its imprimatur, and, certainly, all the views emanating from the British Board of Film Censors disclose an upper-class, flag-waving, orthodoxy. Its Secretary, J. Brooks Wilkinson, admiring the sentiments of *The Four Feathers* (1939) shortly before the outbreak of war, is reputed to have told Alexander Korda: 'The British nation should be grateful to you for producing such a film at such a time.'[15] Richards makes no mention of the possibly curious fact that each of these films involved, at a high level, artists and technicians who were émigrés or refugees. *Sanders of the River* and *The Drum* were produced by Alexander Korda and directed and designed respectively by his brothers Zoltan and Vincent. They were written by Korda's long-time collaborator, Lajos Biro, and photographed by Georges Périnal, whom Korda had brought over from Paris in 1933 to film *The Private Life of Henry VIII*, the film which established Korda as a major force in British cinema. Even the music was written by the émigrés Mischa Spoliansky and Miklós Rosza. The other three films were made for Gaumont-British and were similarly closely associated with émigré film-makers. *Rhodes of Africa* was directed by Berthold Viertel, its designer was Oscar Werndorff; Günther Stapenhorst —- to whom Joseph Goebbels had made overtures and a refugee by choice —- was associate producer on *The Great Barrier*; Mischa Spoliansky and the designer Alfred Junge worked on *King Solomon's Mines*. Whatever the 'cinema of Empire' was, it was not solely an expression of patriotism carried out by the film production companies on behalf of the British government.[16] Richards assumes that the émigré adopts the political assumptions of the host country but he pays little attention to the artistic traditions which the émigré may have brought with him as part of his stock in trade.

Reviewing Zoltan Korda's *The Four Feathers* (1939), Graham Greene wrote:

> The story . . . must be known by this time to everyone — four films have been made of this ham-heroic tale . . . so the plot hardly matters: what is important is the colour, which is almost invariably pleasant and sometimes gives a shock of pleasure . . . What is important is nocturnal London smoking up through Faversham's grey windows: the close up of mulberry bodies straining at the ropes along the Nile: the cracked umber waste round the dried-up wells . . . We forget the silly plot . . .[17]

These films, with their innocuous story-lines, were certainly compatible with national sentiments as seen by the British Board of Film Censors; they could hardly have been otherwise. What makes them memorable — when they are memorable — is, as Greene notes, their physical appearance and the skills which have been employed to relate them. The colour, the imagery and the sound are constituent elements of the fabric which makes up the totality and, as Greene recognizes, are significant components of the theme of the film.

When we consider the films of the 1930s, in which the Europeans played a lesser role, the list of important films is small: *Midshipman Easy* (1935) and *The Stars Look Down* (1939), perhaps, but even the latter, which was directed by Carol Reed and began as a Max Schach–Karl Grune project, was photographed by Mutz Greenbaum, with music by Hans May, had Fred Zelnick as its executive producer and Isadore Goldsmith as producer. Karol Kulik, in her biography of Alexander Korda, notes that the documentary film-maker Basil Wright described the romantic comedy *Storm in a Teacup* (1937) as 'the first British comedy from an English studio . . . a film which is, perhaps for the first time, genuinely British.'[18] *Storm in a Teacup*, however, is a good example of the European aesthetic in British cinema of the time; its photographer was, once again, Mutz Greenbaum, its designer was Andrei Andrejew and it was derived from Bruno Frank's play *Sturm in Wasserglas*.

Tony Aldgate argues that there was, nevertheless, a British domestic cinema of the 1930s, made up of films which includes the working-class comedies of George Formby and Gracie Fields, and which were made with solely British crews.[19] It contributed 'to the remarkable stability of British society during this period. It reflected and reinforced the dominant consensus and sought to generate adherence to the idea that society should continue to remain stable and cohesive as it changed over time.' He draws support from the industrial surveys which were carried out by Simon Rowson and from the popularity polls conducted by Sidney Bernstein, whilst recognizing that they should be treated with some caution. Starting from a different premise, Aldgate arrives at conclusions which are compatible with those of Richards for the 'cinema of Empire'. *Sing As We Go* (1934), *Off the Dole* (1935) and *Feather Your Nest* (1937), however, avoided consideration of the social and political issues which they touched upon. They may have been financially successful, but they were minor films, inexpensively made and technically poor. The Formby comedies were hardly seen in central London. The greater part of the budget was spent on the salary of a single star, a Gracie Fields or a George Formby, and the émigré technician, who could ask a relatively high salary, was rarely involved with them.[20] When the technicians' trade union, the Association of Cinematographic Technicians, provided a written statement to the Ministry of Labour on 28 June 1937, on the subject of foreign technicians in the British film industry, it complained that the eminent lighting cameraman Günther Krampf was working on a film not worthy of his talents, a light comedy starring Jack Hulbert. It could, the union argued, have been photographed by 'a British cameraman'.[21] Krampf had controlled the photography on *Die Büchse der Pandora* (1929) and *Kuhle Wampe* (1932) in Germany and was in continuous demand in Britain.

As we shall see, a major ideological debate raged throughout the 1930s about the nature of British cinema. Dissatisfaction with the calibre of British films began early, but took a fresh direction under the influence of John Grierson and the members of the documentary film movement which he founded. Andrew Higson argues in his important article on the documentary-realist tradition in British cinema,[22] that there is 'at the heart of the documentary idea . . . a powerful differentiation between "realism" and "escapism": between a serious, committed, engaged cinema, and mass entertainment.' It manifested itself in 'a more overt conflict, between this concern for aesthetic principles and experimentation and a concern for education and propaganda'. The debate, nevertheless, existed in a wider context which encompassed the feature film. It included the quite specific concern of whether it was possible for British cinema to extricate itself aesthetically, from Hollywood on the one hand, and from Europe, and predominantly Germany, on the other. The documentary film-makers tended to model their films on developments in Soviet cinema, the films of Eisenstein and Pudovkin especially, and proposed a programme which denied the 'pure cinema' ethos of German art, with its links to Expressionism and all that it implied.[23]

The Contribution of European Artists and Technicians

As early as 1929, P.L. Mannock, who was film critic of the *Daily Herald* and a regular contributor to *Kinematograph Weekly*, wrote:

Half the British directors who have made films this year ought never to be
allowed in studios again. Half the studios should be scrapped forthwith, and
half the heads of production firms should gracefully retire from a business to
which their proved incompetence is a menace . . . What is the use of pretending
that [British films] are not below . . . standard?

This was a theme to which he would constantly return. Mannock notes a
film on which the photographer was not 'allowed to see a foot of his
"takes" for nearly a month' and another on which the director 'could not
see a foot of his work for six weeks'. He is critical of 'our starfinders', 'who
take no notice of a cabaret dancer in the West End named Louise Brooks',
an American dancer and actress who had been transformed into a star
when she was featured in two films directed by G.W. Pabst in Germany,
Die Büchse der Pandora (*Pandora's Box*) and *Das Tagebuch einer Verlorenen*
(*Diary of a Lost Girl*) in 1928/29. Mannock's prescription was:

Import a foreign expert rather than a second-rate Englishman, but make sure
that the Englishman is given a chance to be first-rate. Don't import any art
directors; we have the best in the world. Get the best photography at all costs.
Elevate the story and scenario department by employing people with some
grasp of polished popular entertainment, rather than precious young men of the
Chelsea type . . .[24]

A few months later in *Kinematograph Weekly*, an anonymous 'Scenarist'
wrote of a 'collection of old-fashioned hackneyed plots, poorly contrived,
badly written, uninspired and dreary tripe' which passed for scenarios in
Britain. He found it difficult to conceive that they were the best Britain
could muster and blamed the producers, who knew no better.[25] Mannock
was writing in a similar vein in the spring of 1930: 'The average British
scenario is a wretched business, usually an ill assorted compulsory collaboration . . . which is generally unworthy and frequently contemptible.'[26] As
late as 1939, the Executive Director of D. and P. Studios, Richard Norton,
bemoaned the quality of British scenarios: 'Screenwriters are', he emphasized, 'one of the most important things we must encourage in England.'[27]

The major writers, photographers, producers, and even directors of
feature films in Britain throughout most of the 1930s were not British or,
at least, were not British born. They were, for the most part, welcomed in
the British studio of the early 1930s. They not only raised technical
standards, they sometimes introduced them for the first time. The multi-
lingual film *City of Song*, for example, was much admired as a British film
in 1931. L.C. Moen wrote that there was 'a profound lesson for the trade
in it.' Other British studios, he argued, could do it, 'given the will and the
intelligence *at the top*. For basically, the quality of *City of Song* is solely due
to the result of the willingness of Dr. [Rudolph] Becker to spend anything

necessary to obtain quality'.[28] Becker had previously been director of the foreign department at UFA and had devoted his attentions to the quality of sound. *City of Song* seemed indisputably British, yet this neo-operetta, which was the first of the many films which exploited the talents of singers, was made entirely by Europeans, most of whom were to become exiles. Arnold Pressburger produced it and Carmine Gallone was its director. Design was again by someone who had worked with Dupont, Oscar Werndorff, who subsequently worked for Hitchcock on three of his British films.[29] When the Hungarian photographer Arpad Viragh died during the production, he was replaced by Curt Courant. The only British figure to work on the film at anything like a senior level was Miles Malleson, whose main concern was the dialogue for the English version.

A glance at the 'Technical Section' of *Spotlight* for winter 1935 reveals that no major British production company failed to have at least one European cine-photographer under contract. Gaumont-British sported Mutz Greenbaum, London Films listed Georges Périnal and Hans Schneeberger. The small and under-financed company Criterion Film Productions, which had been created by Douglas Fairbanks Jr., with the Romanian producer Marcel Hellman, listed Günther Krampf. Criterion did not last long but among the émigrés who worked for it were Sergei Nolbandov, who was, at this time, its Production Manager, the editor Conrad von Molo, and a reader, Ern(e)st Borneman. Borneman found that his recommendations were totally ignored, and he divided his time by contributing to the newly created film journal *Sight and Sound* and by writing, under a pseudonym, an extraordinary crime novel, *The Face on the Cutting Room Floor*.[30] Even Basil Dean's Associated Talking Pictures, which was not associated with the employment of foreign technicians, lists Jan Stallich as its studio photographer alongside the relatively unimportant John W. Boyle. The only significant company not to list a European photographer was Herbert Wilcox's British and Dominion.

Of the British photographers listed in the same edition of *Spotlight* only four had notable careers: Freddie Young, Ronald Neame, Desmond Dickinson and Erwin Hillier. Desmond Dickinson 'was so good', wrote Adrian Brunel, the director and writer, 'it seemed incredible that he should have been relegated to shooting cheap films only, while foreign cameramen, infinitely less talented, were freely admitted into the country to shoot in our studios.'[31] Erwin Hillier had been born and educated in Berlin. He had started his film career as assistant to the photographer Fritz Arno Wagner on Fritz Lang's *M* in 1931. The market, it is true, had been conquered by American films, but, in the 1920s, the imagination of the British producer and director had been captured less by Hollywood than it had by Germany and, in particular, by the films and production methods of UFA in Berlin.

Like the photographer, with whom he began to work closely, the art director was another figure of enormous influence. He could enhance the production value of British films at little apparent cost. The key designers of the 1930s in Britain, with the single exception of the London-born Alex Vetchinsky, were again from Europe. When the young Ken Adam, a refugee from Germany at the age of thirteen, entered the industry after the war, his models included Alfred Junge, and the Russian opera designer George Wakhevich,[32] Oscar Werndorff, Ernö Metzner (who had designed seven films for G.W. Pabst in the 1920s), and Alfred Junge were all at Gaumont-British during a period when the art director and the photographer were the dominant figures in generating the visual power of the films. Another influence on Adam was Andrei Andrejew, who was at Toeplitz; his baroque style always distinguished the films on which he worked. Vincent Korda was at London Films. His film career had begun as late as 1931, when his brother used him alongside Alfred Junge on one of his Paris films for Paramount, *Marius*.

The Hollywood art director Paul Holmes identified the transformation that was taking place in British studios when, in 1932, he wrote:

> A valuable advance in realism has been attained through the closer co-operation of the director and cameraman with the art director. This essential co-operation has . . . been lacking in this country . . . German producers, ever in the forefront where scenery is concerned, have always insisted on the closest attention to the building of sets which are intended to help the camera to secure the utmost realism . . . The German studios have always realised that large sums of money and a great deal of time can be saved if the director, camera staff, and art director work in the closest harmony.[33]

As with photographers, each of the European art directors had an individual style, which was incorporated into a broad knowledge of film-making. Junge, Michael Powell observed, 'was head director at Balcon's Lime Grove. . . . he ran it like a machine.'[34] 'It was the first time in England that they had a supervising art director. Junge was a good organiser, a tremendous disciplinarian, and a very good trainer of young people . . . besides being a very great designer himself.'[35] This view of Junge is confirmed by the photographer Christopher Challis:

> Alfred was a martinette [*sic*], he ran the art department like a hospital . . . it was immaculate . . . they literally wiped up your footprints as you went in . . . Alfred was brilliant with matte shots, hanging miniatures and all that sort of thing . . . He would mark on the set with a cross the position of the camera for the main shot and woe betide anyone who tried to shift it . . . He'd designed it from that position and that was it. There was this cross and the size of the lens put on it.[36]

Lazare Meerson, the influential Russian-born designer who was brought to London by Korda, had designed *Sous les Toits de Paris*, amongst others, for René Clair as well as films for Marcel L'Herbier and Jacques Feyder, and is spoken of as one of the two greatest designers of European cinema. 'Meerson, who was always very keen on detail, put most of his work into his sets whilst they were being built; he used plaster work very lavishly.'[37] Like Junge, he understood the whole concept of film production, he knew what the lens could do and would use scale models for the long shots of roofs, gables, clock towers, and silhouetted houses. He would create the illusion of a set which extended indefinitely by reducing the scale of the elements in the design the further they were from the camera. Léon Barsacq makes a number of acute observations about British set design during the 1930s.[38] He writes of 'the apathy and ignorance pervading British film studios' and of the encouragment that Vincent Korda offered to a generation of young men.

The European was less dominant in the areas of directing and editing, although even here he was well represented. Paul Stein, Friedrich Feher, Hans Schwartz, Karl Grune, Ludwig Berger, Berthold Viertel, and the brothers Alexander and Zoltan Korda, all have major directorial credits. Feher's *The Robber Symphony*, for example, which was designed by Ernö Metzner, is described by Elliot Stein as 'one of the great and delightful eccentricities of European cinema in the thirties.'[39] It was said to be the first 'composed' film, the first film shot to a pre-recorded sound-track. Michael Powell claims that, although he has never seen the film, he was 'haunted' by it 'and longed for a film subject where music was the master.'[40] It was, he writes, the inspiration which led him via *The Red Shoes Ballet* to *The Tales of Hoffmann*, which was completely shot to play-back. This kind of experiment, which was distasteful to the 'realist' film-maker by the mid-1930s, was, seemingly, a denial of the use of film as a social and educational weapon. In the spectrum of debate, Powell, who had never 'trusted' documentary, was firmly at the European end. He was to be co-director on a film begun by Ludwig Berger, *The Thief of Bagdad* (1940). Berger, 'the distinguished Continental film producer', noted *Kinematograph Weekly*, who 'is also a great musician and has produced several operas on the Continent, has a revolutionary scheme for shooting the music first on *The Thief of Bagdad*.' It was to be 'the first time that a full musical score' would 'be played back and the sound "mixed" on the set.'[41] The chaos associated with the experiment did not dampen Powell's aesthetic enthusiasms. 'In the end the only sequences shot to pre-composed music were those involving special effects — the gallop of the Flying Horse and the Silvermaid's Dance.'[42]

The European film-maker in Britain during the 1930s was frequently better educated and better read than his equivalent British counterpart. He generated considerable resentment, especially, when he also attracted publicity. Powell felt that the European could converse on a wide range of subjects; he was 'cultivated': a trained composer like Feher, a reputable painter like Vincent Korda, a poet like Berthold Viertel, or students of Arnold Schoenberg, as were Walter Goehr and Allan Gray. Powell was one of the few British-born film makers who was seduced, and not shamed, by this wealth of experience and erudition. He recognized that the particular combination of imagination and technical skill which the European brought to the cinema was not a part of British cultural life, especially where the cinema was concerned. Whenever he could, he associated with the European artist. Powell's partnership with the Hungarian-born scriptwriter Emeric Pressburger began in 1938 when Korda introduced them to each other at a script conference for *The Spy in Black*. Powell's designers, thereafter, were always European: Vincent Korda, Alfred Junge and later Hein Heckroth. Georges Périnal and Erwin Hillier were his main photographers until after the war.

'The Preponderence of Aliens' and the British Response

These colourful figures appear, like figures in an *Arabian Nights* fantasy, in Borneman's novel *The Face on the Cutting Room Floor* and Jeffrey Dell's *Nobody Ordered Wolves*. Jeffrey Dell had been employed by Korda as a writer on films including *Sanders of the River*, which his brother Zoltan had directed. Alexander Korda and his brothers appear as thinly disguised figures alongside the composer Mischa Spoliansky and others. Korda is painted as an extravagant, seductive opportunist, devoid of the malice and megalomania of his Hollywood counterparts, but taking advantage of rather incompetent financiers and accountants.

The reality seems to be close to the fantasy. Basil Dean's description of Korda as 'highly intelligent, unscrupulous, with a genuine love of art and a clear idea of its commercial value . . . belonging to a race of alien buccaneers able to charm the financial bird off its British nest for the express purpose of removing one if not all of its eggs', is the kind of sour, double-edged compliment Dean saved for personalities of whom he was jealous.[43] But he had some grounds for feeling resentment towards Korda. After the war, in 1949, and along with Hugh Quennell, who was Korda's financial adviser, they had both been involved in Group Theatres Ltd. Dean found himself accepting personal liability for Group Theatres' expenditure, having believed that he was acting in accord with their wishes. Korda would operate with a sweeping disregard for the realities of personal finance; he would lose 'other people's money, to be sure, but money all the same.'[44]

The financier Edward Beddington Behrens relates a similar, but little-known anecdote, about Korda. In the mid-1930s, newspapers were full of the story that Korda had purchased United Artists when Korda telephoned Beddington Behrens from New York 'at a time when calls cost £20 a minute, to say, "You've probably read in the papers that I have bought United Artists. I've fixed everything except the money. Can you help?"' Beddington Behrens listened to Korda explaining that, in addition to $5,000,000 (£1,000,000) for the business an extra £1,000,000 was '*absolutely necessary*' [my italics] to prevent the production units going 'bust'. Profits, however, were so low that Beddington Behrens felt unable to justify an issue for the extra £1,000,000 of working capital. Korda's 'comment was: " Well let's not bother about the working capital. Let's buy the business anyhow and hope for the best."'[45]

Max Schach who, along with Karl Grune, had been forced out of Emelka Studios, Munich, in December 1931, came to Britain as a refugee in 1934 and soon established a series of film production companies, the Capitol group, which included Trafalgar, Buckingham, and Cecil. In contrast to the tall Korda, Schach was likened to a 'perky griffin behind an enormous desk' by the journalist Hilde Marchant,[46] so small it was not clear when he was standing behind it. According to Hans Feld, editor of *World Film News*, reputable figures like Erich Pommer kept well away from him.[47] His companies in Britain are considered by Rachel Low as 'tramp' operations, travelling from studio to studio, without homes of their own.

Low makes an unfavourable comparison between Schach and Korda; Schach, she feels, contributed nothing to the industry. Money went directly into people's pockets. Korda created stars, built Denham, provided opportunities for writers and directors, and encouraged the industry to find a significant place for itself in the world market. Whilst it is undeniable that Schach contracted stars, bought rights, and produced little — a point well made in Vicki's cartoons for *World Film News* — Korda's companies, like those of Schach's, also survived on borrowed money. Schach was optimitically welcomed as an inspired figure by the trade press, which saw him as 'safely established as one of our busiest and most prolific producers . . . [who has] . . . produced more films in the last eighteen months than any other individual producer in this country.'[48] Monja Danischewsky, who was employed by Schach in the publicity department of Capitol, describes him as a man 'with immense charm and an irrepressible sense of humour . . . God's gift to the publicity man.'[49] Certainly, the films he produced could be over-budgeted and poorly distributed, but it is difficult to determine from currently available sources that Schach was more of a rogue than Korda. Schach's expensive flop *Love from a Stranger* lost over £80,000 in the combined British and American markets; it made only £10,000 in the USA. Korda was partial to fantasy accountancy, and the mythical production cost of *The Private Life of Henry VIII*, £60,000, became the target budget for a British feature film. In fact it had cost around £93,000. The difference was that it was an enormous box office success. A substantial part of Schach's unpopularity with historians seems to have been that he was considerably less appealing than Korda. Low, whilst criticizing him for his failure to invest in the industry, recognizes that Korda was reliant on the independent peripatetic producer like Schach to use the studios at Denham. 'Denham was a Moloch — it had to be fed', wrote Paul Tabori[50] and, indeed, *Love from a Stranger* was one of the films that had given it sustenance. Korda, with a much more satisfactory distribution arrangement in the USA than Schach, could squander money too, although the story still remains incomplete. Marlene Dietrich was paid £80,000 to be directed by Jacques Feyder in *Knight Without Armour* (1937), a film which finally cost £350,000; his adaptation of H.G. Wells's *The Shape of Things to Come* in 1936, which cost nearly as much, also failed badly. Korda, always optimistic about finance, was asked if it would break even and is reputed to have replied, 'Of course. It was an expensive effort but we're only a few thousand out at the moment.'[51] He did not change over the years and retained the same ebullience long after the war, when the National Film Finance Corporation funded *Bonny Prince Charlie* (1948); at a cost of £750,000, it was another disaster. His genial response to the concerned Harold Wilson, then President of the Board of Trade, was 'Ah, just wait until you see my next.'[52]

When Twickenham, a company which produced little of lasting interest, collapsed in 1937, there was a rash of bankruptcies; Schach's and Korda's companies went down too. Low seems to admire the energy which Julius Hagen brought to Twickenham Films as its Managing Director, although it, too, had been under-financed and had operated on borrowed money. She passes over the criticisms of Hagen's high living, enormous salary and inconsequential films. Low considers Korda 'cautious'. Karol Kulik and Sarah Street note a different evaluation of Schach and Korda, from Bruce Lockhart's diary for 23 August 1938:

Last night Bayliss-Smith, who is a leading chartered accountant and represents the creditors in some of the biggest cinema financial messes in this country, says the cinema industry here has cost the banks and insurance companies about £4,000,000. Most of this is lost by Jews — like Korda and Max Schacht [*sic*]. Latter already lost a packet for the German Government before Hitler. He has now done the same here. In Bayliss-Smith's opinion, and he would not say so lightly, Korda is a much worse man than Schacht. Schacht is just a slick Jew who sees financial moves ahead of the other fellow. Korda is a crook and, according to Bayliss-Smith, an evil man.[53]

The ACT intensified its campaign against the employment of foreigners as the 1930s wore on and sought to persuade the Ministry of Labour to act solely on its recommendations for the granting of work permits, but it lacked conviction. The Parliamentary Secretary, R.A. Butler, noted, 'I cannot see why a self appointed body should demand the right to be consulted on every permit . . .'[54] In spite of the union's protestations, the Ministry did not believe that there was enough suitable British talent to meet the industry's needs and often sought advice elsewhere. The dominance of the European in British cinema was reduced by war and the issue remained in the background until 1944, when the ACT was, once more, experiencing a rising membership. It made its 'objection to promiscuous employment of foreign technicians to the detriment of equally competent British technicians',[55] concentrating its energies, however, towards achieving a reciprocal agreement with the American trade union, the IATSE. There were no more Europeans to come.

There had been a feeling of humiliation when, for example, a foreign film editor fell ill and the film was not given to an Englishman to work on. It was shipped to Europe instead. When Sam Eckman of MGM gave evidence to the Moyne Committee in 1936, he argued that 'there were simply not enough technicians in the country for them to establish their own studio for making quota films'. [56] This, of course, was the very point the ACT were disputing and one which resolves itself once it is realized that aesthetic rather than technical judgements were finally being applied. It was to take four or five years before the British aesthetic began to make serious inroads into the British feature film.

Caustic phrasing in the trade press sometimes accompanied the observation that an Englishman was unemployed whilst a foreign-born technician was working. Initially, it was thought that the reason why the European technician was used and admired was simply *because* of his superior technical skills. He would train his British counterpart and return home. When this failed to occur, the technician, especially, began to believe that the foreigner was actually preventing the establishment of a British film industry. P.L. Mannock, again, in *Kinematograph Weekly*, asked 'Are so Many Foreigners Necessary?' Korda's London Films is the initial target of Mannock's feature, but the shot is soon in all directions:

The chief cameraman and directors of every current Denham film are foreign. This fact could be commented on at length, for it is possible to put up a strong case in their favour. But I cannot see the point of engaging foreign art directors

149

and foreign assistant directors . . . There is far too much of this benevolence and giving responsible studio jobs to foreigners, many of them refugees. I should like to see a little more incredulity when Whitehall is assured of their indispensability on any picture.[57]

Later in 1936 Mannock asked 'Have We Grown too Cosmopolitan?'[58] and John Grierson, writing anonymously in *World Film News*, contributed an almost paranoid article entitled 'Aliens Stifle British Talent'.[59] Grierson noted that:

> the preponderance of aliens in key positions in the industry not only tends to produce a product lacking national character, but also develops an unhealthy inferiority complex in the rest of the technical staff, who are of local growth . . . The alien is concerned with getting immediately good results . . . for he is not likely to have his contract renewed if he fails to deliver the goods pretty quickly. And he always has the anxiety of wondering how long he will be allowed to stay . . . bearing in mind the fact that he was not much sought after when he left his own country . . . For these reasons the alien expert tends to watch his own interests . . . rather than train the staff under him . . .

For Grierson, the exiled technician can do no right, for he proceeds: 'If however, the alien looks forward to settling permanently in the country of his adoption, there is all the more temptation for him not to develop qualities in his subordinates that might bring them on to qualify for the position which he himself holds.'

The foreign technician did not go entirely undefended. David Cunynghame, Production Manager for London Films, at which much of the criticism was directed, responded to protests about foreigners in British studios, writing: 'It must be realised that . . . the British industry needs their support in order to take immediate advantage of the possibility of extending its export trade.' He refutes the many specific charges directed at his company; the eleven foreign cameramen employed at Denham were employed not by London Films alone but by six different companies. 'There is not, at Denham, any particular camera unit entirely composed of foreigners.' At Denham, Cunynghame points out, they 'have been training individuals in all departments for the last four years.'[60] On the whole, however, the belief remained that the British technician was being deliberately excluded from working on British productions by the dubious methods of foreign technicians and cosmopolitan producers who were lining their own pockets whilst exploiting British financial institutions.

There was no significant anti-Semitism within the film industry, which is hardly surprising considering the number of Jews which it employed. *Kinematograph Weekly* was quick to notice any manifestation of it and drew attention to the journal of the Imperial Fascist League, which was edited by Arnold S. Leese. *The Fascist* carried features with attacks on the trade journal *Today's Cinema* which was, it claimed, Jewish controlled.[61] The newly established British Film Institute was 'to be in the hands of a gang of Jews and Socialists'.[62] It argued that the film industry was organized as a sweat-shop by people having 'Jewish nationality'. The trade press did not ignore these attacks which were, otherwise, hardly read and the rantings had negligible influence, except that the term 'alien', which was widely used in the writings of the extreme right, came to be substituted for 'foreigner', even inside the film industry. The book *The Alien Menace*, by Lt.-Col. A.H. Lane, which was published in the early 1930s, lists a number of film personalities whom the author considers to be aliens; it includes the Ostrer brothers, C.M. Woolf, Michael Balcon, Sidney Bernstein, Rudolph Becker, Ludwig Blattner and Harry Day.[63] If all were Jews, only one was a foreigner. The Ostrers, had, for example, been born in London and Blattner had been in Britain since 1897.

Resentment rather than racism remained the root cause of hostility towards the foreign worker and producer in Britain. With the exception, for a short while, of the Unionist MP for North Tottenham, Edward Doran, there was no public voice outside the film industry which commented on foreigners in it. Doran had actually worked in films and was constantly asking questions in the House of Commons relating to Jews, 'undesirable aliens', and moneylenders. Both *The Fascist* and the *Jewish Chronicle* reported his parliamentary activities. He received short shrift in the House, and his anti-Semitism led him into conflict with his constituency association. He lost his seat in 1935, the year, coincidentally, in which Willie Gallacher, the only Communist Member of Parliament before 1945, was elected. The '"parlour anti-Semitism" of much English society', as Richard Griffiths calls it,[64] had no equivalent manifestation with regard to the film industry.

The European photographer was skilled in the use of arc lights in combination with incandescent lamps; his talent had been developed through a system of training, roughly equivalent to an apprenticeship scheme, namely learning on the job from a master-craftsman. It was a luxury non-existent in the British film industry, which operated from a weak industrial base, with a low rate of capital investment and a sense of inferiority in the face of American competition in its own market. The difficulty in describing the distinct contribution of the foreign technician in the 1930s is precisely that which made it so elusive to the Englishman in the industry. It only gradually dawned on film-makers and critics that employment did not necessarily follow from technical ability. Ideology, although no one used the word, was actually the central issue; acquired skills only provided the means by which it could be expressed. The

German conception of cinema, 'pure cinema' as it was generally called, was influential in Hollywood and dominant in Britain. The German-trained artist had an artistic conception of cinema which was linked to a literary and philosophical tradition.

Producers and the trade press certainly recognized the distinction, but it was quite a different matter convincing aspiring cine-photographers, for example, that they had not yet made the grade. Paul Rotha made an astute point when he observed that the 'British film has never been self-sufficient, in that it has never achieved its independence . . . For its obscure source it goes firstly to the American, and secondly, but more remote to discern, to the German film.'[65] Erwin Hillier, who, like Rotha, went to art school, also sees the difference as a combination of technical and aesthetic skills: Jan Stallich, the photographer, 'was very technically minded', a man who 'wouldn't tolerate people telling him how to film . . . He often made gadgets to help his filming . . . Otto Kanturek . . . introduced an excellent camera to this country, the Cinephone . . . Most of us learnt to use arcs in Germany, especially at UFA. My speciality was combining arcs, which gave better contrasting shades, with softer inkies [incandescent lamps].'[66] He makes the point that, in spite of all the jealous resentment that existed, sometimes from surprising sources, training in Britain would not have existed at all had it not been for the émigré in the 1930s.

The photographer's European sensibility, his contribution in fact, can generally be noticed only by its absence in the work of others. Certainly, the uncharacteristically forceful photography of Mutz Greenbaum on *Thunder Rock* in 1942 was admired, but it was photography under the influence of *Citizen Kane* which drew attention to itself. Erwin Hillier's photography on *A Canterbury Tale* and *I Know Where I'm Going*, much of it dark and moody, was also admired, but only in general terms. It was achieved, in the location photography, solely by the use of reflectors and without any supplementary lighting at all. Michael Powell, who directed both films and was, like Hitchcock, deeply influenced by his early contact with German cinema, said: 'He was one of the world's greatest black-and-white photographers',[67] but exactly what marked Hillier out from others of the period is the kind of distinction which seemed inconsequential to the less employable British technician at the time.

The Contrast of Cultures

When we turn to actors and writers, we see a different picture. The problem for the actor emerges with great clarity with Fritz Kortner who, because of his reputation, was able to find work in Britain. Salka Viertel gave her impressions of the London of the early 1930s, when she was on a visit to her husband, Berthold, who was directing at Gaumont-British. 'London was filled with refugees. Elisabeth Bergner had a sensational success in Margaret Kennedy's *Constant Nymph* [*sic*] and was acclaimed as the second Duse. Fritz Kortner and Johanna Hofer, Oscar Homolka, and many others were furiously learning English.'[68] It only gradually dawned on film-makers and critics that Britain and Germany were divided less by technical matters and more by a complex fabric of cultural determinants. Kortner

> despaired because of the language problems and the differences in theatrical traditions . . . 'My reputation as an actor was sufficient,' he wrote in his memoirs, 'to bring me my first film part, but between my profession and me stood the English language.' He often forgot his text during the shooting of the film. But there was also the problem that British actors 'underplay . . . Me, always striving to achieve the utmost in expressiveness was expected to renounce it.'[69]

Although his English improved and he became fascinated by the language, his accent remained and determined the parts which were offered to him.

Anton Walbrook, Conrad Veidt, Walter Rilla, Dolly Haas, Lucie Mannheim, Oscar Homolka, Frederick Valk and others all had to battle against difficulties of language. Haas was given parts which brought her from Russia or Hungary; on one occasion her accent was supposed to be Australian. Both Valk and Walbrook appeared successfully on the London stage in 1939, the latter in Noël Coward's *Design for Living*. Yet accent remained a determining factor in the parts which they were offered. As it could not be eliminated, it had to be incorporated into their rôles. Wilson Kent wrote that Anton Walbrook

> created a precedent in Hollywood . . . he insisted upon always having a teacher with him 'on the set' to correct the slightest fault in his speech. This practice has now become general with the Continental stars. When he came to Denham, to play opposite Anna Neagle in the Victoria pictures, he sent for the teacher, who while in Vienna, had given him his first English lesson. She was Mrs Edith Williams. Since then she has never been absent from the set during . . . filming. She has, in fact, been chiefly responsible for Anton's English developing into a most charming asset of his screen personality.[70]

Mrs Williams, it turns out, helped a number of other actors with their English, amongst them Conrad Veidt. She saw to it that Walbrook retained a slight accent which differentiated his voice and expressed his personality. Screen acting, in Britain, was not considered to require any special technical skills and was drawn substantially from the theatre.

Veidt, like Walbrook, had gone to Hollywood in the late 1920s, but there had been difficulties with his accent. According to the actor Robert Morley, who worked with Veidt briefly as dialogue director on *Under the Red Robe* in 1937, he 'was a master at delivering lines . . . He always spoke them very slowly when every one else spoke rather fast, and softly when everyone else spoke loudly.'[71] He also knew about lighting and always carried a small pocket mirror in order to see how his face was lit, so that he could make recommendations to the photographer.[72] As with Fritz Kortner and Anton Walbrook, Veidt's rôles were determined by his accent. He frequently played a German or mysterious foreigner; in three films he was a spy.

The contrast between the British theatre-trained voice and that of the European was impossible to avoid. Foreignness had to be both created and explained. Lucie Mannheim was avoiding foreign agents in *The Thirty-Nine Steps* (1935), Peter Lorre was one in *The Man Who Knew too Much* (1934). Anton Walbrook was Anna Neagle's choice to play Prince Albert in *Victoria the Great* (1937). His part was written within a new convention; the foreigner, especially the German, could learn English quickly, but he could never speak it perfectly, and had to be frequently corrected by a teacher or by a surrogate. There was frequently a transition scene in which both languages were spoken prior to the film settling down into English. In *Victoria the Great*, Prince Albert and Prince Ernest (Walter Rilla) are shown in a castle in Germany. Albert is told that he must practise his English; he doesn't want to go to Britain with its dreadful climate and food. The scene has already moved from German into English. A dissolve takes us to the ferry on the English Channel; its passengers are experiencing a particularly stormy crossing. The whole sequence offers the traditional film-welcome to Britain. The princes look as if they have been violently sick, and sing in German to maintain their spirits. It has been raining heavily at Dover, too, and their clothes are ruined. England is seen as a most unwelcoming country to the German who is used to adorable countryside, delightful food, and the music of the great Romantic composers. The scene is comic, a self-deprecating joke, but one which captures the experience of the refugee. Walbrook, as Prince Albert, is inappropriately dressed, he can barely speak the language and he lacks a sense of British etiquette.

The same development can be seen in *Heart's Desire*, which was directed by Paul Stein in 1935 with Richard Tauber. Tauber was hardly the conventional screen hero and invariably played a sensitive oaf, or tragic clown. Here he is charmed by a wealthy socialite to leave a Viennese

Weingarten where she has heard him singing, to appear on the London stage. He is obliged to learn a new language, and his manager leads him through some English phrases. He is sent off, at the railway station, by a team of children and friends who sing in German. As he leaves Vienna for London, there is an immediate clash of expectation and desire. He is obliged to accept the matronly dictates of his new employer who is patronizingly amused by the English he has learnt from his phrase-book. When she expresses her discomfort at his smoking, he politely removes himself from her first class compartment and joins his friends, who are all crowded together in the second class. Assured of a warm welcome, he begins the conversation with a shared joke — a question in English from his phrase-book — 'Is this a smoker?' A few seconds pass as he enjoys his cigar and begins to sing a song by Robert Schumann, full of sadness at the world which he is leaving behind. The countryside and the snow-covered mountains can be seen through the window of the train, blurred to emphasize his sense of loss. His friends are quick to bring out a hamper of food, but the scene is quickly interrupted by the English woman (Frances Wilson) who calls him away to the restaurant car. The beautiful scenery and the comradeship are quickly replaced, not by a shot of Dover with the rain bucketing down, but by a high angle view as Tauber looks down on the unattractive traffic-ridden Piccadilly Circus.

One film after another has a sequence in which English and German are spoken only for English to be insisted upon. *The Spy in Black* (1939), Emeric Pressburger's second film for Alexander Korda, has the obligatory transitional scene which enables the film to move from German into English. Valerie Hobson, in this case, instructs her German visitor in the English language. Korda, who had Veidt under contract, had found some difficulty in finding him an appropriate part. Pressburger, therefore, created one which enabled Veidt to be placed in an English film whilst retaining features from his rôles in German cinema. Powell put it this way: 'I knew all the German Expressionist films he had done and . . . [Veidt] said ". . . let him wear black overalls as the motorcyclist, make him a black figure" . . . The way he comes out is just as much the myth of Veidt as the myth of the German spy.'[73] Pressburger makes use of the possibilities arising from a situation where one person speaks faltering English and the other speaks it perfectly. Valerie Hobson is a schoolteacher and a double agent, Veidt's apparent collaborator in the Orkneys. He is a U-boat commander who has just been landed on the coast. They make contact by a signal when she leaves an oil lamp briefly in an uncurtained window. When they meet, they establish their credentials by exchanging a few words in German but she loses no time in insisting solely on English and in correcting Veidt's pronunciation, especially of the word 'butter'.

To some extent, the amusing exchange of pleasantries which takes place reflects Pressburger's own struggles with the English language.

The difficulties of adjustment to Britain and its language were never entirely solved by Pressburger, and this theme reappears throughout his career. When Anton Walbrook, as the German refugee Theo Kretschmar-Schuldorff, in *The Life and Death of Colonel Blimp* (1943) arrives at immigration control to be interrogated by A.E. Matthews, he feels that he is being given marks for an adequate response. The story, which is full of imaginative devices, spans half a century; Pressburger, in his most individual film script, is making manifest the anxieties of a refugee from Nazi Germany. The patriotic, exuberant army officer of the First World War is now noticeably down-at-heel and depressed. In a uniquely personal statement, which is spoken without interruption, Theo explains why he has left Germany for Britain. He (unlike Pressburger himself) was not obliged to leave Germany, he had nothing to fear from Hitler. When Matthews comments that it took him some considerable time to discover where he stood with regard to Hitler, Theo points out that the British, too, seem to have been in no great hurry. When a slightly embarrassed Matthews says 'Quite right', standing, as he is, by a desk, there is little difference between his rôle and that of Valerie Hobson's in *The Spy in Black*. He is awarding Theo credits for a pertinent response. Pressburger's comment on this sequence, in 1970, emphasizes the intensity of his feelings:

> I who lived for quite a while in Germany and had German friends, I wanted to express this feeling of mine that though my mother had died in the concentration camp and I was pre-conditioned about the whole thing, I always believed . . . that there are also good Germans . . . who didn't have to go away from Germany but chose to go away . . . I had that kind of experience [in immigration control] obviously. England is a very, very difficult country for foreigners to come to. Of course, when I came my intention was to stay in England but you have to lie straight away but you're not only dying to stay in England, you can't go anywhere else. And you know to the question, 'How long do you intend to stay here?' you mustn't say, 'I intend to stay forever,' . . . You want to be correct in everything but you are forced to lie straight away so you answer, 'Six months', and then you extend the six months . . . I believe that anyone that comes to the country under the same circumstances that I did cannot love the Immigration Officers.[74]

There are other examples of this in Pressburger's screenwriting: *A Canterbury Tale* (1944) and *I Know Where I'm Going* are conventionally seen as examples of Powell's neo-romantic sensibility,[75] but they also disclose Pressburger's sensitivity to being a stranger in an unfamiliar land with a language and culture to which he is unaccustomed.

In *A Canterbury Tale* the stranger is an American GI, played by a real one, Sgt. John Sweet. He too finds himself bewildered in a foreign environment. Officially, the GI was a welcome guest in Britain, and films and newsreels emphasized that the British and the Americans were not separated by either a common language or by different social conventions. Pressburger incorporates a significant variation in this script and divides the problems of language and culture between two characters. Allison Smith (Sheila Sim), a 'towny' but now a land girl, has the language but not the culture; Bob Johnson, the GI, is, it turns out, a country lad and has the culture but not the language. The film, which was shortened at the time of its release, has recently been restored and is now greatly admired by enthusiasts for the Powell–Pressburger films. It nevertheless remains an awkward and aimless film constructed round a thin story of a group of contemporary pilgrims to Canterbury. They are side-tracked into attempting to discover just who is pouring glue over the heads of girls and frightening them from the streets at night. 'It was one of Emeric's most complicated ideas,' Powell observed, 'but the story itself had an impossible premise.'[76] It contains, however, some of Powell's favourite sequences, one of which 'was beautifully written by Emeric' and set in a blacksmith's workshop. It is one of the most remarkable in the film conveying an interest in the collision of cultures of which Pressburger was extremely conscious, shot with subtlety, without any artificial lighting, by Erwin Hillier.

In *I Know Where I'm Going*, which was made towards the end of 1944, a prissy English girl (Wendy Hiller) travels to Scotland with the intention of marrying a rich man, the head of Consolidated Chemical Industries. She finds herself in a country where she understands neither the language nor the conventions of the culture. Like *A Canterbury Tale*, it was at one level a consideration of the question 'What are we fighting for?' and it came naturally to Pressburger. It 'burst out. . . . I wrote the full script . . . in four days'.[77] Wendy Hiller is transported to Scotland in a montage which rather consciously captures Powell's fondness for *The Wizard of Oz* (it also helps illustrate the relative contributions of Powell and Pressburger to their films). For Powell, it re-creates a cinematic experience from an influential film; for Pressburger, it is a further attempt to exorcise the painful experience of his forced flight to Britain. The moment Wendy Hiller arrives on the Isle of Mull we see an interesting example of the way in which an émigré writer and an English director are able to harmonize their interests. The brilliant, almost show-off sequence of the journey from London to the island, gives way to a reflective of discovery for the protagonist. Gaelic may substitute for English as the incomprehensible language in *I Know Where I'm Going*, but the same sense of bewilderment and difficulty is conveyed. Underneath the stand-offishness of the character portrayed by Wendy Hiller lies a yearning to understand and belong.

The 1936 remake of D.W. Griffith's 1919 *Broken Blossoms* shows how the experience of the émigré can be closely reflected in the films of the period. A comparison of the two versions is especially instructive as Griffith's original film served partly as the base from which the fresh screenplay was written. There was some speculation that Griffith himself would direct it and he did, indeed, travel to England. But in the end it became the first film of the émigré theatre director, Hans Brahm, who, under the name John Brahm, had a Hollywood and a television career. Brahm's then wife, Dolly Haas, played Lucy Burrows, and the film was shot by Curt Courant, another eminent European photographer, who had worked with Jean Renoir and Marcel Carné. It is, therefore, possible to account for at least some of the differences between the two films. Brahm's version has a distinctly European appearance and could have been lit for Fritz Lang. The crowd scenes, with their sense of mob violence and with figures, especially women, screaming out that the little Chinese missionary is a spy, suggests the same influence.

In Griffith's version, the long and beautiful opening shows the Chinese Buddhist as being convinced of the need to travel to Europe as a missionary, when he is confronted by a group of brawling sailors. The journey is not shown at all and neither is his whole period of adjustment to living in the slums of Limehouse, which covers many years. In Brahm's version, from Emlyn Williams's screenplay, the violence is experienced only in England and it is directed at him as an unwelcome foreigner. His arrival at Tilbury is conventionally wet and his clothes are quickly spoiled. The English take advantage of him, he is soon tricked out of his money, he experiences racial abuse, and is unjustifiably sent to prison for inciting a disturbance. The magistrate makes the recommendation that, after serving his sentence, he returns home. The parallels are unmistakable. He never settles happily in England. Later, a man enters the shop in which the disillusioned missionary is working and chortles over a Chinese proverb, once it is translated for him. 'Some of these foreigners have good sense' he observes as he leaves. Artistically, it is no match for Griffith's film, but it is extremely close to the experience of the refugee from Europe.

The Second World War and the Triumph of British Realism

A number of films, in spite of active censorship, reflected, rather than commented, indirectly on the situation of both the refugee in Britain and the situation in Germany. *The Times*, for example, identified the correspondence between the story of Karl Grune's *Abdul the Damned*, the rise of Hitler, and the killing of Roehm.[78] Writers have commented on the relevance of *Secret Agent* (1936) which Alfred Hitchcock directed for Michael Balcon, but the topicality should not be exaggerated. In 1937, some play was also made by the trade press of a scene in *Knight Without Armour* in which refugees throw themselves on the railway line as a train steams round the corner. Writing in 1954, Kurt Singer made further observations about films of the period:

> Long before Charlie Chaplin had done a parody of Hitler in *The Great Dictator*, Laughton had portrayed a ruler gone berserk in his Nero [in Cecil B. De Mille's 1933 *The Sign of the Cross*]. Now he went to Italy to finish *I Claudius* . . . It was a timely story dealing with the assassinations and violent seizure of power in the Roman Empire . . . He played Claudius, the usurper who is later proclaimed a god, as a little man with a stutter and a lame leg . . .[79]

If Singer stretches the reader's credulity it is only because his associations seem tenuous, for it is hardly surprising that films with which the exile was associated should reveal his concerns as well as offer evidence of his background. Clive Coultass observes, more modestly, that even the 'period' feature films like *Lady Hamilton* or the Shakespeare film *Henry V* reflect 'the ethos of a nation at war'.[80]

As we have seen, these themes are not expressed directly and few would argue that they were a significant component in British films of the period. Michael Balcon, the most significant British-born producer, who was deeply concerned about events in Germany under Hitler, later admitted· 'These were, for example, the days of Mussolini's Abyssinian War, The Civil War in Spain with all its implications for the future . . . one cannot escape the conclusion that in our own work we could have been more profitably engaged. Hardly a single film of the period reflects the agony of the times.'[81] Graham Greene's story, for example, about 'a Spanish Government agent who comes to London on a mission during the Civil War and finds the war has followed him here', was considered too 'dangerous' by Korda's 'outfit'.[82] It was later published as *The Confidential Agent*. However charming or interesting some pre-war films were, no British film of the period has the immediacy of John Sommerfield's *May Day* or Murray Constantine's (i.e. Katherine Burdekin's) political fantasy *Swastika Night*, both of which were published in the years before the war. There is no cinematic equivalent to George Orwell's *Coming Up for Air* or to Ernest Borneman's *Love Story*, there is no hero of the screen with the perception of George Bowling or with the anxieties of Joe Banyan. After August 1939, previously sensitive subjects became more acceptable. Some of them made it to the screen, but, unsurprisingly, they were designed to

159

reinforce prevailing myths about Britain and Germany.

By the outbreak of war the European producer was, like Max Schach, out of business or, like Korda, in America. The feature film industry had been significantly made up of Europeans who began to experience internment or other difficulties and interruptions in employment. Some undertook official responsibilities; Mischa Spoliansky, Lucie Mannheim, Herbert Lom, Gerard Heinz and Walter Rilla took time out to work for the BBC on propaganda broadcasts to Germany, such as *Aus der freien Welt*. Erwin Hillier moved between being an ambulance driver and a cameraman; for a short while before the battle of Arnhem, advantage was taken of his fluency in German and he was dropped behind enemy lines in Holland. It is now well established that Alexander Korda, who was in the USA during the early part of the war, played a rôle as a courier and in the gathering of Intelligence information for the British government.[83]

Coultass, like other writers, notices an increasing sense of authenticity and reality in British feature films, although he retains many reservations about some of them. The sense of 'authenticity' can be related to the decline in the dominance of the European film-maker. As we have seen, there was a continuing debate in the 1930s about the nature of British film. Graham Greene's now famous review of *The Marriage of Corbal* in 1936 makes the issue clear. He asks whether it can be considered an English film at all, directed as it was by 'Karl Grune and F. Brunn, photographed by Otto Kanturek, and edited by E. Stokvis [*sic*], with a cast which includes Nils Asther, Ernst Deutsch, and the American Noah Beery.'[84] Greene argues that there are perfectly good 'English technicians capable of producing films of a high enough standard to take their place', technicians who had made *Song of Ceylon, The Voice of Britain, The Turn of the Tide, Nightmail* and *Midshipman Easy*. He, perhaps unwittingly, identifies the documentary movement as offering an alternative vision, a more British one than that of the exile 'with their ignorance of our language and culture'.

After 1939, a British interpretation of realism gradually asserted itself. It was seen to be closer to the social and political requirements of the period than the European fantasies of film directors like Paul Stein, Friedrich Feher and Karl Grune. 'The documentary movement', wrote Michael Balcon, 'was in my view the greatest single influence in British film production and more than anything helped establish a national style . . . In the war, denuded as we were of so many of our people, I naturally turned to the documentary school of film-makers, and as a result Cavalcanti joined Ealing . . .'[85] Cavalcanti, ironically, was not British, but nor was he strictly an exile, having been born in Rio de Janeiro. He had been educated in Europe and had been an influential designer and director in Paris before joining the GPO Film Unit in 1934. He ran the unit after Grierson's departure for Canada, but, as an alien, was anyway unacceptable to the government once war had begun. He was clear that Ealing was a continuation of the documentary tradition, as he saw it.[86] He brought a number of figures, all British, from documentary into features and helped initiate a new generation of feature film-makers. The documentary film-maker Sir Arthur Elton made the point clearly that the 'old school' was effectively left behind: 'Korda, who was a wonderful man, didn't finally come into the battle, which was between the old and the new. The attack was to get the Ministry of Information to base its policies on realism rather than 1914 romance.'[87]

The European had dominated British film production in the 1930s due to a number of interlacing historical features. There was no single dominant reason. The fragile structure of the film industry and its traditional links with — even its dependency on — Germany to support its own production, were factors. There were the aesthetic considerations too which were not fully understood. Britain was an open market for the Europeans, many of whom had been despatched unwillingly into exile. The British had made films in Germany during the 1920s; in the 1930s, Europeans made their films in Britain. The collapse of the film production companies after 1937 reduced or eliminated the machinations of figures like Schach and Korda. The synthesis of the documentary ideal with the conventions of narrative film-making during the war made the European contribution less relevant, whilst it gave the British film-maker confidence. J. Arthur Rank was emerging as the most powerful figure in British film production, and Ealing was developing its own character with a home-grown and homogenous team of young film-makers. The situation for technicians eased; some enlisted in the armed forces; there was a decline in the number of Americans working in Britain. In spite of a shortage of film stock, there were increasing opportunities in features and documentaries because of the financial involvement of the Government. For security reasons, the émigré was sometimes excluded from certain areas of film work. Some were interned for part or the whole of the war. In short, the war offered opportunities to many in the British film industry.

For a while the European and the British approaches to film production co-existed, the former closer to the 'pure cinema' of the 1920s, the latter nearer to the aesthetic of the British documentary. Powell and Pressburger, for example, continued throughout the war and took their essentially European style through to 1950 and *The Tales of Hoffmann*. It was their last film for Korda and one, it will be remembered, which Powell now sees to have its roots in Feher's *The Robber Symphony*, produced a quarter of a century earlier. *The Tales of Hoffmann* is the high water mark of the German tradition in British films. It gives way to a cinema of class and social concern, with films like *Mandy* (1952), *The Cruel Sea* and *Genevieve* (both 1953), and various adaptations of classic plays and novels; a continuation, in fact, of the tradition of British film-making which had been encouraged by Cavalcanti. His own films, *Champagne Charlie* (1944) and *Nicholas Nickelby* (1947) — as does *Genevieve* — not surprisingly retain something of a French appearance.[88]

By the mid-1950s television began to hold the centre ground, within the vision which had been established by Sir John Reith for the BBC. It encouraged an aesthetic and a bourgeois educational function which was closer to the documentary than to the classic feature film, and effectively brought the European influence on British film production to an end.

Notes

1. Thorold Dickinson, *A Discovery of Cinema*, London, 1971, p. 66.
2. George Perry, *The Great British Picture Show*, London, 1974, p. 76. Ernest Betts writes, similarly, in *The Film Business*, London, 1973: 'Production during the 1930s is largely identified with the work of Alexander Korda who may be said to have created or re-created the image of British films during that decade.'
3. Ralph Bond, 'Cinema in the Thirties', in Jon Clark *et al.* (eds), *Culture and Crisis in the Thirties*, London, 1979, p. 224. Bond is being unfair and is exaggerating. As an active and influential member of the ACT, he is being consistent.
4. Alexander Esway, a Hungarian, was something of an exception. He had directed before coming to England, where he made a number of shorts and features. *Thunder in the City*, which he produced, was considered by Graham Greene in *The Spectator* (19 Mar. 1937) to be, almost certainly, the 'worst English film of the quarter'. The story persisted that Esway had come to Britain with a testimonial from Emil Jannings which described him as reliable and quick, which were references to his skills as a chauffeur.
5. Clive Coultass, 'British Feature Films in the Second World War', *Journal of Contemporary History*, vol. 19, 1984, p. 10. In fact, two-thirds of cine-technicians were called up and feature film production was, at around sixty films a year, just under half of the 1938 figure.
6. Donald Spoto, *The Life of Alfred Hitchcock*, London, 1983, p. 68.
7. Paul Rotha, *The Film Till Now*, London, 1930, p. 208.
8. John Grierson, in *New Britain*, 18 Oct. 1933.
9. Siegfried Kracauer, *From Caligari to Hitler*, Princeton, 1947, p. 135.
10. Rachel Low, *Film Making in 1930s Britain*, London, 1985, pp. 91–4.
11. *The Kinematograph Year Book*, 1935, p. 21.
12. *Kinematograph Weekly*, 13 Aug. 1936, p. 12.
13. Ivor Montagu, 'The Decline of the German Film Trade', in John Paddy Carstairs (ed.), *Movie Merry Go Round*, London, 1937, pp. 196–205.

14. See, for example, '"Patriotism with Profit": British Imperial Cinema in the 1930s', in James Curran and Vincent Porter (eds), *British Cinema History*, London, 1983, pp. 245–56.
15. Paul Tabori, *Alexander Korda*, London, 1959, p. 203.
16. Korda, for example, was sensitive to the unsettled political situation and employed Sir Robert Vansittart and Winston Churchill in the late 1930s. Vansittart is described, working on *The Thief of Bagdad*, in Miklós Rózsa, *Double Life: The Autobiography of Miklós Rózsa*, Tunbridge Wells, 1982, pp. 80–5. He was 'chief diplomatic adviser to the British Foreign Office . . . the Grey Eminence, the power behind the throne'. He would be called to the telephone and return 'ashen-faced'.
17. Graham Greene, *The Pleasure Dome*, ed. John Russell Taylor, Oxford, 1980, p. 218.
18. Karol Kulik, *Alexander Korda: The Man Who Could Work Miracles*, London, 1975, p. 208.
19. Tony Aldgate, 'Comedy, Class and Containment: The British Domestic Cinema of the 1930s', in Curran and Porter, *British Cinema History*, p. 270.
20. Anthony Aldgate, *Cinema and History: British Newsreels and the Spanish Civil War*, London, 1974, pp. 54–64. Tony Aldgate, 'Ideological Consensus in British Feature Films, 1935–47', in K.R.M. Short (ed.), *Feature Films as History*, London, 1979.
21. P.R.O. LAB 8/75 136289.
22. Andrew Higson, '"Britain's Outstanding Contribution to the Film": The Documentary-realist Tradition', in Charles Barr (ed.), *All Our Yesterdays*, London, 1986, pp. 74–5. Basil Wright, too, in commenting on three 'educational' documentary films (*Housing Problems*, *Enough to Eat* and *The Smoke Menace*), writes: 'the films . . . did, in my opinion, have their own particular aesthetic . . .' See Basil Wright, *The Long View*, London, 1974, p. 113.
23. The only émigré to find more than passing employment in documentary films was the composer Ernst Hermann Meyer, who was brought in by Cavalcanti as an expert in the anthropological use of sound. In 1948, he was appointed professor and director of the institute of musicology at Humboldt University, Berlin (GDR). Lotte Reiniger made 'silhouette films' for the GPO, but was outside the movement.
24. *Kinematograph Weekly*, 3 Jan. 1929, p. 50.
25. *Kinematograph Weekly*, 20 June 1929, p. 47.
26. *Kinematograph Weekly*, 13 Mar. 1930, p. 34.
27. *Kinematograph Weekly*, 29 June 1939, p. 13.
28. *Kinematograph Weekly*, 22 Jan. 1931, p. 69.
29. *Kinematograph Weekly*, 12 June 1931, p. 20. Becker left Britain soon after, to become managing director of Kuchenmeister Maatschapij fur Sprechend Film, the organization which controlled the film-sound companies, Tobis Films Sonores of Paris, and Tobis of America. Hitchcock and Saville both appreciated the qualities of German artists and technicians.
30. Cameron McCabe, *The Face on the Cutting Room Floor*, London, 1937; new edition (with Afterword and interview with Borneman), 1986; Ernest J. Borneman, 'Sound Rhythm and the Film', *Sight and Sound*, vol. 3, no. 10, 1934, pp. 65–7; Ernest Borneman, *Die Urszene: Das prägende Kindheitserlebnis und seine Folgen*, Frankfurt am Main, 1977.
31. Adrian Brunel, *Nice Work*, London, 1949, p. 180. Brunel, like others, found himself with divided loyalties. Dickinson was being shut out, but on another 'assignment . . . *The Return of the Scarlet Pimpernel* . . .' there was 'an excellent producer . . . in the person of Arnold Pressburger' and much of its effectiveness was due to Lazare Meerson, 'that genius amongst art-directors, as well as to the photography of "Mutz" Green [*sic*] [Mutz Greenbaum, later Max Greene]'. Ibid., p. 181.
32. *Screen International*, 12 Feb. 1977, p. 10; interview with author, 4 August 1986. The Two films which influenced him most were *Caligari* and *Ivan the Terrible*.
33. *Kinematograph Weekly*, 11 Feb. 1932, p. 33.
34. Michael Powell, interview with author, 22 September 1970, in Kevin Gough-Yates, *Michael Powell in Collaboration with Emeric Pressburger*, London, 1971.
35. Michael Powell, interview with author, 30 August 1973, in Kevin Gough-Yates, *Michael Powell*, Brussels, 1973.

36. Christopher Challis, interview with Rex Stapleton, 7 January 1984, in Rex Stapleton, *A Matter of Powell and Pressburger: Group Dynamics and Notions of Authorship*, MA Thesis, Polytechnic of Central London, 1984, p. 17.
37. Quoted in Léon Barsacq, *Caligari's Cabinet and Other Grand Illusions: A History of Film Design*, revised edn, New York, 1976, p. 226. Meerson died in London in 1938.
38. Ibid., p. 90ff.
39. Ibid., p. 228.
40. Michael Powell, *A Life in Movies*, London, 1986, p. 582.
41. *Kinematograph Weekly*, 8 July 1939, p. 29.
42. Miklós Rózsa, *Double Life*, p. 84.
43. Basil Dean, *Mind's Eye*, London, 1973, p. 249. On p. 134, he uses similar phrasing in describing Archie Pitt, the manager and, for a short while, husband of Gracie Fields: 'Archie Pitt was a sad, cautious little man with a commonplace mind and a shrewd idea of the commercial value of the wife he had acquired.'
44. Michael Korda, *Charmed Lives*, London, 1980, p. 75–8. Michael Korda provides many examples of Korda's apparent indifference to money.
45. Edward Beddington Behrens, *Look Back Look Forward*, London, 1963. p. 85.
46. Alan Wood, *Mr. Rank*, London, 1952, p. 93. Early British publicity material on Schach and Grune attempted to disguise the Emelka story behind the later political situation. Schach did not come directly from Germany to England.
47. Hans Feld, interview with author, 12 July 1986. Feld had previously exposed Schach in *Film-Kurier*.
48. *Kinematograph Weekly*, 24 June 1937, p. 34. It was probably accepting him at the estimation of his own publicity department.
49. Monja Danischewsky, *White Russian, Red Face*, London, 1966, p. 105.
50. Paul Tabori, *Alexander Korda*, p. 183.
51. Ibid., p. 16. See also Sarah Street, 'Alexander Korda, Prudential Assurance and British Film Finance in the 1930s', *Historical Journal of Film, Radio and Television*, vol. 6, no. 2, 1986, pp. 161–79. Street, in a devastating foray, documents many examples of Korda's financial impudence. He would borrow from the Prudential and blatantly spend the same amount on a gift for Merle Oberon (whom he married in 1939). London Film Productions was widely considered to be mismanaged.
52. Harold Wilson, *Memoirs: The Making of a Prime Minister, 1916–64*, London, 1986, p. 105.
53. Sir Robert Bruce Lockhart, *The Diaries of Sir Robert Bruce Lockhart*, London, 1973, p. 392. Bayliss-Smith was on the board of some of Schach's companies. Bruce Lockhart's well known anti-Semitism did not prevent him exploring the possibilities of working for Korda after the war. He eventually decided against becoming an adviser to Korda at £12,000 a year. 'Films are unclean and having anything to do with them is moral and physical degradation' he wrote to his son on 8 January, 1948. See *The Diaries of Sir Robert Bruce Lockhart, Volume Two, 1939–65*, London, 1980, p. 646.
54. P.R.O. LAB 8/75 136289.
55. *Kinematograph Weekly*, 20 Apr. 1944, p. 3.
56. Rachel Low, *Film Making*, p. 196.
57. *Kinematograph Weekly*, 20 Aug. 1936. p. 39.
58. *Kinematograph Weekly*, 26 Nov. 1936, p. 37.
59. *World Film News*, 3 Sept. 1936, pp. 20–1. Information on authorship provided by its editor, Hans Feld, interview with author, 12 July 1986.
60. *Kinematograph Weekly*, 3 Sept. 1936, p. 5.
61. *The Fascist*, Nov. 1932 and Jan. 1933. *The Fascist* was the newspaper of the Imperial Fascist League. Leese, a fanatical anti-Semite, lacked the qualities of a political leader.
62. *The Fascist*, Nov. 1932.
63. Arthur Henry Lane, *The Alien Menace*, London, 1934.
64. Richard Griffiths, *Fellow Travellers of the Right*, Oxford, 1983, p. 83.
65. Paul Rotha, *The Film Till Now*, p. 226. Phrasing is slightly modified in later editions.
66. Erwin Hillier, interview with author, 16 April 1987.
67. Michael Powell, in discussion with author at Barbican Centre, Conference as part of

exhibition *A Paradise Lost*, 1 June 1987. Hillier matched studio and location photography so skilfully that no one noticed that its leading actor, Roger Livesey, did not venture to the locations at all.

68. Salka Viertel, *The Kindness of Strangers*, New York, 1964, p. 202. She must be referring to another play by Margaret Kennedy, *Escape Me Never*, in which Bergner played Gemma Jones. Bergner had appeared as Tessa in the *Constant Nymph* at the Königgrätzer Theater, Berlin in 1927.

69. Quoted in Marion Berghahn, *Continental Britons: German-Jewish Refugees from Nazi Germany*, Oxford, 1988, p. 105.

70. Wilson Kent, *The Millgate*, Oct. 1938, p. 74.

71. Robert Morley and Sewell Stokes, *Responsible Gentleman*, London, 1966, p. 89f.

72. Erwin Hillier, interview with author, 16 April 1987.

73. Michael Powell, interview with author, in Gough-Yates, *Michael Powell in Collaboration with Emeric Pressburger*.

74. Emeric Pressburger, interview with author, ibid.

75. See, for example, David Mellor (ed.), *A Paradise Lost: The Neo-Romantic Imagination in Britain 1935–55*, Exh. cat., London, Barbican Art Gallery, 1987.

76. Michael Powell, interview with author, in Gough-Yates, *Michael Powell in Collaboration with Emeric Pressburger*.

77. Emeric Pressburger, interview with author, Ibid. Pressburger, however, would have been unable to compose precise and idiomatic dialogue. It was generally written by Powell. On *49th Parallel* (1941) it was written by Rodney Ackland.

78. *The Times*, 3 Mar. 1935.

79. Kurt Singer, *The Laughton Story*, Philadelphia, 1954, p. 176. *I Claudius* was, in fact, never finished. It was abandoned at the time when Merle Oberon was injured in a car accident.

80. Clive Coultass, 'British Feature Films', p. 10.

81. Michael Balcon, *Michael Balcon Presents . . . A Lifetime of Films*, London, 1969, p. 99. Aldgate in 'Ideological Consensus in British Feature Films, 1935–47', is certainly not naïve but he considers films like Michael Powell's *Red Ensign* (1934) and John Baxter's *Doss House* (1933) to be 'moderately significant' in addressing social and political issues. This is the opposite of my view. I feel that they are only significant in the manner in which they avoid them.

82. Julian Maclaren-Ross, *Memoirs of the Forties*, Harmondsworth, 1984, p. 25.

83. See, especially, H. Montgomery Hyde, *Room 3603: The Story of the British Intelligence Centre in New York during World War II*, New York, 1962; and his *Secret Intelligence Agent*, London, 1982. Korda's involvement with British Intelligence before the war is mentioned in Christopher Andrew, *Secret Service: The Making of the British Intelligence Community*, London, 1985, and colourfully detailed in Anthony Read and David Fisher, *Colonel Z*, London, 1984.

84. Included in Graham Greene, *The Pleasure Dome* pp. 78–9. Greene writes: 'may one express the wish that *émigrés* would set up trades in which their ignorance of our language and culture was less of a handicap. . . . there is nothing to prevent an English film unit being completely staffed by technicians of foreign blood. We have saved our country from American competition only to surrender it to a far more alien control . . . it is not English money that calls the tune, and it is only natural that compatriots should find jobs for each other . . .' His tone is similar to Grierson's in *World Film News* writing shortly afterwards (see note 59).

85. Michael Balcon, *Michael Balcon Presents . . .*, p. 130.

86. Alberto Cavalcanti, '"Alberto Cavalcanti", interviewed by Jim Hillier, Alan Lovell and Sam Rohdie', *Screen*, vol. 13, no. 3, 1972, p. 45.

87. Elizabeth Sussex. *The Rise and Fall of the British Documentary*, London, 1975, p. 120. The 'battle' between the 'old and the new' of the cinema finds its literary equivalent in the arguments surrounding *Mass Observation*, which was launched in 1937. See the interesting study by Stuart Laing, 'Presenting "Things as They Are": John Sommerfield's *May Day* and Mass Observation', in Frank Gloversmith, (ed.), *Class Culture and Social Change:*

A New View of the 1930s, Brighton, 1980.

88. The director of *Genevieve*, Henry (Heinz) Cornelius, although born in South Africa, had studied under Max Reinhardt. He left Berlin in 1933 and arrived in England via Paris in 1935. He was assistant editor on the René Clair film for Korda, *The Ghost Goes West* (1935), and Clair's influence is noticeable in most of the films which he directed.

Rudolf Laban and Kurt Jooss in Exile
Their Relationship and Diverse Influence on Dance in Britain

VALERIE PRESTON-DUNLOP

Introduction

Rudolf Laban (1879–1958), dance reformer, movement philosopher, and 'father of European modern dance', and Kurt Jooss (1901–1979), the leading German modern dance choreographer, were the two figures in dance whose careers as artists were interrupted by the Third Reich but who continued to work in their chosen art form in exile in Britain. The interplay of their careers, the manner in which each dealt with his exile, and their different legacies make fascinating reading. The Elmhirsts of Dartington Hall and the climate of interest in the arts and in education in Britain, the problems and opportunities created by the war, provide a context for the story of their two lives.

The overall pattern can be summarized thus: Kurt Jooss arrived in Britain at the height of his theatrical success. He attempted and, in the main, managed to maintain his company and his choreographic output and to build his international reputation throughout the war. He returned to Germany to re-establish his school and company in Essen after the cessation of hostilities. Rudolf Laban arrived a destitute and broken man. He made no initial impact at all, but eventually changed not only the face of dance in Britain but also the place of the study of human gesture throughout the cultures of the Western world. He remained in Britain until his death.

Rudolf Laban's Career to 1937

Laban had been fully involved in the arts revolution at the beginning of the twentieth century, first in Paris and Vienna (1900–10) as a painter,

167

then in Munich, Zurich and Ascona (1900–19) as a teacher, formulating a programme which set out to liberate dance from music and to establish it as an autonomous art form. The vocabulary of dance had to be freed from the limitations of the traditional steps of the ballet and the restrictions of conventional mime. He set out to find the organizing principles of movement from which the new dance forms could develop. He also realized that until the uplifting spirit of dance was re-kindled, dance was destined to remain an emasculated and marginal art form, a position to which it had been reduced by the Industrial Revolution and by nineteenth-century theatre practice. Laban therefore presented and promoted dance as an art form for both men and women and as participatory, festive actitivity for the whole population.

In 1920, Laban opened a school and started his own dance company in Stuttgart, and was simultaneously guest choreographer for the *Tannhäuser* production at the National Theatre in Mannheim. It was here that he created his first major innovative theatre piece, *Die Geblendeten*, using both the theatre's ballet group and dancers from his company. He continued his theatrical output in Hamburg. His large touring group, the Tanzbühne Laban, worked together until the end of 1924. With them he created full-scale works, such as *Fausts Erlösung* (1922), *Schwingende Tempel* (1922), *Gaukelei* (1923) and *Komödie* (1923). Unable to keep the group going continuously, he nevertheless created *Terpsichore* (1925), *Narrenspiegel* (1926), *Don Juan* (1926), *Ritterballett* (1927), *Nacht* (1927) and *Orpheus* (1927) for short seasons. With his smaller experimental group, the Kammertanzbühne Laban, he and Dussia Bereska created a large repertoire of less ambitious works for a regular and appreciative audience, the best known being the group comedy *Oben und Unten*, the fairy tale *Drachentöterei* and the exotic solo *Orchidée*.

All of Laban's works were experimental. He introduced group improvisation, dance without music, movement pieces with speech choir and percussion played by the dancers. The style of the works ranged from the grotesque and satiric to the ornamental. He gave the same dance with different costumes or with different combinations of dancers, sometimes interchanging the gender of performers. He used unusual performance spaces as well as traditional theatre venues. Above all, he explored ways of finding new movement material, incorporating mundane gestures and small behavioural movements into his dance vocabulary. His works shocked, amused, annoyed and amazed. They were not always well finished, for his creativity was such that once he had overcome the main challenge he left his dancers to see the production through, while he focused on the next creative problem.

Laban (a 'volcano' of energy according to the renowned ballet master,

Aurel Milloss), went on to open schools in the major German cities and in Paris, Rome, Zagreb and Prague. He established a new art form for amateurs, the movement choir, for which he created celebratory group works: *Lichtwende* (1923), *Prometheus* (1923), *Agamemnons Tod* (1924), *Dämmernde Rhythmen* (1926), *Titan* (1927) and *Alltag und Fest* (1929). A major achievement was the creation of a workable notation system for dance, published in 1928. He wrote five books on dance, organized dance congresses, undertook lecture tours, and became the controversial figurehead of the new German dance, with his pupil Mary Wigman as its 'high priestess'.[1]

In 1930, Laban was appointed to the prime position of Ballet Master of the Prussian State Theatres in Berlin. For four seasons he choreographed for the Berlin Opera, and in 1930 and 1931 for the Bayreuth Wagner Festival. It was in this position that Laban found himself an employee of the National Socialist Ministry of Propaganda, under the Reichstheaterkammer. In 1934 he became director of the newly formed Deutsche Tanzbühne, where the Nazi régime hoped to maximize his talents and the publicity value of his name to promote German dance culture internationally. Over the next two years, during which he was appointed head of the Meisterwerkstätten für Tanz, an uneasy and increasingly unpleasant battle of wits developed. The dance festival associated with the Berlin Olympics of August 1936 was the scene for his final confrontation with the authorities. Goebbels's diary reveals that he realized Laban would not conform to the Nazi dictates for the arts. Laban was dismissed and placed under detention. In November 1937, he managed to get out of Germany to Paris, his monumental career in ruins, a refugee in physical and mental *extremis*.

Kurt Jooss's Career to 1934

Jooss, as a music and drama student in Stuttgart, encountered Laban in 1920 and joined his school. He served his apprenticeship as a performer and choreographer in the Tanzbühne Laban, his exceptional talent for dance theatre being evident immediately. He stayed with Laban in Hamburg until 1924, a short period, but one that was seminal to his career. With Sigurd Leeder, a dancer in Hamburg, he decided to set up his own company, the Neue Tanzbühne, when Laban's full-time company became financially non-viable. Both men felt the need for more formal techniques than those used by Laban. Therefore, after studying ballet in Paris and Vienna, they began to explore the choreographic possibilities of combining Laban's choreological experiments with the basic ballet vocabulary. Moving to Essen in 1927, as director of the Laban Hauptschule (today the Tanzabteilung of the Folkwanghochschule), Jooss's distinctive choreographic style gradually emerged with works such as *Pavane* (1929) and the first version of *The Prodigal Son* (1931), works which gave him opportunity to find means of stating his social consciousness in dance. Meanwhile, Leeder developed his outstanding talents as a teacher, systematizing the Jooss/Leeder dance technique.

The turning point in Jooss's career came in 1932, when he won the prestigious International Choreographic Competition in Paris with his now-famous dance drama *Der grüne Tisch* (The Green Table). Opportunities for engagements opened up immediately. But the ballet's satirical comments on war-mongering politicians soon brought him into conflict with the Nazi authorities. He was given the choice of dismissing the Jewish artists working in his company, or of resigning his post. Jooss decided to leave the country. In 1934, taking his whole company with him, he managed to get out to Holland and keep the company together, except for a short, temporary period.

Also in 1934, Sigurd Leeder, with the staff and twenty-three students of the Folkwangschule in Essen, had accepted the invitation of Dorothy and Leonard Elmhirst to come to Dartington Hall, in Devon. The Elmhirsts' support and generosity were profound; they were instrumental in setting up the new Jooss/Leeder School of Dance at Dartington. Soon Jooss, too, came to Dartington to begin his time of exile. Dance studios were built, and also a house for Jooss, his wife Aino Siimola, and their daughter. Rehearsal spaces were then added, and he was soon able to re-form the company.

Laban and Jooss at Dartington: The Beginning of the War

The Elmhirsts' relationship with dance was long-standing. Ever since they had bought and refurbished the medieval hall and built the surrounding courtyard and theatre, dancers had been in residence, along with actors, musicians and all manner of craftsmen. The Elmhirsts' imaginative vision for the estate and its place in the Devon community was enabled by Dorothy's wealth and philanthropic disposition, and by Leonard's experience of rural living gained during his sojourn in India.[2] The Elmhirsts' approach to both the arts and industry reflected this experience.

The invitation to Jooss was not, therefore, extraordinary, but an application of the Elmhirsts' general philosophy to the professional dance world. The company was expected to be, and indeed was, part of the community, performing both in the open air theatre and the Barn Theatre on the estate. But additionally, between 1936 and 1938, the Ballets Jooss toured successfully to America and Europe with their now famous works, including *Pavane* (1929), *Big City* (1932), *Ball in Old Vienna* (1932), *Seven Heroes* (1933), *Prodigal Son* (Version 2, 1933), as well as *The Green Table*, while the Dartington school continued primarily under Leeder's supervision. *Ballade*, *The Mirror* and *Johann Strauss Tonight* were added to the repertoire in 1935. Frederick Cohen was Jooss's composer and Hein Heckroth his designer. The influence of the company at this point was far-reaching. The innovation and high quality of their work gave them great prestige, and they were acclaimed wherever they performed.

It was in 1938 that a teacher in the Jooss/Leeder school, Lisa Ullmann, while on holiday, found Laban destitute in Paris. Although she was not in a position herself to bring him to Britain, she alerted Jooss who invited him to be his guest at Dartington. Laban therefore arrived at Dartington not at the Elmhirsts' invitation, but entirely by the good will and good faith of his student, Jooss. They had always retained an artistic father/son relationship since the Stuttgart days. The two men had a mutual, life-long admiration each for the different talents of the other, Jooss for Laban's vision and inspirational teaching and Laban for Jooss's theatrical prowess. They had worked very closely together on the creation of the notation system, with Leeder, Bereska and Albrecht Knust, as well as on the 1927 and 1928 Dancers' Congresses, and the Wagner Festivals in Bayreuth, in 1930 and 1931. They knew each other well enough to be both supportive and understanding.

Leeder's relationship with Laban was that of a colleague. He was a Laban dancer, but not a Laban student. He was a talented notator and keen to build on Laban's choreological practice. Ullmann, on the other hand, had been a pupil at Lotte Wedekind's Berlin Labanschule. She had experienced the full force of Laban as the revered pinnacle of a training hierarchy, and to whom she was sent to take her examinations. She was in awe of him and also, like nearly all women who came in contact with him, affected by his charismatic personality.

Laban's arrival at Dartington found mixed responses. His innovative ideas on dance, his choreutics (space study), eukinetics (dynamic study), *Tanzschrift* (dance notation) were fundamental to the curriculum of the Jooss/Leeder school, but taught in the style of the Jooss/Leeder system. On the other hand, Laban himself, as a 60-year-old, non-English-speaking, depressive and destitute figure, was of no interest to the students. It was clear that he had no place as a teacher in the school. Nor had he any prospects as a choreographer. He also had no desire to be either of these, although he did give one course in dance history in 1939. The fundamental issue for Laban was to regain his physical health, and to recover from the traumas of seeing his life's work disintegrate, his schools closed, his dance works denigrated, his notation and books banned, his colleagues scattered and his archives abandoned. It was Ullmann who set about nursing him to health, and Dorothy Elmhirst who encouraged him to write by giving him a work space at the Hall. In 1939 he wrote what is now the first half of his posthumously published *Choreutics* (1966) in an attempt to put together the fundamental points of his vision of space and dynamics as the essentials of the language of dance. This was in reality the companion volume he alluded to in *Choreographie* (1926), where he mentioned a 'second part to be written shortly', but one which was never completed at that time. The manuscript was given to Dorothy Elmhirst for safe keeping and was only brought to light again years later.

Jooss stayed at Dartington to run the school in the summer of 1939, while the company toured the USA. But with the outbreak of war in September the school had to close down, and the company was unable to return to Britain, as there was no civilian transport across the Atlantic. Thus Jooss lost his livelihood and became temporarily financially dependent on the Elmhirsts.

Because of the anticipation of a German invasion, early in 1940 Devon was declared a military zone. All enemy aliens had to leave Dartington by June. Many men, including Jooss as a German national, were interned, while several others were deported to Canada or Australia, including Hein Heckroth, Jooss's stage designer, and Willi Soukop, the sculptor. Laban, because of his age and state of health, escaped internment. He and Ullmann were given a temporary home in the Elmhirsts' London flat and eventually, taking Jooss's maid with them, they managed to find lodgings in the evacuation town of Newtown, in Mid-Wales.

The problem for Laban was how to earn enough money to become independent of the Elmhirsts' generosity. The correspondence in the Dartington Records shows that Laban thought of going to the United States. He certainly had no vision of the enormous impact his work would have on Britain later. It was almost by chance that a new chapter in his career began, which took him into areas of work which had only been hinted at in his period in Germany, and firstly into work study.

From Dartington Hall the Elmhirsts experimented with setting up self-sufficient rural industries. F.C. Lawrence was brought in by them to assist in structuring the programme. Hearing of Laban's abilities in movement observation and analysis, Lawrence invited him to help with the Motion Study side of the work. Their co-operation led to the development of the Laban/Lawrence Industrial Rhythm, an observation and training method for manual work. This was the first of several new directions for Laban's career in Britain. His assistants were Lisa Ullmann and the newly recruited Betty Meredith-Jones and Jean Newlove.

Jooss's Wartime Work and Return to Germany

Jooss was soon freed from internment on the Isle of Man and attempted to get a passage to New York to join the company, but this proved impossible. In 1941, the company managed to arrange an extension of their US tour to include South America. This they were able to do with the present repertory (*Spring Tale* and *Chronica* having been added in 1939), but when they returned to New York in January 1942, they badly needed new works. Without Jooss they had no possibility of providing a new programme. They disbanded, some members returning to South America and starting modern dance centres in Chile and Brazil, some of which still exist today. Others were absorbed by the US dance world, while a few were escorted back to London after considerable difficulties, both bureaucratic and in terms of transport and finance. In the meantime, Jooss was able to choreograph the dances for the Sadler's Wells 1942 productions of Mozart's *Magic Flute* and *Marriage of Figaro*.

With the return of twelve of his dancers, Jooss was once again able to create a dance centre. This he did in Cambridge, directing at the Arts Theatre and teaching there, and in the autumn of 1942 with the twelve original dancers he re-formed the Ballets Jooss, with Jooss and Leeder both having to perform again because of the lack of male dancers. *Company at the Manor* (1943) and *Pandora* (1944) were the new works, with Leeder choreographing a second version of *Sailors' Fancy* (1943) and Hans Züllig, a soloist in the company, *Le Bosquet* (1945). He continued throughout the war with this smaller company, performing a contracted repertory for military and civilian audiences whenever and wherever opportunity arose, firmly establishing the Ballets Jooss as a remarkable and popular company. The repertory was of two kinds: dances which commented on society, showing war, power-seeking, tyrannical behaviour and the need for understanding, contrasted with more lighthearted ballets as a dynamic contrast to his main works.

In the immediate post-war period, Jooss and the company went on an ENSA tour to Belgium, Germany, Holland and France, entertaining the British army of occupation. It was not until the autumn of 1949 that Jooss, after lengthy preparations, was able to return permanently to Essen to take over again the directorship of the Dance Department of the Folkwanghochschule and to run his Dance Theater as an independent, but city-subsidized company. The difficult task of re-establishing himself in

Germany was made easier by the quality of work he and his soloists (especially Rolf Alexander, Noelle de Mosa, Hans Züllig and Ulla Soderbaum) were able to offer both in performing and teaching. Jooss was prominent in the post-war summer schools held in Switzerland where the famous modern dancers who had stayed in Europe throughout the war, Wigman, Kreutzberg and Chladek, were invited to teach.

Because of financial considerations, Essen was no longer able to support the company after 1953. However, Jooss's masterpieces *The Green Table* and *Big City* have been mounted extensively by leading dance companies world-wide. This work continues through his daughter Anna Markard, who, using her unique knowledge and the Labanotation scores, has added *Ball in Old Vienna* and *Pavane* to keep four of her father's ballets in the repertory today.

Jooss's Influence

The impact of Jooss's works themselves was evident. Articles in the dance magazines of the pre-war period reveal how extensive his mark on the thinking of other choreographers was. Dame Peggy Van Praagh, writing of her work in the 1930s with the choreographer Anthony Tudor, describes the many visits of the Ballets Jooss and the high regard Tudor and his dancers had for the quality of both the choreography and the performance.

Lilla Bauer, a company member, continued a distinguished career as a teacher of dance, pioneering the dance department at London University's Goldsmiths' College. She made a particular contribution to the Laban/Ullmann Modern Dance Holiday Courses as a teacher, with her insistence on artistry and technical training going hand in hand with creativity. Several Scandinavian students who left the school in 1939 made significant contributions to dance in their country. Birgit Culberg's renowned choreographic work reflects her Jooss training. Bodil Genkel became a distinguished teacher of dance, as did Lavina Nielsen and the Dutchman Lucas Hoving. Maria Fedro, a soloist in the company, continued her career as the movement tutor at the Royal Academy of Dramatic Art. The Laban/Jooss influence on movement in drama was strongly felt in all the major drama schools through company members and graduates from the Jooss/Leeder school and, after the war, from the Leeder School and the Art of Movement Studio. Simone Michelle's career as a solo performer in the USA was followed by her becoming Sigurd Leeder's main assistant in the London school. Joan Turner and Jean Cebron, who became Jooss Ballet company members, are examples of the young dancers she helped to train, while others joined companies such as Paul Taylor's and Alvin Ailey's.

Jooss's influence in Britain was limited, however, for two reasons: firstly, because of the non-British nationality of most of his students, and secondly — and most importantly — because of the prominent position ballet occupied in the British art world. Powerful figures such as Ninette de Valois and Marie Rambert ensured that during the immediate post-war period every assistance was given to re-establish world-class and prestigious national ballet companies. Modern influences on their style were acknowledged to be more derived from the Diaghilev legacy than from the German school, although sometimes the modern look which appeared in their works, such as Ashton's *Symphonic Variations*, cannot deny the Jooss influence.

Laban's Wartime Work: Developments in Industry, Education, Recreation, Dance Notation and Research and Therapy

To return to Laban, the forced departure from Dartington in 1940 interrupted his work with F.C. Lawrence, and both Laban and Ullmann found themselves without means in Mid-Wales. Ullmann, with great perseverance and courage, found teaching work for herself through Keep Fit classes for the Local Education Authority, at first unpaid because she was not eligible for a work permit. She introduced Laban's movement concepts and practice for recreational and educational dance to a largely uncomprehending public. But there were several educationists who had pioneered 'Central European Dance' before the war. Joan Goodrich and Leslie Burrows are examples of people who had studied in Germany with Mary Wigman. They, with Louise Soelberg and Diana Jordan, collected a circle of supporters for Laban-based work. Ullmann's fine teaching began to be in demand. Laban's creative methods were ideal for this group of deeply committed teachers of movement, who were at the forefront of the search for meaningful and appropriate forms of dance for children compatible with the child-centred educational principles of John Dewey. The 1909, 1919 and 1933 Physical Training school syllabi provided dance, of some sort, for all children, but it was the pioneering work of this group of women, with Laban, which made the imaginative leap forward in content which put Britain in the forefront of dance education for the child.

The rapid expansion of Laban's educational work accelerated when he and Ullmann moved, in 1942, to Manchester. Here Sylvia Bodmer, a Laban Tanzbühne member from 1923, became instrumental in the formation of the Modern Dance Holiday Courses, the Laban Art of Movement Guild, and the Manchester Dance Circle, all providing training opportunities for teachers. In 1945, Lisa Ullmann opened the Art of Movement Studio in Manchester with Bodmer and Laban as faculty members. This influential training school started with the same curriculum as the German Labanschulen and with the aim of establishing Laban's Art of Movement (*Bewegungskunst*) in education and theatre, with some training also given for industrial and therapeutic application. For four years the theatre training predominated, producing the group 'The Young Dancers' and starting 'British Dance Theatre' with Hettie Loman. But the recognition of the Art of Movement Studio by the Ministry of Education as a place of training for teachers shifted the emphasis to dance for children and students.

Laban, in the meantime, was able to continue his work with F.C. Lawrence, whose management consultancy firm was centred in Manchester and the industrial Midlands. This led to his publishing *Effort* (1947) with Lawrence, a book with a revolutionary approach to the understanding of human dynamic, and the link between the psychological and the physical. The book proved a seminal text for the system now called Effort/Shape Analysis, widely used in dance research, therapy and personality assessment.

In these years, Laban concentrated on writing in an attempt to consolidate his major concepts. In 1948 he published *Modern Educational Dance*, which became *the* textbook for teachers, especially for dance work in primary schools. Many Teacher Training Colleges in Britain and all Physical Education Colleges ran dance courses based on Laban's work. It was variously called 'Modern Dance', 'Movement Education', 'Creative Dance', 'Movement', which reflects the variety of interpretations which teachers made of Laban's original ideas. Since then, second-generation textbooks have appeared, the most influential being Joan Russell's *Creative Dance in the Primary School* (1965), *A Handbook for Modern Educational Dance* (1963) by Valerie Preston-Dunlop, and *Movement Education* (1971) by Marion North. Ruth Morrison's *A Movement Approach to Educational Gymnastics* (1969) outlined her sensitive and widely followed work in which she made the transition from Swedish 'drill' to much freer work in the gymnasium, firmly based on Laban's principles.

Laban's work also became influential on actors' training, mainly through the British Drama League and Esmé Church's Northern Theatre School in Bradford. Here, Laban, with his assistant Geraldine Stephenson, continued for several years — although only in a part-time capacity — to teach and to produce movement dramas. His book *Mastery of Movement on the Stage* (1950) reflects this side of his work. Later publications show his continuing influence on drama in education. Examples are: Wiles and

Gerrard's *Leap to Life* (1957), Janet Goodridge's *Drama in the Primary School* (1970), and John Hodgson's *Drama in Education* (1972), in all of which Laban is prominent.

Adjacent to the Art of Movement Studio in Manchester was Joan Littlewood and Ewan McColl's Theatre Workshop, of later Stratford East fame. Interaction between the two studios was inevitable, but the strongly political views of the Theatre Workshop were never reflected in the more idealistic philosophy of the dance students, although Laban himself felt in fact more at home in the intellectually stimulating atmosphere of the actors' studio.

The influence of Laban's recreative dance methods used in the *Körper-kultur* work with amateurs in Germany was repeated in the way in which his principles were used to revolutionize some of the established recreational methods in Britain, especially those of the Keep Fit Association. Walli Meier and M. Baranek's *Recreative Movement in Further Education* (1973) shows how the Swedish gymnastic base of Keep Fit was revitalized and opened out by the use of Laban's choreological principles. Additionally, in the 1950s and 1960s the Laban Art of Movement Guild had forty or more affiliated groups all offering recreative dance opportunities.

At Dartington in the Jooss/Leeder school, Laban's *Tanzschrift* was taught. Ann Hutchinson as a student there wrote the first score of *The Green Table* and, when the school closed, went to the USA and, with Irmgard Bartenieff and Helen Priest Rogers, opened the Dance Notation Bureau. It has become the world centre for notating and reconstructing dance works. The establishment, in 1959, one year after Laban's death, of the International Council for Kinetography Laban was necessary because of the widespread use of his notation system, better known now as Labanotation (see *Labanotation Scores: An International Bibliography*, edited by Mary Jane Warner and published in 1984).

Out of the Dance Notation Bureau, and combined with Warren Lamb's work with Laban in the 1950s on movement observation, the analytic method variously known as 'Effort/Shape' and 'Laban-analysis' was developed for use in dance and movement research. It has been further developed into Choreological Studies which are built directly on Laban's insightful work into the nature of human movement in everyday life and in dance. The CORD Journals, the IFMC Journals, *Dance Studies* (ed: Lange) are a few of the publications regularly containing Laban-based research work today.

In May 1942, the Withymead Centre for psychotherapy and art therapy was opened by Gilbert and Irene Champernowne near Exeter, aided financially by the Elmhirsts. Laban was recruited to give guidance on dance and movement therapy, in co-ordination with the Jungian analytical approach practised by the Champernownes. This was not an unknown field for him. He had begun work on the effects of movement creativity on psychological disorders tentatively in Zurich in 1916, at the time when Jung's ideas were becoming distinct from Freud's. These experiments have since developed into professional dance and movement therapy and are widely practised today. The American Dance Therapy Association's entry in *The Psychotherapy Handbook 1980* states: 'the two prime contributors to the discipline are Trudi Schoop with Marion Chace and the followers of Rudolf Laban'. Also directly stemming from Laban is Veronica Sherborne's movement work for mentally handicapped children, now widely used in Europe and the Americas, and Betty Meredith-Jones's work for geriatric patients in the USA.

In London, the Laban Centre for Movement and Dance, as the Art of Movement Studio became in 1972 under Dr Marion North, continues to take forward Laban's vision of the interrelationship of dance forms and modes which he embodied in his plans for a State Dance College in 1929, with Jooss, in Germany. Theatre, therapy, community, research, teaching for beginners, graduate and advanced degrees are offered. Students work under the same roof, sharing the same rigorous and passionate commitment to dance which Laban and Jooss pioneered. Elsewhere, in New York, Ohio, Seattle and many university centres, Laban-based work is offered as an integrated part of the dance curriculum.

Notes

1. Mary Wigman remained in Germany after 1933 and was not therefore part of the dance community forced into exile.
2. He had been invited by Rabindranath Tagore in order to aid rural regeneration and development of self-sufficiency in the village where Tagore lived at the time.

–9–

Carl Ebert, Glyndebourne and the Regeneration of British Opera

ERIK LEVI

The reign of terror that followed Hitler's accession to power caused several musicians to leave Germany. As many as four hundred settled in Britain where they certainly enriched the nation's musical life.[1] Yet their contribution was essentially passive — no single person had the opportunity or, indeed, the strength of character to transform a concert system that had remained the same for hundreds of years. The situation in the field of opera was, however, more fluid. Although opera had flourished in England from the time of Handel, its roots were less firmly entrenched. Performances were almost entirely restricted to short international seasons at Covent Garden. Moreover, there was little opportunity of experiencing opera in the provinces. Clearly, there were considerable possibilities of injecting fresh ideas into a medium that had for too long suffered from insularity and quiescence. Thus, when John Christie proposed the idea of building an entirely new opera house at his country home, Glyndebourne, it was fortuitous that he was able to secure the services of two men, the conductor Fritz Busch and the producer Carl Ebert, both of whom had refused to collaborate with Hitler and had therefore been forced into exile. Their participation in the Glyndebourne Festival seasons from 1934 to 1939[2] was to have unprecedented consequences for the development of musical life in the country. In particular, Carl Ebert's contribution to the art of operatic production effected such a change in the national perception of opera that its impact is still felt to this very day.

To understand the nature and level of Ebert's achievement, it is necessary to give a brief account of his career prior to his arrival at Glyndebourne. He was born in 1887 and trained as an actor, studying under Max Reinhardt at the Deutsches Theater in Berlin. At the outbreak of the First World War, he moved to the Frankfurt Municipal Theatre where he developed an outstanding reputation, creating memorable rôles in such plays as Goethe's *Faust* and *Egmont*, Hölderlin's *Empedokles*, and Ibsen's *Peer Gynt*. Ebert returned to Berlin eight years later, and in the

179

heady cultural atmosphere of the Weimar Republic was given the responsibility of founding a school of Dramatic Art at the Staatliche Hochschule für Musik. It was at this time that he began his lifelong association with the world of opera. However, his first opportunity to produce opera professionally arose when he took over the directorship of the State Theatre at Darmstadt in 1927. The success of his ventures into the operatic field, particularly his revelatory production of Mozart's *Figaro*, elevated him within the space of four years to one of the highest positions in Germany's opera houses, that of director general at the Städtische Oper in Berlin.

Ebert's rapid rise to prominence represented the apex of a movement initiated by Richard Wagner, whose concept of the *Gesamtkunstwerk* desired a more equal balance between the component parts of an opera, between voice and orchestra, drama and music, the eye and the ear. The impact of Wagner's notion of *Gesamtkunstwerk* was tremendous, but there was an inevitable time-lag in the diffusion of its principles. In fact, the first real example occurred twenty years after the composer's death, when Gustav Mahler assumed control of the Vienna Opera from 1897 to 1907. By the 1920s, however, practically all the major opera houses in Germany were deeply concerned about the necessity of creating operatic productions that were stylish and dramatically unified.

The position in Britain was somewhat different. Although Covent Garden had adjusted itself to some of the implications of the Wagnerian revolution, the changes were modest and absurdly backward. For example, five years after Wagner's death in 1883, Sir Augustus Harris had at last persuaded British audiences to accept the fact that French and German operas should not have to be translated into Italian before they could be performed on the British stage. But even this concession hardly altered the British perception of opera, which remained essentially rooted in the pre-Wagnerian concept that the drama existed primarily as a vehicle for the singer. This attitude persisted well into the twentieth century, even though the balance of power had shifted from the singer to the conductor when Sir Thomas Beecham controlled proceedings at Covent Garden. Beecham was not unaware of the reactionary position maintained at Covent Garden, but he blamed the situation entirely upon the fact that the society audiences were interested in neither the music nor the drama. Indeed, this damning indictment of the British operatic public exposed the very problems that had beset any possibility of change. During the nineteenth century, Britain, unlike its Continental neighbours, had failed to encourage its composers to believe that the operatic medium was worthy of serious attention. Opera was in effect merely entertainment. The notion that it concerned itself with matters of political, social and ethical significance simply did not exist.

Beecham certainly raised the quality of musical performance at Covent Garden. During the 1920s and 1930s he introduced a whole stream of first-rate singers such as Friederich Schorr, Alexander Kipnis, Frida Leider and Lauritz Melchior to English audiences. It was by all accounts a golden era in terms of the standards achieved by individual performers. At the same time, however, Beecham seemed oblivious to the idea that a dramatically coherent stage production might enhance the effect of his work as a conductor. An anonymous correspondent writing in the *Musical Times* ruminated upon the situation in the following terms:

> It cannot be said that, as regards stage production, the average Covent Garden performance ranks very high. The task of putting on a dozen or more large-scale works within a short space of time is, of course, an immense one, and the difficulties of rehearsal are very great, particularly in these days of flying prima-donnas, anxious to spend the least possible time between one engagement and the next. Nevertheless the staging and lighting resources at the Royal Opera House are now such that a producer of imagination could work more miracles than we have recently been permitted to see.
>
> There is a regrettable tendency amongst the habitués of Covent Garden to *expect* the productions to be slipshod and second-rate. That Beecham and the Orchestra should be in their usual fine form is much to be thankful for; that Gigli should deal successfully with his much-admired high notes is also a matter for congratulation. But thankfulness and congratulation wilt a little before a stage fight such as we recently witnessed in *Il Trovatore*, or a Triumph Scene in *Aida* during which the procession of worshipful animals . . . was carried so sadly awry as hardly to know whether they were coming or going. These are small matters, but they are symbolic of the prevalent heresy that at Covent Garden, as far as the eye is concerned, almost anything will do.[3]

It was perhaps fortunate that John Christie was dissuaded from his desire to emulate Covent Garden by staging grand operas at Glyndebourne. In concentrating their attention exclusively upon the operas of Mozart (and later Verdi and Donizetti), Busch and Ebert were able to exert a much more profound impact upon the English operatic scene. Indeed Christie demonstrated considerable foresight in allowing both men complete freedom in choosing the repertoire and selecting suitable soloists for each production. The régime that Busch and Ebert imposed on Glyndebourne was totally different from anything hitherto experienced in England. Not only were the singers auditioned by both men, but they were engaged to live and work at the opera house for a period of up to two months. Thus Busch and Ebert created a genuine feeling of an ensemble company in which no singer was allowed to predominate. The atmosphere generated by the spirit of co-operation between singer, musician, producer and conductor was so unique that it was possible to achieve performances of an unusually high degree of musical and dramatic cohesion.

Ebert's contribution to this process was of vital importance. His main concern was to realize the intentions of the composer and to translate them into an effective theatrical language. The real value of his production method lay in the intellectual process of searching for the dramatic potential contained within the composition itself. Ebert was not especially interested in achieving a kind of artificial topicality and always remained loyal to the principal ideas embodied in the operas he produced. However, he demanded from his singers that they should work together as an ensemble and create a truthful and natural mode of expression. In other words, the singers had to be totally convincing in musical and dramatic terms. It was only possible to nurture this special type of singing actor by introducing a comprehensive and rigorous method of rehearsal that required total commitment from every member of the opera company. Such conditions became the norm at Glyndebourne and they provided the model for subsequent developments in the British opera houses.

There can be no doubt that the pioneering performances at the 1934 Glyndebourne Festival initiated the revival in critical estimation of Mozart operas in Britain. Previously, standards of production had declined to such an extent that the dramatic aspects of his works had become seriously undervalued. The reasons for this are partially historical, since Mozart's music did not transfer well to the larger stages of the nineteenth- and twentieth-century opera house. Moreover, its classical style was misunderstood by audiences who clamoured for a more superficially flamboyant and emotionally charged musical idiom. Above all, an opera house like Covent Garden could not cope with the sheer complexity of Mozart's ensembles. At Glyndebourne, however, Busch and Ebert in- sisted upon unlimited rehearsal time in which to mould these ensembles and make them dramatically coherent. In particular, their realization of stage action was of a quality never before experienced in Britain. Critics were quick to perceive that Ebert's rejection of conventional operatic gestures, his demand that singers had to act with a naturalness and spontaneity, illuminated Mozart's dramatic achievement. Eric Blom made this very point in his assessment of the 1934 Festival: 'Ebert's productions abounded in neat touches and intelligent sidelights that made Mozart's music seem more richly allusive than ever.'[4]

William McNaught amplified these sentiments in the following year. It is significant that his criticism, published in a music journal, should spend as much time considering the merits of the production as the actual standard of performance:

Artists brought together from many countries do what they are told to the best of their ability, and out of the assembly of their talents emerges something brighter and better and a stage higher in the artistic scale than any one of them could set up personally. How much this collective goodness is directly to the credit of Mr. Carl Ebert, the producer, one cannot judge. But there is a good deal of Mr. Ebert's work that one can judge positively, and it is so excellent that we may form the same opinion of the other part and look upon Mr. Ebert, if anybody, as the hidden hand of Glyndebourne.[5]

According to McNaught, Mozart's *Die Zauberflöte*, reduced from Covent Garden to Glyndebourne scale, gained in completeness. It was 'carried to the region of light fantasy of which Papageno, the three flirtatious ladies and the dancing blackamoors were rightful inhabitants, instead of being visitors under suspicion of misplaced levity.'[6]

Whilst *Don Giovanni*, *Die Zauberflöte* and *Figaro* were always regarded as masterpieces of music theatre, despite their hitherto inadequate representation on the English stage, the other Mozart operas Ebert produced at Glyndebourne, *Così fan tutte* and *Die Entführung aus dem Serail*, were hardly recognized. Indeed, *Così fan tutte* had been roundly condemned by the nineteenth-century critic Henry Chorley as a

tiresome folly of a fable even more fatally flawed than *Die Zauberflöte*. The utterly stupid trick put on the two girls by their two lovers cannot pass at this time of day and thus, because of utter indifference upon the composer's part, a mine of treasure is drowned for ever and ever. There is no hope for *Così fan tutte* on the stage as the work stands.[7]

Although Beecham revived *Così* with moderate success at Covent Garden in 1910, it would be no exaggeration to state that Ebert's production of this opera at Glyndebourne was largely responsible for the dramatic reversal of attitudes towards the work's qualities. With *Die Entführung aus dem Serail*, Ebert's insistence that the opera should be performed in its original version as a German *singspiel* brought added rewards: 'The spoken dialogue between musical numbers was . . . admirable. Whatever their nationality, the performers rattled off their German accents with a round force and similarity of accent that struck agreeably on ears accustomed to the flaccid German of so many English singers.'[8] Clearly, Ebert had worked with considerable vigour to get his team of international singers to speak German with a uniformity of accent previously unknown in the English opera house. His own contribution to the opera's success, taking on the speaking rôle of Bassa Selim, was also acknowledged as being of vital importance:

Ebert brought a corresponding harmony of action on the stage; personally as an actor, he made his Bassa Selim the centre of the drama. His few words, his long silences, his dark presence took on the inscrutability of destiny. Was it for magnanimity or contempt, love or indifference, that he released Constanze and Belmonte? Was the whole story a comedy or tragedy? As in *Don Giovanni* there is no answer, because Mozart's operas are like life itself — comedy and tragedy in one.[9]

Another distinguishing feature of this production rested with the protrayal of the two lovers Constanze and Belmonte. Many critics have remarked upon the fact that Ebert had transcended the essentially frivolous nature of German *singspiel* by re-emphasizing the tragic circumstances of their situation. Their preparedness to die was reflected in actions that were almost like 'visible music' for the listener. Here was a complete unity of sound, action and colour that was the hallmark of Ebert's insight and vision.

It would be misleading to suggest that everything in these early Glyndebourne productions achieved a uniformly high level of execution. In particular, Christie's insistence that Ebert should collaborate with a rather mediocre stage designer, Hamish Wilson, spoilt the effectiveness of some performances. However, in 1938, Ebert persuaded the Glyndebourne management to engage the services of Caspar Neher, a world-renowned artist, for the production of Verdi's *Macbeth*. Neher had worked closely with Ebert when this opera had been given in Berlin, and its adaptation onto the Glyndebourne stage was accomplished with great skill. In many ways, Ebert's production of *Macbeth*, an opera that had been neglected and misunderstood ever since its first performance in 1847, was even more remarkable than his achievements in Mozart. After all, in his productions of Mozart, Ebert was simply realizing to the full an ideal beauty that had been universally recognized. But Verdi's *Macbeth* required nothing less than a wholesale rehabilitation in order to convince the public that the work was a product of genius. The Verdi scholar Dyneley Hussey clearly appreciated that Ebert's belief in the opera had overriden some of the crudities in the score.

> The success of the opera, which the enthusiastic applause left in no doubt, was due in a large degree to Herr Ebert's imaginative production. . . . The result is for the most part admirable and the beauty of the spectacle, especially in the banquet scene, seizes the imagination. . . . The chorus, with plenty of room to deploy upon the enlarged stage sang and what is more acted magnificently. Their contribution to the banqueting scene was quite as important as that of the principals, and their horror struck attitudes in the finale of Act II at the discovery of Duncan's murder, in which Herr Ebert made no pretence of dramatic action, were most effective.[10]

Desmond Shawe-Taylor reflected upon the impact of the 1939 performance of *Macbeth* in similarly ecstatic tones:

> Never was unity of music and drama more splendidly achieved . . . Even those
> who most admired the genius of Verdi were amazed at the dramatic force
> achieved by passages which had seemed insignificant in the score. I am thinking
> in particular of two moments. First, the sinister effect of the commonplace
> 'garden party' music played during the *absolutely silent* entry of Duncan into
> Macbeth's castle; coming after the passionate outbursts of Lady Macbeth, its
> amiable triviality froze one's blood. Second, the drinking song for Lady Macbeth
> in the banquet scene, a harsh anticipation . . . . . of the joyless *Traviata*
> Brindisi . . . How wonderfully Busch, Ebert and Margherita Grandi between
> them conveyed the mood: 'Enjoy yourselves, it is my order!'[11]

The final challenge of the pre-war Glyndebourne Festivals was a
production of a work far inferior in musical quality to that of Verdi's
Macbeth. In selecting Donizetti's *Don Pasquale*, Ebert clearly realized that
his stage direction would have to attain a standard which would draw the
audience's attention away from the inadequacies of the score. This fact
was readily acknowledged in William McNaught's review, published in
the *Musical Times*:

> Carl Ebert seems to have determined that an opera of this class was as much a
> call upon his best services as anything by Mozart — perhaps even more so, for
> without the beguiling presence of superfine music it was more than ever
> necessary to hold the attention by things well done. So he gave us vivacious,
> merry action that never left a moment unoccupied, was always to the point, and
> contained all those touches of character that can make a 'production' more than
> the sum of its parts. The producer's care was never more necessary, or came
> under closer scrutiny, for the mind readily turned from Donizetti's crudities of
> noise and sought solace in things to be watched . . . the choral scene, sung and
> acted by the household staff at the beginning of Act 2, was a masterpiece of
> delicate, inventive stage management. One wanted to encore it, in order to
> examine its workings after the initial surprise had passed.[12]

McNaught also commented upon Ebert's remarkable ability to make the
central rôle of Malatesta (sung by Mariano Stabile) so convincing:
'Stabile played the part so keenly, with such style and with such ready
play of voice, feature and gesture that this unbelievable character was
never dull, laboured or unreal.'[13] Another review, published in the *Musical
Times*, attempted to summarize the specific achievements of the Glyndebourne Festival. There was no doubt in the critic's mind that

> the art of producing opera has been carried to the highest point of perfection
> known in these days. The all-embracing virtue of Glyndebourne productions is
> that each is a study, both artistic and practical, that draws its inspiration from
> the opera and makes a blend with it. Thus Glyndebourne opera has a strong

and all pervading character. It absorbs its casts however individual their members.[14]

Whilst the critics generally raved about the standards of production at Glyndebourne, there was some evidence that the Covent Garden management was responding to the implications of Ebert's work. In 1937, for example, Beecham engaged Otto Erhardt, a German producer of considerable stature, to revive productions of the *Ring* and *Fidelio*. Emil Preetorius was also brought over to direct a committed production of *Der Fliegende Holländer*. There were encouraging signs of progress at Sadler's Wells Theatre, where Lilian Bayliss had set up a new opera company which attempted to improve standards of theatrical presentation, even if the musical results were less convincing. But these isolated forays into what was still foreign territory were unfortunately interrupted by the outbreak of war.

It can be argued that it was in the post-war period that Ebert's ideas on operatic production really gained ground in Britain. The renaissance almost certainly occurred with the first performance of an opera of genius by a British composer, when Benjamin Britten's *Peter Grimes* was given at the Sadler's Wells Theatre in 1945. There is no evidence to suggest that the production was in any way extraordinary, but the fact that the country had at last produced an operatic masterpiece worthy of comparison with the finest works of the twentieth century gave the world of opera an enormous psychological boost of confidence. Indeed, Sir David Webster, who assumed control of Covent Garden in 1944, was determined to change the old system, where miscellaneous foreign singers appeared on the stage without having had proper rehearsals. He also realized that it was essential, despite the uncertain economic climate of the post-war period, to make fullest use of whatever first-rate material existed irrespective of nationality. In essence, Webster was adopting a principle that was similar in nature to that used by John Christie during the 1930s at Glyndebourne.

In 1949, Webster risked the wrath of both critics and public by appointing the young Peter Brook as Covent Garden's new Artistic Director. It was a bold stroke certainly inspired by the fact that, like Ebert, Brook had learnt his trade in the theatre. However, Brook had little or no musical experience and was more interested in 'good theatre' than in the composer's intentions. He began with a production of Mussorgsky's *Boris Godunov* that demonstrated his ability to tackle certain aspects of grand opera, particularly in terms of compelling crowd scenes. But Brook antagonized musicians, critics and the public when he collaborated with Salvador Dali on Richard Strauss's *Salome*. This production certainly hastened Brook's departure from Covent Garden, but the idea that someone who had initially trained in the theatre could become an effective operatic producer was fortunately not banished for ever. Indeed, the fact that Ebert had returned to Glyndebourne in 1950 spurred other opera companies to seek out producers who were willing to meet the particular challenges offered by the operatic medium. At Covent Garden, this naturally involved engaging a whole list of producers with varying degrees of success. Nevertheless, Sir John Gielgud, who produced Berlioz's *The Trojans* and Britten's *A Midsummer Night's Dream*, and Luchino Visconti, designer as well as director in Verdi's *Don Carlos*, demonstrated that it was possible to achieve convincing music theatre given the right conditions.

Ebert's influence was of course more readily visible at Glyndebourne itself, where the traditions of intensive rehearsal were maintained even in the austere financial conditions of post-war Britain. In addition, Ebert handed down his ideas to a new generation of British opera producers who were inspired to follow his example. Anthony Besch, who worked as Ebert's assistant at Glyndebourne from 1951 to 1957, delineated the special characteristics of his work as: 'a great actor transmitting the intricacies of his art for the benefit and instruction of his fellow artists . . . he will never allow a singer to evade the necessity of acting, for to him a production is the sum of its component parts and he knows the weak link is always the one which the audience will notice first.'[15] According to Besch, Ebert's greatest contribution to the art of operatic production related to 'his ability to interpret a work both from within and without — from the standpoint of the actor-singer who must perform in front of an audience and from that of the composer-author whose work is to be given a faithful representation.'[16] More recently, Sir Peter Hall reiterated similar ideas in an essay directly concerned with the contemporary role of the operatic producer:

> True opera is action made out of music. And it can only be made by long, close collaboration between conductor and director through shared rehearsals. The atmosphere, the action, the character of the drama affect the nature of the music making. And the music making affects the drama. Which comes first? Neither. Opera should be a perfect circle, the drama making music and the music making drama. This ideal was established by Busch and Ebert. . . .[17]

The overwhelming and lasting effect of Ebert's operatic production derived ultimately from his inborn understanding and love of music. His conception of opera was neither of a play adorned with music nor of wonderful music to which were added gestures and scenery. It was a form of art in which both the musical and dramatic action were of equal importance. The musical score acted as the foundation and key to the stage action and scenery. Although the singing voice and orchestral instruments obey different laws of rhythmic and breathing technique from those of the spoken word, Ebert insisted that the singer should utilize gestures that were dramatically convincing yet totally related to particular characteristics of the music. This unity of music and movement was only possible when the people concerned — producer, conductor and stage designer worked together in an intensive yet harmonious manner. It was this unique atmosphere that was generated at Glyndebourne from the very first festival of 1934.

Notes

1. See Birgid Leske and Marion Reinisch, 'Exil in Großbritannien', in *Exil in der Tschecho-slowakei, in Großbritannien, Skandinavien und Palästina*, Leipzig, 1980, esp. the chapter on 'Der Freie Deutsche Kulturbund', para. 'Sektion der Musiker'.
2. For a detailed history of the origins and subsequent development of the Glyndebourne Festival see Spike Hughes, *Glyndebourne: A History of the Festival Opera*, Newton Abbot, 1981.
3. 'The Co-ordination of Opera', *Musical Times*, London, July 1939, pp. 497–9.
4. Eric Blom, 'The Glyndebourne Festival', *Musical Times*, July 1934, pp. 651–2.
5. William McNaught, 'The Glyndebourne Festival', *Musical Times*, July 1935, p. 646.
6. Ibid.
7. Henry Chorley, *Thirty Years of Music Recollections*, London, 1862, p. 138.
8. M.M.S., 'The Glyndebourne Festival', *Musical Times*, Aug. 1935, pp. 744–5.
9. Ibid.
10. Dyneley Hussey, 'Verdi's Macbeth', *Musical Times*, June 1938, p. 466.
11. Desmond Shawe-Taylor, 'Reflections on Glyndebourne', *Opera*, vol. 2, 1951, pp. 386–92.
12. William McNaught, 'Donizetti's *Don Pasquale* at Glyndebourne', *Musical Times*, June 1938, p. 539.
13. Ibid.
14. William McNaught, 'The Glyndebourne Festival 1939', *Musical Times*, July 1939, p. 542.
15. Anthony Besch, 'A Triptych of Producers', *Opera*, vol. 9, 1958, pp. 226–7.
16. Ibid.
17. Peter Hall, 'A Place for Mozart', in J. Higgins (ed.), *Glyndebourne: A Celebration*, London 1984, p. 10.

– 10 –

Theatre behind Barbed Wire
German Refugee Theatre in British Internment

ALAN CLARKE

On 16 May 1940, the day of the dress rehearsal for *Was bringt die Zeitung?*, a topical satirical revue staged by the Kleine Bühne (Little Theatre) of the Free German League of Culture (FDKB) in London, Manfred Fürst and Margarete Hruby — two members of the cast — were arrested and sent to internment camps.* They were amongst the 25,000 German and Austrian refugees who were hauled out of their beds in the middle of the night or fetched from their work-places, or who even delivered themselves unwittingly into the hands of the police: 'The nephew of an Ealing councillor lost a pocket-book containing over £9 in Treasury notes. It was found in a neighbouring suburb by a German, who took it to the nearest police station, where he was thanked, asked his name and detained for internment.'[1]

Under the Aliens Act of 1920 most refugees entering Britain from the Continent in the late 1930s had been classified as 'enemy aliens' of varying degrees of risk, even though the majority were fleeing from Nazi oppression. Now a large proportion of them — including women and children — were rounded up and imprisoned as part of the anti-German campaign which followed the collapse of the 'phoney war'. Initially those interned were taken to transit camps in various parts of England and Scotland where they spent days and even weeks under the most primitive conditions. Many of them were then transported to the Isle of Man, the main centre of internment, where, if they were lucky, they lived in the comparative safety of converted boarding-houses until their release a year or so later. Those less fortunate amongst the male internees were shipped as prisoners-of-war to Australia or Canada. If they arrived safely — one Canadian-bound transport ship, the *Arandora Star*, was torpedoed by a German U-boat resulting in the loss of many lives — those with money or contacts, especially in the USA, had the choice of staying there permanently; the others had to wait cut off from the rest of the world until they could return to the British Isles. Under such circumstances it is understandable that internees in Douglas on the Isle of Man should use this interminable waiting as the theme of an ironical song:

> You get used to it,
> You get used to it,
> The first years are the worst years
> But you get used to it.
> You may scream and you may shout,
> They will never let you out.
> Serves you right, you so and so,
> Well, weren't you a naturalized eskimo?
> Just tell yourself it's wonderful,
> You'll get used to it more and more and more.
> You'll get used to it,
> But when you get used to it,
> You'll find it's just as lousy as before![2]

Conditions in the Internment Camps

Although only a fifth of those arrested were shipped overseas, the process of confinement was for all concerned an enormous physical and psychological burden, especially since over half of them were more than forty years old: 'The anti-Nazis suffered both mentally and physically. They had the indignity of being treated as enemies, and in some cases herded with Nazi civilian prisoners while at the same time they had no news of what was happening "outside".'[3] Those who had previously experienced the horrors of Hitler's concentration camps feared a repetition of the same fate. During the first weeks of the internment, many committed suicide, some even before arriving at a camp:

> . . . a former Professor of Chemistry in a German University, 62 years old, and an international authority on dye-stuffs, . . . had been thrown by the Nazis into a concentration camp, and got to England just before the war. He was engaged in research for utilising sisal waste in submarines. As soon as the release Orders were enacted, the firm applied for his exemption from internment. But no answer had come from the Home Office when the Police came to his home to take him. He begged them to wait until the Home Office replied. They did not; and unable to face internment again, he took poison and killed himself.[4]

Even though, despite such fears, the 'English internment camps had nothing in common with the concentration camps of the Third Reich',[5] they were still extremely unpleasant places. The large number of suicide attempts during the first weeks after arrest were a result not only of the severe mental pressures on those affected but also of the inhospitable environment presented by most of these transitional camps: '[The internees] were pushed into any kind of available transport, and kept for days and even weeks in shocking conditions, in prisons, camps, race-horse stands, derelict factories and half-built houses, and they had to face primitive medical, sanitary and catering conditions in a Britain on which no bombs had fallen and where there was plenty of decent accommodation available.'[6] This treatment of German refugees, even taking into consideration the panic created in this country by Hitler's advance towards the West, cannot be fully justified, especially as British Nazi supporters were being kept in normal prisons. For some time the émigrés had to contend with such conditions as existed in the winter quarters of Bertram Mills Circus or a converted cotton mill in Lancashire: 'We've been put here in an old factory building with a lot of barbed wire and no comforts. The missing window panes cause many draughts which result in colds and sore throats, but the air in the room, in which about 300 sleep, is still bad.'[7] In a camp in Prees Heath in Shropshire, which eventually had to be closed down as a result of public protest, the internees were housed in small tents with about eighteen men in each. This 'temporary' accommodation lasted for over five weeks with the residents not only living under the most basic conditions but completely cut off from the outside world. The depressing atmosphere of this abandoned existence was captured by Kurt Barthel (Kuba) in a poem written at the time:

> 08 — that is a barbed-wire square
> somewhere in England,
> somewhere amongst the heather.
> Here the sun hurts —
> here no mornings are happy —
> here the wind moans so loudly —
> camp in the heather,
> no-one knows where.[8]

Another difficulty faced not only in the transit camps but in most of the internment centres was having to live in the close proximity of German Nazi sympathizers. The tense situation in a converted Devon holiday camp was even reported in a national Sunday newspaper:

In this camp about half the men were Nazis, the rest decided friends of our [the anti-Fascist] cause. The Nazis were organised by a Gestapo man, and behaved with deliberate arrogance and brutality. They went about singing their blood-thirsty Nazi songs, and occasionally they even beat up Jewish internees . . . Life in these conditions was scarcely endurable; there was a daily civil war in the camp.[9]

Similar situations were experienced in the women's camps on the Isle of Man where about 600 to 700 Hitler sympathizers were to be found amongst the 40,000 internees. The Nazis, who were entitled to official representation through the Swiss Embassy, frequently received additional backing from the British camp authorities:

> From the official side, the comment was made that the camp was now regarded as one for Fascists and prisoners-of-war, who were granted a great deal of licence so as to encourage similar freedoms for English prisoners-of-war in Germany. If they were allowed to celebrate Hitler's birthday, we could also hope that English prisoners would be allowed to celebrate the King's birthday in Germany.[10]

The Fascists were permitted to greet each other with 'Sieg Heil', to hang swastikas from their windows and to hold 'illegal' meetings on the cliffs. The anti-Fascists, on the other hand, were strongly forbidden from organizing any kind of meeting, defined as the coming together of more than three people at any one time, and found even their attempts to form a camp newspaper thwarted by the commander's wish to 'please the Nazis'.[11] Occasionally the contact with the Hitler supporters was on an even more intimate level: 'Nazis and refugee internees are housed together. There are cases where Nazi women and refugee women have to share not only their rooms but also their beds. The Nazis threaten and terrorize the refugees . . .'[12] In addition, the social and hygienic conditions were appalling. The women were not permitted to use the bedrooms during the day and therefore had to spend most of their time with their children in the overcrowded lounges of the boarding-houses. Medical care was almost non-existent, and there were cases such as a pregnant woman sharing her bed with a tubercular sufferer, and a child with chicken-pox sleeping in the same room as its mother and a ten year-old.[13]

Most hardship, though, was probably suffered by the men deported overseas to Canada, where the authorities regarded them as genuine Nazis and treated them accordingly. At the start of the war, the British government had made secret arrangements with their Australian and Canadian counterparts to take German prisoners-of-war in case Britain should be threatened by an invasion. However, by summer 1940 only three to four thousand prisoners and Nazi civilians had been taken, so that the Home Office in London — without informing its Commonwealth colleagues — 'topped up' the numbers with anti-Fascist refugees. Thus more than two and a half thousand émigrés were shipped to Canada with prisoners-of-war and Hitler sympathizers, and almost as many again were sent to Australia on their own, as the British Government had 'run out' of genuine Nazis. This did not prevent the troops accompanying the Australian voyagers on the *Dunera* from treating their prisoners like dangerous criminals:

> Our guards would have fitted well in the SS. We were 'frisked', sworn at, kicked and crammed down below in the clammy hold like galley slaves. In this floating prison we were literally treading on each others' stomachs . . . Thus we squatted in our mass coffin, abandoned, fleeced, without shaving gear, soap, towels, clean underwear, not knowing where they intended to transport us to, with the prospect of being helplessly swallowed up if a torpedo should hit us as had happened earlier to a transport ship bound for Canada.[14]

If, when they finally landed on 'terra firma', the Australian internees were to a great extent left alone to organize their camp life as best they could, their fellow sufferers in Canada had a far more depressing situation to overcome. They were still regarded as prisoners-of-war, had to wear the regulation trousers with the broad red stripe and the coat with the red cross on the back, and endured strict military discipline. Only some months after their arrival did the Canadian authorities learn that there were anti-Fascists amongst their prisoners, but even after they had been separated from the actual prisoners-of-war the refugees' treatment did not improve much. Six of them, including the Communist Wilhelm Koenen and the actor Gerhard Hintze, who had complained about the provocative behaviour of the Nazis left in the camp, were even placed in a detention centre reserved for Italian supporters of Mussolini; only a public protest in Britain and a two-day hunger strike by the other interned refugees secured their return.[15]

Although the Canadian inmates suffered more than most, all internees went through a period of extreme hardship and deprivation. The separation from family, friends and supportive organizations; the intimate cohabitation with strangers of different outlooks, political views, religious persuasions, habits and temperaments; the lack of normal comforts; the absence of social responsibilities and useful tasks; the isolation from everyday events; the lack of information about the progress of the war and the length of their confinement, all of these factors exercised a negative influence on the state of mind of the individual internee. In addition, many of them were still suffering from the shock of the apparent betrayal by their British hosts; they had seen Britain as a last bastion against the advance of Fascism and now they found themselves amongst the first victims of the British war effort against the Nazis:

> We have been Hitler's enemies
> For years before the war.
> We knew his plans of bombing and

Invading Britain's shore,
We warned you of his treachery
When you believed in peace,
And now we are His Majesty's
Most loyal internees.[16]

This disillusionment certainly contributed to the growing sense of abandonment which conditioned the general atmosphere in many camps. How dangerous this bitterness and isolation could be is portrayed in a short story by Jan Petersen about life in Canadian internment:

> There were many in the camp who lived an empty and sad prisoner existence, letting themselves drift unresistingly. Day by day they grew more phlegmatic. Their brains stopped working. They fell into useless and purposeless brooding and fantasizing . . . Earlier, in an ordered life, they had gone about their tasks and duties in an honest and conscientious way. Now the constant inactivity wore them down, physically and morally. Their thoughts were sluggish and filthy like swamp bubbles. Soon they had only one topic which they varied incessantly, greedily and consummately: women.[17]

It was against such negative manifestations and outlooks that the more positively minded members of the interned community directed their efforts.

Art and Culture in the Internment Camps

The problem of poor morale amongst the internees was the most immediate concern during the first weeks of internment. Suddenly the norms of civilian life had no more validity, and it was crucial therefore to establish alternative codes of communal behaviour appropriate to the new circumstances, with set routines and collective self-discipline. At first individual communities attempted to establish some order for themselves:

> You will understand that it was only through great comradeship and understanding that the nervousness and irritability amongst the internees could be reduced to a minimum. Eight men crouching together in a small tent day and night, especially when it's raining! In my tent . . . we are at least trying to bring some order to this chaos. 2 to 3 in the afternoon is always quiet time in our tent; each of us can occupy ourselves on our own, sleep or read, or even both together; talking is strictly forbidden and visits, even the most urgent ones, are unwelcome.[18]

Later on, larger management committees were formed to establish similar routines for the whole camp. But creating calm and order 'at home' solved only a part of the internees' problem. The various social, educational and cultural needs of the prisoners also had to be satisfied, and it is interesting that a very similar process of setting up appropriate structures occurred in almost every long-term centre. Firstly, groups were established to cope with the overall organization of the camp and the catering arrangements, closely followed by a cultural committee and the camp newspaper. A variety of such journals appeared — many simply as wall newspapers when the shortage of paper prevented a wider circulation — such as the *Moragh Times, Onchan Pioneer* and *Frauenruf* on the Isle of Man, the *Stacheldraht* in Canada and the Australian *Camp News*. Ironically, the one aspect usually missing from these news-sheets was up-to-date information on the progress of the war outside; the general ban on news information meant that the occasional press items obtained through a sympathetic camp commander, or more usually by illegal means, were in great demand: 'In many camps the ban on newspapers was overcome by smuggling, and in one camp at least a "black exchange" developed. A newspaper could be hired for ninepence for a quarter of an hour.'[19]

Alongside the camp journals, modest libraries were set up as well as the popular schools and 'universities'. Given the large number of middle-class intellectuals amongst the émigrés — in one English camp, for example, there were '3 Nobel Prize winners, 20 Oxford professors and many world-renowned specialists'[20] — the staffing of these 'educational institutions' was usually of a very high standard. Courses were offered in a wide range of subjects from Darwinism to the history of the Middle Ages, the syllabus of one Canadian 'high school' including Arabic, sociology, machine construction and journalism.[21] The education of the younger internees was of particular concern, and many specialist courses and even a 'youth university' were organized to help them complete studies which had been interrupted by their arrest; some were even able to take their matriculation exams whilst still interned.[22] Even more worries were created by the young girls in the women's camps on the Isle of Man: 'They had been taken away in the middle of their training or from school. Because of a reluctance to force them to work or study, they were in real danger of frittering away their time amidst the uncontrollable influences of the peculiar atmosphere of the camp.'[23] Again the activists amongst the internees made every effort to counter such tendencies. An experienced teacher founded a school which became 'the centre of a moral and cultural social life attracting many young and not-so-young women and enabling them to develop their talents'.[24] Many girls worked in the 'kindergartens' — in one camp a deserted golf clubhouse was converted for the purpose — or took part in specially organized youth clubs.

Alongside such educational offerings, sport was also very popular in many centres with regular competitions between teams of internees, like the football tournament in the Australian Hay Camp. Later on, as the conditions in internment gradually improved and the external restrictions on the prisoners were relaxed, possibilities of earning money arose through the sale of hand-made objects, especially toys, to the guards. In some places workshops and even factories were set up, as in Farnham Camp in Canada where camouflage nets, tables and boxes were produced for the army.[25] All these activities helped to encourage more positive attitudes within the camps and prevent the majority of the internees from becoming too introspective.

Within this process, the arts also had a crucial rôle to play, as Rudolf Steiner pointed out in the Australian internment newspaper, *Camp News*: 'Art is the expression of the social order from which it emerges . . . The artist's freedom is his sense of distance from this world . . . Adapting these principles to the world [of the internees] results in the artist facing up to a totally new challenge. His [old] world has ceased to exist, he must find his feet in the new one.'[26] In particular, this meant tackling the wider issues raised by a life of internment: the individual's relationship to the camp community as a whole, and the camp's attitude to the outside world. Artistic activities, both of an individual and a collective nature, were particularly suited to overcoming the most negative aspects of life in a densely populated environment. Thus, together with the other main features of camp organization which sprang into being almost as soon as the refugees settled in, live entertainment and cultural events were soon on offer. In one Canadian camp even a Director of Entertainment Operations was appointed.[27] But if such developments were usually welcomed unreservedly by the majority of the camp population, a few negative voices were raised about whether art was of any use in the internment context. 'F.K.' in *Stacheldraht*, the news-sheet produced in Farnham Camp, complained that such activities were only acceptable in a stable environment where a reasonable aesthetic *niveau* could be achieved:

> Two years of internment have led to one positive experience: culture can neither be maintained nor grow without liberty . . . In consequence culture in [Farnham] was a poor worn-out and underfed lady. If you looked carefully you could even detect some resemblance to life in the Germany of today . . . it soon became clear that men deprived of their liberty cannot stick together in order to live up to a standard of culture . . . [28]

Attitudes like this not only indicated a highly élitist approach to artistic creativity which ignored the concrete conditions in which the artists had to function, but also treated culture as the *aim* of a community rather than a means of improving its spiritual and moral well-being. In contrast to such a blanket condemnation of the creative work undertaken in internment —- 'the shows were poor and the last one a too, too realistic picture of the standards mingled in our camp'[29] — the editor of *Stacheldraht*, Freimut Schwarz, provided a very different assessment of the cultural life in Farnham:

> Even when you free yourself totally from the norms of the prison camp and base your judgement on the standards of normal life, the cultural activities achieved in internment must be viewed with astonishment. Despite working under the most unfavourable conditions, despite the primitive and often inadequate means at their disposal, the results do not compare unfavourably with the standards achieved 'outside'.[30]

An even more authoritative source is the artist John Heartfield, whose critical assessment of an art exhibition of works produced by those in Canadian internment emphasized how successful they were in overcoming their depressing circumstances:

> . . . to be honest we are amazed. Although we were assured that this was not and could not be an art exhibition in the proper sense of the word, but rather a display of products made under the most primitive and unfavourable conditions — we would nevertheless like to comment that the majority of the works exhibited had nothing to fear from a critical appraisal.[31]

Whatever the arguments about the quality of work produced — and the proven reputations of so many of the interned artists as well as some of the poems, stories and drawings which have survived would tend to support Heartfield's evaluation — the breadth of creative output was immense. Poetry, paintings, sketches, music and sculpture were produced; concerts, theatre productions, dance performances and art exhibitions put on; and a whole range of handicrafts undertaken. In one camp Hans José Rehfisch formed a literary circle, in another Kurt Jooss put together a male 'corps de ballet'; Rawicz and Landauer started their famous piano partnership, and the Amadeus String Quartet first got together in internment; the former owner of a craft shop opened a weaving school; in the guest-houses of the Isle of Man pianos were 'borrowed' and an orchestra called into being; overseas, the presence of rare woods led to the production of exotic carvings.[32] If professional artists were in short supply, amateurs filled the gap, as in Wharf Mills.[33] And all this took place in an environment described as 'highly unsuitable for artistic creation'[34] where few of the normal prerequisites for such work were to be found: rehearsal spaces for drama and dance, paper, paint and tools for painting and sculpture, instruments and sheet music for the musicians, and copies of scripts for play productions and readings.

In addition, the internees often faced the discrimination and prejudice of the camp authorities, who in some cases openly sympathized with their Nazi co-prisoners. In Port Erin anti-Fascists were forbidden to view certain films which might 'provide the enemy with information', yet were allowed to see the anti-Communist movie, *Comrade X*, much to the delight of the Hitler supporters.[35] In the transit camp at Huyton, an open-air concert for the internees was stopped by the commander when his guards 'came along and listened, joined in and clapped applause'.[36] In other camps, recitations and sketches in the German language were banned by suspicious officials.

Yet despite such restrictions a colourful cultural life developed in most places with the majority of non-Fascist internees involved as active participants or enthusiastic spectators. The effect of such events on even the most isolated of prisoners was sometimes impressive. Jan Petersen tells of a strongly built yet not especially bright sailor in Canadian internment who found it difficult to establish contact with his fellow captives:

> When a 'cabaret performance' was organized in the camp to alleviate the bleakness of the camp existence for a few hours, he announced: 'I'd like to do something too!' — 'Very well, what?', he was asked. 'Bend iron!' was his answer. Heads shook in amusement and puzzlement; still, a place was found for him in the programme. When it came to his turn, he walked relaxed and quiet to the small improvised stage, placed a finger-thick iron bar between his teeth, bit on it and — bent it crooked with his huge fists. Neither before or after his feat did he say anything. But as he was thanked with laughter and handshakes, his constantly indifferent and unmoving face lit up.[37]

Even though all successes were not quite so identifiable, the consistent efforts of the committed anti-Fascists to involve their fellow sufferers in artistic activities seem to have been a crucial factor in maintaining morale. This is reflected not only in the quantity of the creative work produced in internment but also the subject matter chosen by the artists. Max Zimmering identified three main themes running through this interned art: the refugees' concern with their cultural heritage, problems relating to their confined existence, and their relationship to events 'on the other side of the camp gates'.[38]

For the émigrés the problem of their cultural background, both during internment and later, was a highly controversial subject with a wide variety of views and interpretations laid upon it: '[The concept of a German cultural heritage] can be interpreted very broadly . . . it encompassed a period stretching from German classicism to Hitler's accession to power, because for many culture had ceased to exist with the start of the Third Reich.'[39] This attitude, stemming from an understandable desire to reject the perversion of German culture under the Nazis, was opposed by most of the active anti-Fascists. They pointed out that it ignored the efforts made by the anti-Hitler artists since 1933 and negated the possibility of using the humanist cultural traditions of the German people in the anti-Fascist struggle.[40] At the same time the creations of the past were also seen as sources of inspiration for present-day efforts; the question of heritage was not only the concern of great artistic works but also of modest informal performances, like the impromptu musical soirées:

> When we sing together in the evening, the difference between the Viennese and the Berlin way of saying 'I' doesn't matter . . . Even those who are afraid that every German song has to be a Hitler song, join in with us when we start up the *Song of the Peatbog Soldiers* or when we sing other marching or youth songs . . .[41]

From such experiences the impulses were found to renew the anti-Fascist fight in the cultural field. The close relationship between the cultural traditions of the past and their continuation in internment was reflected in the juxtaposition of performances of classical writers with topical cabaret, which featured in most camp entertainment programmes, or even, as in this example from Onchan Camp on the Isle of Man, with writings by the internees themselves: in October 1940, Peter Ihle and Erich Freund presented extracts from the works of world-famous authors from Aristotle to Thomas Mann under the title 'In Praise of Freedom', while later in the same week Freund also read a selection of poems by the 26-year-old Kurt Barthel (Kuba).[42]

If the respect for German culture was interpreted in different ways, so too was the problem of how to handle attitudes towards the harsh realities of camp life. The senselessness of their enforced confinement obsessed many émigré artists, especially amongst the painters and poets. John Heartfield commented that some of the pictures produced by those in Canadian internment were 'pervaded with a pessimistic tone',[43] whilst an impressive poem, again from Canada, also reflects this feeling of abandonment:

> They stand still by the fence. Sweeping softly
> The evening sinks behind the distant town.
> The quiet songs they are singing
> Are like bright flowers on a forgotten grave.
> They see the bayonets flashing on the barbed wire.
> In the wind many silent longings drift across the field
> To women, who sit in empty rooms
> And wait for them out there in the world.
> Did they weep for long when they had to go?
> In that sad departure how much remained unspoken —

How often did the boy in his barely conscious
Senses ask uneasily after his father.
Then the shrill siren shrieks loud and harsh from the yard.
The last look waves a greeting to the town in the east
Then the prisoners' feet shuffle to roll-call.
Night is here. And before the gates treads the heavy step of the
sentry.[44]

It was understandable that many artists should concern themselves
with their immediate surroundings; the danger was that in concentrating
on camp reality alone they could easily lose sight of the wider perspective.
To avoid this the active anti-Fascists stressed the importance of dealing
directly with the world outside the barbed wire. The demand for special
treatment and a return to normal life was, according to Freimut Schwarz,
one of the main themes of internment art and literature, for despite the
imprisonment there remained 'a kind of dialogue between the internees
and the . . . authorities, which was never quite broken and finally led to
their release'.[45] Such an approach did not always meet with approval or
understanding:

> The criticism often raised about art in interment is that its concern with themes
> [other than those of camp reality] represents a flight from the present. This is
> unjustified; most of the positive achievements arose in an atmosphere of strong
> moral dissatisfaction . . . Internment remained [for the anti-Nazi refugees]
> bitter and unsatisfactory, but far stronger was their determination to participate
> in the reality on the other side of the barbed wire. Hence the 'flight' from the
> narrow reality of the internment camp to the reality of the outside world.[46]

This determination led inevitably to active support of the war effort,
especially after the entry of the Soviet Union into the war. If the formation
of a Pioneer Corps in Huyton Camp by a nephew of Sigmund Freud was
felt by many not only to be an underhand way of avoiding deportation but
a denial of the rights of the German refugees to fight against Hitler as
equals,[47] the desire to give active support to the anti-Fascist struggle was
never lost. This is reflected both in the content of interned art — such as
Carlo Pietzner's large painting 'Coventry', reacting to the senseless
destruction of that historic English city[48] — and in the context, such as the
participation of actors and musicians in 'Aid for Russia' concerts.[49] This
influence is also noticeable in artistic representations of camp life, like
Max Zimmering's poem 'Tower of Refuge' or a drawing from Canada
which strongly impressed John Heartfield:

> . . . most of the [works] . . . betrayed the unshakeable determination best
> expressed in the words: 'Nothing will nor can grind us down!' A drawing

seemed to me to characterize this attitude. It could be seen in an outspread camp newspaper. A long path, leading deep into the distance, fenced in on both sides by high barbed wire. In the foreground we saw, stooping and with heavy steps, a prisoner walking. On the back of his uniform the large red mark which the inmates of Canadian camps have to wear. At the end of this long path of suffering, a radiant sun is shining. This drawing seemed to me a symbol for us all.[50]

Internment Theatre

Within such a situation, theatre was particularly suited both to assist in combating defeatism and isolation and to encourage a more responsible and outward-looking attitude. Its collective nature — both in the production process and the method of reception — helped the internees to create a communal spirit; its immediacy discouraged the tendency towards introspection or hopelessness; the synthesis involving other art forms in set and costume design, musical accompaniment and literary texts supported the sense of a common purpose; and its facility for dealing directly with the social and political issues which most concerned the interned population made it a key element in sustaining morale. An impressive range of theatre performances took place in the camps: one-man shows, Punch and Judy, revues, sketches, readings from the classics, as well as the regular productions of short plays or even full-length dramas. In Farnham Camp, on the other side of the Atlantic, the internees put on more than ten theatre and cabaret productions during their 13-month stay; in Hutchinson Camp, on the Isle of Man, seven full-length plays were staged in 1941 alone, and in the women's camps there at least two plays and numerous informal performances were organized. Only in the transit camps were productions limited mostly to smaller-scale cultural events, although at least two original and important performances emerged in Huyton.

The most unusual theatre venue, however, was between decks on the transport ship *Dunera*, taking 2,500 internees to Australia. Recitals from the works of Goethe, Schiller and Heine together with more modern authors like Kästner, Tucholsky and Weinert were complemented by the setting up of an Austrian cabaret club, the 'Interndl' — named after the popular London émigré theatre, the Laterndl.[51] Here, as elsewhere, the main aim was to counter the heavy physical and psychological pressures of a prison existence, particularly aboard a vulnerable floating target in the midst of war: 'The driving-force behind these activities was only to a small extent the desire for self-gratification; it was much more what I would call a sense of social responsibility.'[52] Thus Max Zimmering saw the contribution of the theatre activists in internment, and it was usually those artists who, like him, had already been involved in refugee organizations like the Kulturbund or the Austrian Centre who initiated such performances.

Whilst those on dry land did not have to rely for their material quite so exclusively on 'what existed in the heads of the thespians, could be drawn out of the memories of literary colleagues or retained by writing it down on toilet paper with smuggled-in pencils',[53] the problem of suitable texts was still acute. Where a writing talent existed amongst the internee population he or she was encouraged to produce work for the stage: in Huyton, Kuba created an original drama; in Australia, regular writers' evenings were arranged, and Max Zimmering provided many of the sketches for the ever-popular revues; in Canada, Paul Dornberger wrote two new plays. Other performances were based on adaptations from favourite books which had survived the many searches and adventures undergone by the internees since their arrest. Occasionally, material sent by friends and supporters back in England, like the FDKB's 'Kunst und Wissen' which regularly reproduced short scenes and sketches, proved suitable for production. More rarely, a sympathetic camp commander was willing to assist in acquiring playtexts. Even so, the selection was very limited and dependent on chance. The importance placed by the anti-Fascists on obtaining suitable plays is shown in a letter written by Wilhelm Koenen from Canadian internment to Thomas Mann in New York requesting copies of dramas, including Brecht's *Fear and Misery of the Third Reich*.[54]

The lack of scripts did not, however, prevent the development of a lively theatre scene in almost every camp. Although the concrete conditions varied from place to place, the general circumstances under which productions took place were similar everywhere. A satirical account of the process is provided by Gerry Wolff, later a leading performer in the GDR but then a member of the Hutchinson Camp drama group:

> It's very simple: you take 1. producer; 2. several copies of a play; 3. a dozen or so people suitable to act the parts; 4. technical staff (actually you can dispense with that but it looks well); 5. draw money from the immense funds of the theatre groups for [paints], costumes, etc.; 6. get a quietly situated hall for rehearsals and 7. get to rehearsing.[55]

Of course, as Wolff knew only too well, the reality was very different with — personnel apart — everything in short supply. To compensate for this lack a great deal of imagination and improvisation was needed, and the delight in experimentation was, as Freimut Schwarz noted, one of the most important and productive features of the camp theatres.[56] This applied in particular to the creation of sets and other technical effects: in

Huyton, great pleasure was taken in the stage curtain with the traditional laughing and crying masks surrounded by barbed wire — cut out of gold and silver paper and stuck on an ordinary black blanket;[57] in Australia, a stage workshop was organized which provided a splendid set for R.C. Sherriff's *Journey's End* 'where at the end the trenches collapsed to perfection';[58] and in Canada, the internees constructed their own stage and devised an original way of portraying God in the 'Prologue in Heaven' to Goethe's *Faust*: 'A piece of board was removed from the false ceiling in the recreation hut and an actor installed above it under the roof; the Divine Voice came booming through the gap.'[59] Such effects, created out of virtually nothing by the painters, sculptors and craftsmen in the camps, made a great impression on their fellow inmates. The technology in the Australian production of *Faust* does, though, seem to have got slightly out of hand: 'If [the] . . . 'Hallelujah' . . . didn't have quite the desired impact, this lay in the disruptions from which the scene suffered, particularly the unsuccessful lighting effects. Where the required impression cannot be obtained with existing, let alone non-existent, means such experiments should be avoided.'[60]

In general, however, the theatre practitioners in internment seem to have accepted the limitations of their situation, and the technical input in most productions provided an enriching contribution. Even then, the onus was placed chiefly on the skills of the actors, amateur and professional — including veteran performers of the London refugee stage like Josef Almas, Gerhard Hinze and Erich Freund and newcomers like Wolff and Michael Mellinger. As well as enthusiasm and talent, great versatility was demanded as is shown by Otto Tausig, who in Hutchinson Camp within the space of a few months appeared in the title role of *Schwejk*, as Dr Bull in *The Man Who Was Thursday*, as Daja in *Nathan der Weise*, as Franz in *Die Räuber*, and as Mrs Barthwick in *The Silver Box*.

This last role highlights a particularly delicate area — the portrayal of the female characters. Where possible this was avoided by putting on plays with all-male casts, such as *Journey's End*, or by keeping the character off-stage, as in the Canadian version of *Faust*: 'The absence of a suitable boy to play Gretchen caused a trickier problem. It was decided to present her voice only. When Faust first meets her in church, and later in her home, she was simply heard, through an open door. It was not hard to cast a suitable falsetto voice to speak her lines.'[61] In other cases, where an appearance could not be avoided, great tact and restraint were needed. In Hutchinson, the director, Fritz Weiss, succeeded in sending 'women' onto the stage 'who did not arouse the slightest feeling of embarrassment which could so easily arise from such masquerading',[62] and Jacques Bachrach seems to have had a similarly sensitive approach in Australia. In Canada, on the other hand, where the 'women problem' was particularly acute and homosexuality a real if temporary issue,[63] the appearance of 'stage females' often made a dubious impact, especially when the effect was heightened by elegant dresses put together from old sugar sacks by a specialist tailor, and make-up obtained through the auspices of a friendly camp commander: 'With open mouths and staring eyes many internees sat through the performances, never letting their attention drop from the 'female' performers. One of these amateur actors thought to have some fun out of his success. He carved wooden shoes with thin, very high heels and strutted about the camp, wiggling his behind.'[64]

Another general worry for the theatre groups was the organization of rehearsal space, as the recreation rooms, lounges and other possible locations were seldom free with, as Wolff comments, 'somebody . . . sure to [be playing] ping-pong and . . . four pianos . . . going at the same time'.[65] The première of *Journey's End* in Australia, for example, had to be postponed for a few weeks because the mess-hut was being used for Jewish holiday celebrations.[66] Rehearsal possibilities, despite the large amount of free time available, were thus rather restricted: for the last week of the production of *Of Mice and Men* in Hutchinson only twenty hours could be set aside, including time for costume calls and dress rehearsals.[67] But despite these difficulties, the theatre performances were high points in internment life, awaited by the camp population with great expectancy, even if some of the accompanying manifestations were less desirable:

> Whether it was an expression of enthusiasm for the theatre or the result of a 'whisper campaign' which preceded the [première] — in any case good seats could fetch on the black market up to ten shillings. It should be emphasised that the entrance tickets had been produced without expense by potato print and distributed in equal numbers to the barracks with democratic fairness. But even here there were well-to-do connoisseurs and snobs who had to experience the première under any circumstances from the front row.[68]

Even this could not diminish the effectiveness of the camp productions, reflected not only in the critical reviews in the camp newspapers but also in the huge popularity which the performers enjoyed amongst their fellow inmates: 'No public is so grateful as that behind barbed wire. We, the members of the camp stage, became popular overnight.'[69]

'Septembertage' in Huyton Camp

The temporary nature of most of the internment camps in England was a strong factor in determining the kind of cultural and performance work undertaken there. Most of the events were spontaneous, improvised affairs, often initiated by the younger prisoners who were able to adapt more quickly to this new kind of existence: 'Even in a camp like Kempton Park, the youth group was able to organize concerts, cabarets and similar social activities.'[70] Most performances remained at this impromptu level, often centred round individual artists like Hugo Baruch and his spontaneous cabarets.[71]

Open criticism of the state of affairs in the transit centres was usually too risky, so a number of clandestine gatherings were organized where political recitations and sketches were performed. Another way of 'rebelling' against the camp restrictions was discovered at Huyton: one of the cooks found a hidden cider store and, during the regular *Hausabende* which took place in the communities with more spacious living-rooms, he served this up as soup to the prisoners, thus allaying the suspicion of the guards.[72]

It was also at Huyton that two of the most original and ambitious theatrical projects occurred, both involving the young Communist poet who later became a major figure in the literary scene of the German Democratic Republic, Kurt Barthel. Kuba, as he was known, was responsible for the direction of *Böhmische Passion* by Louis Fürnberg, with whom he had earlier run an anti-Fascist theatre troupe in Czechoslovakia.[73] The play depicted recent Czech history through a combination of strong poetic images relating the struggles of the ordinary Bohemian people and highly satirical portrayals of the leading politicians involved. Eugen Brehm, who witnessed at least two productions of the piece, found this mixture of 'art and kitsch' puzzling and even accused Kuba of distorting the original for his own political ends.[74] Apart from the fact that such a mixture had been a feature of the earlier collaboration between Kuba and Fürnberg, this technique of adopting different styles to contrast historical figures with ordinary people is not unique — around the same time in America Bertolt Brecht was toying with a similar idea in his adaptation of Hašek's classical novel which later developed into *Schwejk in the Second World War*, in which a stylized depiction of Hitler is counterpointed by some of Brecht's most lyrical songs. Unfortunately little is known of the production of *Böhmische Passion* in Huyton except that it must have had a cast of at least thirty to forty actors, for Brehm noted almost a dozen leading rôles (although some may have been doubled up) as well as a number of speech choirs (*Sprechchöre*). This would make it the largest dramatic enterprise undertaken during the internment period.

Whilst Brehm found Fürnberg's play, for all its apparent contradictions, at least intriguing, he dismissed Kuba's *Septembertage* as a 'hurriedly put-together agit-prop play of the smoothest kind, having an impact only on the converted, but being totally incomprehensible for the mass of Jewish internees born in Germany'.[75] A full account of the production in *Freie Deutsche Kultur*, the magazine of the FDKB, presented a very different picture: 'In my life I have often visited the theatre and seen many great artists and wonderful productions, but one of the deepest impressions which I have experienced was a production by the Youth Group in Huyton Camp.'[76] The following description of the play by the anonymous Kulturbund critic supports the impression that we are dealing here with an original and important contribution to the refugee theatre in British exile. The story concerns a group of young people living in the border area of the Sudetenland, the German-speaking part of Czechoslovakia, which was under threat of annexation by Hitler:

> Hidden in the woods the youngsters . . . wait on guard . . . In vain [the Nazi Stormtroopers] try to force them out of hiding, the village remains united, they are not found . . . [The boys] have formed a singing group, Das neue Leben (The New Life), and have been performing in the surrounding villages, but now times have become too serious, they want to give up singing, the moment for fighting approaches. Then a telegram calls them to Prague, they are to sing on radio and through this show how for centuries the Sudetenland has been culturally linked with the Czech land . . . (They sing on radio and the whole country hears them.) But it is too late, the surrender has already been agreed. They return home but the invasion has begun. They want to fight . . . but the order comes: 'Shooting forbidden! Lay down your arms!' Now they know they have lost . . . They are hunted, they have to flee. But they swear to continue the fight until the day comes when they can return home.[77]

Clearly the play is more than just a smooth piece of agit-prop theatre; it works on a number of levels. Historically, it presented experiences that only a year before many of the refugees had directly undergone themselves — the autobiographical connection is further underlined by Kuba using the same name, 'Das neue Leben', as that of the drama group he and Fürnberg had run in Czechoslovakia[78] — and most of the audience had had to face up to the consequences of a Fascist invasion. At the same time such personal identification with the immediate past was set in a wider perspective, enabling the internees to draw parallels with their present predicament, especially the frustration of not being able to play a direct part in the anti-Fascist struggle. And although in the end the youngsters are defeated, the overall impact of the play comes not from the uselessness of their efforts but from their determination to continue the fight against overwhelming odds. This impression would have been heightened by the presence of many survivors of these events and the fact that, however belatedly, the Nazi advance was being challenged by the major international powers.

Underlying the immediate political concern, however, was a more general theme which occupied German refugee artists in all places of asylum: the rôle of art and culture in the struggle against Fascism. This aspect was treated in *Septembertage* in three ways: through the plot, the form and the context. The question of *Kunst oder Waffen?* (Art or Weapons?) is a dominant concern running right through the play. It is not, though, treated in a mechanical or dogmatic way but shown dialectically, with the balance between the two alternatives constantly shifting according to the prevailing circumstances. At the start, the young people are committed equally to both: preparing to defend their country at the same time as using their musical talents to gain support in the surrounding villages; the more imminent the invasion, the more important their military preparation becomes at the expense of their music; but when it is made clear that their singing can also contribute positively to the anti-Nazi struggle, they seize the opportunity readily; when even this fails, a last desperate attempt at armed opposition is made; finally, both art and arms prove useless, though for the future neither is ruled out. Whilst in the story definite choices have to be made, they are never shown as absolute and any overall conclusions are left open for the audience to debate.

The discussion about the function of art was supported in the action by a number of concrete examples, illustrating the various ways in which it could contribute to the political struggle. Within the overall framework of a dramatic presentation, song, music, poetry, sketches and even classical theatre combined to form an organic entity. The individual elements, whilst often making particular points in their own right, were only fully effective within the total concept. Thus an early inclusion of readings from *Romeo and Juliet* both introduced a thematic parallel to the immediacy of the situation and raised the question of the relevance of more formal art forms to the current struggle; later, the combination of Kuba's poems and Czech folk songs for the radio transmission underlined both what would be suppressed under Fascism and what had survived over the centuries — and would continue to survive in exile; and even the broadcast itself was directly linked in the minds of the audience with the German-language programmes being sent by the BBC to the Nazi-occupied regions.

And, of course, the whole production itself represented the triumph of art over the depressing conditions of the transit camps as well as the internees' recent experiences of sudden arrests, attempted suicides and general abandonment. Although the storyline alone cannot fully convey the impact of the live event, a few examples from the review in *Freie Deutsche Kultur* suggest that in this respect too something special occurred at Huyton. The build-up to the radio transmission, for example, indicates a sensitive handling of the dramatic presentation: 'The next scene shows us the youngsters in front of the microphone. Nervously they enter the broadcasting station, the technical apparatus makes them shy. They are told what they have to do, their fear falls away and they sing out confidently. In a wonderful montage of poems and folk songs and a sketch they show the unity of their land with Prague.'[79] Another powerful moment was when a sympathetic gendarme gave the youngsters rifles and a machine-gun and showed them how to use the weapons; as one of the boys aimed at the audience, 'the expression of hatred on [his] face [was] shocking'. If the ending seems somewhat sentimental for present-day tastes, the feelings aroused in the audience were appropriately mixed: sadness yet hope, isolation yet togetherness, loss yet gain, defeat yet victory:

> The play ends with a melodramatic poem which Kuba spoke from behind the stage in the dialect of his homeland, the youngsters humming a simple tune, the stage darkened, and the last words were:

> 'Mein guter alter Aschberg
> Wir kummen wieder z'samm.'

> 'My dear old Aschberg,
> We'll meet again some day.'[80]

Probably more than any other production put on by German-speaking refugees in British exile, *Septembertage* encapsulated the totality of their experience, including the will to survive and the hope of returning eventually to a peaceful homeland.

'Thunder Rock' on the Isle of Man

In strong contrast to the limited number of major productions in the transit camps on the mainland of Britain, the theatre activity on the Isle of Man was characterized by the large amount of serious drama performed there, as well as a variety of other live theatre events. The rationale behind such offerings — as the Austrian actor Peter Herz pointed out — was not as light-hearted as may have appeared: 'I tried at the time within my immediate circle to fight against the depressing atmosphere of the camp by forming the "Stacheldraht Cabarett" . . . through which new hope, fresh optimism and even a little joy could be planted in the hearts of the abandoned internees.'[81] Amongst the many cabaret offerings individual artists were prominent, like Peter Pojarski, whose *Galgenhumor* is described in Richard Friedenthal's novel *Die Welt in der Nußschale*, and was directed amongst other sensitive targets at the monotonous culinary offerings, the state of camp hygiene, the poor postal service and even the camp authorities.[82] At the other extreme was the bilingual revue *What a Life!*, premièred in September 1940 under the direction of G.M. Höllering — previously a collaborator on Brecht's film of Berlin working-class life, *Kuhle Wampe*, and later to become the owner of the Academy Cinema in London. Originally suggested by the camp commander, the show covered ten aspects of interned existence and was so popular with the British officers that it had to be repeated.[83] Such activities continued even as late as summer 1941, when 'most internees felt as if they already had one foot outside the barbed wire and camp life had become somewhat nervy'.[84] In August, as part of a cultural programme organized by the 'Popular University', Arthur Hellmer directed the Prologue from *Faust*, an extract from *Wallensteins Lager* was put on, and the mechanicals' scene from *A Midsummer Night's Dream* performed.[85] In November Hans J. Rehfisch even managed to organize a full-scale production of *Julius Caesar* at the Gaiety Theatre in Douglas.[86]

In the women's camps too, regular theatre events took place. In Port Erin, Luise Astmann put on a puppet show, *Geographie und Liebe*, a 'topical island play in classical guise';[87] traditional 'Weihnacht' celebrations included an ambitious attempt to 'combine a macabre drama with the Christmas story';[88] and even serious plays like the medieval morality, *Everyman*, and a free interpretation of *Turandot* by Marie Reidemeister were attempted.[89] As in the other camps, the concern was not merely to pass the time agreeably; political considerations could also play a part, as in an afternoon cabaret put on by the 'Youth Players' in front of the camp commander, her staff and a judge from the refugee tribunal: 'The important guests shook our hands. The impression they took away with them could only have been of young people, lively and confident, who even here behind barbed wire have not lost courage. What good and beautiful things these people could achieve if only they could be out there again, in freedom.'[90]

The most consistent theatre work, though, was produced in Hutchinson Camp where, under the direction of Fritz Weiss and with an acting company including Tausig, Wolff, Philo Hauser, Erwin Jacoby and — for a time — Paul Dornberger, an impressive series of classical German and modern English and American plays were put on. Following an earlier version of *Schwejk*, of which little is known, the group adapted G.K. Chesterton's mystical novel *The Man Who Was Thursday*, for presentation in the spring of 1941. Subtitled a 'nightmare' by the author, it was a choice hardly conducive to encouraging an optimistic outlook amongst the internees, reflecting as it does the emergence of anarchism at the turn of the century. Whilst Weiss's direction appears to have played down the symbolic mysticism of the original, as in the shifting of the last scene from 'Sunday's villa' to the more prosaic surroundings of Scotland Yard[91] (although this may equally well have been for reasons of practical staging), this production must to some extent have reinforced the sense of abandonment amongst the interned audience. The same could be said of John Steinbeck's *Of Mice and Men*, which had its première in March. This adapted short story about migrant American farmworkers and their dreams of a secure future does, it is true, invite comparisons with the lives of the internees on the Isle of Man, but here too the overall impact must have been somewhat depressing.

Lessing's *Nathan der Weise*, on the other hand, first performed on 21 April, aroused quite different emotions. At a time when many in Britain and elsewhere equated German culture with Hitler Fascism, such a performance of a German classical play in a country of exile was a strong affirmation of the desire to fight for the 'other Germany'. This work in particular, 'the famous play Hitler banned and burned because of its doctrine of humanity and tolerance',[92] had a special place amongst the exiles in Britain and was later performed by the Österreichische Bühne in London. Encouraged by their success with *Nathan*, the Hutchinson company then undertook in June the difficult task of staging Schiller's *Die Räuber*. Unfortunately little is known of this production either, except that it was performed in modern dress with a set designed by Carlo Pietzner, in which because of limited space the wood scenes were played in the auditorium.[93] No details at all survive of an 'excellent production' in July 1941 of Galsworthy's socially critical drama *The Silver Box*,[94] or of *Die Kassette* by Sternheim.

Luckily, accounts do exist of the production at the end of August 1941 of Robert Ardrey's play *Thunder Rock*, first produced by Elia Kazan in New York in 1939 and later successfully filmed in England with a cast containing many refugee actors (in March 1943 it was also put on by the Austrian exile theatre, the Laterndl). The story tells of a former fighter in the Spanish Civil War, fleeing from the harsh realities of the outside world, who takes on the post of lighthouse-keeper on an isolated rock. During his one-month stay there he is visited by the spirits of those who tried to emigrate following the defeat of the 1848 revolution in Europe; almost a hundred years previously they had been shipwrecked and drowned near this lighthouse. Through his encounter with the ghosts of these refugees, the keeper, Charleston, realizes that his withdrawal is only of use to those who want to delay the elimination of oppression and inhumanity. In the end he decides to rejoin the active struggle against injustice.

For the German internees, after nearly two years behind barbed wire, this rousing call to 'carry on the fight and courageously keep faith with the future'[95] highlighted a problem similar to that dealt with in *Septembertage*: the sense of hopelessness arising from the frustration of not being able to participate directly in the anti-Fascist fight. *Thunder Rock* tackled this theme in a very different yet equally effective way, although — as Fritz Weiss rightly emphasized in an introduction to the play in *The Camp* — the situation faced by the internees was not exactly comparable to that of Charleston:

> I believe . . . this particular play gives expression to many of the problems which are so intimately connected with our life here, with this difference: We refugees still interned are not here trying to escape the issue of our times. On the contrary just like the hero of the play we have come to the conclusion that it is our sacred duty to go out and fight for a new and better world, for the progress of civilization.[96]

The relevance of the play was nevertheless unmistakable, and not only to the internees. The officer in charge of the camp, who had originally suggested the play, also recognized its importance in sustaining the morale of his charges: 'I am certain that this performance will have given you ample opportunity to review your own problems in a different light. It is eminently constructive in so far as it refuses to justify the various moods of escapism and depression to which most of us tend to succumb at times.'[97]

Although Ardrey leaves the final decision to the individual, he does suggest that the way forward can be found only with the help of others, working together in a common cause. 'I have a feeling I'll be seeing you again some place', says Charleston, handing his duty over to another lighthouse-keeper who to all appearances will undergo a similar transformation to his predecessor's. The stirring effect of the play lay not only in its forceful message but also in the way in which it managed to handle a highly personal conflict within a wider historical setting without losing dramatic clarity. The appearance of the ghosts from the past, for instance, is not shown as a mystical event but as the concrete realization of the keeper's thoughts, and the theatrical means by which the political confrontation is presented are realistic, credible and entertaining. The choice of the lighthouse as the place of action works equally well on a literal and a symbolic level, and it is ironic that one of the most famous of all German émigrés in Britain, Albert Einstein, should suggest a similar 'place of asylum' for exiled academics: 'Einstein . . . made the suggestion that a place might be found for some of the younger exiled scholars in light-houses and lightships, presumably as companions of the Keepers, "where they might think out scientific problems of a mathematical or philosophi-

211

cal nature".'[98]

It is highly unlikely that this suggestion was the starting-point for *Thunder Rock*, but it does underline the appropriateness of the central metaphor of the drama. The theatre group in Hutchinson Camp greeted with predictable enthusiasm their discovery of this play, which in its later Laterndl production was regarded as 'the most unforgettable experience of our time in the emigration'.[99] Director Weiss was the first to start reading the script:

> ... behold during the second act I got so enthusiastic that I could hardly control my emotion. I instantly called together those members of the actors' guild which were within easy reach. And never had I experienced such enthusiastic reception amongst our actors. 'We must start with rehearsals immediately, this is the opportunity we have been waiting for', these were only some of the comments. One had in fact the impression that all of us had been released at the same time, so great indeed was the clamour that was going on at that time.[100]

The attraction for the interned refugees was heightened by Ardrey's astute portrayal of the isolated cynic, which corresponded so closely to their own feelings and experiences, as in this example provided by Weiss: 'A friend of mine recently released from internment told me once that he used to build up personages out of his imagination whilst he was held captive in a Nazi camp. He had to give it up, he admitted, for fear of going insane.'[101]

The importance placed on this production is indicated by the wide support given to the theatre company, not only by their fellow inmates and the Camp Captain, but even from London by the actor and FDKB patron, Walter Hudd.[102] Gerry Wolff's previously mentioned description of the production process suggests that the build-up to performance involved a number of difficulties, and even Fritz Weiss admitted that 'it has been far from easy to produce a play with ghosts of flesh and blood on a limited stage like ours'.[103] Despite this, the efforts of the participants, amongst whom Wolff as Charleston, Tausig, Erwin Jacoby and the nineteen-year-old set designer, Jochen Weigert, stood out, were rewarded with a huge success. More than all the other plays put on by the Hutchinson drama group, this production justified the fine reputation which the anti-Fascist theatre practitioners built up during their confinement on the Isle of Man and demonstrated how important their efforts on the cultural front were:

> The work was hard and has cost many anxious moments, but we all without any exception loved the work on this production. And we here, to the greater part refugees from Nazi oppression, are particularly happy to have performed this play, because we feel that, more than any other play before, it gives expression

to our needs and problems. We hope that we will soon be able to leave our 'Lighthouse' to go out and help to fight the menace, which is threatening to overcome our civilization.[104]

Theatre in Canadian Internment

Of all the internment centres, the least documented with regard to the theatre work is Canada, although there are many passing references to a number of interesting plays. The overall impression, however, is that the theatre was less able to establish itself consistently in comparison with other art forms, especially the visual arts. This may have been a result of the lack of community spirit amongst the internees in the face of the extreme difficulties suffered in Canadian internment, even though the anti-Fascists imprisoned there made great efforts to bring about an effective cultural life. Alongside the many improvised and small-scale performances, including readings from Shakespeare, a commemoration of Stefan Zweig, and a special programme on the anniversary of the occupation of Austria and Czechoslovakia,[105] a wide range of works by serious authors were performed. The most active drama group appears to have been in Farnham Camp under the leadership of Gerhard Hinze, where plays by Goethe, Wilde, O'Neill, Chekhov and others were produced. As in Australia, a reading of *Faust* took place as well as a performance of *Journey's End*; in addition, we find the first scene from *The Importance of Being Earnest*, Chekhov's *The Marriage Contract*, Eugene O'Neill's *In the Zone* and a parody of Hugo von Hofmannsthal's *Der Tor und der Tod*, entitled *Tropf und Trommler*, written by Fürstenheim, 'whose profession in England had been pig-breeding, which circumstance made his play still better'.[106] Hinze himself attempted to raise the tone with his performance of songs from Brecht's *Dreigroschenoper* (thus earning the nickname of Kanonen-Hinze), and the final event on 2 November 1941, before the internees were at last shipped back to the British Isles, included a rendering of *Abschied-souper* from Schnitzler's *Anatol*.[107] Elsewhere another Schnitzler play, *The Green Cockatoo*, and a drama about *Oliver Cromwell* were performed, whilst in New Brunswick two interesting productions of pieces by G.B. Shaw occurred. In his discussion of the theatre activities in this last camp, Eric Koch highlighted the difficulties of putting on a full-scale performance:

> Before then they had staged various revues and cabarets . . . But a three-act play, with sets, costumes, and original music, required much more. It could only be undertaken if there was some measure of stability; it required that neither the director nor any of the actors and designers would expect to be

7. Ewald Rosenthal as the Examining Magistrate in *The Good Soldier Schwejk* in the Tatura interment camp, Australia 1941. Drawing by George Blank

released to go to the United States or return to England during rehearsals . . . In short, such a venture presumed abandoning the hopes of attaining imminent freedom, as well as a ready response to [the] imperative 'You'll Get Used to It!'[108]

Nevertheless the production in question, *Androcles and the Lion*, seems to have been an excellent choice with numerous parallels between 'the absurdity of our internment and Shaw's satirical depiction of Christian virtues'. The other Shaw offering, *Man of Destiny*, a one-act drama about Napoleon, was deliberately performed in German, 'so that the officers would not be offended by Shaw's diatribes against the English'. Koch even suggested that this might have been the main reason for the choice of this rarely performed piece.[109] Another unfamiliar play with an all-male cast was *The First Legion* by the American Emmet Lavery, set in a monastery and including the young Anton Diffring, who later made a name for himself on the British stage. Unfortunately there are no further details of two original plays written by Paul Dornberger, *The Last Chance* and *Der junge König*.[110]

'Hay Days' in Australia

If Canada appears the most literary-orientated amongst the centres of interned drama, the most overtly political was surely Hay Camp in the Australian outback. There the émigrés were left more or less to themselves, without the continual comings and goings as on the Isle of Man or the constant confrontations with Nazi prisoners-of-war as in Canada. In addition, there seems to have been a higher proportion of experienced anti-Fascist theatre artists, most of whom had already appeared on the stage of the Kleine Bühne (Little Theatre) in London. These formed the nucleus of the drama group, as Max Zimmering remembered:

> Perhaps it was just an accident, perhaps those of us in Hut 36 had found ourselves together because 'like and like' attract one another — whatever it was, amongst the two dozen inhabitants of our hut there were . . . a painter (Hans Abarbanell), three actors (Josef Almas, Leo Bieber and Hugo Schuster), a man who adapted himself to anything, dramaturg, prompter, prop-man, etc. (that was my brother Siegfried) and finally myself as versifier. We also had our share of promising young talent . . . Of course, the guild from which our Camp Theatre sprang up was not confined to our residence. Actors, singers, musicians and not least writers and journalists were to be found in other huts.[111]

From Hut 36 the ambitious cabaret programme, *Erinnerung an Europa*, a revue in twelve scenes, was organized at the end of 1940 under Almas's direction with texts from Max Zimmering, Jacques Bachrach and Dr Wilhelm Russo, and a set by Abarbanell. This first production developed directly from the need to combat the worst consequences of isolation and confinement amongst the internees:

> Its content attempted to lift the fate of the internees out of the individual consciousness and to place it in the great events of Europe, to give them, despite a global situation which seemed far from rosy, hope for a better future and at the same time to show that — even here in the Australian steppes, behind barbed wire and far from their home in Europe — they were in no way out of circulation or to be regarded as dead.[112]

215

8. Artist's impression of Hay Camp, Australia

This confrontation with the moral and spiritual degeneration which the interned existence brought with it was not only treated in this revue by confronting the audience with reminders of the positive aspects of their European past; it was also done by criticizing the personal attitudes of the camp inmates. This aspect was emphasized by Max Zimmering in his Prologue to *Erinnerung an Europa:*

> You, friends, who've gathered round this stage,

In short scenes we'll present to you
With modesty yet humour too
The great things of our great new age.

Perhaps so great, though, all is not,
As in this camp where we survive,
Yet still we should for greatness strive,
To help to ease our heavy lot.

We play much more than just a game,
For through the action intertwined
A piece of truth you each should find
To help you nearer to your aim.

You each will see within this play
Yourselves as critically perceived;
Be warned, though, do not be deceived
By digs and jibes, it's just our way.

Who sees himself, whose look turns grim
And leaves complaining with a curse,
Of him his friends will think the worse:
Self-criticism's not for him.[113]

The biting yet constructive criticism which underpinned the revue as a whole did not prevent it from becoming an enormous success. The 'experts' declared it 'in the best traditions of the pre-Hitler German and Austrian cabaret' and out of a camp population of a thousand 1,500 seats were taken for the four performances.[114] To satisfy the demand for light-hearted yet high quality entertainment, a second programme, *Hay Days*, was put on, and as late as New Year 1942 Kurt Sternberg organized a *Snow White Revue*.[115] Other events included recitation evenings of classical and modern writers and a series of 'Autorenabende der Camp-Bühne', dedicated both to encouraging new literary and poetic talent and to sustaining the contact between 'the larger community and the individual'.[116]

This concern to provide a broader perspective is also seen in the numerous efforts to promote traditional European culture, though Rolf Stein's adaptation of *Schwejk* provoked — much to the disgust of the rest of the camp — 'a protest from an Austrian monarchist who maintained his sense of allegiance to the Hapsburgs right into the Australian wasteland'.[117] The highpoint of the classical offerings was undoubtedly Bachrach's production of *Faust*. Divided into two separate evenings, the First Part of Goethe's masterpiece, apart from the omitted 'Walpurgisnacht' scene, was performed as a 'kind of playreading', some scenes being acted out 'properly', others merely suggested. Despite the mixture of theatrical approaches, this 'novelty in the history of the stage' — a *Faust* performance behind barbed wire — seems to have been an interesting and thought-provoking effort: ' . . . Speakers and listeners alike showed themselves equal to the only-slightly shortened version and many scenes achieved very vivid effects.'[118] For this production, which attracted 600 spectators, Ernst Hermann Meyer sent specially written musical accompaniments out from England![119] But above all it was the actors who formed the basis of the success, with Almas outstanding in a number of roles, including one somewhat unusual characterization:

> Marthe Schwerdtlein is still rather a problem for a male speaker. And when this speaker is of such quality as Josef Almas, you forget totally that the casting of this rôle is an emergency solution. Of course he is more convincing in the study or on the Easter walk as the speaker of Wagner, even without costume or make-up the figure of the desk-bound student of limited horizons appears true to life.[120]

In the title rôle Bieber was also excellent, Bachrach's 'happiest entrance' as Mephistopheles was in the students' scene, and Gretchen 'whom we can't really afford to have in any proper sense' was played impressively and with tact by the young Michael Rittermann.

It was also Rittermann who directed the last major production at Hay Camp, *Journey's End*. Sherriff's popular play was written in 1919 under the immediate impact of the senseless slaughter of the First World War but was not performed in London until 1928. Even if the *Camp News* felt it had a 'very pro-British tendency' and showed 'the fairness of the British character'[121] — a rather ironic sentiment for the interned anti-Fascists — the real strength of *Journey's End* lay in its critical attitude towards the traditional officer élite in the British army, who up till then had been portrayed as heroically patriotic. Sherriff 'demystified' these heroes in order to bring out the brutality and senselessness of war. Michael Rittermann pinpointed the importance of this production for the camp population: 'Each of the internees, with the exception of a few quite young inmates, could of course remember the first world war; for this reason the play had a tremendous sense of reality for everyone who saw it. This was the reason for our great success in the camp.'[122]

Like their colleagues in the English transit camps, in the boarding-houses of the Isle of Man and the barracks in Canada, the members of the Camp Bühne in Australia were also able to show that even under the worst conditions of internment, culture — and the theatre in particular — had a major rôle to play. Rittermann summed up the feelings of all those, both performers and spectators, who experienced the numerous live performances behind barbed wire: 'The work on this production was wonderful and gave us all endless satisfaction. It was for a camp public unaccustomed to live entertainment enormously valued. We had a great success with it and this understandably delighted us all.'[123]

Notes

*Most of this article is adapted from my unpublished Ph. D. thesis, *Die Rolle des Theaters des 'Freien Deutschen Kulturbundes in Großbritannien' im Kampf gegen den deutschen Faschismus (1938–1947)*, Section II: 'Die Theatertätigkeit der deutschen anti-faschistischen Emigranten während der Internierungsperiode (Mai 1940–Ende 1941)', Berlin (GDR), 1972. Additional material supplied by Günter Berghaus. Translations from German undertaken by myself are indicated by an asterisk.

1. 'West Middlesex Gazette', quoted in *This England: Selections From the 'New Statesman' Column, 1934–1968*, Harmondsworth, 1969, p. 65.
2. From an interview with Gerry Wolff, Berlin 30 November 1971.
3. D.N. Pritt, *The Autobiography of D.N. Pritt*, Part One: 'From Right to Left', London, 1965, p. 236.
4. Mentioned by the English MP Eleanor Rathbone, in a debate in the House of Commons on 10 July 1940; quoted in Norman Bentwich, *The Rescue and Achievement of Refugee Scholars*, The Hague, 1953, p. 30.
5. Julius Berstl, *Odyssee eines Theatermannes*, Berlin (West), 1963, p. 177.*
6. Pritt, *Autobiography*, p. 236.
7. Letter from Wharf Mills, July 1940, quoted in *Arbeitsbericht der Sozialkommission des FDKB in Großbritannien*, London, June 1941.*
8. 'Somewhere in England', a poem written by Kuba in Prees Heath Camp, 1940, published in *Neue Deutsche Literatur*, January 1961, p. 46.*
9. H.N. Brailsford in *Reynold's News*, 14 July 1940; quoted in F. Lafitte, *The Internment of Aliens*, Harmondsworth, 1940, p. 92.
10. *Aus Port Erin*, a stenographed pamphlet, Isle of Man, 16 Sept. 1941.*
11. *Frauenruf*, the illegal weekly paper of the Rushen Women's Internment Camp, Port Erin and Port St Mary, Isle of Man, Sept. 1940, p. 1.
12. From an unidentified pamphlet on *Women's Internment Camps*.
13. Ibid.
14. Max Zimmering, 'Zwei Zigaretten', in *Der gekreuzigte Grischa*, Rudolstadt, 1969, p. 10.*
    According to Michael Rittermann the main reason for this harsh treatment on board the *Dunera* was the anti-Jewish attitude of the commander in charge of the troops. Apparently he was later court-martialled and demoted for this. See interview with Michael Rittermann, London, 18 August, 1988.
15. See D.N. Pritt, *Erinnerungen an Wilhelm Koenen*, London 10 Dec. 1965, pp. 3–4 (translated into German by Emmy Damerius-Koenen); Erich Millstatt, 'Kämpfer aus St. Helens', *Neue Deutsche Literatur*, Nov. 1966, pp. 41 ff.; *Stacheldraht*, interned newspaper, Farnham, Canada, Nov. 1941, p. 3.
16. Quoted in Freimut Schwarz, 'Kulturarbeit in den englischen Internierungscamps', in *Kunst im Exil in Großbritannien 1933–1945*, Berlin (West) 1986, p. 283.
17. Jan Petersen, 'Panik', in *Geschichten aus neun Ländern*, Berlin and Weimar, 1964, p. 180.*
18. 'Prees Heath', in *Freie Deutsche Jugend* (London), 1 Oct. 1941.*
19. Lafitte, *Internment*, p. 118.
20. Walter A. Berendsohn, *Die Humanistische Front*, II. Teil, Worms, 1976, p. 98.*
21. See Max Zimmering, 'Kunst hinter Pfählen', in *Aufbau*, vol. 3, 1948, p. 254.

Alan Clarke

22. See Eric Koch, *Deemed Suspect*, London, 1980, p. 152.
23. Louise Leonhard, 'Frauen im Internment Camp', *Die Zeitung* (London), 1 July 1941, p. 3.*
24. Ibid.*
25. See *Stacheldraht*, Nov. 1941, p. 2; *Zeitspiegel* (London), 18 April 1942, p. 5.
26. Rudolf Steiner, 'Kunst und Künstler im Camp', *Camp News* (Hay Camp), Australia, 1940.*
27. See Koch, *Deemed Suspect*, p. 153.
28. 'F.K.' (Franz Krämer?), 'Kultur', *Stacheldraht*, Nov. 1941, p. 5.
29. Ibid.
30. Freimut Schwarz, 'Kunst hinter Pfählen', *Freie Deutsche Kultur* (London), Feb. 1942.*
31. John Heartfield in *Camp Art in Canada*, publicity brochure for an art exhibition organized by the FDKB in London, 1941.*
32. See Berstl, *Odyssee*, p. 181; Lafitte, *Internment*, p. 118; Zimmering, *Aufbau*, p. 254.
33. *FDKB-Arbeitsbericht.*
34. Zimmering, *Aufbau*, p. 254.*
35. *Aus Port Erin*, 16 Sept. 1941.
36. Lafitte, *Internment*, p. 106.
37. Petersen, 'Panik', p. 178.*
38. Zimmering, *Aufbau*, p. 256.
39. Ibid.*
40. See ibid.
41. 'Prees Heath'.*
42. See *Onchan Pioneer*, 20 Oct. 1940, p. 3.
43. Heartfield, *Camp Art.*
44. A.B., *Abend der Gefangenen*, in the possession of Ernst Hermann Meyer.*
45. Schwarz, *Kunst im Exil*, p. 283.*
46. Schwarz, *Freie Deutsche Kultur.*
47. See Eugen M. Brehm, 'Meine Internierung', *Exil*, no. 2, 1986, p. 48.
48. Schwarz, *Freie Deutsche Kultur.*
49. See 'We want to fight alongside the democracies', *Freie Deutsche Kultur*, Dec. 1941.
50. Heartfield, *Camp Art.*
51. See Zimmering, 'Politische Bühne im Exil', in *Der gekreuzigte Grischa*, pp. 61–2, and in *Aufbau*, p. 254.
52. Zimmering, *Aufbau*, p. 254.*
53. Zimmering, 'Politische Bühne im Exil', p. 61.*
54. See letter from Wilhelm Koenen to Thomas Mann, November 1940, in the possession of Emmy Damerius-Koenen.
55. Gerry (Wolff), 'To produce a play', in *Camp Hutchinson Youth* (Isle of Man), 1 Sept. 1941; also in translation in Zimmering, 'Politische Bühne im Exil', pp. 66–7.
56. See Schwarz, *Kunst im Exil*, p. 285.
57. See 'Theater in Huyton', *Freie Deutsche Kultur*, Dec. 1940.
58. Hugh Rank, 'Our Prisoners of War', *Radio Times* (London), 27 Nov.–3 Dec. 1982, p. 98.
59. Koch, *Deemed Suspect*, p. 154.
60. Dr Wilhelm Russo, ' "Faust" auf der "Camp-Bühne" ', in *Camp News*, Dec. 1940.*
61. Koch, *Deemed Suspect*, p. 154.
62. Zimmering, 'Politische Bühne im Exil', p. 66.*
63. See Koch, *Deemed Suspect*, pp. 157 ff.
64. Petersen, 'Panik', p. 180.*
65. Wolff, 'To produce a play'.
66. See *Camp News*, 16 Apr. 1941.
67. See rehearsal plan written on back of programme for *Of Mice and Men*, 6 March 1941, in the possession of Erwin Jacoby.
68. Zimmering, 'Politische Bühne im Exil', pp. 63–4.*

69. Ibid., p. 64.*
70. Lafitte, *Internment*, p. 118.
71. See Michael Seyfert, 'His Majesty's Most Loyal Internees', in *Gerhard Hirschfeld* (ed), *Exile in Great Britain: Refugees from Hitler's Germany*, Leamington Spa, 1984, p. 180.
72. See Brehm, 'Meine Internierung', p. 49.
73. Hansjörg Schneider, 'Exil in der Tschechoslowakei', in *Exil in der Tschechoslowakei, in Großbritannien, Skandinavien und Palästina*, Leipzig, 1980, p. 119.
74. See Brehm, 'Meine Internierung', p. 51.
75. Ibid.*
76. 'Theater in Huyton', *Freie Deutsche Kultur*, Dec. 1940.*
77. Ibid.*
78. See Schneider, 'Exil inder Tschechoslowakei', p. 119.
79. 'Theater in Huyton', *Freie Deutsche Kultur*, Dec. 1940.*
80. Ibid.*
81. Peter Herz, 'Die Kleinkunstbühne "Blue Danube" in London 1939–1954', in *Österreicher im Exil 1934–1945* Vienna, 1977, p. 451.*
82. See Richard Friedenthal, *Die Welt in der Nußschale*, Munich, 1956, pp. 136 ff.
83. See Seyfert, 'His Majesty's Most Loyal Internees', p. 181.
84. Zimmering, 'Politische Bühne im Exil', p. 65.*
85. See programme for 'Auf der Fest-Wiese', Isle of Man, in possession of Nina Freund.
86. See Hans J. Rehfisch, 'Zeittheater', in *Gebrannte und Gebannte*, FDKB pamphlet, London, May 1942, p. 23.
87. *Frauenruf* (Isle of Man), Sept. 1940, p. 3.
88. 'Frauen im Internment-Camp', *Die Zeitung*, 1 July 1941, p. 3.
89. Programme of *Turandot* by the Ailsa Craig Group, Isle of Man, in the possession of Emmy Damerius-Koenen.
90. 'Lita', 'Youth Players in Port Erin', *Aus Port Erin*, 19 Sept. 1941, p. 2.*
91. See programme for *The Man Who Was Thursday*, in the possession of Erwin Jacoby.
92. Programme for *Nathan der Weise*, in the possession of Erwin Jacoby.
93. From the Wolff interview.
94. See Zimmering, 'Politische Bühne im Exil', p. 65.
95. R.P., '"Leuchtfeur" im Laterndl', *Einheit* (London), 13 Apr. 1943, p. 20.*
96. Friedrich Weiss, 'Thunder Rock', *The Camp* (Isle of Man), 1 Sept. 1941.
97. 'Appreciation of the Camp Captain', *The Camp*, 1 Sept. 1941.
98. Bentwich, *Rescue and Achievement*, p. 14.
99. H.H., 'Thunder Rock', *Freie Tribüne* (London), 31 March 1943, p. 6.*
100. Weiss, 'Thunder Rock'.
101. Ibid.
102. See 'Appreciation of the Camp Captain', *The Camp*.
103. Weiss, 'Thunder Rock'.
104. Ibid.
105. See letter from Dr Freund in *Zeitspiegel*, 13 June 1942, p. 8.
106. 'Culture', *Stacheldraht*, Nov. 1941, p. 7.
107. See 'Our Farewell Party', *Stacheldraht*, Nov. 1941, p. 12.
108. Koch, *Deemed Suspect*, pp. 153–4.
109. Ibid., p. 154.
110. See Wilhelm Sternfeld and Eva Tiedmann, *Deutsche Exil-Literatur 1933–1945*, Heidelberg, 1970.
111. Zimmering, 'Politische Bühne im Exil', p. 63*
112. Zimmering, *Unsterbliches Lachen*, a partly published manuscript, Dresden (undated), p. 11.*
113. Ibid.*
114. See Zimmering, 'Politische Bühne im Exil', p. 63.
115. See Seyfert, 'His Majesty's Most Loyal Internees', p. 182.
116. See Steiner, 'Kunst und Künstler in Camp'.

117. Zimmering, *Unsterbliches Lachen*, p. 14.*
118. Russo, '"Faust"'.
119. From an interview with Ernst Hermann Meyer, Berlin, 2 March 1971.
120. Russo, '"Faust"'.
121. 'The Campman's Diary', *Camp News*, 30 March 1941.
122. Interview with Michael Rittermann, 18 August 1988.
123. Ibid.

Appendix A

Thespis Behind the Wire, or Entertainment in Internment
A Personal Recollection

GEORGE W. BRANDT

The summer of 1940 . . . Dunkirk . . . France had fallen. . . In Britain, German and Austrian nationals were rounded up and interned: a footnote to the war that has been largely forgotten. Except of course by the people involved — like me for instance. To misquote Goethe after the battle of Valmy, 'Ich bin dabei gewesen'.

What a mixed bunch of people we were behind the barbed wire! Recent and not so recent Jewish refugees from Nazism, affluent or down-and-out, orthodox or atheist; anti-Fascists involved in the anti-Hitler struggle, including some International Brigaders; and random stragglers in this century's population shifts — Czechs, Dutchmen, stateless persons; flotsam like that pathetic group of little old German barbers who had been working in England for decades but never bothered to get themselves naturalized.

Nearly half a century later, the experience has lost its sting. In retrospect it seems 'not too bad' — as indeed it wasn't compared to the real horrors of the war. It didn't feel too good at the time though, being put away by what one thought of as one's own side.

These hundreds and hundreds of very diverse people cooped up in a small space generated a good deal of friction; a good deal of intellectual energy as well. Some of this energy went into all sorts of performances. The camp show became an important feature of life, as is apt to be the case among wartime prisoners.

My first show was the one I witnessed at Huyton, Liverpool. I had been delivered there by solo transport with my very own armed escort some time in June 1940 (I forget the exact date). The camp was a recently completed housing estate which had had barbed wire and watch towers thrown around it before any tenants had moved in. We were the first inhabitants. Every square inch of floor space in the empty houses was taken up by suitcases and bodies. It was a hot summer, that summer of the blitzkrieg in the West, so we spent as many hours as possible out of doors, in the streets and backyards of the estate, meeting, arguing, trying to find our bearings. Shortly after arriving I was told there was going to be a camp show.

I went along to this open-air event which happened in the afternoon or early evening, I forget which. A large platform, some five feet high, was surrounded on three or maybe all four sides by a large audience, standing tightly packed like Elizabethan groundlings. The show was a series of cabaret-type turns. A piano, I seem to recall, was the only item on stage. Music was, of course, a feature of all camp shows. Among the inmates there was a formerly well-known composer of *Schlager* who had written a new or adapted an old song for the occasion. He played and sang it and invited the audience to join in. Pleased to be doing something together, we did. I cannot for the life of me remember any of the other turns except for this one: two comedians reading out the current news from a huge sheet of paper. As they went down each column they made their satirical points about the world at large and our situation in particular. Having gone down four columns they looked and looked for another one, couldn't find it and then announced, 'There isn't any Fifth Column here!' This term, coined by Franco to describe his secret supporters in besieged Madrid, was on everybody's lips at the time; the Germans had used Fifth Columns in their attacks in Holland, Belgium and France. We enthusiastically agreed that we were no Fifth Columnists; the declaration was, of course, aimed mainly at the British army personnel watching the show. Strictly speaking it wasn't the whole truth. The vast majority of internees were — passively or in some cases very actively — opposed to Fascism; but there *was* a Nazi element in the camp as well. They weren't very hard to spot. Flushed with hopes of an early German victory they hardly bothered to disguise where they stood.

If that show had given the inmates a sense of solidarity it wasn't to be for long. Overseas transports were shortly to wrench them apart again. Australia was one destination, Canada another; as the prisoners lined up for trans-shipment they didn't know where they were bound for. In July I was sent to Canada on the notorious *Ettrick* which made the Atlantic crossing in convoy in ten days. My first resting-place was Camp L just outside Quebec City, on the same Plains of Abraham where General Wolfe had defeated the French 181 years earlier. Camp L held 793 inmates. Once we had settled down in our huts, some cultural activities started up. The first was an art exhibition. The commandant, Major Wiggs (affectionately referred to as 'Piggy-Wiggy') was impressed. The camp turned into a buzzing hive of art critics.

Next, a camp show was organized. Again, this wasn't a play but another mixed bag of offerings, a *bunter Abend*. Unlike the Huyton show this was an indoor event set in the dining-hut. Tables ranged side by side at one end of the hut made a stage. Was there a curtain? I don't recall. Uprights (were they upended tables? Fibreboard or wooden planks? I don't remember) masked entrances left and right as well as, set far back, upstage centre. The lighting was rudimentary: on or off.

There were some musical turns — of course. Löffler squeezed his accordion — we had heard him practising for hours in our hut before. A professional juggler who had kept juggling even during the Atlantic passage displayed his skill. I had co-authored and directed a piece which poked fun at the internal camp government — a meeting of self-important hut fathers — in which well-known camp characters were lampooned. At the end of the sketch, the committee members suddenly tilted backwards and vanished behind the table at which they had been sitting.

One number was for the ear only — just a radio set placed on stage. Voices were piped in from backstage, comic turns in English and German. One of these was the inevitable Hitler imitation. We were well served by an Austrian who could do a Führer speech at the drop of a hat, guttural accent and all. A line from the Führer's own vocabulary — 'Es ist mein fanatischer Wille . . .!' — sticks in my memory. But what was he feeling fanatical about? I just don't remember.

A sketch I wrote and acted in was a duologue between a Canadian soldier and an internee who consistently talked past each other. This, too, pointed out among other things that we weren't Nazis in improbable disguise. Since Piggy-Wiggy and other officers graced the show with their presence it seemed a good opportunity for putting them straight. They seemed pleased with the efforts of 'their' internees.

A few days later some of us received an amazing invitation, or rather order. We were to play some items from the show again — outside. Outside the camp! It seemed too good to be true. Through the wire on one side we had a panoramic view of the Plains of Abraham sloping down to the majestically wide St Lawrence; on the other side we saw the turrets of the Château Frontenac Hotel peeping over the crest of the hill that bounded our horizon. Would we be getting a chance to see this *terra incognita* at close quarters? We got ready that evening, hearts pounding. Would we be playing at the Château? A private venue? A theatre?

Disillusionment was instantaneous. We were marched not outside the camp, but only out of the inner compound, just a few paces down the road — and there we were, in one of the soldiers' huts. We were to entertain the troops. What a let-down! We went into a huddle to decide what to do next. But since we wanted to prove that we were friendly rather than enemy aliens, friendly we'd better be. We performed. To be honest, the

George W. Brandt

reception we had was OK. Undemonstrative but OK. We got a cup of coffee each and some slices of buttered toast.

There were other events in Camp L. The actor Gerhard Hintze did not actually perform any roles as such but he gave recitals of poetry and, if I recall rightly, passages from plays. His *bühnendeutsch* diction was flawless. For a group of men speaking every known dialect of German (and Austrian), listening to Hintze was more than a pleasure, it was an education. His exquisitely manicured pronunciation was the height of verbal elegance.

In October 1940 the population of Camp L was split up again. A great many of us were transferred to Camp N, outside Sherbrooke, Province of Quebec, where later we were joined by transports from other camps. Unlike our first stopping-off place, Camp N was totally unprepared. It was simply a group of railway repair sheds encrusted with many years' deposit of soot, offering only minimal toilet or other facilities. This is not the place to describe our initial resistance, followed by the long slog of making the place fit for human habitation: that story has been told authoritatively by Eric Koch in his book *Deemed Suspect* (Toronto 1980). Once we had dug ourselves out of the debris, the desire for entertainment returned. Music was pre-eminent: concerts by the violin virtuoso Gerhard Kander, piano recitals by John Neumark (or Newmark) and the Hindemith pupil Helmut Blume who was later to become the Dean of the Faculty of Music at McGill University.

But of course *bunte Abende* or cabarets, though more difficult to set up than music recitals, also happened from time to time. One that comes to mind in particular is the New Year's Eve celebration 1940/41. I was in charge of arranging it, I wrote some of the numbers, acted in it and served as MC. The venue was a good deal more spacious than our dining-hut in Camp L. The mess-hall which was our 'theatre' in Camp N was an enormous railway shed which could hold the entire camp population of 736 men. We rigged a proper stage — timber was readily available — in one corner of the hall, with a small backstage area and some pretence of stage lighting. We got up our basic wardrobe from the clothes we had among ourselves without, as far as I can recall, getting any official help (but I may be doing the authorities less than justice here).

The show had some musical items, of course. There was a comedian who translated some Yiddish expressions into the camp authorities' official jargon. There was a sketch (in English, not in German) in which a top-level British government committee deciding internment policy was portrayed. Needless to say, they were pompous nincompoops.

Suddenly the show was interrupted — an internee in solitary confinement (a punishment actually used for some offences) was brought in to participate in the celebrations. He was in a wooden cage so that his confinement would continue. On closer inspection this figure dressed in the internment uniform with the large red spot on the back of the jacket proved to be a lifesize doll.

I gave a reading of Goethe's *Der Erlkönig* in the grand manner of Hintze, who was no longer with us (he had been sent to another camp from Camp L). This affectionate parody kept being interrupted by announcements and digressions; a man with a deadpan expression entered, stood close to me and just stared; the recital collapsed like Chico Marx's piano. The concluding lines:

> Erreicht den Hof mit Müh und Not,
> In seinen Armen das Kind war tot

were timed — no, not timed: improvised — to come as a crashing anticlimax. Some lifelong friendships were to spring from that ten-minute skit.

At the end of the show I appeared in a cheesecloth outfit and after cutting a few capers addressed the audience thus:

> Schnell wie der Wind — husch! — bin ich da,
> Die allerschönste aller Feen.
> Ich nenne mich Aspasia
> Und flitze her auf Silberschwingen,
> Durch leichte Lüfte leicht getragen,
> Gar wunderlieblich anzusehen.
> Von dunklen, zukunftsschwangren Tagen
> Will ich euch goldne Botschaft bringen . . .
> Ich sage euch die frohe Märe:
> Noch eh des Jahres Kreis verflossen,
> Ist euch der Stacheldraht erschlossen.
> Fast jeder von euch macht Karriere,
> Und mehrere sind Millionäre . . .

> Swift as the wind — whoosh! — here I am,
> Of all the fairies the most fair.
> I'm called Aspasia and I come
> A-fluttering on silver wings,
> On gentle breezes gently borne,
> Wholly delightful to behold.
> Of dark and fateful days to come
> I bring you golden prophecies. . . .
> I give this happy news to you:
> Ere the year's circle is complete
> The wire will disgorge you all.
> You'll most of you have big careers,
> With some becoming millionaires . . .

As a general forecast this wasn't too far out. Many of us were to be released in the course of 1941; some at any rate were to do well in their subsequent lives. But Aspasia made a number of rather more specific and indeed fanciful forecasts about the future of certain well-known camp characters. These in hindsight have turned out to be less than reliable. The end of the recitation coincided with midnight.

> Doch still! Tut's Mitternacht nicht schlagen?
> Hör ich nicht, wie die Stunde kracht?
> Dann kann ich froh: 'Es ist vollbracht!'
> Von Neunzehnhundertvierzig sagen.
> Beschissen war's! Darum hurra!
> Es leb' des Neujahrs Mitternacht!
> So spricht die Fee Aspasia,
> Die drauf sich auf die Socken macht.

> But soft! Is that not midnight's ring?
> Do I not hear the hour boom?
> So I can cheerfully declare
> Of Nineteen Forty: 'It is done!'
> A shitty year! Well then — hooray!
> Long live the New Year's Midnight hour!
> Thus speaks the fay Aspasia
> Who makes a speedy getaway.

I must admit that Camp N never rose to the actual production of a play. Not with live actors anyway. There was, however, a full length puppet show. An experienced puppeteer enlisted a group of enthusiasts to build a miniature theatre complete with a cast of marionettes in order to put on the puppet play of Doctor Faustus. We didn't have a text — but what of it? The script of this traditional play was reconstructed from memory, with new songs and music added. For Faust's visit to the Duke of Parma, a very attractive minuet was written by our resident composer Fritz Grundland, alias Freddie Grant. (His camp song, *You'll Get Used to It*, was subsequently adopted by the Canadian Navy as its theme song.)

The puppets were beautifully made. When Kasperle, Faust's manservant in the puppet play, conjured up devils from hell by citing spells from his master's book of magic, the demons that appeared were marvellously fantasticated. One of them had an extensible neck which could stretch halfway across the stage and then shrink back again. A group of puppeteers were trained to a respectable level of competence. For the performance, actors and singers were seated in the wings. I spoke the title role. There was some music — I forget now whether it was only a piano or strings as well. The minuet was danced very handsomely.

Other camps did in fact mount complete stage plays, notably Camp B at Little River in New Brunswick. They performed the other *Faust* — Goethe's version. In the Prologue in Heaven the voice of God (who remained invisible) came through a hole in the false ceiling from which a tile had been removed. Shaw was a popular author in Camp B. Both *Androcles and the Lion* and *The Man of Destiny* were staged, the latter in German so as not to provoke the Canadian officers with Shaw's anti-English gibes. The part of the mysterious lady was performed by Anton Diffring, who was later to make a name for himself in such British films as *The Colditz Story, I Am a Camera, Fahrenheit 451* and *Where Eagles Dare.* Another ambitious production was Schnitzler's *Der grüne Kakadu.* The play's large cast was no deterrent where manpower was freely available, and the number of female roles was mercifully limited. I should add that I am indebted to Eric Koch for this information about Camp B; I wasn't there myself.

There is no cause to praise these theatrical activities beyond their merits. They served the needs of the moment and that was enough. They were effective morale boosters for participants and spectators alike. Some of the former may have been pointed in the direction of their future careers. For the latter they left memories that cast a rosy glow over an unpleasant episode in their lives. These memories, as the writer of this is only too well aware, are growing fainter and fainter as time moves on.

Appendix B

Tdc 186

A Repertory Theatre in a PoW Camp

CARL WEBER

In October 1944, a column of lorries packed with German prisoners of war drove down a low ridge into the parkgrounds belonging to a manor house in the vicinity of Colchester, Essex. They stopped on a large meadow, enclosed with barbed wire fence, where their cargo was unloaded. The men jumped down from the lorries and viewed with some apprehension the fence, the clusters of trees around the clearing, the folded tents and wooden floor boards stacked on the wet grass, and the grey afternoon sky above. No one could envision that less than a year later a small town of Nissen huts in neat rows, patterned by a grid of paved roads, would occupy this bucolic space, and that the tallest structure in town would be a building with semi-circular steps leading up to its entrance door, a theatre where six nights a week a repertoire of classical plays, along with less ambitious fare, was presented by a company numbering close to fifty performers, designers and technical staff. This "Theater des Camp 186" would indeed become an unusual phenomenon among the cultural activities in British PoW camps; if there was anything comparable, I haven't yet seen documentation of it.

In October 1944, however, there were only rows of pup tents set up by the prisoners, with some large mess tents in between, where the men began to make themselves at home while the fog and rain of early winter turned much of the camp grounds into a morass. I was among the youngest inmates, drafted from high school into the army and having picked the first occasion which offered itself during the German retreat from France into Belgium to surrender to the advancing Allied troops. After a brief stay in a transit camp near Dieppe, I had been among the lucky ones who were shipped to England, processed on the site of a race track near London, and then trucked to Colchester.

When the British camp administration was looking for interpreters, I decided to negotiate my modest school English to advantage and volunteered. Soon I and another young soldier, who was even less proficient in

English, made our home in a tent next to the camp gate; a tent we shared with an old Sergeant Major, a crusty and not all too pleasant professional soldier who was one of the three German 'Lagerführer' (camp leaders) appointed by the British.

It was part of my duty at the gate that I had to translate all sorts of requests by prisoners and the orders which came down from the British camp command in the manor house close by. One day a bespectacled prisoner approached me who wanted to discuss with the Officer on Duty the possibility of using one of the mess tents for a planned theatrical performance. The British captain promised to submit the request to the Camp commander, while I was introduced to a group of prisoners who had discovered their shared interest in the stage. Some had been professional actors, singers, or directors in civilian life, others were students from theatre schools; several just liked performing as a hobby or had acted at home in amateur groups. One of them owned a volume with Schiller plays which somehow he had salvaged during fighting and capture, and they had agreed to put on a performance of Schiller's *Die Räuber* (The Robbers). They still were looking for additional performers and asked me if I would be interested. I was, and after a kind of 'audition' when I was asked to read from the rôle of Spiegelberg (a character I had relished when we read the play in literature class at school), they offered me the part in their planned production. I most gladly accepted and so became one of the founding members of what we later were to call Theater des Camp 186.

The group had been gathered and was guided by two professionals: August Rieger (the bespectacled man who came to the camp gate), a young, wiry actor and director from Vienna who had worked at the Akademie Theater, and Kurt Büchner, a grey-haired, slightly pompous actor in his forties who had been with the Kassel State Theater — or so they told us; it was, of course, not possible to check any credentials. Rieger, indeed, turned out to be a gifted director, and by late November rehearsals were in full swing. The British administration made one of the large mess tents available to us, and we erected a stage in it, using mess tables to build a raised platform. A curtain was sewn from blankets; uniform parts, cotton shirts and long underwear were made into costumes by the actors and a professional tailor who volunteered his services. There even was some dyeing, tea being used for all sorts of yellows or browns, and permanganate, courtesy of the camp pharmacy, for various shades of purple. The set was created with tables put upright, blankets and sheets which were hung or stretched, and whatever furniture pieces were available to us. The lighting was provided by kerosene lamps of regular army stock.

Rieger himself played Franz von Moor; Büchner was his brother Karl, leader of a gang of highway men; among the cast were as Kosinsky the young Willy Stoll, pupil of the famous German actor Will Quadflieg, and later, as Günther Stoll, a quite successful German stage and TV actor; the equally young Wolfgang Feige (as Roller), who also made a very respectable professional career after the war; and, as the old Count Moor, Herbert Scholz, a member of the Communist Youth Organization before 1933 who had managed to survive during Nazi rule by doing small rôles in movies and occasional jobs in suburban music halls (after the war he joined the company of East Berlin's operetta house, the Metropol Theater). The only female part in the play, Amalia, had been eliminated. We were hesitant to cast women with men, and such cutting could dramaturgically be justified in *Die Räuber*. Our performance must have been a curious blend of professional work along with all levels of amateur acting, among the latter my Spiegelberg.

The production opened on Christmas Eve, 1944; the tent was packed with prisoners, sitting on the ground in front of the stage or standing tightly packed in the back, while many more stood outside just listening to the text and trying to get a glimpse through the open entrance of the tent. As I recall, the performance lasted more than three hours, but the audience was totally spellbound: there was hardly a stir, hardly a sound. We assumed this was mainly due to the PoWs' Christmas sentiments, extremely heightened by the prisoners' total lack of information about their families at home, and reinforced by the impact of Schiller's highly charged emotional language as it was presented in such an unusual environment. Whatever the specific cause was, mere sentimentality or a true understanding of Schiller's forceful cry against tyranny and its abuses, at the end the audience was in tears and gave us an ovation. There was no question in anybody's mind that we would continue to perform, at least as long as we could keep our group together. We went on playing *Die Räuber* during weekends, while we prepared our second production.

Our only literary source available was the book with Schiller plays from which we had copied by hand the rôles for *Die Räuber*. It must have been Volume One of a collected works edition, since it contained another early play by Schiller, *Die Verschwörung des Fiesco zu Genua* (The Conspiracy of Fiesco at Genoa). *Fiesco* appealed to us since, again, it was easy to eliminate the rather minor female parts by judicious editing. It also made a clear political statement about tyranny, the abuses of power, and the rulers' contempt for the people which goes along with it. We rehearsed the shortened piece for about five weeks and opened the production in February 1945. Rieger again directed, and the same group of performers, with one or two additions, acted. I had been given the title rôle, not without considerable misgivings on my part, but I did get away with it and this surely became one reason for my eventually considering the theatre as a career. This time, Rieger didn't perform himself; besides the actors already mentioned, there were interesting performances by Karl Wirtz as Andrea Doria, Hans Richert as his son, and Werner Zogbaum as leader of the commoners. Sets and costumes showed considerable improvement in the imaginative use of all kinds of materials available to us, and the nucleus of a technical staff had been formed. The production was successful, though it didn't achieve the tremendous impact of our Christmas opening of *Die Räuber* — as was only to be expected.

The British administration, meantime, had permitted us to erect next to the theatre tent a second large mess tent where all members of the company could be housed. All of us had by now given up other activities we had been involved in, as interpreters, members of the camp's medical staff or of work details, and we were regarded as a 'permanent' company. Moreover, a change in the camp's structure, which was implemented during February/March 1945, created a new situation which offered the occasion to establish a theatre that emulated the model of Germany's many subsidized professional companies.

During March 1945, the British started to transfer most inmates to other camps, and only a rather small number of about 200 PoWs was retained as permanent staff at Camp 186, which now became a transit camp where the ever increasing numbers of arriving new prisoners were processed and then distributed to other locations all over England. During this overhaul, all PoWs 'indigenous' to Camp 186 were screened for their political beliefs by a special commission which arrived from Headquarters of East Anglia. All prisoners had to appear at appointed times singly in front of an officer whom they, of course, first had to salute, before he asked them a few questions. The official salute of the German army was, since the assassination attempt against Hitler in July 1944, the Nazi salute with the right arm raised, the hand stretched out. However, once in England, many of us had made a point of saluting again in the old German army manner, hand at the cap or temple.

After the fall of the fortress Brest in Brittany, early in 1945, large numbers of parachute troopers had arrived at Camp 186, many of them fanatical Nazis. They twice killed fellow prisoners whom they regarded as traitors, dumping the bodies in one of the water-filled ditches along the camp roads so that the British authorities did not have any chance to trace a corpse to his murderers. When the screening commission began its work in a large Nissen hut (such huts were beginning to take the place of tents by early 1945), parachute troopers kept loitering outside to watch through the windows the goings on in the brightly lit interior. No wonder that most prisoners saluted smartly with raised arm and stretched hand, demonstrating their loyalty to the Führer. It soon became obvious that the commission regarded the manner of saluting as a simple but effective litmus test for the political stance of the screened prisoners who, as rumour had it, were graded after the interview from A to D, 'Anti-Fascist' to 'Hardcore Nazi', and then send to camps for Anti-Fascists or Nazis, according to their grading.

We from the theatre saluted the screening officer the old Prussian way, certainly from conviction if not necessarily from sheer heroism: living together in our tent we felt fairly secure and never went out after dark except in groups of two or three. Nevertheless, one evening there was an effort made to pull down our tent, but when we all rushed out in full force, armed with boards and other objects handy for our defence, the attackers vanished into the night. My screening officer turned out to be a Czech major from Prague who, of course, was fluent in German. He had seen our *Fiesco*; after a few questions about my views of Hitler and the Nazi system, he spoke at length about the performance and seemed impressed that we had put on a play about the rise and fall of a tyrant who used his city's political crisis to his own unscrupulous ends. Since the personal statements of most company members did corroborate his favourable impression, his report was probably supportive, if not instrumental, during the subsequent developments which led to the firm establishment of Theater des Camp 186.

However, a first result of the screenings was the transfer of some of our group to other camps. We petitioned the British administration to no avail; Rieger and three or four less important company members had to leave, obviously a result of their interview. But soon we were able to compensate for our losses. Since nearly every day new PoW transports arrived, to be processed and then distributed to other camps, we asked permission to contact theatre professionals and other interested persons in each arriving group. Permission was given, and we were fortunate in recruiting some exceptional talent from those transients. The first new professional to join us was Hans Buehl, formerly of the Municipal Theatre of Koblenz, who became a leading actor and director with us. After his return to Koblenz, he again worked there as an actor, dramaturg and director.

Since we still had no access to German language scripts, Buehl proposed to put together a cabaret-type revue from skits, songs, musical numbers, and other appropriate material of our own invention. The show, *Pech und Schwefel*, consequently was partly authored and also directed by Buehl. It was truly low-brow entertainment: a few operetta arias, sung by H. Scholz; a violin virtuoso piece, called 'The Canary', presented by W.

Zogbaum on a violin he managed to get from a collection of instruments the YMCA had donated to the camp; some rather trite dialogue skits Buehl and K. Büchner jotted down from memory; and an amateur magician's act, made up the programme. The big hit, however, was the final number: H. Buehl, in drag, sang his self-written title song *Pech und Schwefel* (Pitch and Brimstone), which made fun of the various meanings this colloquial German phrase conveys, while he also cavorted in a cancan-style dance. This rather grotesque display each night brought down the house — or rather, the tent — and had to be repeated. There would be nothing remarkable about such an example of the well-known popularity drag shows enjoy in all-male environments, like camps or prisons, if Buehl's skilful, funny and effective female impersonation hadn't demonstrated to us that indeed women's rôles could be convincingly performed by men. And so the next project — our group certainly wasn't timid! — was *Faust, Part 1* which opened, of course, at Easter 1945.

The YMCA had donated a small German language library to the camp; not surprisingly, Goethe's collected works were among the books. *Faust* was an obvious choice in several respects. The newness of theatre in the camp had worn off by now, and after the tremendous acclaim *Pech und Schwefel* had received for its cheap entertainment, the group felt the need of some project that was as respectable as it was attractive to our audience. Germany's revered classic seemed to fit the bill exactly. The production of a drastically condensed version was directed in a conventional, quite boring style by K. Büchner, who also acted an equally conventional Mephisto, while H. Buehl was Faust. The rather tall G. Stoll, in his first of several female rôles, played a very convincing Gretchen. The audience responded with great enthusiasm; one reason surely was Goethe's reputation as Germany's greatest classic writer, another was Stoll's remarkably moving performance which had nothing drag-like, risqué or gauche about it; a third reason may have been sets and costumes which were considerably more sophisticated than in previous productions.

Diligent recruiting among the arriving transports of PoWs added several new members to the company during spring 1945. One of them was a seventeen-year-old parachute trooper with a face like one of Raphael's putti surrounding the Sistine Madonna; he was a pharmacist's son from Berlin's suburb Pankow, his name Klaus Nakschinsky. Though he had little, if any, previous experience, his obvious talent quickly earned him important rôles, and he soon excelled in female parts. After the war he was going to make a spectacular stage career as Klaus Kinski and later became the international star of many movies, the most important being those he did with Werner Herzog.

But it was not merely prisoners interested in performing who were attracted by our theatre. When a young man inquired about joining the group as a designer and told of his studies of architecture and the fine arts, he was most welcome. He became resident designer of the company and, eventually, the architect of its permanent house. In addition to designing, he constructed and painted the sets and also became the creative collaborator of many a production's director. He was Werner Düttmann, later Professor of Architecture at Berlin's Technical University, and a City-Architect of West Berlin. But apart from company members who proceeded to become 'big' names; there were several more of considerable talent who later achieved a professional career in the theatre.

After Germany had capitulated, in May 1945, the British decided to put the vast army of PoWs in the country to carry out constructive work; after all, there were no repercussions to be feared any more for ignoring the Geneva Convention. Most prisoners welcomed this chance to get out of their camps and even earn some modest recompense for their work. As for the theatre group, this measure threatened it with extinction: if the members were put to farm or construction work for eight or more hours a day, rehearsing and performing would become exceedingly difficult if not well-nigh impossible. A petition was submitted to the British commander, asking to exempt us from the general work requirement. To our amazement, our request was not only granted but we also were given permission to sell tickets to our shows, since we didn't share the income all other PoWs received for their work in or outside the camp. The 'money' prisoners were paid with consisted of plastic chips, looking like those in gambling casinos, in denominations of One Penny, Twopence, Six Pence, and One Shilling. Such 'coinage' was only valid in special shops set up in the camps where cigarettes, chewing gum, razor blades, toothpaste, etc. were sold.

Suddenly the theatre had to face the challenge of functioning as a 'commercial' enterprise. One of our group, Heinrich von Heeren, volunteered to handle the business end. He was a Bavarian who had been a Sergeant on General von Stülpnagel's staff in Paris during 1943/44, where he became marginally involved in the 1944 conspiracy to assassinate Hitler and topple the Nazi government. As one of the founding members of the company he hadn't shown great talent as an actor, but in his new job as Administrative Director he excelled. He devised a financial plan which detailed ticket prices and proposed an equal sharing of all income. It was accepted, and henceforth every member, be he an actor, designer, technical or administrative staff, received the same salary based on division of the box office income after deduction of a certain amount towards a financial reserve. Prices were set at sixpence for the wooden armchairs which by now formed the first two rows of seats, twopence for a bench-seat, and one penny for standing room. This was expected to provide each company member with a modest income, not below but certainly not above what other prisoners earned by their work. In some respects, the theatre had become a commercial operation. On the other hand, it was 'subsidized' by the British army. For instance: the camp command managed to find old canvas backdrops and other stage equipment in a closed theatre or music hall in Colchester and had the stuff trucked to the camp, offering greatly needed resources for our stage work shop which also was provided with tools and materials such as nails. This enabled Düttmann to design increasingly complex and sophisticated scenery, while our wigmaker and tailors had the means now to do truly professional work.

Of course, no army regulation acknowledged such frivolous activities as 'theatre' in a prison camp. In the books, all members of the company were counted as part of the camp's work force to be contracted for farm work or other jobs. It must have struck the British command that in a transit camp, where thousands of prisoners were staying and milling around for brief periods, without any news from home and often quite desperate in view of an uncertain future, a theatre might be a stabilizing factor, easing mental pressures, distracting prisoners' minds from their numerous worries, and in addition presenting plays critical of behaviour and thinking patterns which had been favoured by Nazi ideology. Whatever the motivation was, the British administration decided to exempt us from work. However, a pretext had to be created. The solution was simple: we all were declared ailing and unfit for physical work by the German doctor in the camp infirmary, and the British medical officer, responsible for Camp 186, happily signed the necessary papers. This, eventually, would have its consequences.

For the time being, our problems were solved and the company decided to pursue now a more ambitious artistic course. However, there was still the lack of printed texts in German. K. Büchner tried to write down from memory a German farce by Reimann and Schwarz, *Ehe eine Ehe eine Ehe wird* (Before a Marriage Becomes a Marriage), arriving at a quite effective text even if it wasn't letter-perfect. He also staged the trifle, and the cast's uninhibited shenanigans were duly acclaimed by an audience starved of fun and laughter, while no one in the company felt much pride in the result. But successful it was.

A better way of solving the problem of new texts was to be found in translations from English scripts which were, of course, abundantly available. When a Dr Günther Schwab appeared one day in May and offered his expertise as dramaturg and translator, we were delighted. He immediately set to work and adapted R.B. Sheridan's *The Rivals* for the company, a crisp and very actable version which he kept improving and honing during rehearsal. H. Buehl directed and also played Mrs Malaprop with wonderful abandon. Klaus Kinski surprised as a witty, stunningly charming Lydia, H. Scholz's Acres was especially amusing, and I managed to do a fairly successful Captain Absolute. The production achieved considerable historic and aesthetic consistency; there were Düttmann's backdrops and wings emulating, to a degree, the etchings of the period, and costumes which strove for an authentic eighteenth century look. Soon after the successful show had opened, Dr Schwab was transferred to another camp, a much regretted loss.

Again we had to cope with the lack of texts. However, the camp library was gradually stocked up by the YMCA and other institutions, and there were a few drama books among the new arrivals. Apart from Goethe's and Schiller's collected works, by summer 1945 we had some volumes of Shaw, editions of Grillparzer, Kleist, Lessing, a complete Shakespeare in the Schlegel/Tieck translation, and a text of Carl Zuckmayer's *Der Hauptmann von Köpenick*. Among some Reclam paperbacks we even discovered a copy of the Brothers Schönthan farce *Der Raub der Sabinerinnen* (*The Rape of the Sabinian Women*), once a classic staple of the German stage which derived its popularity among theatre people from its topic, namely the hilarious struggles of a small travelling company of players and its actor/manager, pathetic principal Striese; the play was a sort of low-brow variant of *Trelawny of the Wells*. Now there were, at last, a number of texts to choose from, and the company decided to stage a repertoire of plays which either emphasized individual freedom and democratic rule, or criticized Germany's autocratic social and political traditions.

From summer 1945 until February 1946, when a majority of the company were sent home to Germany, an amazing number of productions were staged. There was one more Schiller play, *Don Carlos*, with H. Buehl as Carlos, K. Büchner as King Philip, G. Stoll as Queen Elizabeth, K. Kinski as Princess Eboli, W. Feige as Marquis Posa, and C. Weber as Father Domingo. Of Goethe's works, *Egmont* was produced, with Büchner as Egmont, Kinski as Clara, Buehl as Brackenburg, and Weber as Vansen. Other German classics were Heinrich von Kleist's *Der zerbrochne Krug* (The Broken Pitcher), with Buehl as Judge Adam, Büchner as Councillor Walter, Weber as Clerk Licht, Stoll as Rupprecht, and Kinski as Eve; and an evening of Lessing One-Acts, *Philotas* and *Der Schatz* (The Treasure), with Buehl playing Philotas. There also was the Austrian classic, Franz Grillparzer's *Weh' dem der lügt* (Thou Shalt Not Lie!), with Stoll as Leon, and Kinski, or the newcomer Rolf Lorenz, playing Edrita (it is sometimes difficult for me to recall all of our casts from memory). Of the English repertoire, there was Shakespeare's *Othello*, with Büchner as Othello, Weber as Iago, Stoll as Desdemona; and *King Lear*, with Büchner's Lear, Kinski's Cordelia, Stoll's Regan, R. Lorenz's Goneril, Feige's Edmund, Weber's Edgar, and Scholz's Kent. Shaw was represented by two works: *The Man of Destiny*, Weber playing Bonaparte and Stoll The Lady; and, early in 1946, *The Doctor's Dilemma*, with Buehl as Sir Colenso, Weber as Dubedat, Feige as Dr Blenkinsop, Hofmeister, a newcomer, as Mrs Dubedat, and Büchner, Scholz and Zogbaum as the other members of the medical profession. These productions were mostly staged by Büchner or Buehl, occasionally by Scholz who directed the Kleist and the two Shaw plays. Most texts were quite drastically edited to remove everything which, as we felt, wasn't accessible to our audiences; also all female rôles which weren't absolutely necessary for the plot were cut. In spite of many successful productions when Kinski, or Stoll, or others played women, the company remained very much aware of the problems of female impersonation and tried to avoid the cheap effect of 'drag shows', however popular our 'female' actors had become.

I remember the Shakespeare productions as especially acclaimed, although two other plays became our most successful projects since we had started the theatre with Schiller's *Die Räuber*, at Christmas 1944. One of them was the already mentioned farce *Der Raub der Sabinerinnen*, where Büchner gave his most fully achieved performance as the hapless but indefatigable Director Striese, whose traditional Saxon dialect had the audience in stitches. (Büchner, having the highest military rank of our group as Sergeant Major of the Medical Corps, had been made the official Director of our company, and actually had a lot in common with the play's protagonist.) Others in the cast were Zogbaum as Professor Gollwitz, Kinski as his daughter, Weber as the young actor Sterneck, and Scholz, in a hilarious performance, as his father from Berlin.

Of all our productions, Zuckmayer's *Der Hauptmann von Köpenick* surely was the most ambitious, and I would rate it as our most accomplished artistic achievement. Audience response also surpassed that of most other productions, and no play stayed as long in our repertoire. The company had become large enough by autumn 1945 to cast the numerous rôles of Zuckmayer's canvas of pre-First World War Berlin. Herbert Scholz played the cobbler Voigt who dons the uniform of a Prussian Guards Captain and cons the Mayor of Köpenick into handing over the city's treasury. All other company members played two, three, or four rôles; noteworthy were Stoll, Buehl, and especially Kinski.

Düttmann had designed a backdrop strip with lithograph-like images of old Berlin; it was stretched between two cylindrical pillars, upstage right and left, which were turned by stagehands so the background images could travel slowly or fast when Voigt trotted through the city of Berlin, while they stopped for individual locations when scenes were played in front. This simple but effective device moved the action along without interruption, to great delight of the audience. Costumes had never before been as rich and detailed in all their variety, and I don't think they were ever again in later productions. Buehl staged the show, and the enthusiasm everyone developed for our first production of an important contemporary German work made for truly spirited performances. It was especially gratifying to us that Zuckmayer's satire on Prussian/German *Kadavergehorsam* had such an impact on our audience of former Nazi soldiers.

Operating a 'commercial' theatre where the box-office takings were counted every night, the group soon realized that out there was also an audience interested in mere entertainment, an audience staying away from our classics or ambitious modern works. To attract these spectators, two more cabaret-revue type productions were put on; I only remember the title of one of them, *Berliner Luft* (Berlin Breeze), a quote from one of Paul Lincke's popular tunes of pre-First World War Berlin. The formula of the earlier *Pech und Schwefel* was more or less repeated, providing a similar hodge-podge of songs, skits, drag numbers, and a magician's act thrown in. I don't recall that we repeated our earlier success with them, and they didn't stay long in the repertoire.

By summer 1945 the theatre performed a rotating repertoire of up to five different productions, six days a week. In the beginning each production had been performed during weekends from Friday, later Thursday, till Sunday night, until a new production was ready. But since Camp 186 had become one of the largest transit camps in the country, with new prisoners arriving nearly every day and leaving again after three or four weeks, there was a steady rotation of spectators. At times the camp housed up to 10,000 prisoners. A production could be performed four or five months for our constantly replenished audience, and since the professionals in the group had worked in the German repertory system, it was a logical step to adopt the model of German municipal theatres. The company eventually played Tuesday to Sunday, often changing plays every day; posters with the weekly playbill, laboriously done by hand, one piece at a time, in calligraphy, were put up at all official announcement boards in the camp.

In early summer 1945, the British army proceeded to convert PoW Camp 186 into a more permanent facility which later could be used as barracks for British troops. A unit of the Royal Pioneer Corps moved in and soon set prisoners to work on roads, Nissen huts, and many other structures which were to change the look and the life of the camp. All tents were eventually to be pulled down. The theatre was threatened with losing its premises. A delegation was formed to explain our problem to the Camp Command, and a Major of the Pioneer Corps came forward with the hardly expected solution: to build a permanent theatre according to our specifications. This was an incredible stroke of luck. Major Atkins was a set designer in civilian life and had worked in the Berlin film industry in the early 1930s; he had not only an understanding of our intentions, he obviously agreed with us wholeheartedly. A work detail of construction workers was assigned to the theatre; Werner Düttmann designed a building with an auditorium of approximately 200 seats, a stage, and some other facilities, all to be fitted into the largest of the standardized Nissen hut models used in the camp, and an additional structure for the stage house which became the tallest structure in all of Camp 186. Within a week the theatre was erected. A foundation of concrete was poured for a raked auditorium and a proscenium stage with a small pit; there was a tiny lobby with the box office to the right, and a stage house with enough fly space to bring in small scenery pieces or drops from above, plus a fair amount of wing space. Düttmann added a little fanciful fling to it all: a semicircle of five steps led up to the theatre's entrance, making the building even more conspicuous than it already was by its size. Major Atkins also saw to it that Nissen huts for the company's housing and work-shops were put up next to the theatre. Eventually, this little compound consisted of the theatre, two huts for living space, a smaller and a large hut for workshops and storage of scenery and costumes.

By autumn 1945, the company numbered close to fifty members of artistic, technical and administrative staff, and the enterprise became ever more a small replica of the typical German municipal theatre with its actors, craftsmen and its hangers-on. The camp had lost all of its tents now, and consisted of neat rows of Nissen huts, lined up along cemented or dirt roads. There was a camp hospital, church halls, a library, the theatre, and various workshops set up by the British army, which produced items for the outside world. There also was a very active black market where goods that weren't available in the camp's stores were sold. One enterprising prisoner, who owned a textile company in Zwickau before the war, had started a chocolate factory in the back of a Nissen hut where his cooks made bars from cocoa, sugar and evaporated milk, and which his network of salesmen marketed in the camp. There were tailors who, for a price, fitted and altered your PoW uniform (ill-fitting British army tunics and pants, dyed brown or dark green, with a yellow patch on the back of the blouse and on the front of the right leg), so you looked rather smart in those outfits. In the back room of one of the camp kitchens, the German chef-in-charge had set up a club-like coffee house where prisoners who were in the know could have their 'mocca' or a drink from the illegal distilleries in the camp, one of them operated by the medics in the camp hospital. The most daring, and eventually most scandalous, enterprise in Camp 186 was a factory, operating in a large excavation beneath one of the storage huts, where tables, cabinets, chairs, and other quite fancy pieces of furniture were manufactured by German craftsmen. Their products were moved out of the camp on army lorries and sold on the outside. The whole operation was the brainchild of a Canadian Captain attached to the Pioneer Corps who, for a while, seemed to make quite a bundle from it, until it was all discovered and he was court-martialled. The prisoners couldn't be blamed, of course, they had only acted on orders.

As in any environment where great numbers of men are sequestered for a considerable period — the camp housed at times nearly 10,000 prisoners in transit — homosexuality became an accepted mode of relationship. There was quite an uninhibited display of affection in public, and prostitution flourished at night at some of the construction sites within the camp, which became a sort of 'beat'. In the theatre group, there were a few permanent and several less durable relationships, and naturally they caused rivalries and conflicts which occasionally interfered with the company's work. A few members left the group because of such altercations, but most of them eventually returned.

By early 1946, the Theater des Camp 186 had its firm place in the small city which the camp had become. There was the logo 'TdC 186' on all of its posters, programmes, etc., which had become familiar to every inmate. Some of the actors had attracted fans who attended their important openings and tried to express their appreciation through small gifts. The productions in the new theatre building had profited from its modest, yet serviceable potential; and, as the production of *Der Hauptmann von Köpenick* had demonstrated, quite effective means of staging were now available.

What the company lacked was a truly gifted and visionary director who would have set it on a more adventurous and imaginative course. Theater des Camp 186 presented productions of a remarkably competent professional standard, but the artistic level of a conventional German repertory theatre in a smaller city was rarely transcended. It probably was all that could have been expected from a group dependent on the accidental appearance of new talent among transports of PoWs passing through the camp. Another reason was that the company never got hold of plays by important modern or contemporary playwrights, except for Shaw and one script by Zuckmayer. We had no scripts of Brecht, Horvath, or other important German playwrights, nor anything by Ibsen or Chekhov, for instance. Such texts might have motivated the group to experiment and dare to 'go out on a limb'. Without them, the theatre didn't live up to its unique challenge, namely presenting new models of thought and action to an audience of bewildered, totally disoriented people who had lost not only a war but also all their bearings. Admittedly, such a task might have been more than a group of equally bewildered actors and dilettantes was able to handle, a company thrown together by sheer accident on those park grounds near Colchester where some strangely wise British army officers offered them the means to pursue their dream of a theatre.

The end of TdC 186's story is rather ironical. In February 1946, London decided there was no longer any reason to feed German PoWs who couldn't pitch in and do their share of work. A medical examination of all prisoners who were on sick lists was decreed. This naturally caused our Camp Commander and his Medical Officer considerable embarrassment: there were those forty-odd prisoners in the camp who carried on prancing about on stage while being seriously ill, according to their papers. A commission was soon to be expected to screen all inmates unfit for work. There was no way out but to stick with that generous invention of early 1945, namely that all those actors, painters, tailors, and so forth, had disabling ailments. The German Camp Doctor called all of us to his office in the Camp Hospital. There was also the British Medical Officer. They informed us of the commission's pending arrival and proceeded to instruct us about our 'ailments', first by asking us what kind of serious health problems we had in the past, and then by exactly describing and even rehearsing with us the symptoms of each prisoner's chosen illness. Mine was arthritic rheumatism, because I had mentioned a bout of it which I had years ago, or so I believed; it could also have been a case of sore muscles after rowing. Properly instructed, and certainly willing to employ all our acting talent, we appeared before the commission of three officers from the Medical Corps. We tried to describe and demonstrate our pain, or restriction of movement, or whatever we had been told to do, as convincingly as possible; after all, there was the golden promise of being sent home if our acting convinced this audience of professionals. More than twenty of us succeeded; I was among them. Within two weeks we received our marching orders for Germany. Very few of the actors, one of them the unfortunate Kurt Büchner, didn't pass the screening and had to remain in the camp. There was a tearful leave-taking, and we were on our way across the Channel, back to a Germany we found to be cold and miserable and in ruins, under the grey sky of February 1946.

Theatre in Camp 186 continued for a while, I'm inclined to assume, although I never had any information about it. Those of our friends who had to stay behind in February 1946 expressed their firm intention to continue, however difficult it might be after the loss of more than twenty company members. Nevertheless, if every PoW remaining in England was expected to work after the elimination of all disabled bodies, it is hard to believe that the theatre could have gone on for long in its previous form.

As mentioned above, several 'alumni' of TdC 186 went on to remarkable careers. Klaus Kinski, Günther Stoll, Hans Buehl, Herbert Scholz, Wolfgang Feige, Werner Düttmann: these were friends I met again, or kept hearing and reading about for many years. Others probably worked in the theatre with success though without achieving similar recognition. I joined Brecht's Berliner Ensemble six years after I had left Colchester, and after four years with Brecht and nine years with his company, I went to direct in West Germany, Scandinavia, and eventually New York and other American cities. Now heading Directing Studies at Stanford University's PhD programme in Directing/Criticism, I often wish that my students could once have the good fortune of an experience as challenging and exciting as the one which Theater des Camp 186 confronted us with.

Bibliography

I Autobiographical Writings

C.C. Aronsfeld, 'Refugee No. 562 Remembers . . .', *Jewish Quarterly*, vol. 20, no. 4, Winter 1973, pp. 23–6

Julius Berstl, *Odyssee eines Theatermenschen: Erinnerungen aus sieben Jahrzehnten*, Berlin (West), 1963

Jack Bilbo [i.e. Hugo Baruch], *An Autobiography*, London, 1948

———, *Rebell aus Leidenschaft: Abenteurer-Maler-Philosoph*, Herrenalb 1963 (second ed. under the title: *Käpt'n Bilbo, Rebell aus Leidenschaft: Ein Leben für das Abenteuer*, Munich, 1965)

Max Born, *Mein Leben: Die Erinnerungen des Nobelpreisträgers*, Munich, 1975; Engl. edn: *My Life: Recollections of a Nobel Laureate*, London, 1978

Carl Brinitzer, *Hier spricht London: Von einem der dabei war*, Hamburg, 1969

Elisabeth Castonier, *Stürmisch bis heiter: Memoiren einer Außenseiterin*, Munich, 1964

Fritz Cronheim, *Deutsch-Englische Wanderschaft: Lebensweg im Zeichen Stefan Georges*, Heidelberg, 1977

Eva Figes, *Little Eden: A Child at War*, London, 1978

Grete Fischer, *Dienstboten, Brecht und andere Zeitgenossen in Prag, Berlin, London*, Olten, 1966

Heinrich Fraenkel, *Farewell to Germany*, London, 1959

Richard Friedenthal, *. . . und unversehens ist es Abend: Von und über R.F. Essays, Gedichte, Fragmente, Würdigung, Autobiographisches*, ed. Klaus Piper, Munich, n.d. [1976]

Hermann Friedmann, *Sinnvolle Odyssee: Geschichte eines Lebens und einer Zeit von 1873–1950*, Munich, 1950

Charles Hannam, *A Boy in Your Situation*, London, 1977; German edn: *. . . und dann mußte ich gehen: Die Geschichte eines jüdischen Jungen von 1933 bis 1940*, Würzburg, 1979

———, *Almost an Englishman*, London, 1979

Kurt Hiller, *Rote Ritter: Erlebnisse mit deutschen Kommunisten*, Gelsenkirchen n.d. [1951]

———, *Leben gegen die Zeit*, Reinbek, 1970

Alfred Kerr, *Ich kam nach England: Ein Tagebuch aus dem Nachlaß*, ed. Walter Huder and Thomas Koebner, Bonn, 1979

Judith Kerr, *The Other Way Round*, London, 1975

———, *A Small Person Far Away*, London, 1978

Emmy Koenen, 'Exil in England: Erinnerungen', *Beiträge zur Geschichte der deutschen Arbeiterbewegung*, vol. 20, 1978, pp. 540–63

Arthur Koestler, *The Invisible Writing, Being the Second Volume of Arrow in the Blue: An Autobiography*, London, 1954; German edn: *Die Geheimschrift: Bericht eines Lebens 1932 bis 1940*, Vienna, 1955

Bibliography

Oskar Kokoschka, *Mein Leben*, Munich, 1971, English edn: *My Life*, London, 1974

Jürgen Kuczynski, *Memoiren: Die Erziehung des J.K. zum Kommunisten und Wissenschaftler*, 2nd edn, Berlin (GDR), 1975

Alfred Lomnitz, *'Never Mind, Mr. Lom!' or The Uses of Adversity*, London, 1941

Ernst Hermann Meyer, *Kontraste-Konflikte: Erinnerungen, Gespräche, Kommentare*, ed. Dietrich Brennecke and Mathias Hansen, Berlin (GDR), 1979

Wilhelm Necker, *Es war doch so schön!*, Hanover, 1947

Robert Neumann, *Mein altes Haus in Kent: Erinnerungen an Menschen und Gespenster*, Vienna, 1957; Engl. edn: *The Plague House Papers*, London, 1959

———, *Ein leichtes Leben: Bericht über mich selbst und Zeitgenossen*, Vienna, 1963

Jan Petersen, *Er schrieb es in den Sand: Geschichten aus neun Ländern*, Berlin (GDR), 1960

Lily Pincus, *Verloren-Gewonnen: Mein Weg von Berlin nach London*, Stuttgart, 1980

Theodor Prager, *Zwischen London und Moskau: Bekenntnisse eines Revisionisten. Mit einem Nachwort von Georg Eisler*, Vienna, 1975

Bruno Retzlaff-Kresse, *Illegalität — Kerker — Exil: Erinnerungen aus dem antifaschistischen Kampf*, Berlin (GDR), 1980

Hans Sahl, *Das Exil im Exil: Erinnerungen*, vol. 2 (= Gesammelte Werke, ed. Klaus Schöffling, vol. VI), Zurich (to be published)

Kurt Schwitters, *Wir spielen, bis uns der Tod abholt: Briefe aus fünf Jahrzehnten*, ed. Ernst Nündel, Berlin (West), 1974

Hermann Sinsheimer, *Gelebt im Paradies: Erinnerungen und Begegnungen*, Munich, 1953

Edgar Stern-Rubarth, *. . . aus zuverlässiger Quelle verlautet . . .: Ein Leben für Presse und Politik*, Stuttgart, 1964

Paul Tabori, *They Came to London*, London, 1943

Fred Uhlman, *The Making of an Englishman*, London, 1960

Stephan K. Westmann, *Frauenarzt: Ein Leben unter zwei Flaggen*, London, 1960

———, *A Surgeon's Story*, London, 1962

Walter Zadek (ed.), *Sie flohen vor dem Hakenkreuz: Selbstzeugnisse der Emigration*, Reinbek, 1981

Stefan Zweig, *Die Welt von Gestern: Erinnerungen eines Europäers*, London, 1941; Engl. edn: *The World of Yesterday: An Autobiography*, London, 1943

———, *Tagebücher*, Frankfurt, 1984

II Historical Background Studies

(1) Jewish Emigration, 1933–1945

Kurt R. Grossmann, *Emigration: Geschichte der Hitler Flüchtlinge 1933–1945*, Frankfurt, 1969

Eugene M. Kulischer, *The Displacement of Population in Europe*, Montreal, 1943

———, *Europe on the Move: War and Population Changes 1917–1947*, New York, 1948

Michael R. Marrus, *The Unwanted: European Refugees in the Twentieth Century*, London, 1985

Horst Möller, *Exodus der Kultur: Schriftsteller, Wissenschaftler und Künstler in der Emigration nach 1933*, Munich, 1984

Henry B.M. Murphy, *Flight and Resettlement*, Paris, 1955

Malcolm J. Proudfoot, *European Refugees 1939–52: A Study in Forced Population*

Movement, London, 1957

Werner Rosenstock (ed.), *Dispersion and Resettlement: The Story of the Jews from Central Europe*, London, 1955

————, 'Exodus 1933–39: A Survey of Jewish Emigration from Germany', *Leo Baeck Institute Year Book*, vol. 1, 1956, 373–90

Joseph B. Schechtman, *European Population Transfers 1939–1945*, New York, 1946

Arieh Tartakower and Kurt R. Grossmann, *The Jewish Refugee*, New York, 1944

Mark Wischnitzer, 'Jewish Emigration from Germany 1933–1938', *Jewish Social Studies*, vol. 2, 1940, pp. 23–44

(2)   German-Jewish Emigrés in Great Britain

Normann Angell and Dorothy Frances Buxton, *You and the Refugee: The Morals and Economics of the Problem*, Harmondsworth, 1939

Norman Bentwich, *The Refugees from Germany, April 1933 to December 1935*, London, 1936

————, *I Understand the Risk: The Story of the Refugees from Nazi Oppression Who Fought in the British Forces in the World War*, London, 1950

————, *They Found Refuge: An Account of British Jewry's Work for Victims of Nazi Oppression*, London, 1956

Marion Berghahn, *Continental Britons: German-Jewish Refugees from Nazi Germany*, Oxford, 1988 (originally published as *German-Jewish Refugees in England: The Ambiguities of Assimilation*, London, 1984)

Britain's New Citizens: The Story of the Refugees from Germany and Austria, ed. the Association of Jewish Refugees in Great Britain, London, 1951

Dorothy F. Buxton, *The Economics of the Refugee Problem*, London, n.d. [1939]

Dispersion and Resettlement: The Story of Jews from Central Europe, ed. the Association of Jewish Refugees in Great Britain, London, 1955

Mary Ford, 'The Arrival of Jewish Refugee Children in England, 1938–39', *Immigrants & Minorities*, vol. 2, 1983, pp. 135–51

Karen Gershon (ed.), *We Came as Children: A Collective Autobiography*, London, 1966

Gerhard Hirschfeld (ed.), *Exile in Great Britain: Refugees from Hitler's Germany*, Leamington Spa and New Jersey, 1984

Hermann Kellenbenz, 'German Immigrants in England', in Colin Holmes (ed.), *Immigrants and Minorities in British Society*, London, 1978, pp. 63–80

Rainer Kölmel, *Die Geschichte der deutsch-jüdischen Refugees in Schottland*, PhD Thesis, Heidelberg, 1980

Vivian David Lipman, *Social History of the Jews in England 1850–1950*, London, 1954

M.G. Murchin, *Britains's Jewish Problem*, London, 1939

Gottfried Niedhart (ed.), *Großbritannien als Gast- und Exilland für Deutsche im 19. und 20. Jahrhundert*, Bochum, 1985

James Parkes, *The Jewish Problem in the Modern World*, London, 1939

————, *The Emergence of the Jewish Problem, 1878–1939*, London, 1946

Harold Pollins, *Economic History of the Jews in England*, London, 1982

The Position of Jewish Refugees in England, ed. the Jewish Central Information Office, London, 1945

Cyril Claude Salway, *Refugees and Industry*, London, 1942

Albrecht Schreiber, 'Nicht nur zu Weihnachten: Shalom. In der Emigration Erinnerungen an die Kinderzeit: Jüdische Frauen in London', *Frankfurter Rundschau*, no. 299, 1977, Weihnachtsbeilage, p. v

Bibliography

Walter M. Schwab, *B'nai B'rith: The First Lodge of England: A Record of Fifty Years*, London, 1960

Ari Joshua Sherman, *Island Refuge: Britain and Refugees from the Third Reich 1933–1939*, London, 1973

John Hope Simpson, *Refugees: Preliminary Report of a Survey*. *July 1938*, London, 1938

———, *The Refugee Problem: Report of a Survey*, London, 1939

———, *Refugees: A Review of the Situation since September 1938*, London, 1939

Austin Stevens, *The Dispossessed: German Refugees in Britain*, London, 1975

Bernard Wasserstein, *Britain and the Jews of Europe 1939–1945*, London, 1979

Frances Mary Wilson, *Displaced Persons — Whose Responsibility?*, London, 1947

———, *They Came as Strangers: The Story of Refugees to Great Britain*, London, 1959

(3) Exiled Intellectuals, Artists and Scientists in Britain

Ursula Adam, *Zur Geschichte des Freien Deutschen Kulturbundes in Großbritannien (Ende 1938–Mai 1945)*, PhD Thesis, Berlin (GDR), 1983

———, 'Die deutsche antifaschistische Emigration in Großbritannien in der Zeit nach der Stalingrader Schlacht: Zur Tätigkeit des Freien Deutschen Kulturbundes im Jahre 1943', *Jahrbuch für Geschichte*, vol. 27, 1983, pp. 229–58

———, 'Das Echo auf die Gründung des Kulturbundes zur demokratischen Erneuerung Deutschlands in Großbritannien und dessen geschichtlichen Voraussetzungen', *Weimarer Beiträge*, vol. 31, 1985, 743–54

Hans-Günter Adler, 'Deutsche Exilliteratur in London', *Europäische Ideen*, no. 45/46, 1979, pp. 29–32

Norman Bentwich, *The Rescue and Achievement of Refugee Scholars: The Story of Displaced Scholars and Scientists 1933–1952*, The Hague, 1953

Club 43 (ed.), *Zwanzig Jahre Club 1943*, London, 1963

Cordula Frowein, 'The Exhibition of 20th Century German Art in London 1938: Eine Antwort auf die Ausstellung "Entartete Kunst" in München 1937', *Exilforschung*, vol. 2, 1984, pp. 212–37

Ulla Hahn, 'Der Freie Deutsche Kulturbund in Großbritannien: Eine Skizze seiner Geschichte', in Lutz Winckler (ed.), *Antifaschistische Literatur: Programm, Autoren, Werke*, vol. 2, Kronberg, 1977, pp. 131–95

The Immigrant Generation: Jewish Artists in Britain 1900–1945, Exh. cat., New York: The Jewish Museum, 1983

Jewish Artists of Great Britain 1845–1945, Exh. cat., London: Belgrave Gallery, 1978

Kunst im Exil in Großbritannien 1933–1945, Exh. cat., Berlin (West): Schloß Charlottenburg, 1986

Birgid Leske, Marion Reinisch and Mathias Hansen, 'Exil in Großbritannien', in *Exil in der Tschechoslowakei, in Großbritannien, Skandinavien und in Palästina*, Leipzig, 1980, pp. 147–305

Wolfgang Mock, *Technische Intelligenz im Exil: Vertreibung und Emigration deutschsprachiger Ingenieure nach Großbritannien 1933 bis 1945*, Düsseldorf, 1986

Sylvia M. Patsch, *Österreichische Schriftsteller im Exil in Großbritannien: Ein Kapitel vergessene österreichische Literatur*, Vienna/Munich, 1985

Paul Tabori (ed.), *The PEN in Exile: An Anthology*, London, 1954

——— (ed), *The PEN in Exile: A Second Anthology*, London, 1956

Gabriele Tergit, 'Die Exilsituation in England', in Manfred Durzak (ed.), *Die deutsche Exilliteratur 1933–1945*, Stuttgart, 1973, pp. 135–44

Hans-Albert Walter, *Deutsche Exilliteratur 1933–1950, Vol. 2: Europäisches Appeasement*

Bibliography

und überseeische Asylpraxis, Stuttgart, 1984, pp. 112–41

Bernard Wasserstein, 'Intellectual Emigrés in Britain, 1933–1939', in J.C. Jackman and C.M. Borden (eds), *The Muses Flee Hitler: Cultural Transfer and Adaptation 1930–1945*, Washington DC, 1983, pp. 249–56

Heinz Worner, 'Deutsche antifaschistische Künstler im englischen Exil (1939–1946)', *Bildende Kunst*, vol. 16, 1962, pp. 143–52

1915–1965: Fifty Years of Achievement in the Arts: Commemorative Volume to Mark the Fiftieth Anniversary of the Foundation of the Ben Uri Art Society, ed. Jacob Sonntag, London, 1966

(4) Political Exiles in Great Britain

Hiltrud Bradter, 'Die Beuer-Gruppe im Kampf um den antifaschistischen Einheitsausschuß in der Londoner Emigration', *Wissenschaftliche Zeitschrift der Friedrich Schiller Universität Jena*, vol. 21, 1972, pp. 331–8

Louise Dornemann, 'Die Arbeit des "Allies inside Germany Council" in Großbritannien (1942–1950)', *Beiträge zur Geschichte der Arbeiterbewegung*, vol. 23, 1981, pp. 872–91

Lewis J. Edinger, *German Exile Politics: The Social Democratic Executive Committee in the Nazi Era*, Berkeley, 1956

Anthony Glees, *Exile Politics During the Second World War: The German Social Democrats in Britain*, Oxford, 1982

Siegbert Kahn, 'Zur Entstehung und Tätigkeit der Freien Deutschen Bewegung in Großbritannien', *Mitteilungsblatt der Arbeitsgemeinschaft ehemaliger Offiziere*, vol. 14, no. 4, 1970, pp. 4–8

Jürgen and Marguerite Kuczynski, 'Die "Freie deutsche Bewegung in Großbritannien"', *Mitteilungsblatt der Arbeitsgemeinschaft ehemaliger Offiziere*, vol. 6, no. 7, 1963, pp. 4–6

Dieter Lange, 'Der faschistische Überfall auf die Sowjetunion und die Haltung emigrierter deutscher sozialdemokratischer Führer: Zu den Anfängen einer Zusammenarbeit von Kommunisten und Sozialdemokraten in der englischen Emigration', *Zeitschrift für Geschichtswissenschaft*, vol. 14, 1966, pp. 542–67

——, 'Dokumente der Freien Deutschen Bewegung in Großbritannien', *Zeitschrift für Geschichtswissenschaft*, vol. 9, 1972, pp. 1113–58

Birgid Leske, *Das Ringen der Organisation der KPD in Großbritannien um die Verwirklichung der Einheits- und Volksfrontpolitik der KPD (1934 bis Mai 1945)*, PhD Thesis, Berlin (GDR), 1983

Werner Röder, 'Deutschlandpläne der sozialdemokratischen Emigration in Großbritannien 1942–1945', *Vierteljahreshefte für Zeitgeschichte*, vol. 17, 1969, pp. 72–86

——, *Die deutschen sozialistischen Exilgruppen in Großbritannien, 1940–1945*, Hanover, 1969

Friedrich Stampfer, *Mit dem Gesicht nach Deutschland: Eine Dokumentation über die sozialdemokratische Emigration*, Düsseldorf, 1968

(5) Austrian and Sudetendeutsche Exiles in Great Britain

Martin K. Bachstein, *Wenzel Jaksch und die Sudetendeutsche Sozialdemokratie*, Vienna, 1974

Leopold Grünwald, *In der Fremde für die Heimat: Sudetendeutsches Exil in Ost und West*, Munich, 1982

Bibliography

Georg Knepler, *Five Years of the Austrian Centre*, London, 1944
Eva Kolmer, *Das Austrian Centre: 7 Jahre österreichische Gemeinschaftsarbeit*, London, 1946
Johann Lettner, *Aspekte der österreichisch-jüdischen Emigration in England 1936–1945*, unpublished PhD Thesis, Salzburg, 1972
Helene Maimann, *Politik im Wartesaal: Österreichische Exilpolitik in Großbritannien 1938–1945*, Vienna, 1975
Menschen im Exil: Eine Dokumentation der sudetendeutschen sozialdemokratischen Emigration von 1939 bis 1945, ed. the Seliger Archiv Stuttgart, Stuttgart, 1974
Friedrich Prinz (ed.), *Wenzel Jaksch-Edvard Beneš: Briefe und Dokumente aus dem Londoner Exil 1939–1943*, Cologne, 1973

(6)   The Internment of Enemy Aliens

William Allen and Earl Jowitt, *Some Were Spies*, London, 1954
John Barwick, *Alien Internment Camps in the United Kingdom*, London, 1941
Eugen M. Brehm, 'Meine Internierung', *Exil*, no. 2, 1986, pp. 39–64
Hans Eichner, 'Internierungslager und Lageruniversität', in E. Schwarz and M. Wagner (eds), *Verbannung: Aufzeichnungen deutscher Schriftsteller im Exil*, Hamburg, 1964, pp. 115–21
Stanley Firmin, *They Came to Spy*, London, n.d. [1946]
Peter and Leni Gillman, *'Collar the Lot': How Britain Interned and Expelled its Wartime Refugees*, London, 1980
H. Jaeger, 'Refugees' Internment in Britain 1939–1940: A Survey of Literature', *Wiener Library Bulletin*, vol. 9, 1955, pp. 31–3
Ronald C.D. Jasper, *George Bell, Bishop of Chichester*, London, 1967
Miriam Kochan, *Britain's Internees in the Second World War*, London, 1983
Emmi Koenen, 'Exil England: Leben und Kampf im Frauenlager', *Beiträge zur Geschichte der Arbeiterbewegung*, vol. 20, 1978, pp. 880–95
François Lafitte, *The Internment of Aliens*, Harmondsworth, 1940
Livia Laurent, *A Tale of Internment*, London, 1942
Benzion Patkin, *The Dunera Internees*, Melbourne, 1979
Michael Seyfert, *Im Niemandsland: Deutsche Exilliteratur in britischer Internierung. Ein unbekanntes Kapitel des Zweiten Weltkrieges*, Berlin (West), 1984
Eugen Spier, *The Protecting Power*, London, 1951
Ronald Stent, *A Bespattered Page? The Internment of 'His Majesty's Most Loyal Enemy Aliens'*, London, 1980
Mary D. Stocks, *Eleanor Rathbone: A Biography*, London, 1949

(7)   Living Conditions and Political Climate in the 1930s and 1940s

Robert Benewick, *A Study of British Fascism: Political Violence and Public Order*, London, 1969 (2nd edn under the title: *The Fascist Movement in Britain*, London, 1972)
Noreen Branson and Margot Heinemann, *Britain in the Nineteen Thirties*, London, 1971
Claud Cockburn, *The Devil's Decade*, London, 1973
Colin Cross, *The Fascists in Britain* London, 1961
Frank Gloversmith (ed.), *Class, Culture and Social Change: A New View of the 1930s*, Brighton, 1980
S. Glynn and J. Osborrow, *Interwar Britain: A Social and Economic History*, London, 1976

Bibliography

Louis Golding, *The Jewish Problem*, London, 1938
Richard Griffith, *Fellow Travellers of the Right: British Enthusiasts for Nazi Germany 1933–9*, London, 1980
Colin Holmes, *Anti-Semitism in British Society 1878–1939*, London, 1979
Gisela C. Lebzelter, *Political Anti-Semitism in England 1918–1939*, London, 1978
David Stephen Lewis, *Illusions of Grandeur: Mosley, Fascism and British Society, 1931–81*, Manchester, 1987
Kenneth Lunn and Richard C. Thurlow (eds), *British Fascism: Essays on the Radical Right in Inter-War Britain*, London, 1980
W. F. Mande, *Anti-Semitism and the British Union of Fascists*, London, 1968
Malcolm Muggeridge, *The Thirties, 1930–1940, in Great Britain*, London, 1940
Frederic Mullally, *Fascism Inside England*, London, 1946
James Parkes, *An Enemy of the People: Antisemitism*, Harmondsworth, 1945
I. Rennap, *Anti-Semitism and the Jewish Problem*, London, 1942
Lionel S. Rose (ed.), *Fascism in Britain*, London, 1948
John Stevenson, *Social Conditions in Britain Between the Wars*, Harmondsworth, 1977
—— and Chris Cook, *The Slump: Society and Politics During the Depression*, London, 1979
Richard Thurlow, 'The "Jew Wise": Dimensions in British Political Anti-Semitism, 1918–1939', *Immigrants and Minorities*, vol. 6, 1987, pp. 44–65

(8) Anglo–German Relations, 1933–1945

Maurice Cowling, *The Impact of Hitler: British Politics and British Policy 1933–1940*, Cambridge, 1975
Franklin Reid Gannon, *The British Press and Germany, 1936–1939*, Oxford, 1971
Margaret George, *The Hollow Men: An Examination of British Foreign Policy Between the Years 1933 and 1939*, London, 1965
——, *The Warped Vision: British Foreign Policy 1933–1939*, Pittsburgh, 1969
Martin Gilbert, *Britain and Germany Between the Wars*, London, 1964
Oswald Hauser, *England und das Dritte Reich: Eine dokumentarische Geschichte der englisch–deutschen Beziehungen von 1933 bis 1939 auf Grund unveröffentlichter Akten aus dem britischen Staatsarchiv*, 2 vols, Stuttgart, 1972–1982
Fritz Hesse, *Hitler and the English*, London, 1954
Lothar Kettenacker (ed.), *Das 'Andere Deutschland' im Zweiten Weltkrieg: Emigration und Widerstand in internationaler Perspektive*, Stuttgart, 1977
—— et al. (eds), *Studien zur Geschichte Englands und der deutsch-britischen Beziehungen: Festschrift für Paul Kluke*, Munich, 1981
William Norton Medlicott, *Britain and Germany: The Search for Agreement 1930–1937*, London, 1969
Keith Middlemas, *Diplomacy of Illusion: The British Government and Germany, 1937–1939*, London, 1972
Karl Rohe (ed.), *Die Westmächte und das Dritte Reich 1933–1939: Klassische Großmachtrivalität oder Kampf zwischen Demokratie und Diktatur?*, Paderborn, 1982
Andrew Sharf, *The British Press and Jews under Nazi Rule*, London, 1964
——, *Nazi Racialism and the British Press 1933–1945* (= Noah Baron Memorial Lecture 1963), London, n.d. [1965]

Bibliography

III Theatre in Exile: General Studies

'Antifaschistisch-demokratische und sozialistische deutsche Theatertraditionen 1917/18 bis 1945. Schriftlich vorgelegte Diskussionsgrundlage der Arbeitsgruppe "Sozialistische Traditionen in den darstellenden Künsten"', in *Die darstellenden Künste in der entwickelten sozialistischen Gesellschaft. Positionen und Perspektiven. Arbeitstagung der Sektion Darstellende Kunst, 27. bis 29. November 1972* (= Arbeitshefte der Akademie der Künste der DDR, No. 16), Berlin (GDR), 1973, pp. 115–28

Lisa Appignanesi, *The Cabaret*, London, 1975, pp. 161–70

Klaus Budzinsky, *Pfeffer ins Getriebe: So ist und wurde das Kabarett*, Munich, 1982, pp. 147–168

Deutsches Exildrama und Exiltheater: Akten des Exilliteratur-Symposiums der University of South Carolina 1976, ed. Wolfgang Elfe, James Harding and Günther Holst, Berne, 1977 (= Jahrbuch für Internationale Germanistik, Reihe A, Kongreßberichte, 3)

Marianne Exner, 'Theatre in Exile: The Stage as Tribunal', in Gerhard Schoenberner (ed.), *Artists against Hitler: Persecution, Exile, Resistance*, Bonn, 1984, pp. 29–42

Heinz Greul, *Bretter, die die Zeit bedeuten: Die Kulturgeschichte des Kabaretts*, Cologne, 1967, pp. 341–64

Reinhard Hippen (ed.), *Satire gegen Hitler: Kabarett im Exil*, Zurich, 1986

Rudolf Hösch, *Kabarett von gestern und heute. Nach zeitgenössischen Berichten, Kritiken, Texten und Erinnerungen, Vol 2: 1933–1970*, Berlin (GDR), 1972, pp. 29–58

A. Kahn, 'Kabarett in der Emigration', *Das Literarische Kabarett*, no. 4, 1946

Gudrun Klatt, *Arbeiterklasse und Theater: Agitprop-Tradition — Theater im Exil — Sozialistisches Theater*, Berlin (GDR), 1975

Kunst und Literatur im antifaschistischen Exil 1933–1945 in sieben Bänden, ed. Ludwig Hoffmann *et al.*, Leipzig, 1979–1981

Franz Norbert Mennemeier and Frithjof Trapp (eds), *Deutsche Exildramatik 1933–1950*, Munich, 1980

Werner Mittenzwei, *Das Schicksal des deutschen Theaters im Exil (1933 bis 1945)*, Berlin (GDR), 1978

Uwe Naumann, *Zwischen Tränen und Gelächter: Satirische Faschismuskritik 1933 bis 1945*, Cologne, 1983

Marta Nierendorff, *Exiltheater im Sinnzusammenhang*, Los Angeles, 1977

Reiner Otto and Walter Rösler, *Kabarettgeschichte: Abriß des deutschsprachigen Kabaretts*, Berlin (GDR), 1977, pp. 143–68

John M. Ritchie, *German Literature under National Socialism*, London, 1983, pp. 230–51

Günther Rühle (ed.), *Zeit und Theater 1933–1945, Vol. 6: Diktatur und Exil*, Frankfurt, 1980

Lothar Schirmer (ed.), *Theater im Exil 1933–1945. Ein Symposium der Akademie der Künste*, Berlin (West), 1973

Hansjörg Schneider (ed.), *Stücke aus dem Exil*, Berlin (GDR), 1984

Ernst Schürer, 'German Drama in Exile: A Survey', in J.M. Spalek and R.F. Bell (eds), *Exile: The Writer's Experience*, Chapel Hill, 1982, pp. 48–67

Jennifer Ann Taylor, *The Third Reich in German Drama, 1933–1956* (PhD Thesis, University of London, 1978), Ann Arbor, 1980

Theater im Exil 1933–1945, Exh. cat., Berlin (West): Akademie der Künste, 1973

Bibliography

Frithjof Trapp, *Deutsche Literatur zwischen den Weltkriegen. Vol 2: Literatur im Exil*, Berne, 1983, pp. 56–102

Curt Trepte, 'Archiv Deutsches Theater- und Filmschaffen im Exil', *Mitteilungen der Deutschen Akademie der Künste zu Berlin/DDR*, vol. 5, no. 1, 1967, pp. 11–12

——, 'Deutsches Theater im Exil der Welt', in Helmut Müssener and Gisela Sandqvist (eds), *Protokoll des II. Internationalen Symposiums zur Erforschung des deutschsprachigen Exils nach 1933 in Kopenhagen*, Stockholm, 1972, pp. 520–56

Hans-Christof Wächter, *Theater im Exil: Sozialgeschichte des deutschen Exiltheaters 1933–1945. Mit einem Beitrag von Louis Naef: Theater der deutschen Schweiz*, Munich, 1973

IV   Exile Theatre in Great Britain

Lisa Appignanesi, *The Cabaret*, London, 1975, pp. 164–70

Walter A. Berendsohn, *Die Humanistische Front. Einführung in die deutsche Emigranten-Literatur: Zweiter Teil: Vom Kriegsausbruch 1939 bis Ende 1946*, Worms, 1976, pp. 57–72

Günter Berghaus, 'Theatre in Exile', *Plays and Players*, Sept. 1986, pp. 14–17; Dec. 1986, p. 2

Franz Bönsch, 'Das österreichische Exiltheater "Laterndl" in London', in *Österreicher im Exil 1934–1945: Protokoll des internationalen Symposiums zur Erforschung des österreichischen Exils von 1934 bis 1945, abgehalten vom 3. bis 6. Juni 1975 in Wien*, ed. the Dokumentationsarchiv des österreichischen Widerstandes und Dokumentationsstelle für neuere österreichische Literatur, Vienna, 1977, pp. 441–50

Eugen M. Brehm, 'Meine Internierung', *Exil*, no. 2, 1986, pp. 39–64, esp. pp. 50–1

Alan Clarke, *Die Rolle des Theater des 'Freien Deutschen Kulturbundes' im Kampf gegen den deutschen Faschismus (1938–1947): Ein Beitrag zur Untersuchung des deutschen antifaschistischen Exiltheaters*, unpublished PhD Thesis, Humboldt-Universität Berlin (GDR), 1972

'Deutsches Theater in London: Die "Oesterreichische Bühne"', *Die Zeitung* (London), 30 Jan. 1942, p. 9

Exil in der Tschechoslowakei, in Großbritannien, Skandinavien und Palästina, Leipzig, 1980, pp. 147–305

Erich Freund, 'Deutsches Theater im Londoner Exil', *Theater der Zeit*, Heft 4, 1946, pp. 20–4

Richard Friedenthal, *Die Welt in der Nußschale*, Munich, 1956, pp. 134–42

Lothar Georgi, *Der Bühnenbildner Ernst Stern*, PhD Thesis, Berlin (West), 1971

Peter Herz, 'Die Kleinkunstbühne "Blue Danube" in London 1939–1954', in *Österreicher in Exil 1934 bis 1945*, Vienna, 1977, pp. 451–8

Rudolf Hösch, *Kabarett von gestern und heute. Nach zeitgenössischen Berichten, Kritiken, Texten und Erinnerungen. Vol. II: 1933–1970*, Berlin (GDR), 1972, pp. 48–52

Eric Koch, *Deemed Suspect: A Wartime Blunder*, Toronto, 1980, pp. 153–5

Hartmut Krug, 'Gulliver oder Von Adam bis Adolf. Ein summarisch-dokumentarischer Überblick über deutschsprachiges Theaterschaffen', in *Kunst im Exil in Großbritannien 1933–1945*, Exh. cat., Berlin (West), Schloß Charlottenburg, 1986, pp. 263–70

Bibliography

Egon Larsen, 'Deutsches Theater in London. Ein ungeschriebenes Kapitel Kulturgeschichte', *Zick Zack* (Hanover). vol. 2, 1948, pp. 13–15

—— 'Deutsches Theater in London (1939–1945): Ein unbekanntes Kapitel Kulturgeschichte', *Deutsche Rundschau*, vol. 83, 1957, pp. 378–83

P.E.M. (i.e. Paul Ernst Marcus), 'Stage and Film', in *Britain's New Citizens: The Story of the Refugees from Germany and Austria*, London, 1951, pp. 55–7.

Otto Reiner and Walter Rösler, *Kabarettgeschichte: Abriß des deutschsprachigen Kabaretts*, Berlin (GDR), 1977, pp. 156–62

Friedrich Richter, 'Auf Theatertour in England', in Renate Seydel, (ed) *. . . gelebt für alle Zeiten: Schauspieler über sich und andere*, Berlin (GDR), 1980, pp. 292–307

William Rose, 'German Literary Exiles in England', *German Life and Letters*, NS, vol. 1, 1947–49, pp. 175–84, esp. 177–80

Michael Seyfert, *Im Niemandsland: Deutsche Exilliteratur in britischer Internierung. Ein unbekanntes Kapitel des Zweiten Weltkries*, Berlin (West), 1984, pp. 53–5

—— '"His Majesty's Most Loyal Internees". The Internment and Deportation of German and Austrian Refugees as "Enemy Aliens". Historical, Cultural and Literary Aspects', in Gerhard Hirschfeld (ed.), *Exile in Great Britain: Refugees From Hitler's Germany*, Leamington Spa, 1984, pp. 163–93, esp. pp. 180–3

Hilde Spiel, 'Keine Klage über England', *Ver Sacrum. Neue Hefte für Kunst und Literatur*, vol. 72, 1972, pp. 21–5

Rudolph Spitz, 'Das Laterndl in London', in *Theater im Exil 1933–1945*, Exh. cat., Berlin: Akademie der Künste, 1973, S.28–30

Ernst Stern, *My Life, My Stage*, London/Toronto, 1951

'Theater in Huyton', *Freie Deutsche Kultur* (London), Dec. 1940, pp. 3–4

Curt Trepte, 'Deutsches Theater im Exil der Welt: Ein Übersichtsbericht über die Tätigkeit deutscher Theaterkünstler in der Emigration von 1933–1946', in Helmut Müssener and Gisela Sandqvist (eds), *Protokoll des II. Internationalen Symposiums zur Erforschung des deutschsprachigen Exils nach 1933 in Kopenhagen 1972*, Stockholm, 1972, pp. 520–56, esp. pp. 536–9

Hans-Christof Wächter, *Theater im Exil. Sozialgeschichte des deutschen Exiltheaters 1933–1945*, Munich, 1973, pp. 66–81

Erna Wipplinger, '"Zünden soll d'Latern": Österreichisches Exiltheater in Großbritannien', *Wespennest* (Vienna), no. 56, 1984, pp. 29–38

—— '"Von Adam bis Adolf". Die politisch-satirischen Kleinkunstprogramme der österreichischen Exilbühne "Laterndl"', *Mitteilungen des Instituts für Wissenschaft und Kunst* (Vienna), vol. 40, no. 1/2, 1985, pp. 30–4

Max Zimmering, 'Kunst hinter Pfählen', in *Aufbau. Kulturpolitische Monatsschrift des Kulturbundes zur demokratischen Erneuerung Deutschlands*, vol. 4, 1948, pp. 253–6

——, 'Vierundzwanzig schwarze Schafe', in Helga Bemmann (ed.), *Mitgelacht — Dabeigewesen: Erinnerungen aus sechs Jahrzehnten Kabarett*, Berlin (GDR), 1967, pp. 312–16

——, 'Politische Bühne im Exil', in Max Zimmering, *Der gekreuzigte Grischa. Begegnungen mit Zeitgenossen*, Rudolstadt, 1969, pp. 60–70

V German Film-Makers in Exile

(Periodicals and general histories have not been included unless the émigré features heavily. Neither have books and pamphlets which derive almost entirely from the sources below.)

Rodney Ackland and Elspeth Grant, *The Celluloid Mistress or the Custard Pie of Dr. Caligari*, London, 1954

David Badder, 'Powell and Pressburger: The War Years', *Sight and Sound*, vol. 48, no. 1 (winter 1978–9)

Michael Balcon, *Michael Balcon Presents . . . A Lifetime of Films*, London, 1969

Charles Barr, *Ealing Studios*, London, 1977

Léon Barsacq, *Caligari's Cabinet and Other Grand Illusions: A History of Film Design*, revised edn, New York, 1976

Geoff Brown, *Launder and Gilliat*, London, 1977

Adrian Brunel, *Nice Work: Thirty Years in British Films*, London, 1949

Edward Carrick [i.e. Edward Craig], *Art and Design in the British Film*, London, 1948

Charles Castle, in collaboration with Diana Napier Tauber, *This Was Richard Tauber*, London, 1971

Alberto Cavalcanti, '"Alberto Cavalcanti"', interviewed by Jim Hillier, Alan Lovell, and Sam Rohdie', *Screen*, vol. 13 no. 3, 1972, p. 45

Monja Danischewsky, *White Russian Red Face*, London, 1966

Basil Dean, *Mind's Eye*, London, 1973

Margaret Dickinson and Sarah Street, *Cinema and State: The Film Industry and the Government 1927–84*, London, 1985

Denis Gifford, *The British Film Catalogue 1895–1970*, Newton Abbot, 1973

Ernst Ginsburg, (ed.), *Berthold Viertel, Dichtungen und Dokumente: Gedichte, Prosa, Autobiographische Fragmente*, Munich, 1956

Kevin Gough-Yates, *Michael Powell in Collaboration with Emeric Pressburger*, London, 1971

——, *Michael Powell*, Brussels, 1973

Graham Greene, *The Pleasure Dome*, ed. John Russell Taylor, Oxford, 1980

Maria Hilchenbach, *Kino im Exil*, (= *Kommunikation und Politik*, No 14), Munich, 1982

John Huntley, *British Film Music*, London, 1947

H. Montgomery Hyde, *Room 3603: The Story of the British Intelligence Centre in New York during World War II*, New York, 1962

Wolfgang Klaue, *Alberto Cavalcanti*, Berlin (GDR), 1962

F.D. Klingender and Stuart Legg, *Money Behind the Screen*, London, 1937

Michael Korda, *Charmed Lives*, London, 1980

Fritz Kortner, *Aller Tage Abend*, Munich, 1959

Karol Kulik, *Alexander Korda: The Man Who Could Work Miracles*, London, 1975

Lawrence Langer, *G.B.S. and the Lunatic*, London, 1964

Kurt London, *Film Music*, London, 1936

Rachel Low, *Film Making in 1930s Britain*, London, 1985

Herbert Luft, 'Erich Pommer', *Films in Review*, vol. 10, Nov. 1959

Ivor Montagu, 'The Decline of the German Film Trade', in John Paddy Carstairs (ed.), *Movie Merry Go Round*, London, 1937

Diana Napier Tauber, *Richard Tauber*, London, 1949

Lilli Palmer, *Dicke Lilli — gutes Kind*, Munich, 1974 (Engl. edn: *Change Lobsters and Dance*, London, 1976)

Valerie Pascal, *The Disciple and His Devil*, New York, 1971

George Perry, *TheGreat British Picture Show*, London, 1974

Michael Powell, *A Life in Movies*, London, 1986

Bibliography

Miklós Rózsa, *Double Life: The Autobiography of Miklós Rózsa*, Tunbridge Wells, 1982

Rex Stapleton, *A Matter of Powell and Pressburger: Group Dynamics and Notions of Authorship*, unpublished MA Thesis, Polytechnic of Central London, 1984

Sarah Street, 'Alexander Korda, Prudential Assurance and British Film Finance in the 1930s', *Historical Journal of Film, Radio and Television*, vol. 6, no. 2, 1986

Elizabeth Sussex, *The Rise and Fall of the British Documentary*, London, 1975

Paul Tabori, *Alexander Korda*, London, 1959

Salka Viertel, *The Kindness of Strangers*, New York, 1964

Alan Wood, *Mr. Rank*, London, 1952

Basil Wright, *The Long View*, London, 1974

Novels

Jeffrey Dell, *Nobody Ordered Wolves*, London, 1939

Christopher Isherwood, *Prater Violet*, London, 1946

Cameron Mc Cabe, *The Face on the Cutting Room Floor*, London, 1937 (new edn. with an afterword by Ernest Bornemann, London, 1986)

VI German Opera in Exile

Anthony Besch, 'A Triptych of Producers', *Opera*, vol. 9, 1958, pp. 224–30

Rudolf Bing, *5000 Nights at the Opera*, London, 1972

Eric Blom, *Music in England*, London, 1943

Wilfried Blunt, *John Christie of Glyndebourne*, London, 1968

Fritz Busch, *Aus dem Leben eines Musikers*, Zurich, 1948; 2nd edn. 1952; 3rd edn. Berlin, 1978; 4th edn. Frankfurt 1986; English trans: *Pages From a Musicians Life*, London, 1953

——, *Der Dirigent: Aus dem Nachlaß herausgegeben von Grete Busch und Thomas Meyer*, Zurich, 1961

Grete Busch, *Fritz Busch, Dirigent*, Frankfurt, 1970

Moran Caplat, 'Carl Ebert, 1887–1980', *Opera*, vol. 31, 1980, pp. 645–6

Elizabeth Carson, 'Carl Ebert', *Opera*, vol. 1, 1950, pp. 25–8

A. Christie, 'Fritz Busch: An Appreciation', *Opera*, vol. 2, 1951, p. 697

John Christie, 'Luxury — or Necessity? An Open Letter on Glyndebourne's Policy', *New Theatre*, vol. 5, no. 2, May 1949, pp. 6–7

Bernhard Dopheide, *Fritz Busch: Sein Leben und Wirken in Deutschland, mit einem Ausblick auf die Zeit seiner Emigration*, Tutzig, 1970

John Higgins (ed.), *Glyndebourne: A Celebration*, London, 1970

——, *The Making of an Opera: Don Giovanni at Glyndebourne*, London, 1978

Spike Hughes, *Glyndebourne: A History of the Festival Opera*, London, 1965, 2nd edn Newton Abbot, 1981

In memoriam Fritz Busch, ed. the Brüder-Busch-Gesellschaft, Dahlbruch, 1968

Birgid Leske and Marion Reinisch, 'Exil in Großbritannien', in *Exil in der Tschechoslowakei, in Großbritannien, Skandinavien und Palästina*, Leipzig, 1980, pp. 264–73, 284–9

Desmond Shawe-Taylor, 'Reflections on Glyndebourne', *Opera*, vol. 2, 1951, pp. 386–92

Bibliography

Max Uwe Stieren, 'Glyndebourne: Ein Opernhaus für England', in *Kunst im Exil in Großbritannien, 1933–1945*, Exh. cat., Berlin (West): Schloß Charlottenburg, 1986, pp. 253–6
J. Strachey, 'Fritz Busch 1890–1951', in *Glyndebourne Festival Programme Book*, 1952

VII German Dancers and Choreographers in Exile

Janet Adshead, *The Study of Dance*, London, 1981, pp. 23–4
'Ballets Jooss: A Chronological Table of Their Tours', *Ballet*, vol. 3, no. 4, May 1947, pp. 49–56
Victor Bonham-Carter, *Dartington Hall: The History of an Experiment*, London, 1958, pp. 128–32
Rosemary Brandt, *An Application of Rudolf Laban's Principles of Human Movement to the Generating Principles of Classical Ballet*, MA Thesis, Laban Centre, London, 1987
'British War-Time Ballets: Ballets Jooss', *Dancing Times*, Aug. 1945, pp. 491–2
V. Bruce, *Dance and Dance Drama in Education*, MEd Thesis, Leicester University, 1962
——, 'Dance and Dance Drama in Secondary Modern Girls' Schools', *Laban Art of Movement Guild Magazine*, no. 30, 1963, pp. 42–66
A.B. Clegg, 'Is Physical Education an Art or a Science?', *The Physical Education Year Book*, 1964/65
A.V. Coton, 'The Sigurd Leeder School of Dance', *Movement*, vol. 1, no. 2, Winter 1948, pp. 23–6, 32
——, *The New Ballet: Kurt Jooss and His Work*, London, 1946
Gordon F. Curl, *A Critical Study of Rudolph von Laban's Theory and Practice of Movement*, MEd Thesis, Leicester University, 1967
Constance Dove, 'Kurt Jooss: An Appraisal of His Work', *Laban Art of Movement Guild Magazine*, no. 54, May 1975, pp. 5–17
M. Dunn, 'Movement as an Aid to the Understanding and Development of Personality', in *Movement, Dance and Drama*, Conference Report, Hull University, March 1970
C.D. Ellis, 'The Use of Laban Lawrence Effort Assessments in Promoting Good Industrial Relations', *Laban Art of Movement Guild News Sheet*, no. 10, March 1953, pp. 1–26
Hallie Flanagan, 'Kurt Jooss at Dartington Hall', *Theatre Arts Monthly*, May 1934, pp. 337–9
John Foster, *The Influence of Rudolph Laban*, London, 1977
Ruth Foster, *Knowing in My Bones*, London, 1976
Janet Goodridge, *Drama in the Primary School*, London, 1970
Calouste Gulbenkian Foundation, *Dance Education and Training in Great Britain*, London, 1980, p. 192
——, *The Arts in Schools*, London, 1982, p. 21
Fernau Hall, 'An Interview with Jooss', *Dancing Times*, Nov. 1945, pp. 55–7
R. Herenk (ed.), *The Psychotherapy Handbook*, New York, 1980
John Hodgson, *Drama in Education*, London, 1972
Michael Huxley, 'A British Legacy', *Ballet International*, vol. 8, no. 2, March 1985, pp. 34–5
Diana Jordan, *The Dance as Education*, London, 1938

Bibliography

Margaret Kirby, *Sherborne Movement*, Bristol, 1984

Rudolf von Laban, *Ein Leben für den Tanz*, Dresden, 1935, (Engl. edn, trans. and annotated by Lisa Ullmann: *A Life for Dance*, London, 1975)

——, *Modern Educational Dance*, London, 1948

——, 'The Work of the Art of Movement Studio', *Journal of Physical Education*, vol. 46, no. 137, 1954, pp. 23–30

——, 'The Laban Lecture' (Reprint of a 1939 Speech), *Laban Art of Movement Guild Magazine*, no. 26, 1961, pp. 11–24

——, *Choreutics*, London, 1966

—— and F.C. Lawrence, *Laban Lawrence Industrial Rhythm/ and Lilt in Labour*, Manchester, 1942

——, *Effort*, London, 1947

Hetti Loman, 'The Art of Movement Studio', *Laban Art of Movement Guild News Sheet*, no. 2, July 1948, pp. 5–10

London County Council, *Movement Education for Infants*, London, 1963

Vera Maletic, *Body-Space-Expression: The Development of Rudolf Laban's Movement and Dance Concepts*, Berlin (West), 1987

Anna Markard (ed.), *Kurt Jooss*. Exh. cat., Venice: Teatro La Fenice, 1981

——, 'Kurt Jooss and His Work', *Ballet Review*, vol. 10, no. 1, Spring 1982, pp. 15–67

—— and Hermann Markard, *Jooss*. Exh. cat., Essen: Folkwang Museum, 1985

Walli Meier, 'The Influence of Rudolf Laban's Work on the Development of the Keep Fit Association of England and Wales', *Laban Art of Movement Guild Magazine*, no. 36, May 1966, pp. 30–3

Olive Moore, 'Man of the Month: Rudolf Laban', *Scope. Magazine for Industry*, Oct. 1954 (partly reprinted in *Laban Art of Movement Guild Magazine*, no. 13, Dec. 1954, pp. 37–42)

Friderica Derra de Moroda, 'A Day with Kurt Jooss', *Dancing Times*, May 1935, pp. 140–2

Marion North, *An Introduction to Movement Study and Teaching*, London, 1971

Valerie Preston-Dunlop, *A Handbook for Modern Educational Dance*, London, 1963

——, 'Towards an Understanding of Rudolf Laban and the Third Reich', *Dance Theatre Journal*, July 1988

——, 'Rudolf Jean Baptiste Attila Laban de Varalja', biographical entry in Selma Jean Cohen (ed.), *Dance Perspective Encyclopedia* (to be published)

Walter George Raffe, 'Modern Dance in Wartime England', *Dance Magazine*, Sept. 1943, pp. 11, 32

Joan Russell, *Creative Dance in the Primary School*, London, 1965

Jeanette Rutherston, 'The Central European Dance in England', *Dancing Times*, Dec. 1934, pp. 313–16

Lisa Ullmann, 'Rudolf Laban in England 1938–1958', in Kurt Peters (ed.), *Laban* (= *Tanzarchiv-Reihe*, vol. 19/20), Cologne, 1979, pp. 26–8

Mary Jane Warner, *Labanotation Scores: An International Bibliography*, New York, 1984

John Wiles and Alan Garrard, *Leap to Life*, London, 1957, p. 31

Jane Winearls, 'Sigurd Leeder and His School', in *Tenth Anniversary Festival of the Sigurd Leeder School of Dance*, June 1957, pp. 7–11

Beryl de Zoete, 'The Jooss–Leeder School of Dance at Dartington Hall', *Dancing Times*, Sept. 1939, pp. 626–8

Notes on Contributors

Günter Berghaus trained at the universities of Cologne and Berlin and came to England in 1978. He taught at Bedford College/University of London and is now a lecturer in Drama at Bristol University. His main areas of research are Renaissance and Baroque theatre and twentieth-century avant-garde performance, on which he has written in various English, American and German journals. He has directed a large number of plays and a film on Oskar Schlemmer. His books include studies on Johann Nestroy (Berlin (West), 1978), Andreas Gryphius (Tübingen, 1984) and The Reception of the English Revolution in Germany, 1640–69 (Wiesbaden, 1989). He is currently preparing a volume on Italian Futurist Theatre.

George W. Brandt is Professor Emeritus of Radio, Film and Television Studies at Bristol University. He emigrated from Berlin to England in 1934, read Modern Languages at University College and after his graduation was interned and deported to Canada. He obtained a Master's degree at Manitoba, served in the Canadian army, and worked for the National Film Board of Canada before returning to England. He joined the Drama Department at Bristol University in 1951, where he created the only practical postgraduate film course at any British university. His publications include a verse translation of Calderon's *The Great Stage of the World* (Manchester, 1976) and *British Television Drama* (Cambridge, 1981).

Alan Clarke trained as an actor at the Central School of Speech and Drama, worked in a number of repertory theatres and made an educational television series in the GDR. He read Theatre Studies at the Humboldt University in Berlin, where he completed his Ph.D. with a thesis on *The Theatre of the Free German League of Culture in Great Britain*. Having worked with the Berliner Ensemble, the Deutsches Theater and DEFA, he returned to Britain in 1972. Since then he has lectured in theatre and media studies in both further and higher education. He is currently Head of Performing Arts and Media at a tertiary college in Sheffield. He has written, directed and translated a wide range of plays for the theatre and radio.

N.A. Furness graduated in French and German at King's College, Newcastle upon Tyne, and took his doctorate at the University of Innsbruck, writing his dissertation on Georg Büchner. He taught at the universities of Newcastle and Manchester and has been Professor of German at Edinburgh University since 1969. He has researched various aspects of nineteenth- and twentieth-century German drama and published widely on Büchner, Hebbel, German Expressionism and Ernst Toller.

261

Notes on Contributors

Kevin Gough-Yates was Lecturer in Film at Hornsey College of Art, Central School of Art and Design, Polytechnic of Central London and University of Surrey. He was Deputy Curator of the National Film Archive and, until 1988, head of a postgraduate course in film production. He was founder editor of *Screen*, has contributed to many journals, including *Studio International* and *Marxism Today*, and has written the 'Moving Picture' column for *Art Monthly* since 1979. He has organised many film retrospectives, including the first Powell and Pressburger season, at the National Film Theatre in London, and is currently writing a book on European film-makers exiled to Britain during the 1930s and 1940s.

Gerhard Hirschfeld was until recently a Fellow of the German Historical Institute in London. He is now director of the Library of Contemporary History in Stuttgart. He has published widely on the history of Nazism, the Second World War and on German emigration to Great Britain after 1933. Among his most recent books are *Nazi Rule and Dutch Collaboration* (Berg: Oxford, 1989) and *Collaboration in France* (Berg: Oxford, 1989) a collection of essays on politics and culture in France during the Nazi occupation, edited jointly with Patrick Marsh. He is currently working on a major study of German émigré scholars in Great Britain.

Erik Levi studied in West Berlin, Cambridge and York and is now Lecturer in Music at Royal Holloway and Bedford New College/University of London. He is also a professional musician who has recorded extensively for BBC Radio and commercial record companies. His main area of research is German music between 1919 and 1945. He is the author of an Open University course unit on Busoni, Weill and Hindemith, a contributor to a new book on Hanns Eisler and to the New Grove Dictionary of Opera. He is at present engaged in writing a book on music in the Third Reich.

Valerie Preston-Dunlop is Senior Lecturer in postgraduate dance studies at the Laban Centre for Movement and Dance in London and director of the 'Laban Collection' research project. She has recently reconstructed the choreography of six of Laban's dance works and is preparing a study on Laban's choreographic works for the Forschungsinstitut für Musiktheater at Bayreuth University. She has published a large number of books on dance in education, kinetography, choreutics and dance theory.

Hugh Rorrison is Senior Lecturer in German at the University of Leeds. His main field of research is drama and performance, on which he has written in various academic journals and theatre magazines. He edited several of Brecht's plays, translated Erwin Piscator's *The Political Theatre* and has written a book on *Politics on the Stage in the Weimar Republic*. He is currently translating Brecht's *Arbeitsjournal*.

Jörg Thunecke was educated at Hamburg, Dublin and London University and is now Senior Lecturer in German at Nottingham Polytechnic. His main areas of research are late nineteenth-century prose fiction, exile and National Socialist literature. He has published widely on Busch, Fontane, Raabe, Ebner-Eschenbach, Büchner, Celan, and generally on National Socialist literature. He also edited the Festschrift for Charlotte Jolles (1979), a book on Wilhelm Busch

(1987), and a collection of essays on National Socialist literature (1987). He is currently engaged in editing several volumes of correspondence of various nineteenth- and twentieth-century authors.

Carl Weber was an assistant director, dramaturg and actor at Brecht's Berliner Ensemble. After 1961 he worked as a theatre director in West Germany, Scandinavia, India, Canada and America. In 1966 he joined the staff at the Tisch School of the Arts at New York University and chaired the Department of Directing from 1972 to 1982. Since 1982 he has been Professor of Directing at Stanford University's Ph.D. programme in Directing and Criticism. He has published widely in *Performance Art Journal*, *The Drama Review*, *The Brecht Year Book* et al. and has just finished translating and editing three volumes of plays by Heiner Müller.

Index

Index